BEHIND THE LENS

Filmmaker Jay Holben has been battling in the production trenches for most of his life. For the past 17 years, he's chronicled his adventures in the pages of *American Cinematographer*, *Digital Video*, *Videography*, and *TV Technology*. Now, in *Behind the Lens: Dispatches from the Cinematographic Trenches*, he's compiled nearly 100 of his best articles on everything from camera technology and lenses to tips and techniques for better lighting. Whether you're making independent films, commercials, music videos, documentaries, television shows, event videos, or industrials, this full-color collection provides the tools you need to take your work to the next level and succeed in the world of digital motion imaging.

Featured topics include:

- **Tech**, including the fundamentals of how digital images are formed and how they evolved to match the look of film, as well as image compression and control
- **Optics**, providing a thorough examination of lenses and lens interchangeability, depth of field, filters, flare, quality, MTF, and more
- **Cameras**, instructing you in using exposure tools, ISO, white balance, infrared, and stabilizers
- **Lighting**, featuring advice on using lighting sources and fixtures and how to tackle common lighting problems

Additional tips and tricks cover improving audio, celestial photography, deciding if film school is right for you, and much more.

For over a decade **Jay Holben** worked as a director of photography in Los Angeles on features, commercials, television shows, and music videos. He is a former technical editor and frequent contributing writer for *American Cinematographer*, for seven years he served as technical editor and columnist for *Digital Video* and currently writes a lighting column for *TV Technology*. The author of *A Shot in the Dark: A Creative DIY Guide to Digital Video Lighting on (Almost) No Budget*, Holben is also on faculty for the Global Cinematography Institute. He is now an independent producer and director.

Bound to Create

You are a creator.

Whatever your form of expression — photography, filmmaking, animation, games, audio, media communication, web design, or theatre — you simply want to create without limitation. Bound by nothing except your own creativity and determination.

Focal Press can help.

For over 75 years Focal has published books that support your creative goals. Our founder, Andor Kraszna-Krausz, established Focal in 1938 so you could have access to leading-edge expert knowledge, techniques, and tools that allow you to create without constraint. We strive to create exceptional, engaging, and practical content that helps you master your passion.

Focal Press and you.

Bound to create.

We'd love to hear how we've helped you create. Share your experience: **www.focalpress.com/boundtocreate**

Focal Press
Taylor & Francis Group

BEHIND THE LENS

Dispatches from the Cinematographic Trenches

Jay Holben

Focal Press
Taylor & Francis Group

NEW YORK AND LONDON

First published 2016
by Focal Press
70 Blanchard Road, Suite 402, Burlington, MA 01803

and by Focal Press
2 Park Square, Milton Park, Abingdon, Oxon OX14 4RN

Focal Press is an imprint of the Taylor & Francis Group, an informa business

Library of Congress Cataloging in Publication Data
Holben, Jay.
   Behind the lens : dispatches from the cinematic trenches / Jay Holben.
   pages cm
   Includes bibliographical references.
   1. Cinematography. I. Title.
   TR850.H58 2015
   777—dc23
   2014037507

ISBN: 978 1 138 81347 2 (hbk)
ISBN: 978 1 138 81348 9 (pbk)
ISBN: 978 1 315 74812 2 (ebk)

Typeset in Myriad Pro
by Florence Production Ltd, Stoodleigh, Devon, UK

Printed and bound in India by Replika Press Pvt. Ltd.

For my wife, Jennine.

She has been by my side for every word in these pages. She is, simultaneously, my biggest supporter, my most candid critic and my closest collaborator. It is her incredible support that has allowed me to pursue my crazy passion in this business and none of this would be possible without her.

I love you, Boo. Team KA!

Contents

5 MISC 353

Acknowledgments

A work like this is never accomplished in a vacuum. Although I am the sole author of all of the stories included in this volume, they wouldn't be possible without the participation, patience, dedication, and passion of many other individuals—far too many to name here, but I'll try to cover the most significant ones.

Stephen Pizzello, the editor-in-chief and publisher of *American Cinematographer* magazine. Steve took the first chance on me as a technical journalist, a title I've never really been comfortable with, and he's become a good friend over the years.

David Williams, who has dragged me with him to various publications over the years including *The Hollywood Reporter*, *DV*, and *Geek* magazines. It was Dave who first suggested the idea of this book and it was under his nurturing editorship that DV101 really took form. We've worked together on a number of projects, including HBO's *Femme Fatales*, and I appreciate his continuing friendship.

Christopher Probst and I came up in the trenches together. We moved from the scorching desert of Arizona to Los Angeles with each other, then scratched, clawed and fought our way up through the departments side-by-side. We have continued to relentlessly support one another for years. One of my closest friends and one of the few people on earth I can sit down and talk about modulation transfer function in an honestly passionate way. Chris also served as my technical peer review for this volume—and I'll be eternally grateful for his contributions both in the trenches and here on these pages.

Otto Kitsinger and I have been friends for nearly 20 years and we talk almost daily, although I've only seen him in person four times in the past 15 years. Otto is a phenomenally talented photographer (indeed he photographed one of *Sports Illustrated*'s pictures of the year in 2009). He and I have had technical conversations ad nauseam (sometimes to his chagrin) and he's been a great sounding board and friend over the years.

Jamie Neese, my dearest and best friend on this planet. Jamie and I have worked together since my early days in Los Angeles. Several of the projects I discuss in this book were collaborations with him. He's one of the only directors I'll still put on a light meter for.

In addition to recreating an MTF chart for this book—which I was screaming and pulling out my hair trying to do—Jamie is a strong spirit in between the lines of these pages.

Megan Peckman Belanger, the editor of my first book *A Shot in the Dark: A Creative DIY Guide to Digital Video Lighting on (Almost) No Budget*, who first believed in me, sought me out (hunted me down!) and suffered through horrible tacos to brainstorm that first work. I'm forever thankful for her faith in me.

David Stump, ASC—if I've ever had an unofficial mentor when it comes to the technical world of digital video, it's David. His unending knowledge is a true wellspring from which I have drank on innumerable occasions. It is an honor to teach alongside him at the Global Cinematography Institute and to consider him a friend.

Kimberley Browning is a producer and director with whom I've had the pleasure of working with more than a dozen times. She was one of the earliest supporters of my work as a director. I have served as one of the heads of her education wing of Hollywood Shorts and my lectures there have also shaped many articles that appear here and vice versa. Kimberley's professional partnership and her friendship have been near and dear to me for many, many years.

Ashley Barron, whom I first met when she was the coordinator for the Global Cinematography Institute, and I have collaborated together on several projects (a few mentioned in these pages). Ashley served as my early consultant on the curating of articles you now hold in your hands and I'm grateful for her collaboration, friendship, and guidance.

Finding images to illustrate a technical concept is always a challenge. Many things that I shoot or create for other people, I don't have the rights to use or they are incredibly complicated to procure. Most of the images you see in this book were from a small handful of sources: projects produced by my production company, Adakin Productions; projects and companies where I have intimate connection with the copyright holders; some images borrowed from my first book (with sincere thanks to Cengage Learning); or images I specifically created for use here. Images of charts and flowers get tedious very quickly, so I'm eternally grateful for the models/actors/guinea pigs who have stood in front of my lens and generously allowed their visages to be included here. You'll see a lot of Becka Adams in these pages; we've had a lot of great shoots together—and I appreciate her presence in front of the lens more than I can say. In addition Debbie Diesel came through at the last minute to fill in glaring blanks for me; she's a spirit that's quite addictive! Actress Lisa Jay also appears a number of times in these pages, a beautiful woman with a beautiful soul. In addition to those ladies, I express my sincere gratitude to: Alexandra Preda, Amanda Bolten,

Amber Dawn Lee, Amber Myers, Andrea Fellers, Anne-Michael Smith, April Adams, Areti Athanasopoulos, Barbara Harper, Brian Glanney, Chanel Marriott, DaNae West, Ed Schofield, Glends Suggs, Grace DeSilva, Heather Carr, Karin Pyrak, Jada and Jane Kaufman, Laura Manchester, Lauren Waisnren, Lucas Riney, Mark Gerson, Mason Rae, Megan Reinking, Tamara Lyn, Nathaniel Edwards, Noelle Messier, Shannon Setty, Toby Heilmann, and Tonya Ivey. Many thanks for the last-minute models who grace the cover of this tome: Nayri Gregor, Mike Sullivan, and Benjamin Molyneux.

With rare exception, all of the images in this book were photographed or created by me. For those very few exclusions I have to thank the photographers who allowed their images to be included: Carlis Johnson, Christopher Probst, Claudiu Gilmeanu, James Cole, Maria Angelopoulou, and Otto Kitsinger.

Warmest thanks to my editors at Focal Press, Emily McCloskey, Peter Linsey, and Abigail Stanley who believed in this book and shepherded it to life. My primary education has been from books and I have many, many shelves in my house lined with the evidence of my past learning. By far the majority of my filmmaking books—artistic and technical—are from Focal Press. I am immensely proud and deeply humbled to be on their roster of authors.

Sources and Disclaimers

SOURCES

This book is comprised of articles and selections from:

Holben, Jay. *A Shot in the Dark*: *A Creative DIY Guide to Digital Video Lighting on (Almost) No Budget*. Boston: Course Technology PTR, Cengage Learning, 2012.

American Cinematographer magazine. Pizzello, Stephen, ed. Hollywood: ASC Press.

Digital Video magazine. Clapp, Cristina, ed. New York: NewBay Media.

DV magazine. Williams, David, ed. New York: NewBay Media.

TV Technology magazine. Butts, Tom, ed. New York: NewBay Media.

Videography magazine. Clapp, Cristina, ed. New York: NewBay Media.

DISCLAIMERS

The world of digital video is an RGB (red, green, and blue) world. The world of publishing is a CMYK (cyan, magenta, yellow, and black) world. They often play very nicely together—except where pure red, green, and blue is concerned. Anytime that you see technically precise color chips in this volume—color bars or color charts, etc.—every effort was taken to represent these images as correctly as possible within the limitations of the print color space. Please forgive any discrepancies.

Any recommendations in this book are intended to be executed by qualified individuals. The author or publishers assume no responsibility for the reader's actions. Proceed at your own risk.

Individuals are advised to incorporate all standard and recommended safety gear, always follow manufacturer's instructions on all electrical components.

While all recommendations in this book have been tested for safety and functionality, it is not possible to overstate the importance of safe practices wherever dealing with delicate and potentially dangerous equipment and situations. Please shoot safely.

Author Biography

Jay Holben spent more than a decade working as a director of photography. As a technical journalist, Holben has been a lead contributing writer for *American Cinematographer* magazine for nearly two decades. For seven years, he served as technical editor for *Digital Video* magazine, he is the current lighting columnist for *TV Technology* magazine, and has been a contributor to *Videography* and *The Hollywood Reporter*.

As the author of the highly-lauded independent lighting manual: *A Shot in the Dark: A Creative DIY Guide to Digital Video Lighting on (Almost) No Budget*, Holben was been able to bring his on-set experiences to new filmmakers. In addition to frequent speaking engagements, he holds a faculty position at the Global Cinematography Institute.

With *Behind the Lens*, Holben strives to influence and inform today's entrenched production technicians with regaling stories from the front-lines.

He is currently an independent producer and director living in Los Angeles.

Foreword

The digital age of filmmaking has, to some degree, democratized cinematography. The level to which aspiring filmmakers have access to high-quality, low-cost cameras and workflows has spawned a revolution in storytelling. The overwhelming new supply of content is evolving new mechanisms for fitting that content to the proper demographic demand. New social media mechanisms are now evolving to sort the diamonds from the lumps of coal. Accordingly, the number of people calling themselves cinematographers has increased by an order of magnitude.

Today, a cinematographer is responsible to a director, to producers, and to investors to provide them with the highest quality imaging system that they can afford, and the cinematographer's choice can make the difference between the success or the failure of a project. Producers and directors hire you to create art for them, to be the guardian of the image, to press for quality and beauty at every turn, but they hire you to do that on a budget. The modern cinematographer must be three things: an artist, a technician, and a businessperson. We cinematographers are judged by all of our colleagues and employers: the studios, producers, directors, editors, and post-producers, based on *all three* of these criteria.

In this environment, how does a cinematographer differentiate his or her work from the rest of the thundering herd?

Put simply: education.

In order to differentiate themselves in this new environment, cinematographers must now constantly and energetically research, test and be familiar with the entire spectrum of hardware and software available for their work. They must educate and inform themselves in the technology vigorously and continuously.

There will always come a moment of truth early on any given project when the cinematographer is asked: "What camera should we use?" Cinematographers who have done their homework can answer authentically. Educated and informed, they can answer the question without having to lean on the crutch of their own greater familiarity or comfort level with one camera system or another, they can answer the question by prescribing the best camera for the script, and they can freely choose the absolute best-quality camera and workflow that they can possibly afford with the money the project has.

Part of that education includes reading. Critical reading is important to the success of cinematographers engaging in the relatively new arena of digital cinema, whether you are a 30-year pro or a film student. Jay Holben is a working professional who understands the criteria well enough to have survived and thrived from the film industry through the digital revolution. Not only have I known Jay as a talented and knowledgeable member of the cinematographic community for many years, I've had the pleasure of teaching alongside him and seeing, first-hand, his knowledge and grasp of the technological intricacies of cinematography as well as his natural ability to explain the complicated in most simple terms. This collection of articles he has put into *Behind the Lens* will help you to learn this new technology without having to sort through the mountain of sales pitches or trade show brochure hyperbole. Value that experience and read this work with an appreciation of the wisdom being imparted.

David Stump, ASC

David Stump, ASC, a recipient of an Academy Award for Scientific and Technical Achievement, is a member of the Producer's Guild of America (PGA), the Visual Effects Society (VES), the Society of Motion Picture & Television Engineers (SMPTE), the Academy of Television Arts & Sciences (ATAS), and the Academy of Motion Picture Arts and Sciences (AMPAS) in addition to being the chairman of the Camera and Metadata Subcommittees of the American Society of Cinematographer's Technical Committee.

Introduction

Film production is a battlefield. There's no coincidence that the structure of a film crew is very militaristic in nature. Our schedules, battle plans, the way we move in convoy-fashion, the trials and tribulations of each day on set—overcoming great obstacles to create the art of the final project: these are the battles we fight in the production trenches. My boots are caked with dirt of more than 25 years of production—and I have the battle scars and battle stories to prove it. It's a hard business and it takes its toll on its participants, both mentally and physically. Film production is not for the faint of heart. It's a passion that gets into your blood. And some blood—along with sweat and tears—is left on the battlefield every job.

You hold in your hands a battle journal, of sorts. A chronology of my professional experience, primarily in the world of cinematography (with some other dabblings) offered here to help the reader gain a further understanding of the art and science of cinematography.

HOW THIS ALL CAME ABOUT

Once upon a time (all the best books start that way, don't they?), before the digital age, before the Internet, there was an "online" service (accessed through the squeaking and squawking of a 1,200 baud modem) called Prodigy. A young, aspiring filmmaker, way too big for his britches, decided to start his own forum called "Behind the Lens" to answer questions about Hollywood and filmmaking.

As you've probably already guessed, the audacious little aspiring filmmaker was *me*, and although I had no authority and no experience at that point, I was a voracious reader about everything having to do with movies and I did pretty well with that little forum.

The Internet became a thoroughfare in my career path and the World Wide Web grew before my eyes. The next big phase was America Online and a chat room called "Hollywood Tonight"—where the most adult conversation was over which Kodak emulsion had the best contrast—and I met some truly extraordinary individuals in that chatroom (including a burgeoning cinematographer who would go on to earn an Academy Award for a little movie called *Titanic*, Russell Carpenter, ASC, among many others). As AOL waned, this forum evolved into the Cinematography Mailing List, run by British cinematographer Geoff Boyle, which I was an active member of for many years.

I never had any intention of having a side career as a journalist. My first article with *American Cinematographer* magazine was really just a fluke. Since I spent a great deal of my off-time in front of my computer, I did a significant amount of research on software that could help me learn more and propel my filmmaking career. This research became "Desktop Cinematography," my very first article published in the April 1997 issue of *American Cinematographer* magazine. I haven't stopped writing for *AC* since. In the intervening 18 years since that first article, I have written more than 200 stories for *American Cinematographer*. When I started with *AC*, Stephen Pizzello, now the editor-in-chief and publisher, was a fairly new executive editor and his senior editor was David Williams.

When David Williams left *American Cinematographer* for an editor position on special issues with *The Hollywood Reporter*, he brought me along with him as a contributor to the prominent trade publication. All the while, I continued my real career as a filmmaker—mostly as a gaffer and then cinematographer during this period.

Then came MySpace.

Yeah, MySpace. Remember that?

I became active in the Filmmaker Forum on MySpace. By this time, I was well into my career and much more qualified to answer the questions in the forum. Here, I resurrected the "Behind the Lens" series and wrote a number of tutorials, articles, and answers to user's questions.

By now it was 2007 and editor David Williams had taken over the popular *DV* magazine and, once again, asked me to be a contributor. David then asked me to serve as the technical editor for the publication, a position I held for a couple of years at *American Cinematographer*, alongside my good friend Christopher Probst. In addition, David asked me to contribute a column and I suggested a variation on the "Behind the Lens" series, which he dubbed "DV101." At that time David told me, "If you write this [column] long enough, you could collect it all into a book." An idea that, certainly, germinated in my head.

Monthly, for the next seven years, in addition to reviews and other stories for *DV* (which, later, became *Digital Video* when it merged with its sister-publication *Videography*), I wrote the DV101 column. And, as David had predicted, they began to mount up.

When Vilmos Zsigmond, ASC, and Yuri Neyman, ASC, approached me to become a member of their faculty at the Global Cinematography Institute, many of my DV101 columns became the foundation for my lectures—and vice versa. Topics discussed in class often became a new column. I realized, as I formulated a curriculum for my Introduction to Optics class, that four or five of my DV101 courses became a solid basis for that class. Although the stories had been scattered throughout the years, compiling them together covered a lot of ground.

Indeed, David had been right. Each month there was no particular rhyme or reason to the columns, but after seven years and more than 70 DV101 columns, I realized there's a lot of information that isn't typically covered in other resources.

That's what you're holding now. Compiled within these pages is the result of my blood, sweat, and tears over the past decade or so. Not just DV101, but blogs I wrote for dv.com, articles I wrote for *Videography* magazine, *TV Technology* magazine, *American Cinematographer* magazine, in addition to some new writing just for this book.

WHAT IS THIS BOOK?

As this is a compilation of many separate articles, I've gone through and categorized and curated them into a logical order. The book is divided into five parts: Tech, Camera, Optics, Lighting, and Misc. As it is a collection of separate pieces, you can easily pick and choose which articles are of most need to you—or you can read through from beginning to end. There is a definite logic to the way things have been laid out, so some topics first discussed in early pieces may be revisited later. In some cases I've combined two articles of a similar nature into one. In all cases, each article has been carefully updated and, often, expanded from its original form. As they were separate pieces, however, there is a little bit of redundancy between some articles that I've decided to leave intact. I believe that going over the same material, perhaps in different contexts, helps the reader to gain a better understanding of the topic.

This is, by no means, a complete textbook on cinematography. However, the collective of these individual stories goes a long way toward creating a unique look into that world.

In addition, I've worked hard to eliminate any information that is or may be obsolete in the near future. The information here should be relevant at least five years—until there's substantial technological advancement in the digital revolution. The articles on lighting and production will always be germane.

WHO IS THIS GUY?

Without going into tedious detail, professionally, I have embodied nearly every job in film production (including development and post) in the past 25 years, with the exception of hair/makeup and music composition. My primary background, however, is as a cinematographer. I was a director of photography for about ten years and I was a gaffer before that.

Although I officially "retired" as a cinematographer in 2006 to pursue my directing and producing career, I remain very closely involved with technology and continue to do practical reviews, keeping well abreast of the latest and greatest toys.

WHY I TEACH

Some self-reflection on learning and sharing.

I got into this business because I wanted to share. I wanted to share the stories and ideas in my head with people and making movies seemed the best, most amazing way to do that. *Star Wars* is what really opened my eyes and made me want to be a filmmaker; what a wonderful way to share your imagination with millions of people!

An extension of that sharing became teaching. Anyone who knows me knows I can talk for days and days about the business and the art and craft of filmmaking. I love this business, I love this art, I love to share it with people who are interested in it. I also found that teaching was the best way to test myself on what I've learned. As I was learning about the industry and, more specifically, about the art and science of cinematography, I would share this information with other people, which forced me to clearly understand what I was talking about so I could instruct others on what I had learned (my poor mother and girlfriend (future wife) bore the brunt of these early "lessons," bless them).

Over the years, as I have progressed in my own career, I have made a commitment to helping others learn. This has been done in various venues: online, in filmmaking community forums and answering one-on-one questions, through my writing with *American Cinematographer* and contributions to textbooks, through workshops and seminars that I have taught over the years, and through my work with *The Hollywood Reporter*, *DV*, *Videography*, and *TV Technology*.

With each article I write, with each seminar I teach, I strive to learn something new. I work to not only solidify the previous lessons and experiences in my own mind, but expand my knowledge and understanding right along with those whom I am writing to, teaching, instructing, or mentoring. I never stop learning, which is part of the joy of teaching.

So, gear up! Head out! The great battles are still ahead.

Happy shooting.

Jay Holben
Los Angeles, California
April 2015

PART 1
TECH

How a Digital Image is Born

Let's take a few minutes and step back and start from scratch. The information to follow might seem a little simplistic, but it's going to make sure we're all on the same page before we move deeper into more important terms and concepts.

We're going to assume that we're shooting a scene—actually this scene with actress Lisa Jay.

Actress Lisa Jay from *Tranquility Inc*. Tranquility Inc © Adakin Productions.

In order to capture this image, the light reflecting off the objects in the scene enters the camera's lens and is projected onto the sensor inside the camera.

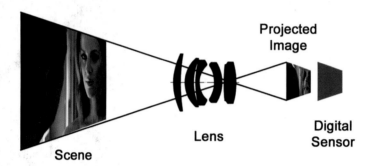

Projected Image

Lens

Digital Sensor

Scene

The image to the right is an approximation of how the sensor sees the image.

The photons of light reflecting off of objects in the scene are projected through the camera lens onto the sensor, which is made up of millions of little microscopic photosensitive components called sensels or photosites. Each photosite has a potential "well," which we can think of as a "bucket," that collects the number of photons it "sees" in a given period of time. Imagine

Each of the little rectangles in this image represents a photosite on the sensor.

thousands of little buckets set out under a tree on a rainy day. As the rain falls, it is collected in the buckets. However, if there are branches of the tree over some of the buckets, not as much rain will be collected in those buckets as ones where there is no interference. This is just like the light and dark areas of an image being projected onto the sensor. Some photosites receive much more "rain" than others.

Once the given period of time for a single exposure has lapsed, the photosite counts the number of photons it has in its bucket and converts the collected energy into an electrical voltage. Remember that photons are particle-waves of electromagnetic energy, so this accumulated energy can easily convert into a small electrical charge. The more photons a photosite has collected, the higher the resulting voltage.

That voltage is then changed in an analog-to-digital converter to digital bits. The higher the voltage, the higher the digital bit code value. This digital code value represents how much light that single photosite saw in that exposure.

The sensor, however, is colorblind. It cannot determine the wavelengths (colors) of photons striking it, it can only count the total number of photons it sees in a given period of time.

The image to the right is really how the sensor sees the image—in black and white.

If we peek at that closer, it's easier to get a more solid idea of what's happening. Let's take a look at just Lisa's eye in the next image.

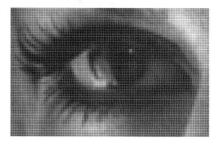

Each of the individual squares in the image of Lisa's eye represent a photosite and all that those photosites "see" is the illumination that strikes them. Some of those photosites don't see much light at all—like the ones in the pupil of Lisa's eye—while others see a lot of photons, like the highlights in her eye. All of them see the scene as some percentage between black (no light) and white light (maximum brightness possible).

A closer look helps to illustrate how much light each photosite/sensel receives. Some see no light at all, some see bright highlights.

Since the photosites are colorblind—and the resulting digital bits only represent the luminance values of the scene as it was captured, we need a way to determine the actual color of the light that strikes each of the photosites. That's where we get into three-chip cameras (one chip sensitive to red, one to blue, and one to green light) or a color filter array (CFA) over a single sensor so that each photosite will only receive one range of wavelengths of light—red, green, or blue.

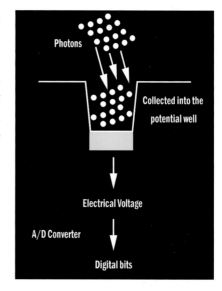

The anatomy of a photosite: photons of light are captured in a potential well and are passed through a silicon substrate that converts their energy into electrical voltage. An analog-to-digital converter changes the voltages into digital bits.

Demystifying Digital: How Digital Cameras Capture a Color Image

At this year's Digital Video Expo I got the opportunity to teach one of my favorite lectures, *The Flavors of HD* (which is also the basis for my Digital Cinematography class at the Global Cinematography Institute), or as it was known this year: *Demystifying Digital*. It's a favorite because I get to discuss so many different aspects of what makes up a digital format and really open people's eyes to the differences in formats and how to understand them. This year we expanded the session from its typical hour and a half into a day-long session and I was able to cover a lot more ground. After getting feedback from some of the session attendees, I decided to share some of the elements from that session in this column.

One of the fundamental things I discuss is how digital cameras capture a color image, and to start there I've got to set some ground rules.

WHEN IS A PIXEL NOT A PIXEL?

I blame this one more on manufacturers and hype than individuals with the misunderstanding, but we have to make a distinction between a sensor *photosite* and a *pixel*.

A photosite is a light-sensitive cell on a digital sensor (CCD or CMOS) that captures photons of light and then—through an analog to digital converter—turns those photons into bits to create a single point element of a digital picture.

A pixel—which is short for *picture element*—is a component of *color* (comprised of red, green, and blue levels) in a final image. In order to create digital images we have to have millions of pixels packed tightly together—each is a single solid color—but together, they form a full picture.

There is a significant distinction to be made here. A pixel is an element of the final picture, but a photosite is a light gathering cell on a sensor. Photosites are merely a well to gather light and they are colorblind. They can only see values of brightness, not colors of the light. In order to create a color image, made up of millions of pixels, we have to find a way to discern red, green, and blue content of the picture and there's two primary ways of doing that.

THREE BLIND CHIPS

Since the sensors themselves are colorblind, if we just let them gather light, there would be no way to determine the color values of the scene we're photographing. So we have to trick the sensors a bit.

The first method of doing this trickery and gathering RGB information is to use three discreet sensors in the camera (3 CCD or 3 CMOS sensors) to capture color information: one that will gather the red portion of the image, one for the green, and one for the blue light. To do this, after the light passes through the lens into the body of the camera, it strikes a prismatic beam splitter that separates out the light into its red, green, and blue primary color wavelengths. Each color of light is then sent off in a different direction toward an individual sensor inside the camera.

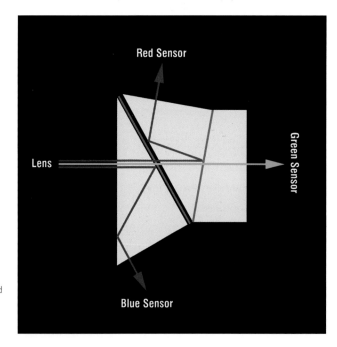

A cross-section of a dichroic prism from a three-chip camera. Full spectrum light enters the lens and is projected onto the prism. The blue light reflects off a dichroic mirror and off the inside of the prism and is projected onto a sensor. The red light passes through the first mirror, but reflects off a second dichroic mirror and off the surface of the prism to project onto a second sensor. The green light passes directly through both mirrors to project onto a third sensor. Each sensor only receives light from one color.

So each sensor only receives one color of light: one red, one green, and one blue. Each sensor, with its own array of millions of photosites, will receive only one color of light, but the camera will combine the information from these three sensors to create a color photo from the RGB information. "Full Raster" or "Native" are terms that refer to three-chip cameras where the number of photosites on each of the sensors is equal to the number of pixels in the recorded image. If each of the sensors has 1,920 × 1,080 photosites, then each pixel is made up of information from three photosites to get its Full Raster RGB information.

There are several problems with three-chip cameras: there is a loss of light through the beam splitter, making the camera less sensitive to light; three sensors and a beam splitter take up a lot of room, making compact cameras with large sensors an impossibility and the distance between the back of the lens and the sensors is too great for use with lenses designed for motion picture or still cameras. Three-chip cameras require lenses specifically designed for use with those cameras, and there are much fewer lenses available. Many three-chip cameras have fixed lenses.

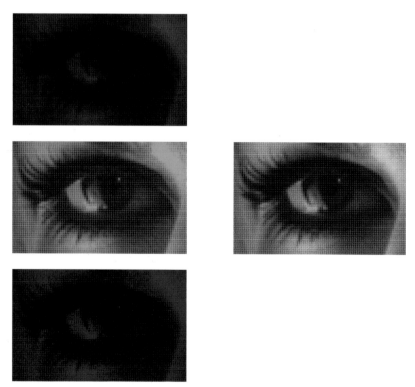

The red, green, and blue images represent the light from the scene that is projected onto the individual sensors in the three-chip camera. The camera's computer combines this information to create the full-color image.

THE SENSOR STANDS ALONE

The second method for gathering RGB information is from a single sensor. When you have a single sensor in a camera, you can have a physically larger sensor in a more compact space—as with HDSLR cameras that feature Super35 (or larger) sized sensors—and the larger the sensor, the less depth of field in your images, and the more sensitive to light the sensor can be. With just one sensor in the camera, the distance from the back of the lens to the sensor can be the same as in film cameras, opening up an entire world of lens choices.

The problem with a single sensor is that you have to find a way to gather all three colors of light with one colorblind sensor. To do this, manufacturers employ a color filter array (CFA) on the sensor. This means that a colored filter is physically "placed" on each of the photosites on the sensor so that only one wavelength of light can pass through that color into that particular photosite. So some photosites will be filtered green, some red, and some blue. Each filtered photosite will only gather the photons that are in those particular wavelengths of color.

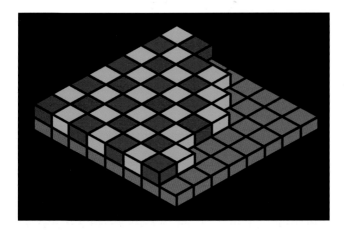

The Bayer pattern color filter array, a mosaic (checkerboard) of blue and green and green and red: 1/2 of the photosites are colored green, 1/4 are blue, and 1/4 are red.

The most typical color array is called the Bayer (pronounced buy-ur) pattern array, named after Bryce E. Bayer, who developed the pattern for Eastman Kodak in the mid-1970s. The Bayer pattern features a green, blue, green, and red checkerboard pattern. Note that there are twice as many green filtered photosites as there are red or blue. This is because the human eye is more sensitive to changes in the luminance (brightness) of an image than it is to changes in the chrominance (color) of an image. There is inherently more luminance information in the green channel, so we use twice as many green colored photosites to gather the most important information and the other half of the photosites are equally divided between blue and red.

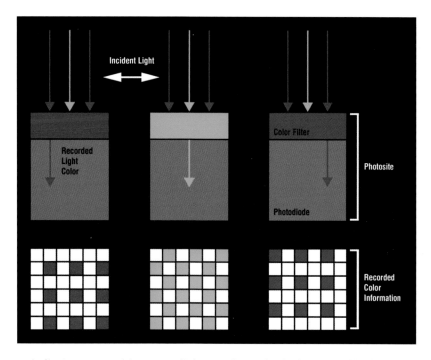

This image illustrates the filtration process and the amount of information from each color that is received by the sensor. Notice that each photosite only collects one color of light and rejects the other two. Also notice the limited color information gathered in the red and blue spectrum.

The individual photosites gather their single color photons, create electrons from them, and feed those into the analog-to-digital converter to create digital bits. That information then goes into the camera's processor and is fed into a de-Bayering or demosaicing algorithm that interpolates the image information to derive full RGB color for each pixel of the final image. That's a somewhat fancy way of saying that the camera's computer looks at the information coming off of the sensor—with only one color per photosite—and makes an educated guess at the other two "missing" color values for each photosite to generate the full RGB information in each pixel of the final image. This "guessing" involves incredibly complex mathematical calculations, and there are different methods for determining the guess (nearest neighbor, linear, cubic, cubic spline, etc.), but it still is just a guess. In cameras with a single sensor where the number of photosites are equal to the number of pixels in the final image, about 67% of the image is interpolated—or mathematically guessed. Some higher-end single sensor cameras utilize sensors with more photosites than output pixels so that it can gather more red, green, and blue information to make up the final image with less guesswork. A camera that has three times as many photosites, each equally filtered red, green, and blue (not like Bayer pattern with more green) can actually act just like a three-chip camera and gather true RGB information for each final pixel.

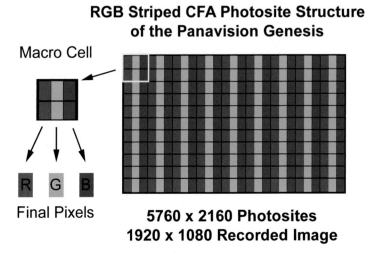

**RGB Striped CFA Photosite Structure
of the Panavision Genesis**

Macro Cell

R G B

Final Pixels

**5760 x 2160 Photosites
1920 x 1080 Recorded Image**

The Panavision Genesis camera used an RGB striped array, not a Bayer pattern. In addition, even though it had 5,760 × 2,160, it combined information from six photosites to create three pixels so the final image was a *super-sampled* 1,920 × 1,080 image.

The sensor in the Panavision Genesis and the Sony F35 is a 5,760 × 2,160 photosite sensor that uses a red, green, and blue striped pattern (as opposed to a Bayer pattern mosaic). This striped pattern is then combined so that two photosites of red, two photosites of green, and two photosites of blue information are combined together to create ONE pixel of information. This is called "super-sampling" and it results in true RGB information from a single sensor. The final image is a 1,920 × 1,080 image (5,760/3 is 1,920). Unfortunately, this is not a common technique.

Most single sensor cameras, however, employ the Bayer pattern filter—and although the number of photosites in the sensor may be equal to the number of pixels in the final image, the majority of the information in those pixels is not based on actual photons to digital bits, but rather mathematical approximations of what the de-Bayering algorithm believes were the number of photons from uncaptured colors. Although the algorithms are advanced and complex, they are often wrong—especially in areas where there are sharp edges in the image—and if you blow up a de-Bayered image, you will see strange color pixels side-by-side (also a factor of anti-aliasing filters incorporated to help hide de-Bayering artifacts). This lack of color fidelity actually reduces the overall resolution of the image, as compared to a camera that generates full RGB information for each pixel.

The Film Look— Aspect Ratio

A 35mm anamorphic film print with analog and digital soundtracks.

For a very long time, there was a constant struggle between film and video. Film was seen as the ultimate visual art form and video was seen as the fast-food of motion pictures. Even those who worked, daily, in the video industry—news, live television, documentaries—often looked up to the filmmakers who shot 35mm film, as the crème-de-la-crème. There were those who believed that video would someday replace film, and those who laughed at that idea.

Time has proven that those few, lunatic fringe, who believed that video would someday replace film to be (mostly) right; although it certainly took time. From the 1950s, with the proliferation of television and into the 1960s with the emergence of the video camera, individuals have touted the death of film. Why did it take almost 60 years to see video take a stronghold in the film world? Mostly it took nearly six decades for technology to catch up to the technical and aesthetic qualities of motion picture film.

THE "FILM LOOK"

There were a few things that had to happen to make video a viable replacement for film—one of them was the "film look."

"Film look" has long been coveted among narrative video/digital filmmakers. Many years ago when I first started as a cinematographer, I shot a pair of feature films on Betacam (a standard definition analog professional video format) and, in postproduction, we went through the official Film Look process on one of them (in the early 1990s, Film Look was a company that specialized in making video look like movies). Back then it was an alchemy of image softening, adding simulated flicker and grain—a virtual hodgepodge of destructive image filters to make video look more like film.

There are four primary factors that have been determined to define the film look—and when video technology was able to match each of these, it got closer to replacing film. In the 2010s, digital video technology reached a point at which it could match film (and exceed, in some cases) aesthetically and technically in all four categories.

- Aspect ratio
- Frame rate
- Sensor size
- Resolution

In 2012, we reached what I call the "Digital Event Horizon"—the point at which the number of movies released theatrically in the United States that were originated digitally outnumbered the number of films that were originated on motion picture film (47% film, 49% digital, 4% a combination of the two). Six decades after video started to proliferate our lives, it tipped the balance in the last remaining vestige of film origination—theatrical movies.

In this article, we'll tackle the first of the four categories that make video look like film.

ASPECT RATIO

To understand how aspect ratio relates to the "film look," I'm going to delve into a bit of history here on the evolution of wide-screen.

When film first came into being, at the turn of the twentieth century, Thomas Edison and

The 1.33:1 aspect ratio is derived from the width of the image being 1.33 times longer than the height. When we represent image ratios, the :1 always represents the height and the other number represents the width.

George Eastman collaborated and settled on a four perforation frame that was 35mm wide. This—somewhat arbitrary—decision became the standard for motion pictures. The picture aspect ratio wasn't entirely square, but it was close to it: 1.33:1. This means that the length of the image was 1.33 times longer (or wider) than the height. This is also sometimes expressed as 4:3 (four divided by three is 1.33).

It's not a perfect square, but it is a very squat rectangle. Film people usually refer to aspect ratios with the height of the picture always being equal to one such as 1.33:1 or 1.78:1. Video people usually refer to aspect ratios in whole numbers like 4:3 or 16:9. The numbers relate to each other, as four divided by three is 1.33 and sixteen divided by nine is 1.78.

1.33:1 (4:3) remained the motion picture standard for half a century. Nearly all movies made from the invention of film until the 1950s were shot and presented in this 1.33:1 aspect ratio. That was the window of movies—until the invention of television.

Television adopted the same near-square aspect ratio of the movies and TVs were made in the 1.33:1 ratio. This made sense, as half a century of filmed material was generated in this aspect ratio.

Then, as television grew in popularity and more and more people were buying televisions, there was a perception that less and less people were going out to the movies. Motion picture studios felt they had to do *something* to bring audiences back. What was different about the movies that they couldn't get on TV?

Spectacle.

By "spectacle," I mean *scope*, *grandeur*, *epic feel*, and, well, gimmicks. We'll stay away from the innumerable gimmicks (stereo sound, 3D pictures, smell-o-vision) in this article and just go for the grandeur, or rather, "*scope.*" One thing that movies had that TV didn't was *size*, and filmmakers realized they could increase that size and create something that couldn't be found on the box at home.

Enter widescreen.

Now in the 1950s there were a number of widescreen processes, far too many to go into any kind of detail here, but suffice to say out of the "widescreen wars" two aspect ratios emerged in the United States: wide, 1.85:1 (could be called 37:20, but isn't . . .) and super wide 2.35:1 (47:20?).

Again, these numbers represent the ratio of length to height. So a 1.85:1 aspect ratio has a screen shape with a length that is 1.85 (or nearly twice) that of the height. If your picture is 10' high, in 1.85:1 it will be 18.5' long.

This is what the ratios look like next to each other:

When television started broadcasting movies that had been shot in 1.85:1 or 2.35:1, they had a problem: How do you fit a rectangular picture into a near-square?

Well, it's simple. You chop off the sides.

And that's exactly what they did.

The most common worst-case scenario were the films shot in 2.35:1 widescreen. Cropping those down to 1.33:1 eliminated more than 40% of the picture!

This got really bad if the filmmaker had a two-shot where one character was on the extreme left and one character was on the extreme right of the frame. When it was broadcast on television, one of them would be completely cut out!

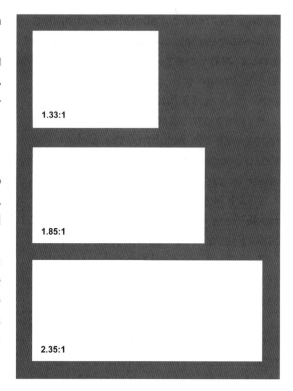

A visual comparison of the three most common US aspect ratios up until the adoption of HDTV in the 1990s.

An example of an anamorphic 2.39:1 (formerly 2.35:1, a SMPTE change in the 1970s altered this to 2.39:1, see sidebar on page 19) aspect ratio image, as seen in the theater in its full width. Last of the Mohicans © Twentieth Century Fox.

The same 2.39:1 image, cropped to 1.33:1 for television. Last of the Mohicans © Twentieth Century Fox.

So broadcasters invented the "pan and scan" technique. By floating the 1.33:1 cropping zone within the frame of the 2.35:1 image, they could show the "most important" section of the image and cut off the rest.

This is what happens in the "pan and scan" process—the 1.33:1 window (red box) is literally moved across the frame within the 2.39:1 to show the "most important parts." Last of the Mohicans © Twentieth Century Fox.

The same 2.39:1 image "letterboxed" within the 1.33:1 television screen. By reducing the size of the image, we can contain the full picture within the smaller rectangle and merely black out the portions of the unused screen. Last of the Mohicans © Twentieth Century Fox.

If there were two characters speaking in a single shot and one had to be cut off in the 1.33:1 frame, they would simply "pan" over to the other character when they started speaking. These "pans" were a product of the movement of the 1.33:1 window cut out of the 2.35:1 frame and were never in the original photography!

An ugly solution, for sure.

In the 1970s and 80s, home video took off and exploded as a whole new entertainment powerhouse. Although we struggled through the VHS and Beta wars, with VHS the clear victor, the formats never really stopped there. In the late 1980s and early 90s, laserdiscs were very popular among movie fans. The new digital format, a precursor to DVDs, was about the same size as a 33⅓" RPM vinyl record and offered unparalleled image clarity, sound clarity and, for real film aficionados, the new concept of "letterboxing."

True film fans decided there was *another* way to fit a rectangle picture in a square box; simply make the rectangle smaller so that the sides fit and then put black bars at the top and bottom. Voilà! You have a smaller picture, but at least you're seeing the *whole* image!

A cult following emerged in support of letterboxing (*wider is better!*). And it started to permeate throughout popular culture. Companies started broadcasting certain commercials letterboxed to give themselves a more sophisticated, higher-end, "film look." Movie review

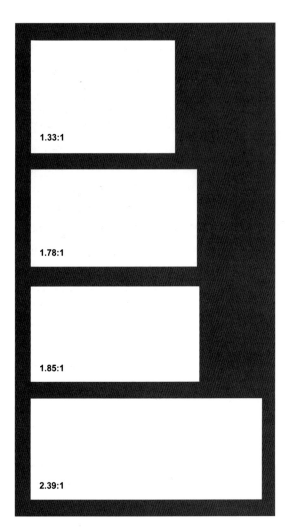

A visual representation of the modern aspect ratios most commonly used in the US.

shows on television started broadcasting clips of the films letterboxed. Even VHS releases like Michael Mann's *The Last of the Mohicans* were released letterboxed. Although not everyone was a fan of it, the black bars became synonymous with "movies."

Welcome to the 1990s. Laserdiscs are on every film collector's shelves, letterboxing is permeating the pop culture, and "high-definition" is looming on the horizon.

Enter 16:9.

With the advent of HD comes the creation of a wholly new aspect ratio, 1.78:1 or 16:9. A mathematical compromise between 2.39:1 (see sidebar page 19) and 1.33:1, slightly less wide than standard US widescreen (1.85:1), this new ratio became the standard for high definition.

So how does this historical diatribe relate to you, you ask? Simple, by using the widescreen and the letterbox format you can go a long way toward adding a "film look" to your project.

Today, nearly all cameras now shoot in 16:9 (1.78:1) mode, although some older standard definition cameras still shoot 1.33:1. This is the new television standard since the birth of high-definition. But, you can still achieve a more "filmic" look by presenting your project in 2.39:1 aspect ratio with letterboxing in the 16:9 image.

This image of actress Becka Adams from *Nameless* is a native 1.78:1 (16:9) image.

The same image of Becka, now "letterboxed" to create a 2.39:1 image within the 1.78:1 picture creates a more "cinematic" image.

2.35:1 becomes 2.39:1

One important distinction with regards to widescreen aspect ratios: SMPTE—the Society of Motion Picture and Television Engineers, one of the collective bodies in the industry who sets the standards—made a change to the size of the film frame in 1973 to accommodate multitrack stereo sound. This change significantly altered the frame size for anamorphic motion pictures. From that point on, there has never been a 2.35:1 movie projected in theaters as the aspect ratio changed to 2.39:1 (often called 2.40:1). So most movies (with some exceptions in other formats) from the 1950s to 1973 in the super widescreen format are 2.35:1, after 1973 they are 2.39:1.

The difference in the shots above is merely adding a letterbox. In my opinion, the letterboxed images are immediately more "filmic" than the full frame image. This is the power of letterboxing and widescreen to add to the "film look" for your project.

The Final Stages of Motion Picture Film

I've long said that film will reign forever as the primary choice of filmmakers, but time has proven me wrong. Although we have our die-hard filmmakers who insist on shooting film (Christopher Nolan and Quentin Tarantino among them), many filmmakers are embracing the new digital tools.

There's no doubt that digital is here to stay and that it will replace film. Unfortunately it won't matter what the filmmakers want if there are no more film labs or no more film manufacturers.

At the time of this writing, in 2015, we have one manufacturer of motion picture film left: Eastman Kodak. In 2012, Kodak filed Chapter 11 bankruptcy proceedings. They pulled out of it, and still remain in business today, but the future looks grim. For a company that used to manufacturer film for consumer still cameras (gone now), print films (about 90% gone at this time), camera negatives for television (more than 90% gone), music videos (nearly 100% gone), news (100% gone), sports (99% gone), and home movies (100% gone)—now has only one outlet: motion picture film stocks. As I already noted, in 2012, we passed a threshold in the digital revolution with 49% of the theatrically released films in the United States originated digitally.

So, for the first time since the digital revolution, the final frontier of film versus digital has crossed the tipping point.

There's no going back and film will never again be the dominant medium for any aspect of motion picture entertainment. As long as Kodak continues to manufacturer film and labs exist to develop and scan that film, then some filmmakers will continue to choose film. The day Kodak can no longer afford to continue to manufacturer film for just a small handful of filmmakers, or no single lab can afford to stay open or keep the real estate necessary for film developer tanks, film will die for good. It is highly possible that day is in the not-too-distant future.

The shame in this goes way beyond nostalgia into a potential serious detriment for motion picture archival. Digital does not have any legitimate long-term solution for the archiving of motion picture images. Film is still a human-readable medium that can last for more than 1,000 years if properly maintained. Digital evolves so quickly, requires machines to read the information and digital archival mediums (hard drives, LTO tape) degrade quickly. If we don't find a legitimate long-term solution for digital and film does, indeed, die—it's possible that we could lose the legacy of all films that are made today for future generations.

Death of a Standard ... Goodbye to 1.85:1?

For me, this is a sad observation over the past two decades—the 1.85:1 aspect ratio is dying.

From the 1950s to the late 1990s, the aspect ratio 2.39:1 (2.35:1 prior to 1973's SMPTE change) was achieved, primarily, in one of two ways—either through the use of anamorphic lenses or through an optical printing process with Super35 film (created in the 1950s, but brought back into vogue in the 1990s). This aspect ratio was primarily used for "epic" films: adventures and action pictures where the larger scope added to the fantastic nature of the story. The vast majority of pictures produced in the US between 1950 and the late 1990s, however, were the standard 1.85:1 aspect ratio. 2.35:1 (or, later, 2.39:1) was the rare exception.

Anamorphic lenses are more expensive, larger, slower (need more light) and more finicky than standard spherical lenses. Therefore they are more difficult to work with. They are also not as plentiful as standard spherical lenses and can sometimes be difficult to get your hands on—even for the biggest cinematographers in the business—especially if you're shooting a project with multiple cameras.

Super35 is a format that ignores the area of the negative that is generally intended for the sound and records the image on the "full frame." To get 2.39:1 out of Super35, the cinematographer exposes the full frame and then crops the image vertically in post. In the days of film prints for theatrical distribution, an optical printer is then required to extract that cropped image and blow it up—anamorphic—on a print for projection.

For many cinematographers this was an undesirable method because you're dealing with a much smaller vertical area of the negative and adding an optical printer step that degrades the image. Although Super35 allowed you to use standard spherical lenses to achieve a 2.39:1 aspect ratio, the quality of the final product suffered.

Along comes HDTV. In the 1990s the 16:9 or 1.78:1 aspect ratio was developed for HDTV. I've never met a cinematographer who wasn't baffled and frustrated by this new format.

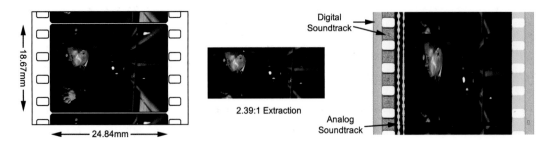

An illustration of the Super35 workflow. The camera records "full frame" utilizing the full four perforation high area perf-to-perf (leaving no room for the soundtrack that will, later, be necessary). From that image, a 2.39:1 aspect ratio (really only the image between the center two perforations) is extracted and then optically squeezed to fit onto an anamorphic print. Notice that the width of the anamorphic image is less than the originally photographed image because there needs to be room for the optical soundtrack (just left of the picture). Digital soundtracks run outside of the perforations or between them. Photo by Carlis Johnson.

Prior to the 1990s, it didn't exist. Now, suddenly, we have a new format and it's decided that this will be the de facto standard for HD cameras and HDTVs. Let's not consider the fact that prior to the invention of this format we have 100 years of movies and TV all shot in different aspect ratios—*none* of which are 1.78:1 . . .

In the early 2000s we started to see widescreen TVs becoming more and more prevalent. Now, with the death of CRT televisions, if you're shopping for a new TV, there are no CRT options nor are there any 1.33:1 options anymore.

Suddenly it's the 1950s all over again. Home theaters are drawing people away from going to the movies. It's been happening quietly, without fanfare, but we've seen the motion picture business going through the same "we're better!" gimmicks now that we did in the 1950s: 3D is back; IMAX is getting more and more popular for mainstream releases; larger theater screens, stadium seating and—yes, you guessed it—more and more "Cinemascope" (2.39:1) movies than ever before.

I started to note this trend in 2005 and 2006 when I was seeing romantic comedies and straight dramas (NOT epic adventures) in the theaters in 2.39:1 aspect ratio. I started to realize then what was going on and have been tracking this trend ever since.

In 1990, 78.2% of the theatrically released films were 1.85:1. Of the films that received a wide release (studio pictures seen on more than 500 screens), 79.3% of them were 1.85:1 and 18.9% were 2.39:1. Of course not a single film released was 1.78:1 as the format didn't really exist yet. There were eight films released in the US in the European widescreen standard of 1.66:1.

In 2001 we start to see an increase in "scope" films, 51.8% were 1.85:1 and 45.5% were 2.39:1. Of the wide releases in 2001, 46.3% were 1.85:1 and 53.68% were 2.39:1.

This was even more dramatic in 2010. Of all the films released, 35.8% were 1.85:1, 54.8% were 2.39:1, and 3.7% were 1.78:1. Of the wide releases, only 28.8% were 1.85 and 69.6% were 2.39:1.

That's a pretty major jump from 18.9% of studio releases in 1990 to 69.6% in 2010. There's also an increase in those years in Super35 2.39:1 films from 1.8% in 1990 to 28.7% in 2010. This is due to the increasing availability and decreasing cost of digital intermediates, which eliminate the optical printer step to create an anamorphic print from a cropped Super35 negative and thereby eliminate the quality loss. This makes Super35 a very appealing format for "scope" pictures, which can be shot with standard, non-anamorphic, lenses.

In today's digital age, we have similar choices to create 2.39:1 films. The image can be shot "full sensor" (most sensors are 16:9 native aspect ratio) and cropped in post (letterboxed) to create 2.39:1, or there are some cameras that can work with anamorphic lenses to create an anamorphic 2.39:1 aspect ratio. In either case, we've eliminated the need for an optical step to create the aspect ratio and both techniques—cropping and anamorphic lenses—are commonly used with digital films.

What puts a stronger death nail into the coffin of 1.85:1 is the switch to 16:9 TVs and the lack of concern by DVD, Blu-Ray, and streaming manufacturers to "over-zoom" 1.85:1 films to fill the 16:9 screen (cropping the sides a bit to eliminate the slight letterbox). Now, granted, the difference between the formats is very minor. 1.85:1 is less than 4% "wider" than 1.78:1 and, realistically speaking, no two theaters will have the same precise masking in either the projector or curtains—you'll always be seeing slightly less than "pure" 1.85:1—but what troubles me is the 16:9 craze seems to be setting back all the ground covered by the letterboxing movement of the 1990s.

The 1.33:1 aspect ratio for theatrical films was killed by the rise in television in the 1950s. In 1991 there was one 1.33:1 film released theatrically, and one in 2010. That's a far cry from nearly 100% in the 1940s and 50s. If the trend that we're seeing now continues, 1.85:1 may very well be replaced with 1.78:1 theatrical releases, or—more probably—primarily 2.39:1 releases.

Just food for thought.

1.5 TECH

The Film Look— Frame Rates

As we've discussed before, there are four main properties to the "film look":

- Aspect ratio
- Frame rate
- Sensor size
- Resolution

This article will discuss the second factor: frame rates.

In the early days of the evolution of motion pictures, Thomas Edison and George Eastman started to set basic standards for the new medium. They determined the size of the film—35mm—the number of perforations per frame—four—and the speed at which the film would travel through the camera.

Physiologists aren't entirely sure why human beings can see a series of still images shown in rapid succession and the brain interprets that as motion. Early on there was the theory of *persistence of vision*; later the theory of the *phi phenomenon*. Most agree it's an optical illusion of sorts that was first observed in child's toys like a Kinetoscope. Edison and Eastman determined that the slowest they could present the still images, and still achieve a smooth motion image was between 16 and 24 frames per second. With the invention of sound in the 1930s, this standard settled firmly at 24 frames per second as the slowest the film could travel and still have quality sound.

We've been locked into this frame rate for nearly 100 years. There are some who consider this a flaw in motion picture imagery—and they're not necessarily wrong. It was a compromise, no doubt. 24 frames per second was the minimum speed possible to achieve good images and sound. Faster frame rates produced sharper images and better sound, but also used more film and therefore increased costs and decreased the amount of time that a single reel of film could hold.

24 frames per second is, technically speaking, too slow to really eliminate the flicker of the image from the black moments between frames as the shutter closes to advance the next frame. This was solved in theatrical projectors by splitting the shutter into two openings that would allow two independent presentations of each frame, thereby achieving a 48 images per second, but still with only 24 unique images per second.

This frame rate, however, has become deeply ingrained in our consciousness as the "look of movies."

When television was invented, the engineers behind the innovation had to break up the single frames into individual fields. A television image is "scanned" onto the screen in horizontal lines—480 of them for standard definition. To break up the image into halves, the engineers found a way to alternate lines so that the first field of the image was the odd lines (1, 3, 5, 7, 9) and the second field of the image was the even lines (2, 4, 6, 8). They are presented in very rapid succession and appear to be one image. In the United States, this rapid succession happens 60 times a second—to match with the cadence of our electrical service, which alternates between positive and negative polarity 60 times a second (60Hz). These 60 fields combine together to create 30 discrete frames per second (it takes two fields to create a frame). This is called *interlacing*, as the individual lines of each field of the image interlace together to form a full picture.

A simplified depiction of interlacing: the odd lines (right) are presented to the viewer first within 1/60 of a second and the even lines (left) are presented next. The combination of these two fields create the illusion of a full frame (center) every 1/30 of a second.

So television is presented at 30 frames. In many other countries around the world, this happens based on their electrical cycles at 50Hz or 25 frames per second.

Television network executives realized that filling hours of television time with content was expensive! How would they ever fill all the hours in a week? Well . . . There was an entire wealth of movies that had been made for the last half century before television became popular that were available—thousands and thousands of hours of movies they could show! They had one big problem, however. They had to solve the issue of translating the frame rates of 24 frames per second of movies into 30 frames for television.

They did this through the *telecine* or 2:3 pull-down process.

This process takes four frames of film A, B, C, and D and converts them to five frames of video by dividing up the fields in a 2:3 cadence. Remember that a television frame is made up of two fields, so the first frame of film (A) is recorded into the first two fields of frame 1 of video. The second frame of film (B) is recorded onto the two fields of frame 2 of video *and* the first field of frame 3. Then the third frame of film (C) is recorded onto the second field of the 3 frame of video and the first field of the fourth frame of video. Then the fourth frame of film (D) is recorded onto the second field of the fourth frame of video and the two fields of the fifth frame of video. This cadence of two fields and three fields per frame of film expands the time from 24 frames per second to 30 frames per second. This is how we've seen movies on television since the invention of the small screen.

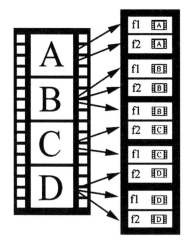

A visual depiction of the telecine process that converts 24 frames per second to 30 frames per second.

You'll note that the combination of two different frames of film into two fields of one frame of video creates an "alien" frame. It happens very quickly so that we can't notice the image anomaly. Interlacing, in general, creates image anomalies. Since the image is shown every other line for ⅟₆₀ of a second and then every other line the next ⅟₆₀ of a second, if the action being recorded is faster than ⅟₆₀ of a second then you can have a difference in the position of your subject from one field to the next in the final frame which creates a "combing" effect.

The problems of interlacing when there is movement from the subject in frame from the first 1/60 second field to the second 1/60 second field. You end up with a "combing" effect that degrades the image considerably.

But wait ... things get even more complicated ...

When color television came out, the engineers had to find a way to insert the color information into the existing signal so as to not require an entire re-vamp of the existing television hardware and network components. They decided to slow down the frame rate by a fraction of a second (.03) and utilize that area of the signal to insert the color information. From the 1950s our television in the United States changed to 29.97 frames per second.

So when you see the nightly news, a sitcom, or soap operas, you're watching them at 29.97 frames per second.

When we shoot video at 24 frames per second, to compensate for this .03 second time change, we shoot video at 23.976 frames per second. It's an unfortunate legacy that we're stuck with since the invention of color TV. We *could* get away from it in a wholly digital world with modern progressive televisions, but it would take a good decade—and a serious commitment by all manufacturers of any equipment for video and audio—to slowly phase out the fractional frame rates. I don't see that kind of cooperation happening anytime soon.

This is a very common problem in television that is so fast that you can't really see, but it does serve to degrade the overall image quality. The very process of interlacing reduces image resolution about 30%.

Now, even though we've converted 24 frames to 30 frames for television, we're still only seeing 24 discreet images per second. The speed of the film images has not changed. The *feeling* of that frame rate remains the same whether it's shown in the theater at 24 frames per second or on television at 30 frames per second. Take a look at the nightly news compared to a movie on TV and you'll *feel* a substantial difference in the image. I say *feel*, because it is an emotional and physical reaction to the different frame rate. There is also a psychological, temporal experience that is wholly different between 24 frames per second and 30 or higher.

With all of this in mind, it is important to note that there are flaws in the image because of this slow frame rate. With a standard shutter in the camera at 180 degrees, when the film runs 24 frames per second we get a $\frac{1}{48}$ of a second exposure of light to each frame. If you've ever played with still photography and shutter speeds, you know that the faster you make an exposure the more you can stop action. The slower your exposure time, the more you blur the action.

1/60 1/1000 1/4000

In all three images, the fan blades are traveling at the same constant speed. With a 1/60 of a second exposure, the blades travel a significant distance in their circular path within that time frame so that they appear just as one blur. When we decrease the exposure time to 1/1,000 of a second, the exposure is short enough that the blades travel only a very short distance—so the blur is significantly reduced and we can tell there are three distinct blades in the fan. When we decrease the exposure time even further to 1/4,000 of a second, the exposure is short enough that the blades do not travel at all during that time and they appear to have been stopped when the exposure was taken.

So the slower the exposure time, the more we capture motion blur in fast moving objects. At ¼₈ of a second, the object doesn't have to move all that fast to get blur. This blur, however, *is part of the film look*. That's significant enough to repeat, this flaw *is part of the film look*. We associate motion blur with movie images because that's the way we've seen them for more than 100 years.

There is, currently, a movement in the motion picture industry to increase the frame rate of theatrical motion pictures to eliminate the motion blur and sharpen the image to make it feel more "lifelike." There is no doubt that higher frame rate images do produce sharper pictures that have more "reality" to them—and this methodology is fantastic for ride simulation films, live concert films, nature documentary, sports, and the like, where reality of the experience enhances the audience's experience. It is, however, a significant detriment to a narrative, imaginary or dramatic experience—in my opinion.

Having gone through that diatribe, let's get back to the first step in making digital imagery look like film: the 24-frames-per-second frame rate.

This was first introduced in a digital camera with the Sony HDW-F900 CineAlta camera that was a joint venture between Sony, George Lucas, and Panavision in the late 1990s. Further, they didn't just create a camera that shot 24 frames per second, but that shot 24 *progressive* frames per second.

Motion pictures are created one complete picture at a time, there is no interlacing, and the visual experience is vastly superior to an interlaced image. So Sony came up with the idea of creating what they called PsF or *progressive segmented frames*. These were single, discreet, or *progressive* images that were captured one every ¼₄ of a second and then that single image was broken up into individual lines and split into odd and even lines. This way they would still create an interlaced image that could be seen on any television, but the image would never suffer from the possible time differential between fields because the fields were divided up from one single frame. This was our first 24p (the p meaning *progressive*) camera and it was actually 24 PsF.

Panasonic was the first to introduce this technology in a prosumer camera with the standard definition AG-DVX100 camcorder.

Undoubtedly 24p was the first major frontier to making electronic imagery look like film.

An image of a Panavised (altered by the company Panavision to accept their lenses and accessories and make the camera more robust), Sony HDW-F900 HD camera from the set of *The Night Before*. Photo by James Cole.

The original Panasonic AG-DVX100 camera. Image courtesy of Panasonic.

The Film Look— Resolution

Resolution is a term that is thrown around with reckless abandon like mashed potatoes at a food fight. Unfortunately, it's a term that is rarely used properly.

While many people refer to resolution simply as the pixel counts in the final display image or as the number of photosites on a camera's sensor, neither of them are actually resolutions: 1,920 × 1,080 is *not* resolution, it's merely the number of pixels in an image. Likewise, the Red Epic may have 5,120 × 2,700 active photosites on its sensor, but that is not a definition of resolution, either.

Resolution is reliant upon, *yet independent of*, the number of photosites on a sensor and the final number of pixels within the display image.

Resolution, by definition, is the ability of a camera (or lens, compression algorithm, or display) to resolve detail within a scene. It is measured by resolving fine detail between high-contrast elements—namely fine black and white lines next to each other. Modulation transfer function (MTF, which will be discussed in the Optics portion of this book), is a method for measuring the resolving power (resolution) of a lens, or an optical system. It is tested by photographing high-contrast black and white lines of increasing spatial frequency—meaning they're getting narrower and narrower, and fitting more and more of them into the same space so that the frequency of alternating lines increases within a given space. A lens that can resolve detail from a high spatial frequency image is said to have a high resolution.

In the digital world, resolution is also dependent on the number of samples that are taken from a given scene. The more samples taken, the more accurately the original image can be reproduced in the digital picture.

Simplifying this idea, if we take the basic shape of an ellipse and sample that shape at five points, we have a very small sample size and the resulting digital shape will not accurately

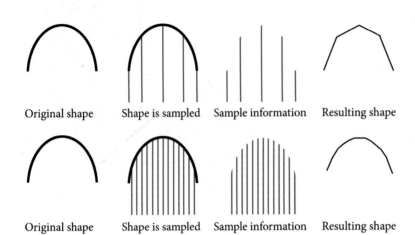

Original shape   Shape is sampled   Sample information   Resulting shape

Original shape   Shape is sampled   Sample information   Resulting shape

The higher the number of samples taken, the more accurate the digital representation of the original subject. We start with the ellipse shape (top left) and we sample that five times. The result of that low-resolution sampling is an angular shape that only slightly reflects the actual ellipse we were attempting to recreate. In the second instance (bottom line), we sample the ellipse many more times and we end up with a shape that more closely represents the original.

represent the original form. If we increase the number of samples, we can record more of the gradual curve of the ellipse and the resulting digital image more accurately reflects the original.

Each photosite on a digital sensor can be thought of as a device that takes a single sample of an image. It would stand to reason, then, that the higher the sample rate, the more potential resolution we can have. This is where photosite and pixel counts relate, but do not define a camera or system's resolution.

As it turns out, we need twice the number of samples to reproduce a given resolution without introducing artifacting or aliasing. This is the basis of Nyquist-Shannon theorem.

Harry Nyquist was an engineer at AT&T's (which later became Bell Telephone Labs) Department of Development and Research from 1917 to 1934. Claude Shannon was a mathematician who is credited for developing digital circuit design theory in 1937. The two (in addition to simultaneous, independent research by both E.T. Whittaker and Vladimir Kotelnikov) formulated a theorem that postulated that any sampling rate must be at least twice the highest frequency present in order to reconstruct the original signal.

In other words, for X samples, we can only resolve X/2 resolution without interference.

This may be hard to grasp, but let's take a look at this concept in a simplified version: resolution is defined as the system's ability to differentiate detail between high contrast elements. So if we have black and white lines, we need two of them—one black and one white—in order to tell the distinction between them and define resolution. The smallest that we can get any single element in a digital image is the size of a pixel. So if we have a

1,920 × 1,080 image, the smallest that we can get details into that image is 1,920 pixels or lines across the screen and 1,080 down. For 1,920 lines, we need one black line and one white line in order to define resolution via contrast, so we have—at maximum—960 line pairs (1,920/2 = 960).

That's the Nyquist limit.

It's a simplification of it, but that's the general gist.

For 1,920 samples, we can only resolve 960 lines of resolution. Beyond that point, the detail is too fine for the camera or display to discern and we begin to get artifacting like aliasing and moiré.

Moiré is a common problem with digital images and it happens when the frequency of detail within the scene is higher than the system's ability to resolve that detail. With an HD image, if we have any element of that image that features higher detail than 960 line pairs per picture width, then that detail will have moiré artifacting.

It stands to reason, then, that the higher the sampling rate, the better our resolution can be—and this is true. The more photosites we have on a camera's sensor, the higher the frequency of our digital samples of an image

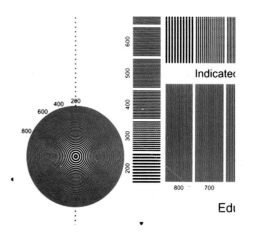

This is what happens when the spatial frequency of the image being captured exceeds the Nyquist limit—we see artifacting. Instead of clean concentric circles, we see odd anomalous patterns that are a result of the sensor's inability to resolve the detail in the image.

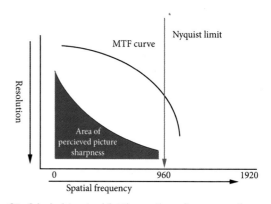

Otto Schade determined that the area the audience sees as the sharpest is the square of the area under the MTF curve—or the areas of low spatial frequency.

and the higher our Nyquist limit. If we increase the number of photosites on our sensor to 4,096, we can now resolve 2,048 lines of resolution in the image. This is the *theoretical* maximum, however, not necessarily the actual resolution.

Every component of an imaging system has its own resolution limits. The lens, the digital recording format, and the display all have their own resolution limitations and the highest resolution possible is determined by the maximum of the lowest resolution component in the chain.

Looking at the two images side-by-side—which image has the most sharpness?

Most people would chose the image on the right as sharper, but, looking closer at the image we see it isn't sharper in detail, but simply higher in contrast. Most people perceive higher contrast as sharper image.

Further, there's a very interesting distinction to be made between actual resolution—meaning the system's ability to reproduce fine details—and perceived sharpness as seen by the human eye.

This is where Otto Schade comes in. Schade, an engineer at RCA, performed extensive studies on the human response to perceived picture sharpness. He found that what humans experience as appearing sharp from a normal viewing distance is equal to the square of the area under the MTF curve.

This means that what we see as sharp is really defined by the low spatial frequency resolution elements of an image.

Just like lenses, human eyes are also more attuned toward lower spatial frequencies, so we see larger elements—with high contrast—as defining the sharpness of an image. In addition, human eyes will perceive higher contrast of low detail as sharper than actual high detail in a lower contrast image. You can have all the detail in the world, but if there isn't significant contrast in the image, it will be seen as lacking sharpness to the eye. Ever play with sharpening filters in a program like Photoshop? What you're actually doing is increasing the contrast in high-contrast lines in the image. By increasing that contrast, the apparent sharpness of the image is increased.

So what is the lesson to be learned here? Resolution is not just the pixel count in an image, but it is dependent upon pixels and can only be a maximum of half of the pixels in an image. Generally, even though we may have a high resolution image, if there isn't sufficient contrast in low spatial frequency areas of the image, it will not be perceived as sharp to the human eye.

The Film Look—Sensor Size: Size Matters

Don't be lied to! Size matters!

Well, as far as sensors are concerned.

Why?

Focus. Rather, depth of field. And field of view.

When we first entered the digital arena, technology only allowed our sensors to be so big—up to ⅔"—which meant that video always had more depth of field than film. Achieving the shallow, creamy, filmic depth of field became one of the last great frontiers of digital imagery.

Depth of field is defined by the size of the circle of confusion (see Optics section), which is defined by the size of the target (imager). In its most simplistic form, the smaller the image target, the greater the depth of field.

To that end, camera manufacturers have been reaching for the goal of matching the depth of field of 35mm film, specifically Super35 film. When we were able to manufacturer sensors to the size of Super35 film, first with the Panavision Genesis and Arri D20, followed quickly by the Red One, we were finally able to achieve that filmic depth of field in a digital system.

Super35 has become a "class" of sensor sizes. None of the cameras actually have exactly the same size sensor and none of them are precisely the size of a Super35 negative, but they're all close enough to achieve the same feel as film.

WHY SUPER35?

The original size of the film frame was determined, somewhat arbitrarily, by Thomas Edison and George Eastman. Edison asked Eastman to manufacture film for him "about this wide" stretching his fingers out about an inch and a third apart. Eastman went away and created film that was 35mm (1.37″) wide. Sprockets in the sides of the film were necessary to move it through the camera and through the projector, so the actual image area was between the sprockets.

When sound came into play in the 1930s, the area on the film reserved for the image was reduced in order to accommodate the optical sound track. This became the Academy standard for movies and, later, television.

In the 1950s, during the aspect ratio craze, the Tushinsky Brothers created Superscope 235, which had very little success until it was revived by cinematographer Joe Dutton in the early 1980s. The format required a revamping of the camera gate to

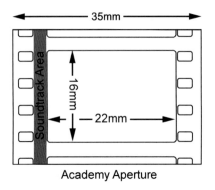

Academy Aperture

A look at the Academy 35mm frame, notice the imaging area is shortened to make room for the soundtrack that will be added later.

open it up and extend the image into the area reserved for the soundtrack and a recentering of the lens mount. The thought process was that leaving this area blank wasn't necessary on the camera negative and one could record a larger image if they utilized this area and optically reduced the picture later to accommodate the soundtrack. Super35 allowed the cinematographer to expose the full negative area "perf-to-perf."

Early problems with Super35 were that it required an additional optical printing step to reduce the image to fit into the proper print area, which reduced the overall quality of the image through the additional step. With the rise of telecine and the ubiquity of digital post, this became a moot issue as there was no additional step—it could be done digitally, with no image degradation—and the popularity of Super35 rose substantially in the 1990s.

The format was also popular for shooting films that would be released theatrically in one aspect ratio and on videotape in another. Director James Cameron was a fan of Super35 because it negated the need for a pan-and-scan with 2.39:1 movies. He could compose the image in-camera for a 2.39:1 theatrical release by cropping off the top and bottom of the image for the theater and "open up" the frame to show the full 1.33:1 frame for television. This actually meant that video releases would show *more* image than was seen theatrically (as long as the filmmakers were careful and didn't let the microphone boom or dolly tracks sneak into the top or bottom of the frame!).

Super35 as exposed

Center crop for 2.39:1 theatrical release

2.39:1 letterboxed TV (4:3) version

"Open matte" full-frame TV (4:3) version

A look at the Super35 workflow. The camera exposes the maximum area of the film (top left) and a 2.39:1 area is cropped out of the center of the image for theatrical projection. At home (on an older 4:3 TV) the image could be letterboxed to maintain the theatrical aspect ratio or (bottom right) "opened up" to show the full frame as it was exposed. Nameless © Adakin Productions.

The bottom line, however, is that Super35 was the format that exposed the most area of a 35mm negative, so that became the de facto standard to match (or beat) in the digital world.

SIDE-BY-SIDE

Let's take a look at several formats side-by-side.

Sensor Size Comparison Chart

1/2" Professional HD
6.4mm x 4.8mm (1.33:1)
Sony PDW-F335 XDCAM

2/3" Professional HD
8.79mm x 6.6mm (1.33:1)
Panasonic AG-HPX3000

Super35 Class

Canon 7D APS-C
22.2mm x 14.8mm (1.5:1)

Panavision Genesis
23.62mm x 13.28mm (1.78:1)

Red Epic
25.6mm x 14.58mm

Arri Alexa
23.76mm x 17.82mm

Super35 Motion Picture
24.89mm x 18.67mm (1.33:1)

Larger than Super35

Red Dragon
30mm x 15.8mm (1.89:1)

Canon 5D MKIII
36mm x 24mm (1.5:1)

Phantom65
51.2mm x 28mm (1.83:1)

A scale visual comparison of various sensors, notice the Super35 class, which are all of a similar size, and the sensors that are *larger* than Super35.

Note that cameras like the Red Epic, Arri Alexa, Panavision Genesis, and HDSLRs like the Canon EOS 7D all fall into the Super35 category. The Red Epic Dragon and Canon EOS 5D Mk III, however, are *larger* than Super35. Does this mean those cameras have less depth of field than Super35?

Yup. It certainly does.

It also, however, means that those cameras require lenses that project image circles big enough to cover the larger sensor area. Lenses designed for Super35 cameras (all cinema lenses designed after 1990 and many before) will not work on larger sensor cameras.

Larger than Super35-sized sensors give rise to higher photosite count sensors (aka 6K Dragon or 36.3K sensor of the Nikon D800 HDSLR), but these cameras require lenses designed for still cameras, or larger, in order to cover the full sensor.

Within the Super35-sized category, there is a delicate balance regarding the number of photosites possible to contain in the fixed size. More photosites mean that they are smaller in size, therefore less sensitive to light and more prone to noise. Less photosites mean less sampling and less image resolution. It's a balancing act that every manufacturer needs to consider.

LARGER EQUALS WIDER

I'm going to let you in on a little secret. Larger target sizes also have less depth of field because the larger target creates a wider field of view for the same focal length lens, therefore it requires getting the camera closer to the subject to achieve the same framing; reducing the focal distance reduces the depth of field.

We all talk about circle of confusion—and that's important, for sure—but the easy way to look at it is if you're using the same lens with a smaller sensor camera and a larger sensor camera, the larger sensor camera is going to have to be closer to your subject to get the same framing. Closer = less depth of field.

Let's take a look at a 50mm lens on several different format cameras and the field of view we get.

- Super8—6.5°
- Super16—13.9°
- Super35—27°
- 65mm—55.5°
- ¼"—4.5°

- ⅓"—6°
- ½"—8°
- ⅔"—11°
- APS-C—25°
- Full Frame—39.6°

50mm lens field of views from various digital formats

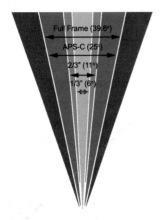

50mm lens field of views from various film formats

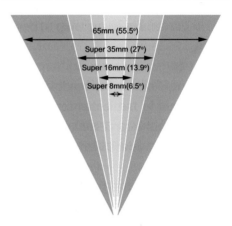

Both images depict the field of view of a 50mm lens. The left are fields of view of the *same* 50mm lens on digital cameras and the right are film formats.

As the sensors get larger, the field of view, for the same focal length lens, gets wider.

This also means that it's easier to get a wide field of view, with less chance of distortion, with a larger sensor. If you're shooting landscapes, this is a benefit, for sure.

BIGGER!

Does it behoove us to get larger and larger sensors—well beyond Super35?

Yes and no.

Larger sensors would be more sensitive to light, have more resolution, create higher integrity digital sampled images, but they would also leave behind a wonderful wealth of lenses that have been manufactured over the past 100 years for 35mm motion picture cameras. If you're OK with shooting with still lenses, then yes, we can get larger and larger, but there are significant problems with using still lenses on motion cameras, focus being one of the biggest. The smaller focal scales on still lenses are very difficult to work with in a motion environment. Incompatibility with a plethora of camera accessories is another problem.

However, as Red has already shown us, the marketing war, previously fought primarily over "K"s (2K, 4K, 6K), now has a new battlefield—sensor size. We will be seeing cameras with larger and larger sensors.

Where will it stop? Your guess is as good as mine.

Bits and Bytes: The Bottleneck of Data Rates

In spite of the fact that we're more than a decade into the digital revolution of high-definition (and beyond) moving images, there is still a very narrow bottleneck that keeps digital shooters from getting everything they want: data. The sheer amount of information that needs to be recorded from today's high-definition and cinema-definition cameras is staggering, and we—as of yet—don't have the technology to do so.

In order to understand how data flows and the problems it creates, we need to understand the basics of digital information—so we'll start with the very building blocks.

BITS AND BYTES

In the world of binary communication, one bit can define two states of being: on/off, zero/one, black/white, whatever the information may be, one bit can describe two states, generally polar opposites.

If one bit can define two states, then two bits can define four states; makes sense, right? We continue to increase exponentially with the addition of each bit. Three bits equals eight states ($2 \times 2 \times 2 = 8$), four bits equals 16 states ($2 \times 2 \times 2 \times 2 = 16$), and so forth, like this:

1 bit	=	2 states	5 bits	=	32 states
2 bits	=	4 states	6 bits	=	64 states
3 bits	=	8 states	7 bits	=	128 states
4 bits	=	16 states	8 bits	=	256 states

9 bits = 512 states   13 bits = 8,192 states

10 bits = 1,024 states   14 bits = 16,384 states

11 bits = 2,048 states   15 bits = 32,768 states

12 bits = 4,096 states   16 bits = 65,536 states

Note that in a binary system, working on a factor of two—and not ten—numbers that we're used to seeing as clean, round numbers, aren't. In fact, our normal modifiers like kilo (k), meaning 1,000 or mega (M), meaning 1,000,000, aren't round numbers, either. One kilobit (kb) is actually 1,024 bits (b), not 1,000. One megabit (Mb) is 1,024,000 bits, not 1,000,000 bits. That often causes confusion. When you buy a hard drive, the drive is classified in a base-10 system, so that one terabyte (TB) is one trillion (1,000,000,000,000) bytes, however, since data is measured on a binary scale, you can only actually fit 931.32 gigabytes (GB) on that drive (999,997,235,528 bytes (B)).

MORE BITS IS BETTER

Relatively speaking, the more bits we have to define any particular piece of information, the more it can be accurately defined. If we're trying to create a gray scale that defines gradations between black and white, the more bits we have, the more subtly and accurately we can represent that scale.

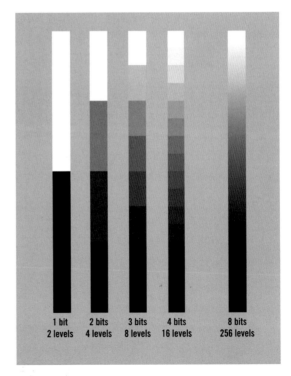

Defining stages between black and white. In a 1-bit system, there can only be two states, black and white. In a 2-bit system there can be four stages, so two gradiations between black and white. In a three-bit system there can be eight stages and we begin to have more subtle stages between black and white. Then in a 4-bit system we get 16 stages between black and white. If we bump up to an 8-bit system, we now have 256 stages between black and white and we can create a much more subtle, gradual transition between the two extremes. As we increase our bit depth, the differences between the extremes (black and white, in this case) can be defined with more and more detail.

1 bit / 2 levels   2 bits / 4 levels   3 bits / 8 levels   4 bits / 16 levels   8 bits / 256 levels

If we're looking at 8-bit RGB delivery systems, as most exhibition/display formats are, we find that we have eight bits of red, eight bits of green, and eight bits of blue information. Since each eight bits represent 256 individual states or levels, 8-bit RGB can reproduce 16,777,216 different colors (256 × 256 × 256). This is, arguably, all that the human eye is capable of seeing. Although when we work with digital images, it's nice to have more room to pick our final eight bits from, which is why many camera systems are 10, 12, or even 16 bits. Colors increase exponentially with higher bit rates. In a 10-bit system you have 1,073,741,824 colors available (1,024 × 1,024 × 1,024). In a 16-bit system you have 281,474,976,710,656 colors (65,536 × 65,536 × 65,536)—now *that's* a big crayon box. Actually, the colors available in a 16-bit system are well beyond the human range of vision, most of them will get discarded when we reach an exhibition format—be that a motion picture theater screen via Digital Cinema Projection, or a home television or a computer screen or even a mobile phone. Having 16 bits of information at the capture stages gives us more flexibility, especially in terms of dynamic range, to choose our final eight bits (or 12 bits in some rare cases such as digital cinema projectors) later on.

If we look at what a full 10-bit RGB HD signal *should* be, we'll see there's a great deal of information to be recorded. How much? Well, it starts with the pixel count. To get your total pixels in a single image, multiply the horizontal count by the vertical count. Multiply that number by ten for the number of bits of information per pixel, and then multiply that by three, because we're dealing with a tri-stimulus system that has three colors: red, green, and blue.

Once we arrive at the total bits in this single image, we've got to reduce that number down to a more manageable size, so we convert to kilobits (kb) by dividing the total by 1,024 (the binary version of 1,000), and then further reduce to megabits by, again, dividing by 1,024 again. This gives us our total in megabits (Mb), which we can further breakdown into megabytes by dividing that total by eight (eight bits to a byte (B)).

$$1{,}920 \times 1{,}080 = 2{,}073{,}600 \text{ pixels}$$

$$\times 10 \text{ bits per pixel} = 20{,}736{,}000 \text{ bits}$$

$$\times 3 \text{ (R,G,B)} = 62{,}208{,}000 \text{ bits}$$

$$/1{,}024 = 60{,}750\text{Kb (kilobits)}$$

$$/1{,}024 = 59.33\text{Mb (megabits)}$$

$$/8 = 7.42\text{MB (megabytes)}$$

So, 1,920 × 1,080 10-bit uncompressed RGB video is 7.42MB (59.33Mb) per frame.

Except we don't just record one picture, we record 24 (23.976) pictures per second—so we take that number and multiply it by 23.976 to get = 177.9MB (1423.22Mb) per second.

That's an extraordinary amount of information.

THE BOTTLENECK—RECORD MEDIA

To put that number in context, let's look at the highest possible data rates for some common types of videotape (remember that stuff we *used* to record images onto?):

MiniDV/HDV	=	3.125MB/s (25Mb/s)
DVC	=	6.25MB/s (50Mb/s)
DVCPro (HD)	=	12.5MB/s (100Mb/s)
HDCAM	=	17.5MB/s (140Mb/s)
HDCAM-SR (SQ)	=	55MB/s (440Mb/s)
HDCAM-SR (HQ)	=	110MB/s (880Mb/s)

Looking at that chart of tape types, we see that even the *highest* data-rate video tape, HDCAM-SR (HQ), can only record 880Mb/s, which is just a bit more than half the required data rate for full 10-bit uncompressed HD video.

This creates a significant problem. Our best, fastest (and of course largest and most expensive) common videotape can't record all of the information from a full HD signal. So . . . how do we do it?

We *compress* the information from the camera in order to reduce the data rate and fit it onto the medium. This, ladies and gentlemen, is where that ugly compression comes in— in order to fit the pretty images we want into the limitations of the media we have, we have to compress it (discard information) to reduce the overall data rate. Some formats, such as HDV or AVCCAM have considerable compression applied to get HD images onto media that records at 3.125MB/s (25Mb/s). Some media, such as DVCPro HD or HDCAM has much higher data rates so less compression is required.

This is a major reason for the move to tapeless acquisition. Hard drives and especially solid state media, have a much higher data rate to be able to record more information.

However, we're chasing our own tails a bit as we're getting cameras with higher and higher photosite counts—well beyond HD—into 4K, 5K, and 6K images (with 8K not too far off). With larger photosite counts on imagers, and larger pixel counts in the resulting recorded images, the data rates are going up and up. The Red Epic MX has a full-sensor image area of 5,120 × 2,700 and is a 16-bit system, although it is not a tri-stimulus camera (it has a Bayer pattern color array on a single sensor) so the Epic has a data rate of 221,184,000 bits per frame.

Let's break it down:

5,120 × 2,700 = 13,824,000 pixels per frame

× 16 bits per pixel = 221,184,000 bits

/1,024 = 216,000Kb (Kilobits)

/1,024 = 210.94Mb (Megabits)

/8 = 26.37MB (Megabytes)

5K 16-bit is 26.37MB (210.94Mb) per frame

× 23.976 = 632.18MB (5057.44Mb) per second

With data rates of this magnitude, videotape is not an option. Neither are standard connections to external hard drives:

FireWire 400: 49.15MB/s (393.22Mb/s)

USB 2.0: 60MB/s (480Mb/s)

FireWire 800: 98.3MB/s (786.43Mb/s)

This leads manufacturers to find ways to get the media closer to the information bus in the camera, namely, today's solid-state media drives like P2, SxS, and RedMag drives.

Now with 4K and HD data rates in mind, it's readily apparent to see how much compression is happening in formats like AVCHD with an HD record data rate of 25Mb/s, or even XDCAM with 35 or 50Mb/s. Panasonic's DVCPro HD and AVC-I formats are both 100Mb/s, which allows for less compression of the same HD signal (although they incorporate other techniques to reduce data rates). It should go without saying that formats with the least compression are more viable in image integrity and much easier to manipulate in postproduction without severe degradation of the image.

Let's look back at the Red Epic's data rate (before compression) of 632.18MB (5,057.44Mb) per second. That's at 24 (23.976) frames per second. What about when the Epic shoots 60fps? That's a staggering 1,582MB (12,657Mb) per second of data. Even with Red's lowest compression of 3:1, that's still 264MB (2,110Mb) per second of data. That should give you some idea how fast the data transfer rates of the RedMags are—quantum times faster than any videotape.

As cameras continue to increase bit depth and photosite counts, our needs for faster and faster record media is urgent. There is no media, currently, that can record the immense data coming off of a camera like the Red Epic at 60 frames per second without compression. Perhaps in a couple of years there will be—but, by then, people will be demanding 120 frames per second from the Epic's new 6K dragon sensor *without* compression. Someday, that may be possible. Today, however, it's still a dream.

A look inside a standard hard drive.

The "Raw" Deal: What's Involved in Recording Raw Imagery?

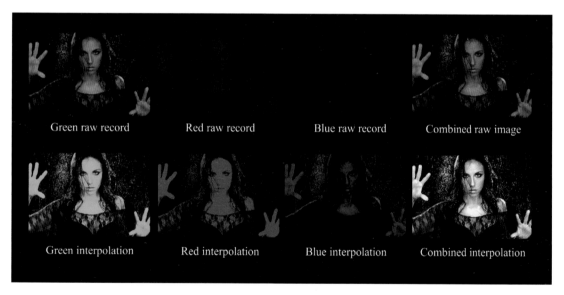

A visual representation of the Bayer process. The top row illustrates how the sensor captures the green, red, and blue information from the image and combines that to make a muddy, ugly image. It is the interpolation process (bottom line) that fills in the missing colors to create a colorful image.

Digital imaging has evolved considerably over the course of the last two decades. In video—especially for a "cinematic" look—we have graduated from analog to digital, standard definition to high-definition, 30 frames per second to 24 frames per second, interlaced to progressive, small sensor to large sensor, fixed lens to interchangeable lenses, moderate light sensitivity to high ISOs, high definition to "cinema" resolution . . . all of these advancements have elevated the quality of digital motion picture images substantially; each is a quantum leap in image quality and—especially—the "filmic" or "cinematic" image quality.

Today we have a new evolutionary link in digital imagery: the uprising of raw image recording. Raw has become the new buzzword. Note that it's *raw*, not *RAW* or *Raw*—it is not an acronym, it's not someone's name, it is not a proper noun; it doesn't deserve a chariot or secret service agents, nor does it deserve an unnecessary capital letter, let alone three. Just raw.

Raw is actually just an adjective to describe the kind of image file that is being recorded. In its most simple definition—raw describes data that is recorded without any image processing or compression of any kind. After the analog to digital conversion happens at the camera's sensor, you are recording the "raw" data from the sensor's photosites.

Raw only applies to single-sensor cameras and it describes a state in the image-making process before any demosaicing (de-Bayering) has taken place, before color processing or file processing has taken place. The raw image file is not really even an image, by any definition, yet. It's purely data reported from each photosite on the sensor. That means that each "pixel" in the raw image contains information from only *one* color—either red, green, or blue.

When you are recording a digital image to an image file, the camera has to apply the de-Bayering algorithm between the sensor and the record media. This takes a considerable amount of processing power and—much like setting the camera on "auto"—it is allowing the hardware to make decisions for you. Now, most cameras do this extremely well, but there are always compromises.

There are also several other steps that the image goes through before it is recorded:

- The white balance setting is applied.
- Colorimetric interpretation algorithms are applied.
- Gamma correction is applied.
- Noise reduction is applied.
- Antialiasing filters are applied.
- Image sharpening (compensating for antialiasing) is applied.
- Image compression algorithm is applied.
- Color dissemination (dictated by compression algorithm) is applied.

All of this is applied to the image before it is recorded.

When you shoot in raw mode, you bypass all of these functions and only the raw data off of the sensor is recorded. This allows you to utilize software in your postproduction workflow to have more control and flexibility in all of these image process steps.

In addition, most sensors are capable of capturing 12-bit data off of the sensor, but many record formats are limited to 8-bit. This means once the camera does the de-Bayering and coloring and image sharpening, it discards four bits worth of data for every one captured when recording the final image. In 12-bit data, you have 4,096 levels of information per photosite. In 8-bit data, you have 256 levels per photosite. That's 16 times more color information in 12-bit than 8-bit. Most of that is not discernible to the human eye, but the higher bit depth allows the camera to capture more subtle gradations between colors and more subtle gradations between highlight and shadow. In short, you have more color information and more dynamic range with the raw data off the sensor than you do in your final image. If you record the raw information off of the sensor, then you can use software later to make your own choices about what 3,840 bits you'll be "throwing away" when you create the final image.

A raw workflow isn't all a bed of roses, however; there are some downfalls. Firstly, your post process is elongated as the de-Bayering and image processing has to happen after-the-fact. Although some software is extremely powerful in performing these functions, they are notably slower than the in-camera processors. This will increase the ingest time for your raw footage before you can work with it. Some non-linear editing systems (NLEs) can work with native raw files, but you're forcing the computer to do a substantial amount of work that will invariably impede the rest of your processes.

On set, shooting raw takes away one of the greatest advantages to shooting digital (as opposed to film) as you no longer necessarily have "what you see is what you get" (WYSIWYG) on your monitors. The raw image has to be processed through a LUT in order to de-Bayer and mimic the image processing that will happen later in post. This is either done with an in-camera processor that is feeding out a simulated final image (via HDMI or HD-SDI), or through an additional image-processing piece of hardware before going to the monitor. In either case, you are looking at an approximate image, not your final image.

Further, if whoever is processing the image in post does not pay attention to the metadata associated with the raw files, or the notes from the cinematographer, the intentions on set can be quickly and easily lost in the post process.

A final problem that I've started to notice is a production "laziness" brought on by a "fix-it-in-post" mentality. Since things like white balance, gamma range, highlight and shadow protection are *slightly* less of a concern with a raw image (as there is more manipulation room later), more filmmakers tend to ignore these aspects as they can "fix" them later. This can be a very dangerous habit. In my professional opinion, it is always better to work to get the final, polished image at the lens rather than in postproduction.

Some people get confused with raw and color dissemination. Keep in mind that raw is *only* a third of the color information needed to create the final image. Each "pixel" only has one color of information and the other two have to be interpolated in order to complete the picture. You *cannot* have 4:4:4 *and* raw, they are mutually exclusive terms. If the image has been de-Bayered and the color information has been interpolated—meaning it is no longer raw—*then* your camera and/or record format can choose to represent all of the interpolated (and captured) color information (4:4:4) or discard some (4:2:2, 4:1:1. 4:2:0, etc.).

There are some cameras that provide uncompressed video via an alternate output. This is not to be confused with raw. An uncompressed signal has been de-Bayered; white balance, colorimetric interpretation, gamma correction, antialiasing, and sharpening have all been applied, you are merely getting the image before additional compression and/or color dissemination happens at the recording stage. This image feed has to be recorded via an external recorder as there currently does not exist a record system in-camera fast enough to capture uncompressed HD video.

At the end of the day, raw, like any other option in capturing motion images, is a tool to be utilized, and in many cases it is a very beneficial workflow to allow for more creative freedom in post-production. It is not, however, the answer to all solutions. Shooting live events (for live broadcast), news, and documentary, I would not want to use a raw workflow. I'm starting to hear people talk about raw as being the be-all-and-end-all and the ultimate future of all workflows, but it is not the only option and most certainly is not an excuse to be lazy with lighting, exposure, and other camera functions that define the technical and artistic aspects of the final image.

Digital Cameras and Color: The 411 on 4:4:4, 4:2:2, and 4:2:0

Many people get confused when it comes to discussing how digital cameras capture and record color information—as the two are mutually exclusive. Color information can be captured via three discreet sensors in the camera (one sensitive to red, one blue, and one green light) or it can be captured via a single sensor with a color filter array. This color information is then processed and, quite often, compressed or altered before recording.

Before we go further, let's recap a little bit about data rates. In a theoretical "perfect" HD signal, we have 1,920 × 1,080 pixels in the final image and in a 10-bit system that gives us 20,723,000 bits of information. We multiply that by three (for red, green, and blue) and get 62,208,000 bits of information *per frame*. Reducing that down, we get 7.42 Megabytes of data per frame. If we're recording at 24 frames per second, that's 177.9MB per second, or 1,423 Mega*bits* per second. That's a lot of data. The problem is, we don't have—practically— anything that can record that kind of data. The bottleneck comes in the form of the record media.

Looking at just one type of common media today, the CompactFlash card, a SanDisc Extreme Pro is an amazingly fast record card that is capable of 100MB/s (not your typical CF card, a 128GB sized card at 100MB/s sells for $1,500). But even that superfast card can't record the 177.98MB/s of the theoretical full HD signal. Typical record media can record 30–40MB/s with some exceptions going up to 100MB/s. Even the highest performing record media, however, isn't fast enough to record all the data—so we have to reduce the amount of data recorded to fit onto the media. One method of reducing data is color dissemination.

Color dissemination is based on the same principal as the Bayer pattern color array: that human vision is more sensitive to changes in luminance (brightness) than we are to changes in chrominance (color). Therefore the brightness information of an image is more important, and the most brightness information is included in the green channel of a color image.

We've all seen the numbers: 4:4:4, 4:2:2, and 4:2:0 before, and pretty much everyone knows that 4:4:4 is better than 4:2:2, which is better than 4:2:0—but what do these numbers really mean? This is the breakdown of the color dissemination scheme. The numbers represent:

- Green (luminance)
- Red (chrominance)
- Blue (chrominance)

In each of these dissemination schemes, they're working off of a four-pixel sampling pattern (the pattern repeats every four pixels throughout the image). In an HD image, we have 1,920 pixels across the image. So starting with the first four pixels of the image, in a 4:4:4 color scheme, the information is sampled from the green channel in all four pixels (the first number in 4:4:4), in the red channel from all four pixels (the second number in 4:4:4), and in the blue channel from all four pixels (the third number in 4:4:4). In other words, no color information is discarded. This is the best-case scenario.

In the 4:2:2 color dissemination scheme, all four pixels in the sequence send their green information to the record media (the first number in 4:2:2). But only two pixels in the sequence of four send their red and blue information to the record media (the second and third numbers in 4:2:2). What happens in 4:2:2 is the first pixel in the sequence sends all of its color information—green, red, and blue—to the record media. The next pixel, however, only sends the green information and discards the red and blue. The third pixel, again, sends all information—red, green, and blue—and the fourth pixel only sends green. In this manner, we are able to discard 50% of the color information from the image, significantly reducing the data rate, and yet because human vision is more sensitive to changes in brightness (green) than color (red/blue), we don't discern a loss in the image.

In a 4:1:1 color dissemination scheme, the first pixel in the series of four sends all three channels of information—green, red and blue—but the subsequent three pixels only send green and discard the red and blue information. Again, the 1:1 represents that in the sequence of four pixels, only one pixel sends its red and blue information to the record media.

4:2:0 is a little trickier. This is a method of really reducing the data rate, used in formats like HDV and AVCHD; very low bit rate formats. Again, utilizing a sequence of every four pixels, 4:2:0 takes a different approach and not only reduces color within the horizontal lines of the image, but the vertical too. So, for the first line of the image, in a four pixel sequence, the first pixel samples the green and red information, the next the green only, the third pixel is green and red, and the fourth is green only. This continues all the way down the line for the first horizontal line of the image. No blue information is sampled at all from the first line and only 50% of the red information is sampled. For the next line of the image, the sequence samples green and blue from the first pixel, then just green, then green and blue again, then just green. No red information is sampled from the second line of the image. This pattern repeats with the odd lines sampling green and red and the even lines sampling green and blue. This color scheme reduces a significant amount of information. Although it is indiscernible to all but the most trained eye, when this image goes into postproduction there is so little color information in the image that it becomes exceptionally difficult to manipulate at all.

It's very important to understand that color dissemination happens *after* the analog to digital conversion inside the camera and *after* any color array demosaicing. There are several cameras out on the market that have single-sensor Bayer pattern sensors in them, but record a 4:4:4 image. There is a contradiction there because, although the camera isn't discarding any color information before it records it to whatever format, it only has 33% of color information to start with, and the rest is interpolated through the demosaicing algorithm. 4:4:4, in these cases, means that the full interpolated color is recorded.

4:4:4									
Pixels									
		1	2	3	4	5	6	7	8	→
	1	GRB	GRB	GRB	GRB	GRB	GRB	GRB	GRB	
	2	GRB	GRB	GRB	GRB	GRB	GRB	GRB	GRB	
	3	GRB	GRB	GRB	GRB	GRB	GRB	GRB	GRB	
Lines in the Image	4	GRB	GRB	GRB	GRB	GRB	GRB	GRB	GRB	
	5	GRB	GRB	GRB	GRB	GRB	GRB	GRB	GRB	
	6	GRB	GRB	GRB	GRB	GRB	GRB	GRB	GRB	
	7	GRB	GRB	GRB	GRB	GRB	GRB	GRB	GRB	
	8	GRB	GRB	GRB	GRB	GRB	GRB	GRB	GRB	

4:2:2									
Pixels									
	1	2	3	4	5	6	7	8	→
1	GRB	G	GRB	G	GRB	G	GRB	G	
2	GRB	G	GRB	G	GRB	G	GRB	G	
3	GRB	G	GRB	G	GRB	G	GRB	G	
4	GRB	G	GRB	G	GRB	G	GRB	G	
5	GRB	G	GRB	G	GRB	G	GRB	G	
6	GRB	G	GRB	G	GRB	G	GRB	G	
7	GRB	G	GRB	G	GRB	G	GRB	G	
8	GRB	G	GRB	G	GRB	G	GRB	G	

(Lines in the Image)

4:1:1									
Pixels									
	1	2	3	4	5	6	7	8	→
1	GRB	G	G	G	GRB	G	G	G	
2	GRB	G	G	G	GRB	G	G	G	
3	GRB	G	G	G	GRB	G	G	G	
4	GRB	G	G	G	GRB	G	G	G	
5	GRB	G	G	G	GRB	G	G	G	
6	GRB	G	G	G	GRB	G	G	G	
7	GRB	G	G	G	GRB	G	G	G	
8	GRB	G	G	G	GRB	G	G	G	

(Lines in the Image)

4:2:0									
Pixels									
	1	2	3	4	5	6	7	8	→
1	GR	G	GR	G	GR	G	GR	G	
2	GB	G	GB	G	GB	G	GB	G	
3	GR	G	GR	G	GR	G	GR	G	
4	GB	G	GB	G	GB	G	GB	G	
5	GR	G	GR	G	GR	G	GR	G	
6	GB	G	GB	G	GB	G	GB	G	
7	GR	G	GR	G	GR	G	GR	G	
8	GB	G	GB	G	GB	G	GB	G	

(Lines in the Image)

Maintaining Your Image Integrity: Masterclass on Monitor Calibration

I can't stress enough about the importance of a professional calibrated monitor on set to maintain image integrity. Without a professional-grade monitor, that you can precisely calibrate, the image you're looking at while shooting is—at best—a guess at what the image might look like.

Even when working with raw cameras, maintaining consistency over the image and making quantitative judgments over your exposure, color, contrast, and lighting quality can't be done, with any real precision, without a calibrated tool to monitor the image—for some that tool could be a light meter and experience, for most it's a monitor.

LED monitors have come of age in the last few years. Where they were previously quite inferior to CRT (cathode ray tube) monitors—which are now obsolete—LED technology has improved considerably to be a viable production tool.

Without proper calibration, however, you might as well be looking at an Etch-A-Sketch image of your scene.

To properly calibrate your monitor, your camera needs to be able to generate SMPTE color bars. For many years—and still—I advocate the use of SMPTE (Society of Motion Picture and Television Engineers) Engineering Guideline EG 1–1990 color bars.

The importance of these bars are the top two portions: the large row of bars at the top, which take up about two-thirds of the image, are 75% intensity white, yellow, cyan, green, magenta, red, and blue. Beneath that is a small row of rectangular bars: blue, black, magenta, black, cyan, black, and gray.

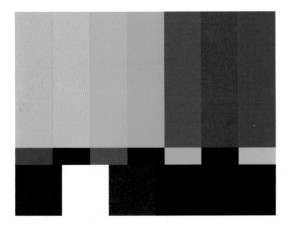

The traditional SMPTE color bars featuring three sections, the top 75% bars, the second row of complimentary bars and the PLUGE in the base.

GRAY	YELLOW	CYAN	GREEN	MAGENTA	RED		BLUE
BLUE	BLACK	MAGENTA	BLACK	CYAN	BLACK		GRAY
-I	WHITE	+Q		BLACK	BLK -4	BLK	BLK +4	BLACK

The composition of the SMPTE color bars.

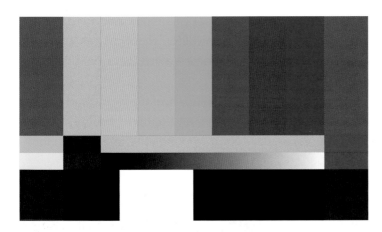

The revised HD standard color bars, still with 75% colors that fall within 4:3 area, but without complimentary bars—replaced by 75% white and an additional step in the PLUGE.

A revision to the SMPTE standard in 2002, developed by the Japanese Association of Radio Industry and Businesses (ARIB) is now prevalent in some HD and digital cinema cameras, and although they're similar, there are important differences to understand.

ARIB STD-B28 otherwise known as SMPTE RP 219–2002, can be frustrating if you don't know what you're looking for. The second row of alternating bars is gone, replaced by a solid long rectangle of 75% white (gray). The concepts are the same, but the important areas of the bars are slightly different.

In both cases, to utilize the bars to calibrate your monitor, you'll need a professional grade monitor with a "blue check" or "blue only" function, along with individual controls over chroma (color), phase (tint), brightness, and contrast. If you do not have a monitor with a blue function, you can procure a filter to simulate this effect. A Kodak Wratten 47B filter is best for this, or you can use a Wratten 98 filter. While looking at the color bars, hold the filter to your eye for a few seconds as you adjust your chroma and phase (or color and tint on some monitors). You only want to do this for a few seconds at a time, as your eye will start to compensate for the blue and bias your judgment of the monitor calibration.

The blue check function button on a professional monitor.

You can also use these blue filters to more precisely calibrate your flip-out LCD, onboard LCD, or color viewfinder (viewing tools that don't have blue-only functions)—none of which are optimal tools for fine image judgments, but they can be (and often are) used in a pinch.

CALIBRATION USING SMPTE EG 1–1990 BARS

You start your calibration with your contrast setting. Generally you're going to want your contrast to be as high as possible before overdriving it. To do this, turn the contrast all the way up and look at the three large squares at the bottom left-hand corner of the color bars. The second one in is a large white box. If you're overdriving your contrast, this box will "dance" a bit, or vibrate; seeming to be animated. Just turn down your contrast until that animation stops. On many HD monitors, it's not possible to overdrive the contrast. I'll usually back it off a bit from max to about 80–90%, depending on the monitor.

Next, we'll set the chroma and phase color adjustments. You do this by turning on the "blue check" function on your monitor.

When a monitor is set to "blue check" or "blue only," the red and green color outputs are turned off so that the image is monochromatic blue. When this happens, the top two sets of color bars appear as alternating blue and black. When chroma and phase are correctly aligned, the two sets of bars (long and short) blend into one another with the blues matching.

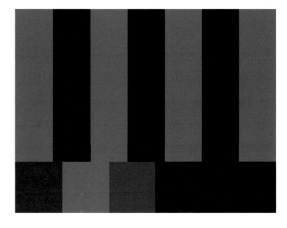

When the "blue check" or "blue only" function is enabled, the image becomes monochromatic blue and the bars become blue or black.

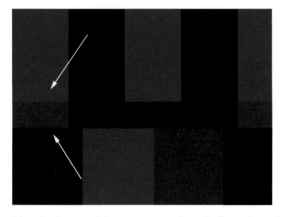 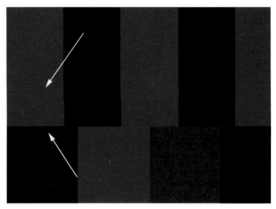

When the chroma and phase are not properly set, the first and second set of bars will not match. When the settings are correct, they blend seamlessly into one color.

When the colors are improperly calibrated, these rows will appear as very distinct variations of blue. To calibrate, make small adjustments to chroma *and* phase (alternating between them) while watching the two sets of bars. You'll need to adjust a little of each as you go to get it as precise as possible, but you'll see the bars get closer and closer in hue until the blues in the two rows are as close to matching as you can get them.

Once you've set your contrast, chroma and phase, it's time to set your brightness. Turn the "blue check" off so you're seeing full color bars again.

Now you're looking at the PLUGE (picture line-up generating equipment), which is the three thin black

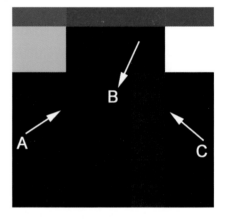

The PLUGE signal area. A represents blacker than black, B represents black, and C represents dark gray, just above black.

rectangular blocks toward the lower right-hand side. These three blocks represent blacker than black (A), black (B), and lighter than black (C). Slowly adjust the brightness until you can *barely* just see the third block (C). The other two should blend into the surrounding black, so that you are just *barely* seeing the third block only.

Now you've properly calibrated your monitor. The phase, chroma, contrast, and brightness levels are properly set and you're ready to rock and roll.

CALIBRATION USING SMPTE RP 219–2002 BARS

There are no alternating rows of color bars in the 2002 update, which can be a bit confusing, but have no fear, they still work the same way. The ARIB bars were designed to work with both 4:3 and 16:9 signals. The important color bars, again 75% intensity, sit within a 4:3 aspect ratio in the image. The outsides of those bars are filled with gray.

40% Gray	75% White	Yellow	Cyan	Green	Magenta	Red	Blue	40% Gray
100%C$_Y$	* 1	75% White						100%B
100%Y$_L$	Y-Ramp							100%R
15% Gray	0% Black	100% White	0% Black / -2% / 0% / +2% / 0% / +4%				0% Black	15% Gray

The composition of the revised HD color bars.

Instead of a second row of alternating colors, the ARIB signal features only a single 75% white line, which is called the "chroma set signal." When you turn on "blue only" on your monitor, you will be adjusting your chroma and phase until the large blue bars at top blend seamlessly into the long white bar beneath them. Using the 1990 bars, you're mixing cyan and magenta and blue and white. Those colors will appear as smooth single colors under "blue check" when the calibration is correct. Yellow, green, and red all become black when you're in "blue only" mode.

With the ARIB 2002 bars, you're still blending cyan/magenta and blue/white, but, they're not next to each other. Instead, you have a long line of white (75%) under the yellow, cyan, green, magenta, red, and blue color bars. When you go into "blue only" mode, yellow, green, and red will become black bars. Adjusting chroma and phase will blend the cyan, magenta, and blue bars in with the white bar under them.

NOTE! The small rectangular bars at far right and far left are 100% cyan (100% yellow under that) on the left and 100% blue (100% red under that) on the right. These will *not* match up with the center bars (which are all at 75%).

You still use the large 100% white square in the bottom row to set your contrast and the new PLUGE bars give you four levels of black to set your brightness. There is a large square of black, then a small strip of blacker-than-black (−2%), followed by black, followed by 2% gray, then black, then 4% gray, then black again. To properly set the brightness, you want to turn it up or down until you *just barely* see the 2% black stripe and the 4% is slightly more visible. The other areas of the bars are irrelevant to monitor calibration.

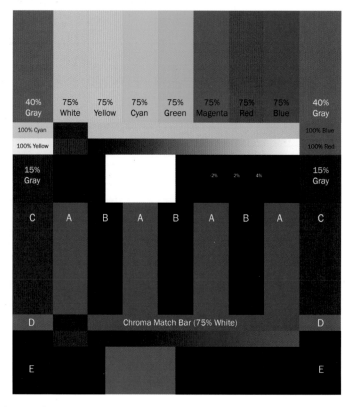

With the revised standard, you're adjusting chroma and phase to match the sections labeled A with the Chroma Match Bar. Note that the other sections—B, C, D, and E—do *not* match in proper calibration.

GENERAL NOTES

In the best-case scenario, these bars should be generated by your camera, but not every camera is capable of generating bars—frustrating as that may be. For instance, HDSLRs, like the Canon EOS series and the Nikon D series, don't generate color bars. In that case, I carry a small media card with me for each camera. For me, that's primarily the Canon EOS 7D.

The easiest way I've found to do this is to use Adobe Photoshop and the *Place* command, which allows you to place elements within a graphical file without changing its wrapping or coding structure.

To do this, use a small media card (generally ones that are now so small that they're obsolete— mine is an old 512MB compact flash card that came with a P&S camera in 2004— that card is now so small it can barely hold ten JPEG images from the 7D), take a photograph in JPG mode with the lens cap on just to get a simple, clean black frame. Pull the card and, using a reader on your computer, open that image in Photoshop and use the *Place* command from the File menu to place whichever color bars you prefer (they're easily found around the web) into that black image. This will allow you to add to an existing file without changing its actual structure. Then simply save the file back on the card. Now those bars can be played back in the camera and seen on your monitor so you can calibrate it properly. Since you used the *Place* command and didn't alter the file structure, the camera thinks those color bars are an image that it photographed, so you'll see a thumbnail and a preview of those bars on your rear LCD screen or any monitor connected to your camera.

In the best-case scenario, your monitor is positioned in a place where there is no extraneous light hitting the screen. In many situations, I'll build a black tent around the monitor to keep all light off of it and duck into the tent to view the monitor, but that's not always convenient or even possible. Even if you can do this, it's also important to understand that the monitor shouldn't be in *total* blackness. It's best to either have a soft glow (optimally of 6,500K, which is the native color temperature of most monitors) behind the monitor or a little light hitting the front frame of the monitor *without* hitting the screen. This takes some careful positioning of a small light fixture with barn doors so that the light just skips across the frame of the monitor. The glow behind or the light on the frame of the monitor is important to give your eye a neutral reference and keep your eye refreshed, especially if you have the monitor in an otherwise pitch-black tent.

We don't always have the option of providing a perfect environment for the monitor, however, so we have to make do with what we can do. Protect the monitor from stray light as much as you can and remember to calibrate it *every time* you move the monitor to a different location. If the monitor stays in one location all day long you really only need to calibrate it once per day, or once in the morning and once after lunch. If it moves around from set to set and location to location, you need to recalibrate every time you put it in a new space.

If you are away from a field monitor when you're shooting, you can certainly use your camera's viewfinder and/or flip-out LCD screen, but know that you're seeing a compromised version of your image. I would also highly recommend that you use the same methods described above to calibrate those viewing devices as best you can; at the very least, use the PLUGE to set your contrast and brightness levels. If you're using your viewfinder, you probably only need to do this once a day, as your "environment" is pretty stable inside the eye-cup. If you're using your flip-out or back-of-camera LCD screen, you should check your calibration often. Also, be extremely conscious of the angle of the LCD screen to your eye. Look at the screen as flat-on as you can so that you're not looking up or down or from the side at the screen.

The bottom line is that, in order to best utilize digital video's WYSIWYG, you need to have the proper calibrated monitor to see the best image, otherwise you're really just shooting in the dark.

PART 2
OPTICS

2.1 OPTICS

Deep into Depth of Field: Understanding a "Filmic" Depth of Field

Achieving that "filmic" depth of field was a holy grail among digital shooters for a long time—giving birth to a plethora of lens adapters—but now that larger sensors are more ubiquitous and affordable, the adapters are, by and large, obsolete and digital cinematographers can mimic the look and feel of 35mm motion picture depth of field with a native large sensor camera.

A shot from *Alone*, a short film I directed, photographed by Jayson Crothers. Here we used very shallow depth of field to create a mood. Alone © Adakin Productions. Jayson Crothers, Director of photography.

Depth of field (DOF) is an optical phenomenon whereby a certain range of space within an image is rendered into acceptable focus through a combination of target size, lens aperture size, and focus distance.

Why is shallow DOF so coveted? Not only does it provide a more "film-like" image, it provides the visual storyteller with an essential tool for focusing the audience's attention on a specific portion of the frame. It communicates to the audience that *this space* is what is important in this scene.

All of this is pretty common knowledge these days. However, in the past couple weeks, I've run across several instances where confusion and misnomers surrounding depth of field are still quite prevalent—even among professionals. I'll make a concerted effort to allay these misunderstandings and set the record straight on depth of field.

A demonstration of the importance of depth of field in visual storytelling. With selective focus, we can help the guide the audience's eye and show them what is important in the image. Here, actress Debbie Diesel holds a beautiful gift from her love—with deep depth of field, the ring gets lost in the background. When we shoot with very shallow depth of field, it's clear that she is holding a ring.

DEFINING THE FIELD

The physics of optics dictate that only one single plane of a photographic image is actually in focus. Light rays from the area of the scene that the lens is focused on pass though the lens and are projected onto the target plane (the sensor). Only that single point in space is actually "in focus." The rest of the image—in front of and behind that focused plane—falls into varying states of unfocused imagery that, depending on certain variables, can be considered "acceptable" or "unacceptable" focus. This area of "acceptable focus," in front of and behind the plane of focus, is called the depth of field.

Before I get too deep into the technical aspects of depth of field, it's very important to understand that this is an *extremely* subjective topic. The charts and calculators (thanks to modern iApps, DOF calculators are readily abundant) are based on mathematical calculations and *theoretical* optical elements. All depth of field calculators will give you an approximation of the area of acceptable focus for a given format. The focus doesn't just drop off sharply beyond those numbers; it's a very soft falloff and the DOF numbers are merely approximate guides based on certain mathematical assumptions. A lesser quality, lower-resolution lens (one with low sharpness and low contrast) may actually appear to have *more* depth of field because the image is naturally soft and the area where the "acceptable" sharpness falls to "unacceptable" is harder to determine. With a very sharp, high contrast lens, the depth of field can appear to be much less because the differences between "acceptable" and "unacceptable" are much more clearly discerned.

HYPER CONFUSION

To mathematically determine depth of field, you must first determine the specific lens' hyperfocal distance. The hyperfocal is an optical anomaly wherein, at a specific focal distance, for any given aperture and focal length, the acceptable focus is half that focal distance to infinity. Every lens, at every aperture, has a specific hyperfocal distance, but most "normal" lenses' hyperfocals are beyond a point of practical usage. Here are a couple of examples, based on 35mm motion picture lenses, at an aperture of *f/4*:

25mm—H = 20′ 2″

35mm—H = 39′ 7″

40mm—H = 51′ 8″

50mm—H = 80′ 9″

75mm—H = 181′ 8″

As you can see, the longer the lens, the further the hyperfocal setting. Most lenses don't have focal settings for any distance beyond 20′ so, in these instances, you're already focused on infinity, which makes the hyperfocal distance rather moot. The wider the lens, and the smaller the aperture, the closer the hyperfocal distance will be. This leads to some misconceptions about wider lenses having extraordinary depth of field, as with wider lenses, it's often more possible to utilize the hyperfocal function. The depth of field properties— aside from the anomaly of hyperfocal—remain consistent among focal lengths, however, as I'll explain in further detail a little later.

The hyperfocal distance for any given lens and aperture is calculated by taking the square of the lens' focal length divided by the product of the *f*-stop number and the circle of confusion (stick with me, that sounds daunting, but it's not as bad as it sounds).

$$H = \frac{F^2}{(f)(CoC)}$$

The circle of confusion is sometimes, well, confusing. In the most basic terms if we can realize that a picture is made up of millions and millions of points of lights and, within the plane of focus, those points will be photographed as sharp points. Beyond the plane of focus, as they get further and further out of focus, they begin to become larger and larger points, taking on the actual spherical shape of the optics of the lens.

To demonstrate this, I took three small flashlights and stood on them on their ends about two feet away from each other. I then set the camera on the floor to shoot a photo of the three flashlights.

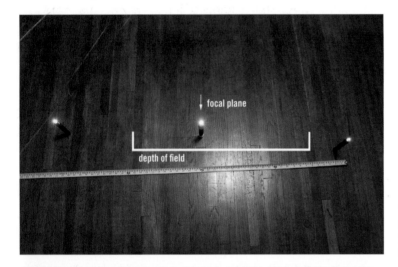

The behind-the-scenes of an illustration of circle of confusion. The camera is positioned out of the image at the far left and focused on the middle flashlight.

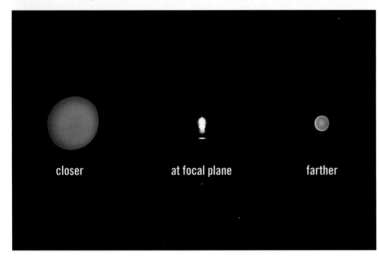

A demonstration of circle of confusion. The middle light, where the focus was set, appears as a sharp shape, but the other two lights appear as spheres, with no distinct shape.

I focused the camera on the middle flashlight. The white bracket in the image denotes the depth of field for that lens at that aperture and focal distance. The two far flashlights fall outside of the depth of field. Just below it is the resulting image.

Looking at the resulting photograph, the center flashlight bulb, the one I focused on, is shown as a sharp shape. We can see the shape of the light bulb and, even, the indentation at the base of the bulb is clear. The other two flashlights are much further away from that plane of focus and we can no longer discern the details of the bulb shape, they simply become out-of-focus spheres.

So we know that the plane of focus features sharp points of light that become more and more sphere-like, and larger, as they get further away from that plane.

Within the depth of field, for a given lens, aperture and focal length, the points of light are getting larger and more sphere-like, but they're still small enough to appear as points to our eyes and, hence, they still appear to be "in focus." That individual point hasn't gotten too large so that we lose the sharpness of the object. The mathematical point at which the out-of-focus sphere becomes too large and we lose the sense of detail so that the point is no longer considered to be "in focus" is defined by the circle of confusion.

The circle of confusion number is constant for any given format/sensor size. It is important to note, however, that this number is subjective and the real-world definition of what is in focus or not depends on the quality of the lens and even the quality and size of the final display. On an iPhone screen, the image might appear to have considerably more depth of field than it would if projected onto a full cinema screen. The circle of confusion number is a theoretical maximum, based on the format size. Leading to even more confusion, depending on the calculator you use, there are variations as to the base standard circles of confusion used for each format. Here are the numbers utilized by Toland, Chemical Wedding's Digital American Cinematographer Manual iApp, and by David Eubank's pCAM, two applications available for iPhone or iPod or other digital devices:

	Toland	pCAM
⅓" sensor	.00043"	.0002"
½" sensor	.00063"	.00028"
⅔" sensor	.00085"	.00035"
Super35-sized sensor	.001"	.00075"
35mm film	.001"	.00085"
Full-frame still-sized sensor	.00118"	.00114"

Although the circles of confusion numbers are considerably different in some cases between the two calculators, the practical results are nearly identical. For any truly critical applications it is always advisable to test the specific equipment you'll be using before your actual shoot.

Once we have our given circle of confusion numbers, we can calculate the hyperfocal distance for any lens and aperture (formula above). When you have that number, you can then calculate your depth of field. Formulas for depth of field are:

$$\text{Depth of field (close)} = \frac{(H)(S)}{H + (S\text{-}F)}$$

H = Hyperfocal, S = Subject distance, F = Focal length of the lens

$$\text{Depth of field (far)} = \frac{(H)(S)}{H - (S\text{-}F)}$$

Now, don't be so scared of the math. Although the formulas are useful to get a better understanding of what is happening, with modern calculators readily available, the math isn't something you need to deal with on a daily basis (there won't be a test later, I promise).

THE TRUTH ABOUT DEPTH

The important factors to take away here, besides the math, are an understanding that the most significant aspects of depth of field are:

- Format size (circle of confusion)
- Aperture
- Subject distance
- *Lens focal length*

Notice the emphasis on the last factor above: lens focal length. This is because longer focal length lenses, for a given focal distance, have less depth of field compared to shorter focal length lenses at the same focal distance. However, for a given field of view, changing your focal length will *not affect your depth of field*. Let's discuss this a bit further.

LONGER LENSES HAVE LESS DEPTH OF FIELD

This can be a confusing statement because there is truth in it, but when you compare apples to apples, it is incorrect.

An f-stop number (one of our significant contributors to DOF) is determined mathematically as the relationship between the diameter of the aperture opening and the focal length of the lens.

$$f = \frac{F}{a}$$

f = f-stop, F = Focal length, a = aperture (diameter of the opening)

So a 50mm lens that has a 25mm diameter aperture opening has an f-stop of f/2 (50/25 = 2).

If you look at a 100mm lens, an f/2 aperture is actually a 50mm diameter opening—twice as large as the f/2 on the 50mm lens. We know from the list above that the size of the aperture is one of the top factors in determining depth of field, so the f/2 on the 100mm lens has less depth of field than the f/2 on the 50mm lens, simply by the fact that it is twice as large a diameter opening. This is where the misnomer actually is true: longer lenses, for a given aperture, have less depth of field.

HOWEVER (and this is a big *HOWEVER*), when you're comparing apples to apples, things change. Many people believe—*incorrectly*—that they can control their depth of field by simply switching lenses. I've heard it almost a million times before (and even seen it in textbooks): if you want less depth of field in a shot, put on a longer lens and back the camera off.

Unfortunately, this is not true. If you are trying to maintain the same shot—keep the subject the same relative size in the frame—when you switch lenses (longer focal length) and back off (further subject distance) you will *maintain the same depth of field properties*. This is because you're switching your focal length, but you're also changing your focal distance by physically moving the camera further back. The two changes cancel each other out.

If we are shooting a medium close up of an actor on a 50mm lens from 5' away and we switch to a 100mm lens, in order to maintain the same field of view of that actor—to keep the same medium close up—we have to now move the camera back to 10' away from the actor. Although the 100mm lens has less depth of field at 5' than the 50mm lens does, when we move the 100mm lens back to 10' away—it now has *the exact same depth of field as the wider lens at a closer focus*.

- A 50mm lens, at an *f*/4, focused at 5′ has a depth of field from 4′ 9″ to 5′ 3″ for a total acceptable focus area of 5″
- A 100mm lens, at *f*/4, focused at 10′ has a depth of field from 9′ 9″ to 10′ 3″ for a total acceptable focus area of 5″

Notice that when we shifted to a longer lens, and moved the camera to maintain the same shot, the depth of field *did not change*.

So, although longer lenses do have less depth of field, by nature, in practical application, they have the same optical properties. The only way to change your depth of field (in most situations) is to increase the size of your lens aperture. The wider your aperture, the less depth of field you'll have. Inversely, the smaller your aperture, the more depth of field you'll have.

PROOF IN THE PUDDING

28mm @ f/5.6 @ 2′   50mm @ f/5.6 @ 3′6″   100mm @ f/5.6 @ 7′2″

An examination of changing focal length, but maintaining subject size, which does not change the depth of field.

By way of example, I set up a very quick demonstration as I was writing this column. I placed three playing cards about 8″ apart from each other, and took out my Canon EOS 7D with my 28–135mm lens to do some quick illustration. The lens is an *f*/5.6 at its widest aperture at the long end of the zoom, so I picked 5.6 as my base aperture. Starting with the 28mm lens at 2′ away from the center card, I took an exposure and then, maintaining the aperture, changed my zoom to a 50mm lens and moved the camera back to 3′ 6″ to approximately match the center card as the same size in the frame, and took another exposure. Then I changed the focal length to 100mm and moved back to 7′ 2″ and took a third exposure.

I didn't get the distances perfect—and, doing this too quickly, I was slightly off on my critical focus on the third exposure, but the rough demonstration stands to prove the point.

Card in focus plane @ 28mm/2' Card in focus plane @ 50mm/3'7" Card in focus plane @ 100mm/7'2"

Farthest card @ 28mm/2' Farthest card @ 50mm/3'7" Farthest card @ 100mm/7'2"

A closer look, clearly demonstrating that change in focal length, but maintaining subject size, does not change depth of field.

Because in the first exposure, the closest card is actually closer than the lens' minimum focus range, we're only going to look at the middle and back card for comparison. Notice that as I change focal lengths and focus distances, the relative depth of field between the two cards *does not change*. The focus is *slightly* clearer in the third exposure, because my critical focus was off (you can clearly see that in the top card) and I focused slightly *beyond* the card, so the far card is *slightly* more in focus—but the relationship of depth of field between them does not change.

FIELD NOTES

Depth of Field Pull in *Miracles*

Ernest Holzman, ASC, was the cinematographer on a short-lived television series, *Miracles*, which featured one of the best pilots I had ever seen up to that date. Holzman executed a remarkable shot in the pilot episode—a depth of field pull—a change of depth of field in-shot.

The following is an excerpt from my article "Divine Intervention" which appeared in *American Cinematographer* magazine, February 2003.

Holzman and [director Matt] Reeves made focus a key part of their visual storytelling, using it as a narrative device in nearly every scene. Many sequences and shots begin completely out of focus, and the characters then step into the plane of focus. After he goes on sabbatical to find his faith, Callan [the show's lead character, played by Skeet

FIELD NOTES

Screen captures from the short-lived series *Miracles*. In the pilot episode, director of photography Ernest Holzman incorporated a depth of field pull in-shot. These images are all taken from the same shot. *Miracles* © Touchstone Television.

Ulrich] is called back to investigate a potential "real deal": a young boy with an incurable blood disease who has the ability to heal other people. Callan discovers that he has been dreaming about this boy for some time, and during an intimate conversation with the dying child, he discovers that the boy has been dreaming about him as well. This moment of clarity is accentuated by Holzman's use of the limited-focus concept, which takes the scene to the next level. "In a very broad sense, this is a detective story," the cinematographer maintains. "Callan is looking for the truth behind this kid's special qualities. When they have this meeting of the minds, I thought it would be very interesting to [increase] the depth of field to create the antithesis of the limited depth we've been using in every other shot. We wanted to show that a moment of clarity was taking place."

To achieve this, Holzman lit the scene to an aperture stop of T11, but he began shooting the scene at a T2.8 with an 11.2° shutter; this made the boy clearly focused in the foreground, while Callan was completely out of focus in the background. As the shot continued, Holzman utilized a pair of interlocked FTZSAC controls to slowly open the shutter angle and close down the T-stop. By the end of the scene, he had progressed to a T11 and a 180° shutter, which slowly brought Callan into clear focus while maintaining sharp focus on the boy. "I loved that the overall effect was extremely subtle," enthuses Reeves. "We had it happen over a length of time so that as the truth is dawning on the character, we're slowly bringing him into focus. You don't notice the depth change and you're not losing focus on the kid. It's very subtle."

"Almost no one has noticed it," Holzman adds. "But that's how I approach my photography—I like it to be very invisible. It's like a music cue that really works: you feel it, you experience it, it helps you understand the story, but you're not really aware of it being there. That's what I'm striving for."

Optical Illusions: Understanding Interchanging Optics

In the world of digital video, there is much ado about depth of field—and deservedly so. Decreased depth of field is one of the more attractive attributes of the "film look." However, many digital video shooters don't have a firm grasp on field of view. Whereas depth of field denotes the area before and after the plane of focus that will appear in an acceptable range of sharpness, field of view denotes the total area (both horizontally and vertically) that will be captured by a given lens onto a given target.

What we're going to talk about here is "crop factor," a term that gets thrown around quite a bit, but not everyone seems to really understand what it means. By "crop factor," we're talking about a change in apparent focal length of a lens when moving from one medium to another, with a smaller sensor size.

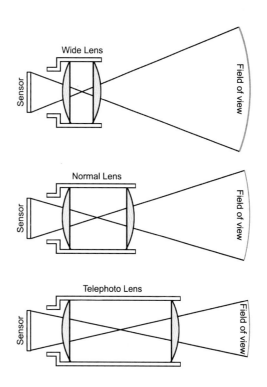

A visual representation of various focal length lenses. Although they have different field of views, the image projected is always the same size.

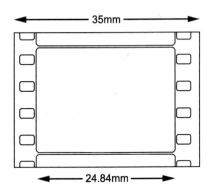

The dimensions of a piece of 35mm motion picture film.

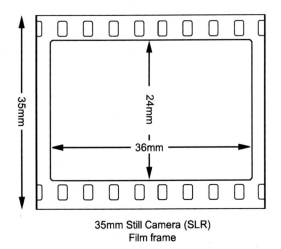

35mm Still Camera (SLR)
Film frame

Comparison of image size of 35mm film as oriented vertically in a motion picture camera as opposed to the same 35mm film oriented horizontally in a still camera.

A lens is designed to capture the light from a given field of view and project that light onto a given target size. No matter what the field of view—perhaps very wide with a wide lens or very narrow with a long lens—the image is projected onto the same size target at the back of the lens. With today's extraordinary selection of sensor sizes (¼", ⅓", ½", ⅔", Super35, full-frame still camera, etc), many people are turning to smaller, more inexpensive sensor sizes and then utilizing higher quality lenses intended for larger formats. This often yields an improvement in the quality, sharpness, and contrast of the lenses, but also alters the respective focal length of the re-purposed lens.

There is a lot of confusion about this topic and many people place more importance on it than is necessary—so I'll try to clear up some of that here.

HDSLR cameras often feature large sensors and in many such cases, larger than Super35 film. Why is this? Both still-photography cameras and motion-picture cameras utilize the same 35mm film, so why would the sizes in HDSLR cameras be different?

It comes down to orientation.

A piece of 35mm photographic film is 35mm wide from side to side. However, in order to transport each frame within the camera, we have to have perforations on the sides of the film. The remaining image area, between these perforations, is an area of roughly 24mm wide.

In a motion picture camera, film runs vertically through the picture gate. This means that the width of the image was determined by the width between the perforations. Super35 format exposed the most negative area between the perforations, about 24mm, with an image area four perforations high, that resulted in 19mm of vertical height per frame.

In a 35mm still camera, the film runs *horizontally* through the camera. This means that the 24mm limitation between the perforations now becomes the *height* of the image and we can use a much wider area of the negative, up to 36mm (creating a 1.5:1 aspect ratio), to get a nice image area for still photographs.

This is an important distinction when working with HDSLR cameras as there are different categories of sensors. "Full frame" sensors feature the full size of the 36mm horizontal still frame area. "Crop sensors" are significantly smaller than this; which includes the size of Super35 motion picture film, and smaller.

A "full frame" camera features a sensor the size of a traditional 35mm still frame at 36mm × 24mm large. Compared to the standard Super35 motion picture frame size at 24.89mm × 18.76mm, the still frame is nearly twice the size of the Super35 film frame. This means that lenses designed for a full-frame camera have to project their image onto the larger 36mm × 24mm area while lenses made specifically for smaller format sizes, such as motion picture cameras, often are designed to only cover the smaller target dimensions.

Lenses, which are circular, project a circular image; not a rectangular one. So every lens has a certain amount of image that is "wasted" because the target (digital sensor or film) is only "seeing" a portion of that projected image. Lenses designed for a particular format are optimized to project their sphere, called the "image circle," to evenly cover the actual rectangular target size with little waste.

If we take a 50mm focal length lens designed to work with the full-frame 35mm still camera, and use it on a "crop" (smaller) sensor, such as an APS-C (Canon) or DX (Nikon), which are both closer to the size of the

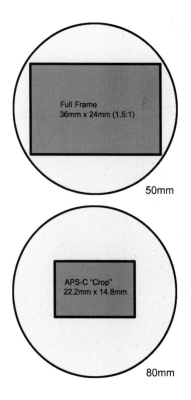

When utilizing a lens designed to project an image circle on a larger target on a smaller target camera, the field of view will be altered by the sensor seeing only a portion of the image circle.

24 × 18mm Super35 film frame, the lens is projecting its image over a considerably larger area than the actual physical size of the sensor. As a result, we have a lot more wasted image because the sensor only "sees" a small portion of the lens' image.

This alters the field of view of the lens and, alters the apparent focal length. What was, originally, a 50mm lens on the full-frame camera, is now the equivalent of an 80mm lens on the crop frame. It is *very* important to understand that this only changes the *apparent* focal length. It does not change the overall properties of the lens. It merely "crops" off portions of the image circle so that the field of view from that lens is different between the cameras.

The smaller the sensor size, the longer the apparent focal length of any given lens. The image below shows an approximation of using a 50mm lens from a full-frame still camera, from the same physical distance to the subject, on several smaller sensor cameras. This is not to imply that the larger lens can (or should) be used with any camera, it's merely an example of how apparent focal length is changed by changing the sensor size.

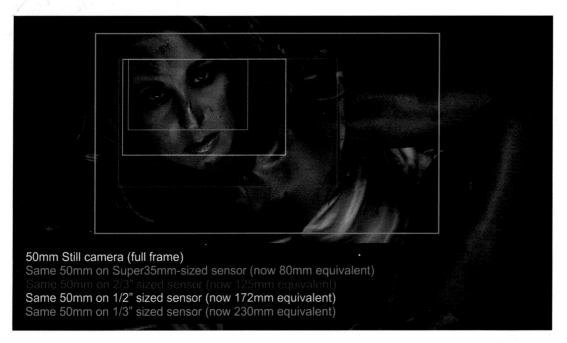

50mm Still camera (full frame)
Same 50mm on Super35mm-sized sensor (now 80mm equivalent)
Same 50mm on 2/3" sized sensor (now 125mm equivalent)
Same 50mm on 1/2" sized sensor (now 172mm equivalent)
Same 50mm on 1/3" sized sensor (now 230mm equivalent)

A visual depiction of utilizing a 50mm lens designed for a 35mm SLR on various smaller sized sensors and the adjusted field of view that results.

Determining what apparent focal length you will be seeing from any given lens on a different format often requires a little research and some basic geometry skills.

First, you need to know the actual physical dimensions of the sensors in each of the cameras—the larger format you're borrowing a lens from and the smaller format you'll be using it on. Not all manufacturers readily provide this information, but this is the age of the Internet, and with some digging you can find the information you're looking for.

If we're working with a lens made for the, say, Canon 5D Mk III, with a sensor size of 36mm × 24mm, and intend to use it on a Canon EOS 7D (with a sensor size of 22.2mm × 14.8mm), we will need to find out the lens equivalency (crop factor) in order to deduce its new apparent focal length. In order to do that, we need to find the diagonal measurements of each of the sensors.

This requires cracking out a little high school geometry and good ol' Pythagorean theorem to find the hypotenuse of a right triangle: $A^2 + B^2 = C^2$. A and B represent the length and width of the chip, so for the 5D we have $36^2 + 24^2 = C^2$ (C= diagonal): 1,296 + 576 = 1,872. We figure out the square root of 1,872 and get a diagonal of 43.27mm. For the 7D's sensor, we find 492.84mm + 219.04mm = 711.88mm. The square root of that is a 26.68mm diagonal. Finally, divide the diagonal of the larger sensor by the diagonal of the smaller sensor and we get a factor of 1.62×.

So a lens from a 5D Mk III on a 7D will have an apparent focal length of 1.62× longer. A 50mm becomes an 81mm. A 10mm becomes a 16mm and so forth.

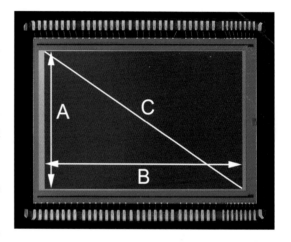

When calculating changes in field of view while using lenses designed for other cameras, the diagonal or hypotenuse of the sensor is the factor you need to compare. To calculate the diagonal, take the height of the sensor squared plus the width of the sensor squared and find the square root of the sum.

These calculations were of paramount importance to cinematographers who first made the leap from film to digital with ⅔" cameras. Understanding the 2.5× lens factor was important in making lens selections and becoming comfortable with the new medium.

A 50 IS A 50

What's really important to realize is that this crop factor is only relevant if you're used to working with the larger format and you're now working with a smaller sensor. In truth, there's no change in apparent focal length by moving a lens from one format to another—only the resulting field-of-view changes *relative to the format it came from.*

There's a phrase in optics: "A 50 is a 50 is a 50."

What does this mean?

It means that any lens, of any focal length, when moved to different mediums, still behaves as that focal length lens would in the new medium.

To understand that a little better, let's talk about "normal" perspective.

For a Super35 motion picture camera, 50mm is considered a "normal" perspective, giving a field of view and magnification that, roughly, approximates that of human vision. For Super16, which is about half the size of 35mm, a 25mm lens is considered "normal" perspective. That means a 25mm lens on a Super16 camera has a field of view that is, roughly, equivalent to a 50mm lens on a Super35 camera.

If we were to take the 50mm lens from the Super35 camera and put it on the Super16 camera, it will have far less field of view in 16mm than it did in 35mm, as explained above. If we were *comparing* that new field of view *back to the Super35* camera, we could say that the new field of view of the 50mm lens on the Super16 camera is, roughly, equivalent to a 100mm lens on the Super35 camera. This is where the crop factor comes in. When comparing the adjusted field of view back to the original format, we multiply the lens' focal length by the crop factor.

However notice that the "normal" perspective in Super16 is a 25mm lens, twice as wide as the "normal" perspective 50mm in Super35. When we take the lens from the larger format and put it on the smaller format—it behaves *exactly* as a 50mm lens would on a Super16 camera—it just turns out that the field of view in Super16 is half that of the field of view in Super35 for any given focal length lens.

As sensors get smaller, field of views get tighter for any given focal length.

So if I take a 50mm lens, designed for use on a full-frame HDSLR camera and use it on a Super35-sized sensor, a 16mm-sized sensor, or an 8mm-sized sensor—it will always have the same field of view as a 50mm lens would in the new format. In Super8, a "normal" lens is a 16mm lens—a 50mm would be a long lens in Super8, but it's a "normal" lens in Super35.

This means if you're working in a medium you're used to working in and you are using lenses borrowed from a larger format—crop factor means nothing to you. The lens will behave exactly as that focal length lens that you're used to. If you're used to working in a larger format and you are using a smaller format camera, then crop factor (whether borrowing lenses or not) will help you to understand the relationship between focal length and the field of view you're used to.

Hence, a 50 is a 50 is a 50.

Making the Switch: Lens Mounts and Interchangeability

Today, with a prevalence of large single-sensor cameras, the options for lenses for cinematographers has grown exponentially. Not every lens will work with every camera, however. Previously, I discussed crop factors and utilizing lenses designed for larger target (sensor) areas on smaller targets and the changes in apparent focal length/field of view, but choosing a lens for your camera can get even a little more complicated when you start to consider the different types of lens mounts and their *register*, or *flange focal distances*.

In the SLR and DSL world, each camera manufacturer uses their own type of lens mount. Typically, each type of mount is proprietary and does not interchange with other manufacturer's mounts without a physical adapter between the lens and the camera. In many video cameras, there are some standard types of mounts that nearly all camera manufacturers use, but this isn't the case when you're using SLR lenses. Leica, Nikon, Canon, Olympus, and Pentax all use different lens mounts, and not all are interchangeable without an adapter.

In the motion picture film-camera world, although there are myriad types of lens mounts for myriad cameras, the Arri PL (Positive Lock) mount arose as a universal professional standard for both 16mm and 35mm motion picture cameras. Many extraordinary lenses have been manufactured by all of the great lens makers in the PL mount. The second most prevalent mount in the motion picture world is the Panavision (PV) mount.

In order to know if you can harness the wealth of lenses manufactured for a particular camera on your new single-sensor HD camera, you have to know a few things first.

As discussed earlier, although we all work in a rectangular world where our images are concerned, lenses project the image in a circular pattern. In order for a lens to work with a given format, the diameter of the projected image circle must be equal to or greater than the hypotenuse of its rectangular target. If the lens is designed for the format, or very closely, you will have an excellent match. Many large-sensor cameras are now using the Super35 film (24.89mm × 13.98 in 16:9 aspect ratio) aperture size as the standard. In the stills world, this is classified as the APS-C (Advanced Photo System, Type C) "crop" group.

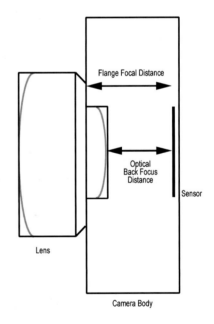

Flange focal distance (register) is measured from the sensor to the contact point between the body of the camera and the lens. Optical back focus is measured from the rear element of the lens to the sensor.

Any lens designed for work with Super35 film cameras, will also cover the area of an APS-C sensor. This image area, however, is considerably smaller than that of standard still cameras (36mm × 24mm), which means lenses designed for still cameras can be used on Super35 sensor cameras, but there will be a decreased field of view and increased apparent focal length, or what is commonly called the "crop factor." Lenses designed for use with Super35mm/APS-C targets cannot be used with "full-frame" cameras as the lens will not cover the full sensor.

There's an additional factor to consider when you're looking to interchange lenses from one format camera to another. In a single-target camera, such as the HDSLR or large single-sensor digital cinema camera, there is a fixed distance from the rear of any lens mounted on the camera to the sensor plane. This distance is called the *flange focal distance*, or sometimes called the *register*. It is measured from the point at which the back of the lens mount connects with the front of the camera's mount to the target/sensor itself—the point at which metal connects to metal to the film/sensor plane. This distance is different for different camera manufacturers, different types of cameras and different photographic mediums.

The reason why this distance is important is that all lenses designed for a particular camera system are designed to work with that fixed flange focal distance. This is how Canon knows that all of their EF lenses will work with any Canon EF body—because every Canon body has a fixed flange distance of 44mm. In the digital motion-picture camera world, all cameras that have PL mounts have a fixed flange focal distance of 52mm. This large flange distance was created to accommodate the rotating shutter utilized in reflex motion-picture film cameras, but it also makes these lenses compatible with a lot of other camera systems.

You can use a lens designed for a *larger* flange focal distance on a camera with a *smaller* flange distance by merely applying a lens adapter that increases the physical distance of the lens from the smaller camera's sensor. However, you cannot really use a lens designed for a smaller flange distance on a larger camera. In this case, the lens will not be able to focus to infinity (or even closer distances) and your lens' inscribed focus marks will also be off.

Interestingly, expanding the flange focal distance greater than the lens is designed for will turn the lens into a macro lens, increasing its close-focus ability (decreasing the minimum focus distance). This is, generally, what a borescope tube does to lenses, making them have extreme close-focus capabilities.

In optical design, many lenses have rear elements that are actually positioned behind the mounting point—and there is a difference between the flange focal distance and the *optical back-focus* distance, which is the measurement from the plane of the rear optical element of the lens to the target.

When designing optics, it is considerably easier to manufacture a higher quality lens if the rear element is very close to the target. The more distance that the lens has to project the image, the more aberrations are a challenge to manufacture out. In digital cameras that don't require a spinning shutter or a reflex mirror,

Fujifilm X-Pro1	17.7mm
Sony Alpha NEX E-Mount	18mm
Micro 4/3	20mm
Minolta/Leica M bayonet	27.80mm
Leitz/Minolta CL, Minolta CLE	27.80mm
Olympus E, Panasonic Lumix DMC-L, Leica Digilux	38.67mm
Canon FD	42.00mm
Canon EOS EF "Full Frame"	44.00mm
Canon EOS EF-S APS-C	44.00mm
Pentax K	45.46mm
Olympus OM	46mm
Nikon F-mount	46.5mm
Leica R	47.00mm
Contax-N	48mm
Arri PL	52mm
Panavision PV mount	57.15mm

the lens can be positioned very close to the target, which allows the manufacturer to create inexpensive, high-quality lenses. In addition, these cameras with very small flange focal distances can be easily adapted to work with higher-end lenses created for larger flange focal distances, such as the PL and PV lenses.

A Micro 4/3 camera (micro for the lack of a reflex mirror), has an extraordinarily shallow flange focal distance of just 20mm, making it easily adaptable with nearly any lens out there (as long as the physical barrel diameter of the lens does not exceed that of the camera's mount). This includes lenses that will work with Micro 4/3, 4/3, APS-C, Super35, APS-H, and full-frame cameras. It is this shallow flange focal distance that makes it possible for the Micro 4/3 camera to accept many different types of lenses.

The chart above details several different camera and lens systems and their flange focal distances. Generally speaking, if you have a camera with a small flange focal distance, you can use more variety of lenses with that camera (with an appropriate adapter).

Thanks to Guy McVicker, manager of optics at Panavision, Hollywood, for his assistance with this column.

A Closer Look: Diopters

I recently had a conversation on Facebook with a friend who was looking to purchase a new camera for a family member who makes jewelry. She was concerned about getting the best macro lens possible to photograph the details of the jewelry. While macro lenses can be fantastic, the category of "macro" covers a lot of ground that may or may not actually represent a lens with excellent close-focus ability. Good, real macro lenses can be very expensive and I suggested that she could purchase the standard kit lens with the camera, and get a set of diopters (also sometimes known as close-up adapters). These optical filters come in many size diameters and are often screwed to the front of a lens to allow it to focus increasingly closer, depending on the strength of the diopter applied. This way, my friend could have an extreme close-up lens without the expense of a specialty macro lens.

A Schneider 138mm diameter +3 diopter.

Diopters are positive supplementary lenses that are, in the most basic sense, glorified magnifying glasses that attach to the front of an existing lens. The glass element is a simple meniscus (curved) lens. These adapters are commonly called diopters, close-up attachments or proxars. Diopter is actually an optical term referring to a lens with a focal length of 1 meter. This means, if you have a +1 diopter and you attach it to a lens set at infinity focus, the focus distance is now 1m (3.28'). Where it gets slightly confusing is that higher power diopters reduce the minimum focus distance—so a +2 diopter on a lens set at infinity will reduce the minimum focus to 0.5m (1.64'). A +3 diopter will reduce the focus to ⅓ of a meter (11.8") and so forth. Common diopters come in +½, +1, +2, +3, +4, and +5, but they can also come in fractional diopters, +3.2, +3.5, and can even go as high as +7.

By attaching a diopter to a lens you are, in essence, reducing the minimum focus and magnifying the image to get the camera closer. This, in turn, renders a larger, close-focused image of the subject being photographed. The measurements above are with diopters used on a lens focused at infinity, but if you adjust the lens' focus to something *less* than infinity, you can get a lot closer. If your camera's lens has a minimum focus of 3', with a +3 diopter, you can now focus at 13", thereby getting the camera much closer to your subject and getting a "macro" shot. In addition, diopters can be stacked together to form even higher power magnification. A +3 and +4 diopter, together, will equal a +7 and a minimum distance of 5.5", at least.

Users should exercise caution when stacking diopters as they can quickly degrade the image. When stacking, the highest power diopter should be closest to the actual lens. In addition, it's a general rule of thumb to shoot with diopters at a fairly deep stop—above a F4 or F5.6, if possible, to help reduce some image degradation from the addition of these simple lenses.

One of the main image degradation effects from a simple meniscus lenses is chromatic aberration, when various color wavelengths of light are refracted by the lens and don't meet at a fixed focal point, you start to see color fringing around the image. To combat this, higher-end diopters are made achromatic, with two lens elements, to correct for the chromatic aberration. These diopters are considerably more expensive, although still—in many cases— cheaper than high-end macro lenses. Some people mistakenly refer to all diopters as "achromats," but that term is only applicable to the dual element lenses and not the simple diopters.

The photo of a page from my grandfather's Portuguese prayer book was taken with a Canon EOS 7D with a 55mm lens from a distance of 10.75", the lens' minimum focus.

The second photo was the same page, with combined Schneider Achromat +3 and +2 diopters at a distance of 7.75". Note that not only is the shot much closer to the physical page, but that the depth of field is extremely

A shot of my grandfather's Portuguese prayer book as close as I could get the lens.

shallow. Both shots are at the same *f*-stop and no additional optical devices are employed. The depth of field is reduced merely because the camera is closer to the subject and the focal distance is so short that the depth of field is only a fraction of an inch.

Additionally, split-field diopters are also available. These are lenses that are, literally, split—that is they're cut right down the middle of the lens element so that the lens holder has half an open space and half a diopter. This allows the cinematographer to apply the close-focus application of the diopter to only a portion of the frame and utilize the lens's inscribed focus setting for the other portion of the frame. Director Brian DePalma is well known for his use of split-field diopters, as well as cinematographer Stephen H. Burum, ASC, who has worked with DePalma on a number of occasions.

The split-field diopters do, however, create a clearly visible distortion line between the close focus and normal element of the frame. This can either be incorporated into the

The same shot with the help of diopters gets substantially closer. Note the extremely limited depth of field comes from the camera being so close to the subject.

A split-field diopter. The diopter is literally sliced in half so that half of the frame is diopter and half of the frame is open air.

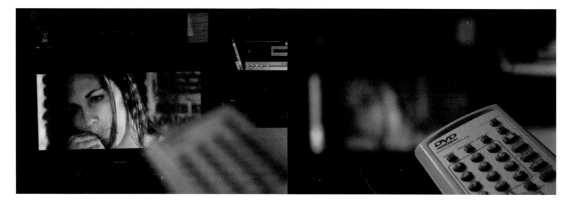

The left demonstrates the shot focused on the television across the room, the right is focused on the remote. At this aperture, it is not possible to hold both the television and remote in focus.

At the same aperture as the previous images, now incorporating a split-field diopter, we can now have both the remote and the television in focus. Note the distinct line of focus where the diopter is cut.

artistic vision of the image, or cleverly hidden through framing and "concealing" the transition with some dark vertical line in the composition. The image above was taken using a Schneider +3 split field diopter.

Diopters can be attached to nearly any lens, which makes them a perfect choice for fixed-lens cameras that have no macro option or prime lens users with a large lens kit. If you have a number of lenses, the best-case scenario is to get a set of diopters equal to the lens diameter of your largest lens, and then purchase inexpensive step-down rings (if you intend to screw-on the diopters), or a large enough matte-box that will accommodate the diameter size required to cover all of your lenses. But in doing so, you will only need one set of diopters to work with any lens in your package.

Split-Field Diopters Used in Popular Movies

For a further examination of uses of split-field diopters, let's look at a few frame captures from a few classic movies.

Some directors and cinematographers take great pains to hide the transition in the split-field diopter, while some make it part of the shot for effect. In either case, it allows two different aspects of a frame to be in focus at the same time without utilizing a ton of light and a deep, deep *f*-stop on the lens.

The Untouchables, directed by Brian DePalma, photographed by Stephen H. Burum, ASC. © Paramount Pictures.

The Untouchables, directed by Brian DePalma, photographed by Stephen H. Burum, ASC. © Paramount Pictures.

Jaws, directed by Steven Spielberg, photographed by Bill Butler, ASC. Jaws © Universal Pictures.

FIELD NOTES

Close Encounters of the Third Kind, directed by Steven Spielberg, photographed by Vilmos Zsigmond, ASC. Close Encounters of the Third Kind © Columbia/Tristar.

Reservoir Dogs, directed by Quentin Tarantino, photographed by Andrzej Sekula. Reservoir Dogs © Artisan Entertainment.

Star Trek: The Motion Picture, directed by Robert Wise, photographed by Richard H. Kline, ASC. Star Trek The Motion Picture © Paramount Pictures / CBS.

2.5 OPTICS

Through the Looking Glass: Lens Adapters

Although relatively small-sized camcorders have served to get more and more videographers into the HD arena, there are several trade-offs to smaller chip sizes and one of them is wide angle shots.

The smaller imagers of ⅓" and less cameras make it increasingly difficult to inexpensively manufacture quality lenses, especially with wide angles of view.

A 0.7× wide angle converter attached to the front of a Canon 20 × zoom lens.

ANGLE OF VIEW

The angle of view (AOV), or field of view, describes the degree of view a particular lens can capture. A 180° AOV would see everything including the edges of the lens itself!

Many, many years ago, when I was first teaching myself photography, I sat on the floor of my mother's living room with my 35mm SLR, a roll of masking tape, two plastic cups, a tape measure, and a protractor. The AOVs I was reading about just didn't seem right to me, and I wanted to see if they related to real-world optics. I set the camera down on the floor and carefully positioned each plastic cup at exactly the same distance from the lens and moved them to the very extreme of the horizontal view from the camera. I then taped a line with the masking tape from each cup to the lens, thereby creating a large "V" angle on the floor. Using my trusty protractor (left over from high-school geometry), I measured the angle of the tape V and—low-and-behold—it matched the published angle of view for that focal length precisely.

Any lens has two angles of view, one for the horizontal plane and one for the vertical. For our purposes here, we'll only look at horizontal AOVs.

MM IS MM—TARGET SIZE DEFINES AOV

All focal lengths, no matter what the format, are optically the same. A 50mm lens for a 35mm motion picture camera has the same distance between the nodal point (roughly the center of the lens where the light rays converge) and the focal plane (film/sensor) as does a 50mm lens on a ⅙" consumer camcorder. Modern zoom lenses, and primes with multiple elements, can cheat this physical distance to a degree, but the optical properties remain the same. In a 35mm motion picture camera, the diagonal of the frame aperture (Academy) is 1.07"—a pretty sizeable target on which to project a very wide angle of view. With a motion picture camera and a 12mm lens, which is very wide, you can have a field of view of 92.1° without significant distortion. That same 12mm lens on a ⅓" camera, which has a diagonal of .236", will only give you an angle of view of 28°! The smaller target for the lens gives a considerably narrower angle of view. This is what makes achieving wide-angle shots on small chip cameras very challenging.

ENTER THE ADAPTER

This is where lens adapters or converters come into play. I'm not talking about adapters that allow film lenses to be used on digital cameras, I'm talking about *optical* adapters, which attach to the camera's lens to decrease the focal length and that, in turn, increases the angle of view. Adding the additional optical elements, allows you to cheat the maximum angle of view to achieve wider shots.

There are, of course, limitations as to how wide you can go with any adapter before you begin to distort the image. Rectilinear wide lenses (those in which real-world straight lines are represented as straight lines in the image) are difficult to manufacturer. The wider the angle of view, the more likely it is to distort the image. Fisheye lenses, the antithesis of rectilinear, provide extreme wide angles of view, but also extreme distortion of the image.

Lens adapters are calibrated by their conversion factor. A 0.7× will mean you simply multiply your focal length by that conversion factor to see how wide your converted focal length will be.

On one particular ⅓″ camera with 20× zoom lens the widest end of the zoom is 5.4mm, which has an angle of view of 54.8°. With a 0.7× adapter we can convert that 5.4mm to 3.78mm and result in a new angle of view of 73°; an increase of almost 25% (and now roughly the equivalent of an 18mm lens on a 35mm motion picture camera).

A shot with a standard 18mm lens on an APS-C camera.

Beyond that, you start to get into image distortion and fisheye lenses. Adding a converter with a factor of 0.4× turns the 5.4mm into a 2.2mm lens with an angle of view of 103.6°, but with significant image distortion.

The same shot with a 0.65× wide angle attachment.

TO AFOCAL OR NOT TO AFOCAL?

Some adapters are *afocal* adapters, meaning that they create no specific focal point themselves (the light rays passing through the adapter do not converge), but rather merely resize the image by optically altering the lens's focal length. A non-afocal adapter works by creating a new focal point for a given lens. Some adapters are negative optical elements projecting the image *in front* of the lens, requiring a macro focus lens to work. The benefit of this, if you have the right lens to work with it, is the ability to create a very wide angle of view with a very small and lightweight adapter. An afocal adapter can weigh as much as a pound and a half whereas a non-afocal adapter can be as light as one ounce.

A shot with a standard 18mm lens on an APS-C camera.

The same shot with a fisheye wide angle adapter attachment.

The disadvantage to a non-afocal adapter is that it will only work if the lens can focus on the new focal point (in this case, requiring a macro lens to focus on the image projected mere inches in front of the lens) and will only work on a fixed focal length, which means you can't zoom through it.

It may seem like an odd technique to have a wide-angle adapter and then zoom through it, but there are many times—especially in run-and-gun situations—where you'll need to recompose an image quickly and being able to still have your full range of zoom (albeit shortened by the adapter's conversion factor) is a very handy thing to have.

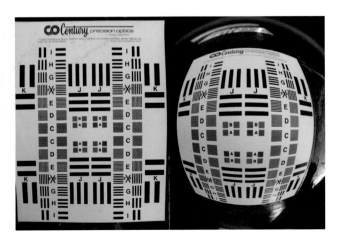

Comparing a wide angle lens to a fisheye lens. Note the extreme distortion of the significantly wider image with the fisheye lens.

Through Colored Glass: Lens Filtration

For many videographers, the farthest they delve into lens filtration is a UV filter constantly affixed to their lens. Filters, for many, seem to be a terrifying undiscovered country. In this column, I'll try to demystify the art and science of lens filtration.

Filters come primarily in two main shapes: circular and square (or rectangular). Circular filters are designed to screw directly onto the threaded rings on your lens whereas square filters require a mattebox to hold them in place. The benefit to certain square filters is that you can position them more precisely in front of the lens. This is beneficial for graduated filters that have transitions from one effect to another or from a clear to effect so that you can precisely position that transition. Typical rectangular sizes are 4″ × 4″, 4″ × 5.125″ (called "Panavision") and 6″ × 6″. To get the most versatility from your filters, it's always best to have a mattebox and a filter size that easily covers all of your lenses.

Filters are also made of different types of materials. Most filters are glass, but some less expensive alternatives are made from plastic or resin.

If you're going with the screw-on type filter, you need to know the diameter of your lens to know which filter size to choose. Most lenses have this information printed right on it. The diameter symbol is a circle with a diagonal line through it and this is followed by a number, usually represented in millimeters; that's your filter size.

Filters come in four major categories: correction, diffusion/contrast, effect, and what I call "special duty."

The circle with the line through it (Ø) represents diameter measurement. This number is printed on most lenses and represents the size of the threads on the lens for filter attachment.

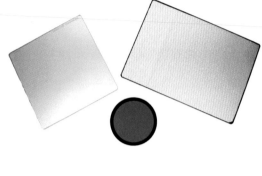

Some various sizes and shapes of camera filters.

CORRECTION FILTERS

These are the most common types of filters used. There are two major types of correction filters, exposure correction and color correction. Exposure correction, or neutral density (ND) filters, reduce the amount of light passing through the lens without altering the color or contrast. Most video cameras have built-in ND filters, but on some less expensive cameras these are not actual filters, rather an electronic signal manipulation—it's important to know the difference. Many videographers feel that additional ND filters aren't necessary, but they do offer a lot more control. Neutral density filters come in various strengths (represented in Log E density) with each three points equaling one stop (half the amount) of light loss:

Filter	Stop loss	Light transmission
ND 0.3	1 stop	½
ND 0.6	2 stop	¼
ND 0.9	3 stop	⅛
ND 1.2	4 stop	¹⁄₁₆

Many video cameras represent their internal ND filtration in fractions, as opposed to densities, and you're likely to see ⅟₁₆ (1.2 or four stop) or ⅟₆₄ (1.8 or six stop). In addition, most cameras only offer two fixed ND choices, which is why you have more control with external filters.

Color correction filters come in many different types. There are four major categories of color correction: blue, orange, magenta, and green. Each of them affects the opposite color spectrum.

Blue filters are used to stop red and orange wavelengths from passing through the filter to correct tungsten light to daylight. Orange filters stop blue light from passing through and help correct daylight to tungsten. Two primary color correction filters are the Wratten 85B, which is an orange filter that converts daylight color temperature to tungsten (5,600K to 3,200K) and the Wratten 80A, which is a blue filter that converts tungsten color temperature to daylight (3,200K to 5,600K). Magenta filters are used to counteract the high green content in industrial fluorescent lights and green filters are used to add green content.

All color filters, whether color correction or color effect, work on a subtractive system —meaning they *stop* various wavelengths of light from passing through and therefore usually require some kind of exposure compensation. In the case of the 80A, which is a deep blue filter (cutting out orange, red, and yellow wavelengths) there is a loss of

Clean, no filter

With ND .6 grad diagonally over 1/2 of image

Utilizing a ND (neutral density) graduated filter we can see the blown out sky in the top image, with no filter, and the detail in the clouds possible to capture with the ND grad in front of the lens. The grad line is placed above the buildings to still see detail in the shadows, but bring down the exposure in the sky.

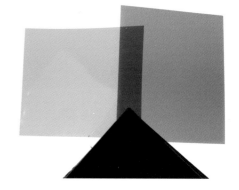

CTO and CTB filters.

about two stops. The 85B filter is, generally, only a loss of two-thirds of a stop. It is therefore normally preferable to correct daylight to tungsten rather than vice versa.

There are many different strengths of color correction filters, which offer various conversions between color temperatures. In the blue range (converting tungsten toward daylight) you have 80A, 80B, 80C, 80D, 82, 82A, 82B, 82C. In the orange family (converting daylight toward tungsten) family you have 81, 81A, 81B, 81C, 81EF, 85, 85B, 85C. Each filter offers a different amount of color correction with 85 and 80A being the most correction. Most videographers do not use color correction filters, as cameras have internal filters to convert for daylight and tungsten and white balance adjustments for infinite degrees between. It's important, however, to understand that—just like film emulsion—digital sensors have a native color temperature. If your sensor has a native color temperature of 5,600K (daylight) and you're shooting in tungsten light, with very little blue content, you're "starving" that sensor of the light that it wants to see. This can create "noisy" images. It is preferable, in these situations, to use a color correction filter to block out some of the orange and allow the sensor to see more of its native color temperature to get a cleaner image. Manufacturers rarely publish the native color of their sensor and it'll take testing or digging to find that out.

DIFFUSION/CONTRAST FILTERS

Diffusion and contrast filters are probably the next most common used. There are many different types of diffusion, but they all work generally on the same two principles of spreading light or reducing contrast in fine lines.

The Tiffen ProMist type of filter is speckled with white or black dots that reflect light passing through to spread the light into the shadow or highlight areas and soften the overall picture. The Pancro Mitchell Diffusion works a little differently by refracting the light rays from high contrast areas

A side-by-side example of a diffusion filter on model Debbie Diesel. In this case the Tiffen 1/2 Black ProMist, which smooths out the shadows, softening the picture.

to diffuse the light. Generally diffusion filters work to "soften" the image by reducing contrast. Fog filters emulate a "fog" or "mist" effect, which will also significantly reduce the scene contrast. In addition to the white or black dot diffusions, nets and other textures are available that produce similar results. Contrast filters utilize the same principle by spreading light into the shadow areas to raise those exposures and reduce the overall contrast range of the image. With all these filters, the videographer needs to exercise caution—especially with nets or diffusion designed for use with film cameras—as the depth of field can be so significant with smaller video cameras that the filter itself is often within acceptable focus and the viewer then sees the texture of the filter rather than the effect it's supposed to cause. The best way to know what will work is to test various filters with your specific camera and lens choices. Also look for filters specially designed for use with small-chip video cameras.

It's also important to note that various strengths of diffusion filters are required for various focal length lenses. You need less diffusion for the longer lenses (which magnify the image more) and more diffusion for wider lenses (less magnification) to achieve the same overall effect. If you start shooting a scene with a wide-angle lens and a #1 Schneider Classic Soft and then move to a longer lens, you might consider bumping down to a half or quarter strength filter to get the same effect as the #1 on the wider lens. Again, testing is your best route to determine what works best for you.

EFFECT FILTERS

Effect filters come in many different types. Color effect filters can emulate day-for-night or a sunset sky or give your overall scene a Mars-esque red hue. Image effect filters can create star patterns around highlights or a kaleidoscope-like image with multiple views of the same subject.

A popular effect filter is the Skintone Enhancer, a slightly warm, slightly magenta filter that adds a "healthy" tan to skin tones.

No Filter | With Skintone Enhancer

Model Shannon Setty with no filtration (left) and with the aid of a Skintone Enhancer (right) which adds a warm, tan "glow" to her skin.

Other effects filters are star filters or streak filters. Star filters (built in to many ENG cameras) take bright highlights and flare them out in long streaks. That same concept is done with streak filters, which mimic the effects of anamorphic lens flares.

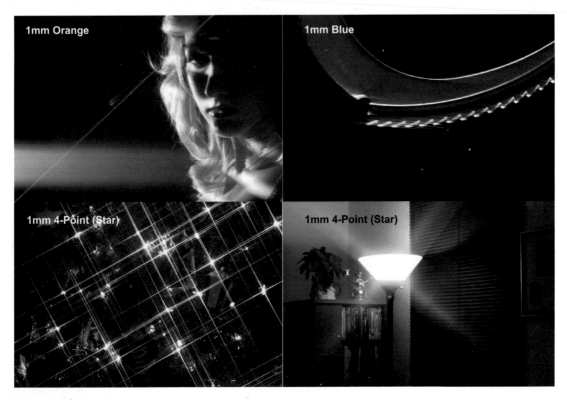

Examples of several flare filters. Top left is an orange Streak filter, which adds an anamorphic like horizontal streak to highlights. Top right is a blue Streak filter. Bottom left is a classic Star filter on point sources of light on a Christmas tree and bottom right is the same Star filter on a softer light source.

SPECIAL-DUTY FILTERS

Finally, special-duty filters, such as color enhancers and polarizers, have specific uses. Color enhancers or red/green Didymium filters increase saturation of red and green. If you're photographing a red barn or a forest of green trees—this might come in handy to really help those colors pop.

Polarizers, in addition to cutting a lot of light—generally one and a half to two stops— will help to reduce or eliminate reflections off shiny surfaces from certain angles or serve to increase saturation in a blue sky in certain angles. Polarizers normally only come in a circular variety—whether or not they'll be used in a mattebox—as they depend on a specific rotation to polarize the angle of light to the lens. As these are very handy filters, I'm going to delve into the polarizer a little deeper.

A polarizer is a relatively unique special-duty filter. It is made up of millions of submicroscopic crystals arranged in parallel rows creating a screen. This parallel pattern allows light rays traveling in specific directions to pass through while blocking rays radiating contrary to the pattern.

Imagine threading a jump rope through a picket fence. Two people hold the rope taut, facing each other, across the fence. If one person begins to wiggle the rope up and down, the waves created will transfer through the fence to the other person as the rope freely moves up and down between the slats in the picket fence. If the first person switches directions and wiggles the rope side to side, the waves will stop at the fence, not passing through, and the person outside will be holding a steady rope. This is the principle of polarization —stopping waves from passing through the "fence" in the filter, unless they're traveling in a parallel pattern to the orientation of the filter.

When light reflects off of shiny surfaces, such as glass or water, it becomes polarized— meaning that it travels in straight lines, rather than radiating in all directions. These specular highlights, or specular reflections (specular meaning mirror-like), can therefore be filtered out under the right circumstances with a polarizing filter.

Cutting reflections off of glass surfaces works best when the camera is at an oblique angle to the glass—typically about 30°, as shown in the two photographs on this page.

In the top image, the polarizer is rotated to have no effect on the scene. The reflection from the window washes out the cover. In the lower image, nothing has changed but the rotation of the polarizer, which is now filtering *out* the polarized specular reflection off the manual so

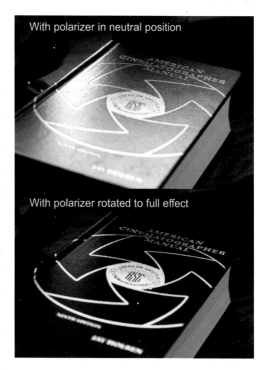

The results of working with a polarizer filter. The top image of the *American Cinematographer Manual* is taken with the filter in a neutral position and the bottom image is taken with the polarizer rotated to eliminate the most reflection off the cover of the book.

that we can clearly see the cover. All the rest of the light in the scene is radiating in all directions and is, therefore, unaffected by the filter. Only the specular (polarized) reflection is filtered out.

Polarizers are also known for darkening blue skies. This is because light reflects off of moisture and dust particulates in the air the same way that light reflects off of shiny surfaces and these reflected rays—which serve to wash out the blue color—can be filtered out. This effect is best achieved at a position 90° to the sun.

This would mean you would be photographing your subject with the sun at your right or left shoulder to achieve the most polarization and darkening/saturating of the sky. If the sun is directly behind you or directly in your lens, the polarizer will have no effect whatsoever. This also happens, to greater and lesser degrees, with other colors reflecting off other surfaces (such as flowers or colored glass), but rarely as extremely as the daytime sky.

With polarizer in neutral position

With polarizer rotated to full effect

A classic example of the importance of a polarizer. Windshield reflection is a significant problem when shooting car scenes. Without the polarizer, the reflection obliterates the talent in the car. With the polarizer rotated to the most effective position, we can clearly see model Jennine Dwyer behind the wheel.

A polarizer can also help to darken bright blue skies to get a deeper blue.

To use a polarizer, you rotate the filter itself until the effect you want is achieved. Polarizers don't necessarily eliminate reflections altogether, nor do they work in every situation, but they can minimize unwanted reflections in many instances.

Due to the dense crystals in the filter, polarizers cut out a lot of light—about 1¾–2 stops of light—just like a neutral density filter and you must compensate your exposure for that loss. Because of this, many photographers use polarizers automatically in exterior situations to reduce more light coming into the camera. In addition, as polarizers are normally circular and mount directly to the threads on the camera lens, it keeps the filter slots in your mattebox open for additional filters.

Polarizing filters are used in a lot of sunglasses to help cut down on glare and reflection as well as in some 3D installations. For 3D viewing, each eye of the 3D glasses has a polarized filter on it, each rotated 90° to the other so that each blocks part of the projected image and allows the brain to recombine the images to form a 3D effect.

Two polarizers together can create a kind of variable neutral density filter. At the height of polarization, when both filters are rotated 90° to each other, the filters will become nearly opaque and allow no light to pass through. When they are parallel with each other, they will be translucent again. This is also a technique for creating a "fading" filter in front of the lens.

Polarizers work indoors just as well as they do outdoors as far as eliminating reflections, but they are rarely used inside because of the amount of light that is lost through the filter.

FIELD NOTES

From the Trenches—*Free Enterprise*

Back when I was a gaffer, I worked on a low budget feature called *Free Enterprise* with William Shatner and Eric McCormack. For an early scene, Eric is perusing a Toys R Us with his friends, played by Rafer Weigel, Phil LaMarr, and Jonathan Slavin. When we scouted the location, cinematographer Chuck Barbee was concerned about the standard cool white fluorescents—literally thousands of them—in the 20′-tall ceiling. There was no way we could replace the fluorescents with color correct daylight tubes—not on this budget. Because of my knowledge of filters, I told Chuck that we didn't have to—that we could use a Tiffen FLD filter on the camera. The FLD is a slight magenta filter that corrects out the green of

A screen capture from the cult hit *Free Enterprise*. Here we left the cool white fluorescents as they were and incorporated an FLD filter on the lens to correct out the green spike. Free Enterprise © Anchor Bay Entertainment.

A shot of Eric McCormack from *Free Enterprise*. The FLD corrected the horrible green tone from the cool white fluorescents and we utilized standard cool white tubes in Kino Flo fixtures to give the edge light on Eric's left side. Free Enterprise © Anchor Bay Entertainment.

cool white fluorescent light to a daylight color temp. If we shot with daylight balanced film and used the FLD, then we put standard cool white tubes in our Kino Flo fixtures and lit the actors with the same ugly fluorescent light, it would all be balanced and the filter would correct out the ugliness making the image work. Chuck was skeptical, he had never worked with an FLD before and had never lit with the ugly utility cool white bulbs before, but we shot a test using Kodak 5247 daylight balanced film in a still camera with an FLD in the Toys R Us, developed that into positive slides (like film print) and Chuck saw that the FLD beautifully corrected out the ugliness. We didn't have to replace any of the existing tubes, we lit with just a couple Kino fixtures to help shape the light on the actor's faces and shot out the store very quickly! And that's just one case where an understanding of filters and a knowledge of what filters were available that saved the day!

One Plus One Equals Blue: Calculating Camera Filters

I received an email a couple weeks ago from a filmmaker who was shooting an action sequence for a low budget independent film with 15 HDSLR cameras. It was a daylight exterior sequence and he knew that he was going to be fighting the changing sun all day long and he was trying to find an expedient way to keep the cameras white balanced throughout the day to help reduce the color timing requirements later on. As I explained to him, there are a couple of options:

A) You can white balance once in the morning and once after lunch and fix it later;

B) You can continue to white balance all day, but that can introduce bias as well if the cameras aren't all balanced in the same place and under the same light. If clouds come in between white balancing camera 1 and camera 15, you're going to have different balances;

C) You can use color-correction filters and quickly apply them throughout the day.

He liked option C, but didn't know anything about color-correction filters at all.

I realized, through our conversations, that many digital shooters, especially in the HD and HDSLR worlds, have probably never considered color-correction filters. With digital camera's abilities to white balance in a wide variety of situations, why would you ever consider using old-school filters? This shoot was a perfect example where the old-school concepts still apply.

Color-correction filters come in two primary "flavors": orange and blue (although the next most prevalent correction filters deal with green and magenta). In gels, these would be CTO and CTB, but in camera filters, they're identified by Wratten filter numbers, named after Fredrick Wratten who invented the filtration system that was eventually purchased by Eastman Kodak.

Filters are manufactured and sold by Tiffen, Schneider, Formatt, Cokin, and many other vendors. The two primary Wratten numbers are 80 (blue) and 85 (orange). Like CTO and CTB, color-correction filters are also available in varying strengths: 80A, 80B, 80C, 80D, 85, 85B, 85C. Knowing when to use which requires a bit of math.

Color correction is not a linear process. An 85C will convert 5,600 Kelvin to 3,850, a change of 1,750K. That same filter, however, will only correct 5,000K to 3,560K, a change of 1,440K.

Knowing how a filter will convert any given color temperature requires the use of mireds or microreciprocal degrees. This requires converting Kelvin temperatures to mireds by dividing 1,000,000 by the Kelvin temperature.

Mired = 1,000,000 / Kelvin temperature

You take the target mired and subtract the mired to be converted.

Table of filters and mireds:

Filter	Light loss	Mired shift value
80A	2	−131
80B	1⅔	−112
80C	1	−81
80D	⅓	−56
85	⅔	+112
85B	⅔	+131
85C	⅓	+81

The use of correction filters requires knowing what your current temperature is and what temperature you want to convert to. The best way of knowing your color temperatures is through the use of a tricolor color temp meter.

Here are some common color temperatures and their mired values:

	Kelvin	Mireds
Candle	2,000	500
Dawn	2,000	500
Standard tungsten bulb	2,900	345
Photo tungsten bulb	3,200	313
Morning/Afternoon sun	4,400	227
Midday sun	5,600	179
Midday sun plus sky	6,500	154
Cloudy sky	6,800	147
Clear blue sky	10,000	100

So 5,600K has a mired value of 179 and 3,200K has a mired value of 313. We want to correct the 5,600K to 3,200K, so we take our target mired, 313 and subtract the mired to be converted, 179, and we find a mired shift of 134.

Looking at the filter list above, an 85B will correct +131, which gets us nearly exactly where we want to be.

Sometimes, in order to achieve a conversion, you need to stack or use multiple filters. Filters are available in a wide variety of shapes and sizes from circular screw-on to attach directly to the threads on your lens, or in square/rectangular for mattebox use.

Tiffen also offers decamired filters, which are named for their mired shift values divided by ten (deca) so a B1.5 is a blue filter with a mired shift value of –15. A R6 is a red decamired filter with a shift of +60.

Although digital cameras have wonderful flexibility in their white balance function, there are situations where it is good to understand the old-school methods to help make your workflow more efficient.

For more on mireds, see "The Magic of Mireds" in the section on Lighting.

Light Reading: Learning to Create and Control Lens Flare

Back when I was a wee lad and an electrician working in films, a cinematographer once looked at me and said, "Do you know the difference between an accidental flare and an intentional one?" I thought for a moment and had to admit, I did not. He said, "Your day rate."

I had to laugh. What is, optically, an aberration and a fault of the optics can also be seen as quite beautiful and organic addition to the frame and mood of the scene.

A lens flare results from non-imaging light that enters the lens and is reflected off of the various surfaces within the lens to be photographed by the sensor. This means the flare is not part of the scene being photographed, but rather is an artifact created by the lens itself.

TO SHADE OR NOT TO SHADE?

Avoiding flares requires shielding the lens from stray light. The first line of defense against flares is a lens shade: a piece of plastic (or metal) that attaches to the front of the camera lens to extend the barrel slightly and cut off stray light.

A mattebox accomplishes the same task, but much more efficiently. Mattebox covers, French flags, eyebrows, and side flags go further to eliminate stray light. If you're looking to eliminate flares in your shot, this is the way to do it for all kinds of flares except those created by a light source that is directly in the shot.

A LITTLE TOP COAT

Most modern lenses are manufactured to cut down flaring. This is because a flare actually reduces the performance of a lens by reducing imaging contrast, therefore reducing resolution and sharpness. The less a lens flares, the more it can retain its contrast and sharpness. Lens manufacturers reduce flaring by utilizing thin coatings on the lens elements that cancel out reflections. How this works is pretty fascinating.

One of the ways that light behaves is like a wave and there are laws of physics governing the cancellation of waves that are at opposite frequencies. This is how lens coatings work. Some light that strikes the surface of the lens is reflected back and this reduces the amount of light being transmitted through the lens. When we apply a thin coating on top of the lens surface—usually silicon monoxide (SiO) or Magnesium fluoride (MgF_2)—most of the light will pass through the coating and lens surface with minimal refraction. Some light, however, will pass through the coating and be reflected off the surface of the lens, while some light will be reflected off the surface of the coating. The thickness of the coating refracts the reflecting light slightly so that the surface reflection and the coating reflection actually end up in opposite phases to each other and cancel each other out, thereby eliminating the reflection.

Some lenses only have one coated surface, and some have multi-surface coatings. As a general rule of thumb, the more coatings, the more transmission of light through the lens, and the less flaring occurs.

SEEING THE LIGHT

There are three primary categories of lens flare:

Ghost Flare

Ghost flare happens when a bright source within the frame reflects off of one lens element onto another element at a different position and it creates a dimmer mirror reflection of the light source in a different part of the frame.

Ghosting flare is very hard to fight as it's caused by a light source or a significant highlight within the frame that is reflecting off of one or more elements within the lens and being re-photographed. If the sun is in frame or a bright light source, you're more likely going to have a ghosting problem. This happens a lot at night with car headlamps—and there's not really a way that you can fight it. The only immediate solutions are to eliminate the source of the flare or change lenses.

A ghost flare—the direct reflection of a highlight in the frame that is reflected off one or more surfaces of glass within the lens and re-photographed in a different position. We see that here, halfway down the middle flashlight.

Spot Flare

Spot flare is a strong light that hits the lens surface from off-axis and creates two or more reflections within the lens elements, these reflections generally take on the shape of the lens' iris.

Spot flare can be avoided by incorporating a lens shade or mattebox, flags, etc. Anything that will cut the offending light off the lens.

You'll recognize spot flares as the multiple spheres that happen when the sun hits the lens at the right angle.

Spot flare occurs when hard light strikes the lens and is reflected and re-photographed off multiple elements within the lens. The result is a series of circular flares that can be different sizes and colors depending on the coatings on the lens elements. Model Becka Adams.

Veiling Flare

Veiling flare is also sometimes called veiling glare and is indirect light that is reflected off one or more surfaces within the lens and reduces image contrast and sharpness. It is generally shapeless.

Just like spot flares, veiling flare can be controlled by eliminating errant light from hitting the lens.

Veiling flare occurs when light from an obtuse angle strikes the lens, but does not create a point reflection, rather a gauzy reduction in contrast. Here the image of model Debbie Diesel is significantly affected by veiling flare.

Although lens coating was first developed in the 1930s, the first major refinements to the process came in the 1960s, but the real advancements came in the 1990s. This means that older lenses tend to flare more and have less light efficiency than newer lenses. There are, however, occasions when flaring is desirable to the overall style of the image and some very modern lenses can be very hard to flare, which leads the savvy cinematographer to reach for older "vintage" glass.

Model/actress Anne-Michael Smith poses among several technical references for a lens test. Here we see the left column are results of a flare test of an older (1970s) Kowa Prominar lens, while the right column are results of a modern Arri Zeiss Master Prime. We can observe that the modern lens reduces flare significantly, especially with direct flare.

In this lens test, note the difference between lenses of two different eras. The newer Zeiss Master Prime holds its contrast much better even under harsh flaring conditions. The spot flare, especially with the Kowa Prominar is more pronounced than the Master Prime and likewise, the veiling flare affects more of the overall frame than the Master Prime.

Even though a flare is an optical aberration, it can be a wonderful addition to any shot or scene. A flare can add a magical quality and is generally accepted by the audience as an organic part of the frame.

The flare from a Kowa Prominar lens, notice the warm color and "sunburst" like flare quality.

The flare from Zeiss Master Prime, notice the cooler, more neutral color and cleaner flare spots.

Paul Cameron on *Total Recall*

Philip K. Dick's science-fiction stories have lent themselves to a rich array of feature films, among them *A Scanner Darkly*, *The Adjustment Bureau*, *Minority Report*, and, of course, *Blade Runner*, but his short story "We Can Remember It for You Wholesale" has proven popular enough with Hollywood to warrant two adaptations: Paul Verhoeven's 1990 release *Total Recall* was the first and the 2012 *Total Recall* reboot was directed by Len Wiseman and shot by Paul Cameron, ASC.

Cameron, whose credits include *Man on Fire*, *Gone in 60 Seconds*, and the ASC Award-nominated *Collateral*, chose to shoot *Total Recall* with Red Epic cameras, secured through Panavision, although at that time it was a brand-new camera.

"We decided to use Cs and Es [series Panavision Anamorphic lenses]," Cameron states. "[Panavision optical engineer] Dan Sasaki had them shipped to us, along with some special 'flare lenses,' which were basically some of the C-Series anamorphics with little ventricular mirrors added to increase the flare characteristics.

Screen captures from *Total Recall*, Paul Cameron, ASC, director of photography. Shot in anamorphic with Panavision C and E series lenses, some lenses were specially altered to accentuate their flare properties. Total Recall © Sony Pictures.

FIELD NOTES

"*Total Recall* became a film about lens flares!" he laughs. "We were pushing it all the time, aiming little Xenon flashlights right at the lens or putting pin-sized sources into the frame. They add a lot of visual punctuation. I like flares, but Len *loves* flares, so we really went for it. We'd be setting up a shot and discussing the details, and Len would walk across the room shaking his hands, showing me where he wanted the flare. It was a lot of fun to make that happen."

For more on Total Recall, *see the full story in* American Cinematographer Magazine, *August 2012.*

What Makes a Good Lens? Part I: Sizing Up How to Properly Size Up Optics

With the HDSLR craze sweeping this phase of the digital revolution, many shooters are now encountering a situation where their lens choices have gone from a single fixed zoom lens, to a wide wealth of fantastic lens choices—and navigating the waters of the options can be daunting.

So, what is good? What is bad? And how do you choose the best lens possible? Do you always have to spend a fortune to get a good lens?

RECOGNIZING THE PROBLEMS

Every lens is different. No lens is perfect and no lens is perfect for every job. By the very nature of optics, every lens is a collection of compromises to optimize its performance for a specific task or range of tasks. Below are some of the imperfections that you need to examine before making a lens choice.

Build quality

Mechanical quality

Chromatic aberration

Distortion

Breathing

Falloff

External Inspection

- **Build quality:** Inexpensive lenses have a plastic build; better quality lenses have aluminum or other metal build. There should be a metal lens mount. The lens should feel well constructed, robust, even if it is lightweight.

- **Mechanical quality:** The lens mechanisms should move smoothly, easily and uniformly, without rough spots, grinding or easy spots. Test the focus ring, zoom ring, and aperture controls for smooth, easy action.

Photographic Inspection

- **Chromatic aberration** is a defect that happens when a particular wavelength of light is not focused at the same point as the other wavelengths. It is represented in the image by a ghosting or fringing of color around the edges of an object. This is the most common optical defect and is generally corrected by additional lens elements. Chromatic aberration is worst at wider apertures and high contrast between objects in frame.

- **Distortion** takes place when light rays don't strike the lens in parallel patterns. They diverge or converge as they strike the lens, turning what should be straight lines in the image into convex (barrel distortion) or concave (pin cushion).

- **Breathing** is a defect whereby the focal length seems to change slightly (zooming effect) when focusing the lens. This happens most often with zoom lenses, but can also happen with primes.

- **Falloff** is a defect that happens when the center of an image is brighter than the edges, also called vignetting. It is most notable at wide apertures.

Lens Attributes

The benefits and strengths of lenses:

- Speed
- Resolution
- Contrast
- Color
- Bokeh

- **Speed** is determined as the widest aperture possible on that lens: $f/1$ being a theoretical widest aperture and an extremely fast lens (note there are some exceptions of a lens with an aperture bigger than $f/1$, such as the Zeiss $f/.07$ that Stanley Kubrick and John Alcott used on *Barry Lyndon*, but these are extremely rare) and $f/5.6$ being a slow lens. Prime lenses are most often faster than zooms because they require fewer optical elements. A high-quality zoom lens has a constant aperture across the entire zoom range, a more economical zoom lens may lose speed as you zoom into the telephoto end of the lens.

- **Resolution** is the lens' ability to reproduce details, typically measured by modulation transfer function (MTF) charts (to be discussed later). All photographic lenses perform best at the center of the image.

- **Contrast** is often misunderstood with regard to lenses. This doesn't refer to the lens' ability to reproduce tones between black and white, but rather its ability to differentiate between similar hues in close proximity. Contrast is closely related to resolution and together they define the lens' overall sharpness.

- **Lens color** varies, sometimes considerably, from lens to lens—even within a family of lenses. There are many factors that contribute to the lens' color including the individual glass elements, their various coatings, the age of the coatings, and so forth. Some lenses have a warmer tone, some a cooler.

- **Bokeh** has become a pretty highly over-used term. It is actually coined from the Japanese work "boke" meaning "blur" or "haze" and photographers use the term to describe the quality of the out-of-focus aspects of an image through a given lens. Bokeh can be manipulated, but is not determined, by the number of blades in the lens' iris. The more blades, the softer and more circular the out-of-focus highlights become.

2.10 OPTICS

What Makes a Good Lens? Part II: Considering Lens Style and Focus Style

In the previous article I talked about all of the different aspects of lenses—build quality, mechanical quality, chromatic aberration, distortion, breathing, falloff, speed, resolution, contrast, color, and bokeh—all in an effort to answer one question: what makes a lens bad or good?

There's yet a couple final factors to talk about, one of which is the style of lens, be that still, ENG, or cine, which are three of the most popular styles.

Still lenses are designed to be compact. They're designed to focus the image quickly and momentarily. Most modern DSLR lenses are auto-focus lenses and work with sophisticated mechanics to keep the focus fast, smooth and quiet. They are designed to focus while looking through the lens at the camera's ground glass.

ENG-style lenses are made for one-man-band shooting. They are compact zoom lenses with handgrip and zoom rocker built right into them. They are designed for on-the-shoulder shooting and to compose and focus an image quickly, again, by looking through the lens through the camera's viewfinder.

Cine-style lenses aren't as compact. They're a little larger with expanded focus scales that allow for smooth tracking of focus on a subject in continuous motion. These lenses are designed for a camera assistant to adjust the focus, independent of the operator, while looking at the barrel of the lens and the subject being focused. They're designed to integrate easily with other cine-style equipment.

Flare is another factor to consider, but it's tough to say whether flares are a good or bad thing. Most modern lenses have special coatings to reduce flares, but sometimes you *want* a good flare and have to scout out those older "inferior" lenses for that great look.

A final consideration is the focus style of the lens: external or internal focus. An external focus lens will actually change in size as you focus the lens, the elements protrude as you change focus. This can cause major issues with filters in a mattebox, or even if you have a screw-on polarizer, as the barrel of the lens can also rotate as you focus, changing the filter's polarity. An internal focus lens, generally more expensive, keeps all of the moving elements inside within the confines of the lens. This also goes for zoom lenses, some inexpensive zooms will actually expand in size as you zoom to the telephoto end of the lens. These are important considerations depending on your shooting style.

The real difficulty in determining whether a lens is good or bad arises from the actual application of that lens. For a cinematographer working on traditional Hollywood-style single-camera scripted narrative projects, ENG-style or still-style lenses are not good. They don't integrate easily into the typical production workflow. That's not to say that those lenses are *bad*—they're just not right for the application. On the flipside, a cine-style lens would be a nightmare for a videographer out in the field shooting documentary or news footage.

Further complicating the issue, when it comes to what is a good or bad, price isn't always a good determination. If you have two lenses of equal specs (speed/focal range/internal or external focus/zoom) then, generally, the more expensive lens will be your better choice. However, there are some excellent, relatively inexpensive lenses manufactured by Tamron or Sigma for DSLRs that are of excellent quality. On the cine-style side of things, Schneider and Zeiss are both making extremely high-quality, excellent performing DSLR mount cine-style prime lenses that are inexpensive compared to the "big boys." Red manufactured the Red Pro Primes, a relatively inexpensive professional PL prime set that are really quite impressive. Many people dismissed them because of their price—but in my tests, they held up in sharpness, resolution, contrast, and flare quality to high-end modern cinema lenses.

Instead of trying to tell a good lens from a bad one, just look for the lenses that are the highest quality, best price you can afford. If you're shooting cine-style, it's a great idea to have cine-style lenses. The expanded focus scale makes a major difference in production. Get the lens with the fastest aperture you can afford. If you're looking at zoom lenses, try to find a constant aperture lens. Many inexpensive zooms have variable apertures that might be presented like $f/3.5$–5.6. This means that if you start out wide at full aperture when you zoom in on the lens to the further, more telephoto end, your relative maximum aperture shrinks in size. At its widest point, that lens is an $f3.5$, but at the longest point, the maximum aperture is, effectively, an *f*/5.6. That is an inferior lens to a zoom with a constant aperture, and it can be a liability when you're shooting.

Look for lenses with good, strong builds. The better constructed lenses will last longer, put up with more rigors of production abuse and, generally, function better for a longer period of time. Many modern cinema lenses are optimized for the wide end of the lens aperture, meaning the optics are specially calibrated to perform to their best near the wide aperture, so that isn't as much of a consideration as it was 30 years ago.

Bokeh is a nice attribute, but really more of a sales pitch than a requirement for a good, functioning lens. If good bokeh is important to you and you don't have access to MTF charts, look for lenses with a higher blade count to the iris—the more blades, the softer and more organic the out-of-focus highlights will be. If you only have a five blade iris, your out-of-focus highlights will take on a distinctive pentagon shape, but an 18 blade iris creates soft, organic highlights. I'll discuss how to tell good bokeh in a lens a little more when we talk about MTF charts.

In a perfect world, you get to test the lenses before you buy them. Try to get out to a camera shop and get the lens in your hands for a few minutes. Talk with trusted professionals about their lens choices—and ask them *why* they like particular lenses. What one professional might consider a "bad" lens, another might use as their primary tool. No lens is perfect. No lens will be best for every job. Every lens has some quality that is beneficial and some imperfections.

Test as often as you can. Side-by-side tests can tell you a lot about different lenses and qualities. Don't fret so much about what is good or bad—just what is right for you, your projects and your budget.

Modulation Transfer Function: Understanding Lens Resolution

OK, bear with me . . . this is actually much deeper, technically, than I normally venture in this column, but it's an important topic to understand.

This month, I'm going to talk about modulation transfer function. It's a fun mouthful of words; try it—*modulation transfer function*. You can almost hear Marvin the Martian asking, "Where is my elunium pu36 modulation transfer function?"

No?

OK, maybe that's just me . . .

Modulation transfer function (MTF) is a methodology for measuring the resolving power of a lens, or an entire imaging system for that matter.

THE BASICS OF MTF

Let's break it down:

- What are we modulating?
- What are we transferring?

No lens is 100% perfect. In fact, it's physically impossible to have a lens that doesn't alter the light passing through it to some degree. A phenomenal lens might transfer 95% of the light cleanly through its glass; a not-so-good lens might only transfer 70%. There will always be some loss of light and, more importantly, loss of contrast.

Now, I already snuck in one of the aspects of MTF: transference. We're transferring light through a substance—in this case a lens—and that transference will *not* be complete; there will be a variation of the light that comes out the other side. This variation is called a *modulation*. The light transferring through the lens has been modulated, or changed, from its initial state as it passes through the lens.

That's the basis of modulation transfer function—how is light passing through a lens or any component of an imaging system and how is it changed by the lens or that imaging chain itself.

CONTRAST, CONTRAST, CONTRAST

Mostly what we're looking at when we're measuring MTF is resolution via contrast. MTF test charts are, primarily, alternating areas of high-contrast black and white lines or wedges at increasing frequency within a given space. It's important to understand that contrast and resolution are closely related, even dependent upon one another. Without contrast, you cannot have resolution. Imagine a white line on a white piece of paper—if there is no contrast between the white line and the paper, there can be no resolution of the image to see the line.

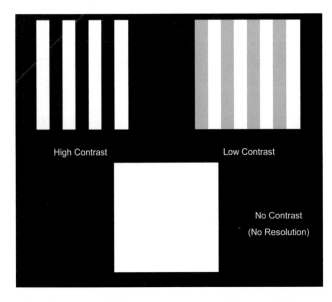

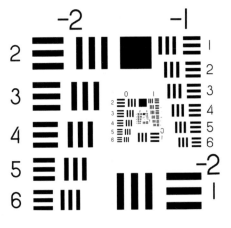

The original USAF 1951 resolution chart.

Contrast and resolution are very closely related. Without contrast, there can be no resolution.

The design for most MTF or resolution charts is based on a test chart that was created in 1951 for the US Air Force to determine the highest resolution optics for reconnaissance photography. The chart features groupings of black and white lines that get smaller and smaller. In its most simple terms, the lens with the highest resolving power will see the smallest lines clearly as black and white stripes. Modern versions of the USAF 1951 chart feature the same concept of alternating lines of increasing spatial frequency—as the lines become narrower, we are increasing the spatial frequency with which lines are appearing in a given space, which are generally measured in line pairs per millimeter (LP/mm) or, sometimes, lines per millimeter (L/mm). Those two can be a bit confusing if you're not paying attention,

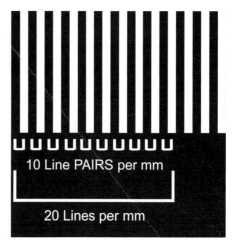

Line pairs per millimeter and lines per millimeter are two ways to represent the same measurement.

but they're two different ways to measure the same thing. If you have 20 lines per millimeter, you have 10 line pairs (a pair being one black and one white line).

The first thing we note when looking at blocks of lines that increase in spatial frequency is that it gets harder to see the individual lines as they get narrower and closer together. Even with just your eyes, you might see those lines close up, but, if you step away from the test chart, the higher frequency lines will quickly become just gray blocks that you can no longer tell black from white; they blend into one. When you lose contrast, you lose resolution and vice versa.

The same thing happens when the image of that chart is projected through a lens. There will always be a loss of contrast, meaning that the blacks won't be quite as black and the whites won't be quite as white. There is often also a loss of sharpness, where the lines may appear to be out of focus.

If we look at a portion of a test chart of very high contrast, low spatial frequency black and white lines, maybe 10LP/mm—and let's, arbitrarily, say that this series of lines has a contrast ratio of 600:1 (the white is 600 times brighter than the black). Our lens, however, can only resolve this spatial frequency with a contrast ratio of 500:1, so we lose some of the richness of the blacks, and, in most cases, we lose a bit of the sharpness of the transition between black and white. This is our modulation of transfer. The image being projected by the lens is not exactly what is being seen.

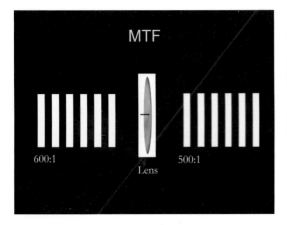

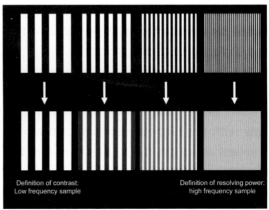

When light passes through a lens it is modulated. The blacks and whites are more gray and the sharp lines blur slightly. The image is never perfectly reproduced.

As spatial frequency (detail) in the image increases, contrast reproduction will decrease.

It's important to note that as contrast increases in spatial frequency—the lines on the chart get closer together—contrast reproduction drops. Every lens ever made has this property and will render lower spatial frequency with better contrast and better resolution than it will higher spatial frequency images. The lens' contrast reproduction is defined by how well it transfers low frequency contrast and its resolution is defined by how well it transfers high frequency contrast.

FORMING THE CURVE

There are two primary ways in which the MTF of a lens can be represented on a chart: by measuring its performance over increas-ing spatial frequency, or by measuring a single spatial frequency across the width of the lens. Both measurements are important and reveal a lot about the performance capabilities of that lens.

As we already know, the contrast reproduction of any lens will drop off as spatial frequency increases. If we have a chart that along the Y (vertical) axis we have a percentage scale, represented in decimals from 0 to 100% or 0 to 1 (i.e., .1 = 10%, .5 = 50% and 1 =100%) this represents our transference, the percentage at which the frequency is passed through the lens. 95% would be extremely efficient and accurate transference with little modulation, 30% would be poor transference with a lot of modulation. Along the X (horizontal) axis, we have our spatial frequency increasing as we go off to the right. Starting, say, at 10LP/mm and increasing to 50LP/mm. We already know that the modulation will increase as spatial frequency increases so when we plot the performance on this chart it will start high and then gently slope off in transfer performance as the spatial frequency increases. This slope on the chart forms the MTF curve and you can tell, at a glance, how the lens performs at a given resolution (frequency).

The second way to plot MTF on a chart is to, again, use the Y axis as percentage of transference (contrast reproduction), but your spatial frequency remains consistent. Instead, your X axis is scaled in millimeters with the far left (0) representing the center of the lens and each number representing a distance (in millimeters) away from the center toward the edge of the lens. Performance at the edges of the lens will always be less than that at the center of the lens.

There's a lot of information in that curve, but it doesn't paint the whole picture. Each of the curves, above, show us one aspect— either increasing spatial frequency contrast reproduction or performance from center to edge of the lens. On most MTF charts, the manufacturer tries to show you *both*. That means we're looking at multiple lines on one chart.

In this case, our Y (vertical) axis still represents contrast reproduction from 0 to 100. Our X (horizontal) axis represents the center to edge of the lens. Each line within the chart represents a different spatial resolution measured across the lens *and/or* a different

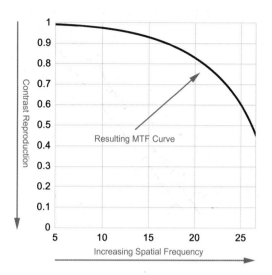

A basic MTF curve representing decreasing contrast over increasing spatial resolution.

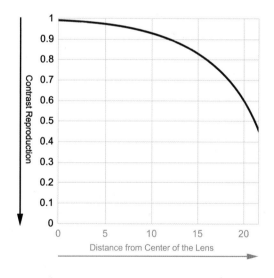

Another, more popular, way of representing MTF is using the X axis of the chart as distance from the center of the lens. As we know that lens performance will always be better at the center than at the edges, the result is, also, a curve. Here different spatial frequencies will be represented by different thickness of lines in the chart.

aperture at which the test was conducted. Most lenses will perform better at deeper stops (for many years a general rule of thumb was that the "sweet spot" of a lens was at least two stops closed from the lens' maximum aperture). Modern cine lenses are, generally, optimized to perform best closer to their maximum aperture.

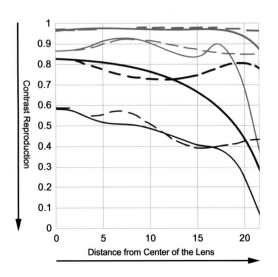

In the chart above, we have lines of different thickness, different color and solid and dotted lines. The thick lines represent measurements taken at 10LP/mm, a very low spatial frequency. The thin lines represent 30LP/mm, a moderate spatial frequency. Blue lines represent the chart shot at *f*/8 and black lines represent the chart shot at the lens' maximum aperture. Finally, the dotted lines represent those same attributes, except

The MTF chart of a Canon 50mm lens. The thick lines are measurements at 10LP/mm, the thin lines are at 30LP/mm. Blue lines are shot at *f*/8 and black lines are shot wide open. The dotted lines represent measurements from diagonal lines on the chart (not present in the Century Precision chart, but on other resolution charts).

instead of looking at vertical or horizontal lines of contrast, we're looking at diagonal lines of contrast on the chart. As it turns out—the closer the dotted line is to the solid line (same contrast representation of diagonal lines on the chart to horizontal/vertical lines) the better the bokeh is for that lens. The more those lines diverge from one another, the more you'll see the shape of your iris in your bokeh. So the chart above gives us a lot of information about this lens. We see at a deep stop (*f*/8) and low spatial frequency of 10LP/mm we have nearly 98% contrast reproduction across most of the lens except the very far edge. We see at 30LP/mm, wide open, our contrast reproduction is very poor—starting at 50% in the center of the lens and dropping to about 15% at the edge. This is a lens that performs significantly better stopped down. Will this lens work for you if you need a fast, sharp lens? Certainly not.

When you understand the basics of MTF, you can look at any lens manufacturer's published specs and get a quick idea of how that lens will perform in terms of contrast and resolution. There are, of course, many, many other attributes to every lens that cannot be determined through MTF charts (color, aberrations, breathing, etc.), but you can get a quick idea about how that lens might perform for you in terms of contrast and resolution.

Further into MTF:
A Specific Look

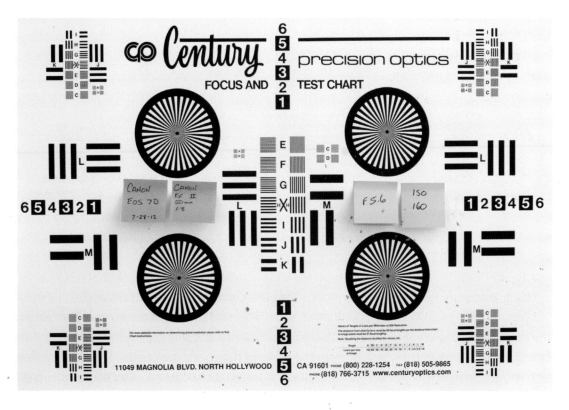

The Century Precision Optics lens resolution test chart.

So let's take a look at one lens. In this case I chose a Canon EF II 50mm 1.8—what I recently learned has been nicknamed the "nifty fifty"—it's an inexpensive EF prime (about $90) and fast, so something I picked up a few years back.

Canon EF II 50mm 1.8

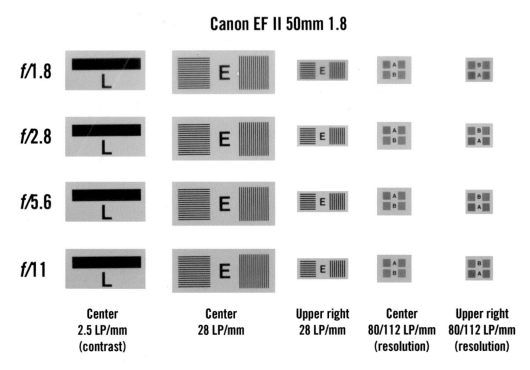

| | Center 2.5 LP/mm (contrast) | Center 28 LP/mm | Upper right 28 LP/mm | Center 80/112 LP/mm (resolution) | Upper right 80/112 LP/mm (resolution) |

Details from a test of Canon's "nifty-fifty" 50mm EF II f/1.8 lens. The rows are various apertures, the columns are details of various portions of the test chart (seen in the previous image).

Using a Century Precision Optics chart, I shot the chart at f/1.8, f/2.8, f/5.6 and f/11. Focus was set manually (using focus zoom assist on a Canon EOS 7D) and never changed during the exposures. The chart was set at the proper distance of 50 focal lengths away—in this case 2,500mm or 8.2'. Let's look at a couple areas of the chart: the center "L" section which is 2.5LP/mm, the center "E" section, which is 28LP/mm, the center A/B section which is 80 and 112LP/mm respectively, and then we'll look at the far upper right-hand corner of the lens at the E and A/B sections.

We can see, at a glance, that this lens performs best at f/5.6. The contrast representation, while not 100%, is good and we can discern contrast between the lines at A/B—even at the far edge of the lens. At f/1.8, this lens performs pretty poorly—even at the 2.5LP/mm area,

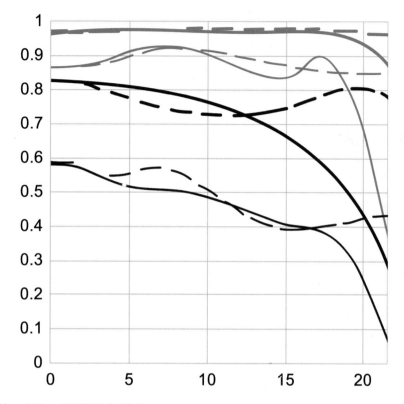

The MTF chart of Canon's 50mm EF II f/1.8 "nifty-fifty" lens.

contrast at *f*/1.8 is pretty low, as is sharpness, that single bar shown here at "L" is not sharp, nor is the black good and rich.

Looking back at the MTF curve from earlier, this is Canon's published MTF chart for the EF II 50mm 1.8 that I just tested. We can see that between my tests and Canon's results, Canon is pretty accurate and honest in their representation. On my chart, the "E" section represents 28LP/mm, very close to Canon's 30LP/mm (black lines). If we look at the thin black line, measuring 30LP/mm at *f*/1.8, we'll see that my findings are pretty close to theirs—the MTF is about 58% at the center of the lens in the E area, and way down to less than 10% at the far edge of the lens.

A FEW PARTING BLOWS

At the risk of complicating a complicated situation further, there are a few more aspects to MTF that should be clarified. Not everyone measures MTF the same. For example, a popular website, dpreview.com, which features extraordinary reviews of digital cameras and lenses (primarily of the still variety), measures their MTF in MTF50—which means that they give you the spatial frequency number at which the MTF has dropped to 50%. Instead of reporting the MTF for a given spatial frequency, they report the spatial frequency for a given MTF (50%).

A very important note is that MTF doesn't stop at the lens. Camera filters have MTF. Sensors have MTF. Filter packs on the sensors have MTF. The recording format often has an MTF. The exhibition format has an MTF. The exhibition medium/display has an MTF and, finally, our eyes have an MTF. All of these, together, combine to create the total MTF for any given camera and display system (called the *optical* transfer function). This is key to starting to understand the real nuance behind what we normally, loosely, refer to as resolution in our images. Real resolution is *not* merely a count of the pixels in the final display, it's a combination of the MTF curves of all the elements within that capture and viewing system. When we're talking about camera MTFs, we're generally talking about OTF (optical transfer function), which is more descriptive of the kinds of loss to transfer function that can happen through the low-pass optical filter in the camera, through the compression codec, etc. Many times you'll see OTF (or camera MTF) measured in *line widths per picture height* (LW/PH) or *line pairs per picture width* (LP/PW)—this is only a *slightly* different form of measurement. If we have an image that is 1,920 × 1,080 *lines* then our cycles (one cycle being one pair of lines), or line widths, measuring in pairs, would be 960 wide and 540 tall. Theoretically, a 1,920 × 1,080 system should be able to resolve 960 line pairs across the image and 540 line pairs down the height of the image.

That, my dear readers, is the simple basics of MTF. There *will* be a test later.

PART 3
CAMERA

3.1 CAMERA

What's the Best Camera?

Above all else, whenever I do lectures or workshops or meet filmmakers at a networking event, the number one question people always ask me: "What's the best camera?"

I know what they're really asking is "What is the best camera *for me—that I can afford*?" At least that's almost always what I infer from the question.

Answering the question isn't easy, nor is there really any right answer. I try, very hard, to impress upon anyone inquiring along these lines— it is NOT the camera that matters as much as the people behind it.

One of the things that I teach in my camera and lighting workshops is to take a look at *Airplane II* and *Blade Runner*—both shot in 1981 with Panavision cameras and lenses and Kodak film stocks. The equipment is the same, but the looks are very, very different.

A frame capture from 1982's *Airplane II: The Sequel*. Airplane II © Paramount Pictures.

A frame capture from 1982's *Blade Runner*. Blade Runner © Warner Bros.

I recall, many years ago, after a director had begged me to shoot DV (up until that point my career had almost exclusively been shooting 35mm film), I was horribly disappointed with the results. I shot a single scene for him and wound up re-lighting it four times to try and get a look that I was happy with, but in the end blamed it on *that damn video format*. About a month later I got a chance to see *Sweet*, a short film shot on DV by Allen Daviau, ASC (*ET*, *Empire of the Sun*, *The Color Purple*, *The Astronaut's Wife*, *Van Helsing*), that blew my mind. Allen embraced the pros and cons of the digital format and created a beautiful short that humbled and shamed me.

I should have known better.

In my case, it wasn't the format's fault, it was the cinematographer who didn't have a good understanding of that format. After that, I shot nearly 20 more projects on DV until I felt that I had "mastered" the format and I could be as happy with the results as I was with my 35mm work—albeit embracing the different aesthetic that format brings.

Over the course of my cinematographic career, I have had the opportunity to shoot with dozens of different cameras, dozens of different formats and have come to a keen understanding and respect for nearly every option out there.

Now back to the question at hand: what is the best camera?

In order to get close to answering this question, we have to answer about a dozen other questions first:

- What are you shooting? Is it a scripted narrative? Documentary? Reality? Sports? Commercial? Music video? Wedding/event? Nature?

- What is your budget? Remember that the cost of the camera isn't the only thing to consider, you'll also need accessories: tripod, lenses, mattebox, dolly, monitor, follow-focus, shoulder rig, etc.

- Where do you plan on having your projects seen? Are they going to theaters, home video, Internet, television, mobile apps?

- What is your shooting style? Do you have a full crew? Are you a one-person production? Do you shoot fast and run-and-gun? Do you have full control over every shot?

- What is your postproduction like? Do you do everything yourself at home? Do you work with a high-end professional facility?

All of these questions influence the answer as to which is the best camera.

If, in our limited space here, we examine only one variable—the genre you'll be shooting—we'll quickly see that not every camera is suitable for every kind of project.

NARRATIVE (MOVIES, TELEVISION, WEBSERIES)

You're generally looking for a "cinema-like" camera. In today's day and age, that means a large sensor camera that can shoot 24p and, most often, have "cinema-style" accessories. These cameras have to be versatile to shoot handheld, on tripods, dollies, cranes, but they can be physically larger and—typically—each shot is planned out and orchestrated. Focus marks are taken, rehearsals done, and each shot is executed in a relatively short period of time.

DOCUMENTARY

In most cases for documentaries you want a smaller physical camera that is easier to move around with, is less intimidating to subjects who aren't used to having a camera around, and less conspicuous to be able to gather more fly-on-the-wall type of footage. You definitely want a camera that can have long recording run times since, when doing interviews, you don't want to stop so often to reload or download your footage.

REALITY TV

You're more than likely moving a lot following subjects, a larger shoulder-mount camera is a must. Longer record times are necessary and cameras with ENG-style functions are better for that genre of shooting.

WEDDINGS AND EVENTS

More often than not a physically smaller camera is preferable. It's easier to get in among the people and be less obtrusive. You'll most likely be doing your own post work, so having an easy workflow is key. Light sensitivity is key as most weddings and/or receptions take place in dim lighting.

SPORTS/NATURE

Generally higher speed frame rates are a must in shooting sports. You'll want to stay away from cameras with CMOS chip issues as you'll be moving quickly and "jello" effect can ruin your shots. Smaller chip cameras with more depth of field are often preferable to cover the fast moving action.

INDUSTRIAL/CORPORATE

In some cases, size matters. Often when you're working for a corporate client, they want to have high confidence in your professionalism and they're paying for your expertise. Often, they want to *see* that expertise and it really helps to have a larger, more impressive, camera. Although you might be a genius with a palmcorder, that isn't going to impress your corporate client. Here you're looking for a full-size professional rig that integrates well with professional sound recording. I'd recommend a medium-sized sensor in the ½" to ⅔" category to get better, more professional lenses and have the flexibility of interchangeable lenses for going from interviews to shooting macro work of products or technology.

MUSIC VIDEO/COMMERCIAL

The needs here are similar to those of narrative filmmaking; the larger the sensor, the better. 24p is going to be a standard, but you're also going to want a camera that shoots off-speed, especially high-speed for slow-motion work. You definitely want a camera with interchangeable lenses to get dynamic views that are required of these genres.

If you look at all of these different requirements for the different genres of shooting, there is not one camera out on the market that is *perfect* or *best* for all of those types of shooting. If you are one of those kinds of shooters who do all of the above, I'm sorry to say, there isn't one magic camera package that will work for you for everything. Today there seems to be more and more popularity for the HDSLR cameras, and I'm a big fan as well, but they certainly aren't the end-all-be-all—and just because they make great images *for their price range*, doesn't mean that they're the right tools for every project.

There are other factors to consider, of course, not the least of which is your budget. How much money do you have to spend? Do you have $500 or $50,000? You might also consider the legacy of your equipment history; if you've owned Sony cameras for years, chances are many of your Sony accessories will work with the purchase of a new Sony camera better than with a Panasonic or JVC—and likewise for the other manufacturers.

It is also important to consider where and how your projects will be seen. If you're shooting a documentary that you believe is perfect for the BBC, you better be sure you know the BBC's broadcasting specs—many networks have minimum bitrates that are required for material to air on their stations. Your 21Mb/s camera might make pretty pictures, but also might not make it through quality check for the network you're trying to get your project aired on.

In the end, the answer to the question is truly as complex as the factors involved. There is no one best camera; no camera is perfect for *every* job.

The chart below lists some of my *opinions* on good cameras for some genres. This is *not* a definitive list, it does not cover every possible scenario, it does not cover every possible camera—it's merely a starting guide of my thoughts on some suitable cameras for certain types of projects.

Genre	Camera Size	Sensor	Speeds	Run Times	Suggestion(s)
Narrative	Med to large	Large	24p, 60p+	4–12 minutes	Red Epic, Arri Alexa, Sony F35, Canon EOS 7D
Documentary	Small	Small to med	24p, 30p	60+ minutes	Panasonic AG-AC160, Sony HXRNX5U
Reality	Shoulder	Medium	24p, 30p	60+ minutes	Sony PDWF335L, Panasonic AG-HPX370, Canon C300
Wedding/ Event	Small	Small	24p, 30p	60+ minutes	JVC GY-HM150U, Panasonic AG-HPX250PJ
Sports/Nature	Shoulder	Small to med	30p, 60p (720)	30–60 minutes	Sony PDW700, Panasonic AJ-HPX2700
Industrial/ Corporate	Shoulder	Med to large	24p, 30p	30+ minutes	Panasonic AJ-HPX3700, Sony HDW650F
Music Video/ Commercials	Med to large	Large	24p, hi-speed	4–12 minutes	Arri Alexa, Red Epic, Sony F35, Canon EOS 7D

Now it's possible that you shoot many of these types of productions and can't afford the cameras I'm suggesting—in that case, I would recommend trying to find the closest equivalent that falls into the parameters that you need for your projects. The truth is that most people who ask me "What is the best camera?" already think they have an answer. No, my friends, the Canon EOS 5D MkII is a great camera, but it is not the best, nor is it right for everything. Seriously. Take your time and—most of all, ask other professionals who are shooting the same types of projects that you are—you may be surprised at the answers you'll get.

ISO, EI, ASA, and YOU

ISO is one of those terms that we all take a little for granted. Once you get the general gist of ISO, it seems simple. So simple, in fact, that when I thought of this column on ISO, I first thought that it would be *too* simple and nothing to really talk about—until I started to try and put it all into words—and realized that ISO is a deceptively complex subject.

ISO is an acronym for International Organization for Standardization, the standards body who defines the particular parameters by which sensitivity of film emulsion was

A digital light meter showing ISO and stop reading.

measured (among many other standards). Before the ISO had this honor, ASA (the American Standards Association) was the American standard, with DIN (Deutsches Institut fur Normung; German Institute for Standardization) handling the European standard.

ASA and ISO both operate off the same numerical scale wherein the higher the rating, the more sensitive the emulsion is to light. It's based on a factor of two, as are all other elements of the exposure triangle (shutter speed, aperture, and sensitivity), so that when the number doubles, so does the sensitivity of the stock. A 200 ISO is twice as sensitive as a 100 and a 400 ISO is four times as sensitive as a 100.

The most common ISO numbers are: 50, 100, 125, 160, 200, 250, 320, 400, 500, 640, 800, 1,000, 1,250, 1,600, 2,000, 2,500, 3,200, 4,000, 5,000, and 6,400. In recent years, this scale has expanded to include 8,000, 10,000, 12,800, 25,600, 51,200, 102,400, and 204,800!

Remember that each doubling of a number represents a doubling of sensitivity (or an addition of one stop), so that 102,400 ISO has more than 1,000 times an increased sensitivity to light than 100 ISO!

Some people also refer to sensitivity with the abbreviation EI, for Exposure Index. EI is, essentially, the same as ISO, but it incorporates other factors that relate to the exposure triangle. For instance, if you're shooting at 100 ISO, but using a 0.3 ND filter,

A roll of Kodak Vision emulsion rated at 500 ISO (Tungsten).

your Exposure Index is now equal to 50 ISO. Many people use ISO, ASA, and EI interchangeably—it should just be noted that EI may refer to more than just the sensitivity of the sensor.

When dealing with film emulsions, faster speed films with higher ISOs actually had a different physical makeup than slower speeds. The silver halide crystals were larger, to gather more light. When you used a 500 ISO film stock, it was physically different than a 50 ISO film stock. Because faster films had larger light-sensitive crystals, those made a difference in the final image, which had more visible grain in it. The faster the film, the more grainy the image.

SIGNAL AMPLIFICATION

Exposure and ISO works differently in the digital world. No matter how many sensors are in the camera (three in the case of a three-chip or four in the case of quad HD, etc.) there is only one *type* of sensor (CCD or CMOS typically) and only one set sensitivity to light. Every sensor has its own base sensitivity, its own native ISO—but it's extremely rare for manufacturers to actually let you know what that native ISO is! Some manufacturers report a completely esoteric (and useless) piece of information about the minimum illumination necessary. That usually looks something like this:

4.5 lux (Shutter speed ⅟₆₀, Gain +21dB)

What this is telling us is that at the highest gain, the minimum amount of illumination necessary to form a picture is 4.5 lux. This information is rarely, if ever, useful in a real-world application. It's like saying your new car has a top speed of 210mph! WOW! Impressive! But how often will you actually be able to drive at 210mph, and is the vehicle performance (and safety) even reasonable at that speed? What you really want to know is: how does the car perform at speeds between 35mph and 55mph—normal, everyday speeds. A camera may be capable of 4.5 lux with +21dB of gain or 204,800 ISO—but the image created will rarely, if ever, be desirable or even usable within those parameters.

Before we get deeper into what is desirable or not, let's talk about how a digital sensor provides different ISOs. Since the sensor itself cannot be changed out—like a film stock— you always have the same base sensitivity in the camera. When you're increasing your ISO, you're electronically amplifying the signal to "see" more into the shadow/underexposure area of an image. This amplification is much like the same kind of signal boosting that an audio amplifier does; taking a weak voltage signal and amplifying it to increase its output. This amplification, or *gain*, is measured in decibels (dB), the same way sound is measured. Remember that a sensor creates its image by having photons of light focused onto the individual photosites on the sensor and each photosite collects as many photons as it can within the given exposure time (see "How a Digital Image is Born" in section 1). In a "properly" exposed image, the average number all of the photosites will collect is about half their potential photons in their collection "wells."

If you think of each photosite's collection well as a bucket that collects photons of light in a given period of time then it's easier to visualize how this works. The bucket size is determined by the size of the photodiode on the photosite, which varies from sensor to sensor. The higher the number of photosites, or the smaller the physical dimensions of the sensor, typically, the smaller the photodiode, hence the smaller the bucket and the less sensitive to light that sensor is. These photons are converted into an electrical voltage by the sensor and then that voltage is turned into digital bits by the camera's analog-to-digital converter.

If the bucket doesn't collect any photons at all, then that photosite has no light information and, hence, no voltage to turn into bits and the resulting pixel will be black. If the bucket fills completely, that photosite will create its highest voltage and highest bit count; the resulting pixel will be white. If the bucket only collects a couple of photons from a very dark image, there might not be enough information to actually make a photo. The resulting voltage might be so low that the low bit count will be so close to black there will be no detail in the final image. By increasing the signal gain, we amplify the electrical current created from the photons, which results in a higher voltage and a higher bit count for that photosite.

IT'S GETTING LOUD IN HERE

However, when we start to apply amplification, we also start to amplify a lot of information that we don't normally see; information that the camera confuses for voltage from photons. This extraneous information (heat from the sensor itself, variation in transistor noise, photon spill, etc.) confuses the camera's image processing circuitry and the result is *noise*, which appears as random speckles in the image and can significantly degrade image quality.

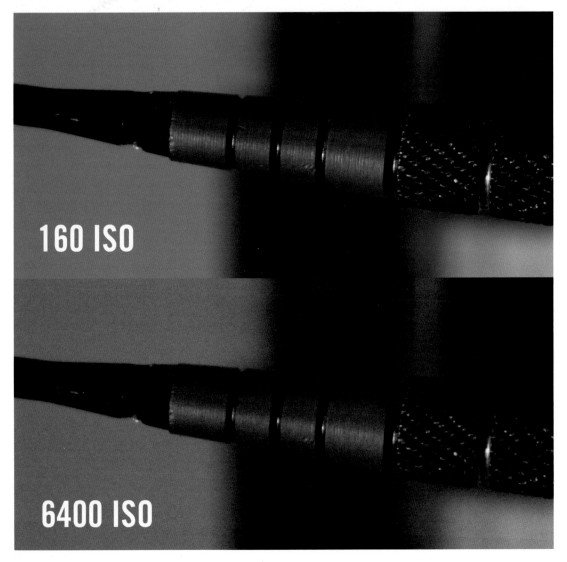

An example of two images, the top shot at 160 ISO and the bottom shot at 6,400 ISO, note the noise in the higher ISO image, and slight degradation of the blacks on the higher ISO image as well.

Imagine taking a photograph to a copy machine and making a copy. Then take the copy and make a copy of that. Then take *that* copy and make a copy of that. The quality will degrade substantially with each copy—and become "noisier." The same kind of thing happens the more you amplify a signal.

The noise you get from amplification, sometimes affectionately referred to as "digital grain," is an artifact that degrades the quality of the image. The more you amplify the signal, the more noise will be apparent in the final image. This is on par with what happens with film—the higher the sensitivity, the more grain—but it's not the same in digital because we're not actually getting larger pixels, we're getting junk information which comes across as dancing "snow" or "static" in the image.

How much noise is acceptable is entirely subjective. This is where the notion of what

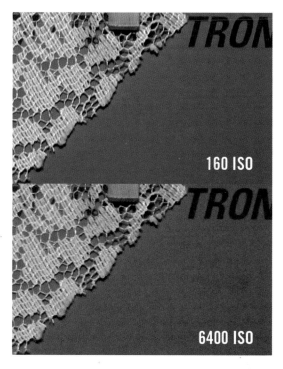

Another example of low and high ISO, the top image shot at 160 ISO and the bottom shot at 6,400 ISO. Again, a lot of noise is introduced in the higher ISO and reduced contrast.

is desirable comes into play. Some shooters don't mind a little noise in their image—they feel it adds a "filmic" quality reminiscent to grain. In some situations, it has become entirely acceptable to have significant noise in the image. Watch any of the paranormal investigation reality shows on TV and when they're shooting in pitch blackness, the audience is used to seeing an extremely noisy image. In normal situations, however, noise is not desirable. It's a flaw in the image, not a benefit. So we want to shoot at the lowest gain setting possible—for a given situation—in order to reduce the noise.

So . . .

A typical function panel on the side of an ENG video camera. The H, M, L area designates high, medium, and low gain settings. The specific designation of what is high, medium or low is set in the menus by the user.

HOW DOES GAIN RELATE TO ISO?

When you increase the ISO in your digital camera, you are simply increasing the gain. In the digital world, ISO is merely a way of renaming gain measurements from decibels (dB) to a terminology that is more readily understood by film users. In gain, each +6dB is the equivalent to a doubling of the electrical signal, or the increase of one stop of light. In ISO, every doubling of number represents a doubling of the signal gain, or an increase in one stop. So a change from 100 ISO to 200 ISO is the same, virtually, as adding +6dB of gain to the image. You have amplified the signal by a factor of two; or increased your exposure by one stop. Change that to 400 ISO and you've now added +12dB of gain or two stops; 800 ISO gets you up to +18dB and three stops, and so forth.

Most digital cameras that measure their amplification in dB of gain won't allow you to amplify the image beyond +18 or +21dB, which is typically very, very noisy. Many recent digital cameras, such as HDSLRs like the Canon EOS 5D Mk III, 1D X, Nikon D4 or Nikon D800, continue to push the gain well beyond this three to four stop range. From a base of 100 (or 200) ISO to as far as 204,800 ISO, which represents an increase of eight stops or the equivalent of +48dB of gain!

It's important to note that these uber-high ISOs of 204,800, 102,400, 51,200, 25,600, 12,800 and 10,000 are *not* necessarily intended to be used under normal conditions. In most cameras the super-high ISOs are part of an "extended" range—clearly denoting that their use is at the user's caution. However, with higher and higher extreme ISOs being implemented in newer cameras, it generally means that the lower, more common ISOs, are cleaner (less noisy) and more advanced as a result of the extended range and technological advances necessary to make that possible.

So the trick is to always shoot at the lowest ISO for the cleanest image, right?

Not so fast.

This was absolutely true of film. The lower the ISO, the smaller and tighter the grain structure and the cleaner, sharper and less grainy the resulting properly exposed image would be.

In the digital world, as I said before, most manufacturers don't actually tell you the base ISO of their sensor. So, what happens when you shoot at an ISO *lower* than the base level? Another way of asking this would be—what happens when you shoot with *negative* gain?

If we go back to the bucket analogy, what happens when you overfill a bucket? Whatever you're filling it with spills out all over the place, doesn't it? This happens when too many photons are collected by the individual photosites, when they fill, they reach their limit and tend to spill their contents over onto other photosites. This creates noise, as well. It also

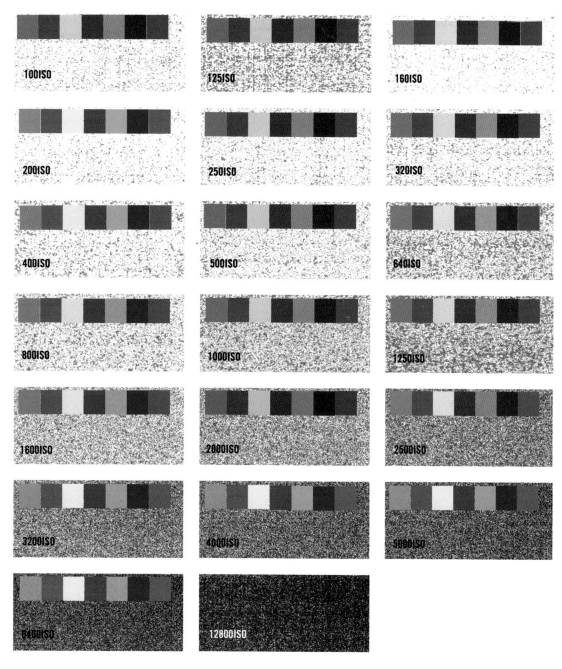

The results of testing ISO on the Canon EOS 7D. The large portion of each image was a photograph taken with the lens cap on at the designated ISO. Each image was taken into Photoshop, blown up, inverted, and the levels were adjusted to bring out the most noise in the image. Then that same setting was applied equally to every image. The color chips were cut and pasted from an image taken at that ISO in natural light, open shade. The color chips represent a more "real-world" (as opposed to extreme) version of what an image would look like at that ISO.

limits the details in the highlights of the image. In the digital world—once you reach that ceiling of the bit count for a pixel (256 bits in an 8-bit system), there's no further you can go. That's pure white and there is no longer any detail available. Once you "clip" and go to peak white, that's it, you can't go back.

So shooting at a lower ISO than the camera's base setting can also lead to noise and a limited dynamic range. Some camera manufacturers, in their "extended" ISO range will offer a lower option, of 100 or 50 ISO, but many are denoting—again—this is not the optimum setting for the camera.

There's another little catch. Not all ISO settings are created equal. I've heard stirrings before that "you should only use *whole* number ISOs 100, 200, 400, 800, etc." and "never use the ⅓ stop increments: 125, 160, 240, 320, 500, 640, etc." This didn't make a lot of sense to me until I started thoroughly testing cameras—and it depends heavily on the specific camera you're discussing.

One method for testing gain/noise for your camera is to put the lens cap on and shoot at various ISO or gain settings. Then take the resulting footage into postproduction, create a negative (white instead of black) and adjust the gamma until you accentuate the noise level as much as possible. Apply this same exact setting to each clip—to make them the same— and the results are quite surprising. This noise is mostly represented by magenta (negative of green) blotches in the image. Remember that noise is a factor of amplification of the sensor signal—so it can be readily seen even if there is no light hitting the sensor at all.

On the previous page are the results of doing this technique with my Canon EOS 7D. These images are the result of shooting with the lens cap on at various ISOs, and then manipulating them in post to accentuate the noise. In addition, I shot a color chip chart under open shade in natural daylight under the various ISO settings and cut-and-pasted those chips onto the manipulated image to get an idea of real-world noise compared to processed worst-case scenario. The color pieces are from actual images and have not been manipulated in post at all.

If you look at these results—you'll see something very interesting. 100 ISO is pretty clean, as is 200 ISO, but 125 is *not* clean at all. In fact it's actually worse than 400 or even 800 ISO! 160 ISO is the cleanest when you look at the enhanced noise in the lens cap capture. 640 ISO is the next anomaly in the bunch, which is decidedly noisier than 800 and only slightly better than 1,000.

This plays contrary to the notion that lower ISOs are always cleaner than higher ISOs.

The reason why this is happening has to do with how digital cameras create each ISO rating. Starting with the camera's base ISO—which is, primarily, a mystery for each camera—

whole number increments (full stops, or doubling) from there are a simple matter of applying gain. Assuming that 100 ISO is the base for the camera, 200, 400, 800, and 1,600 are achieved by simply applying gain.

The ⅓ stop increments are reached somewhat differently. They utilize gain *and processing* through the camera's circuitry. From 100 to 200 (*if* 100 is the base), is a whole stop. From 200 to 250 is a stop plus additional processing, what could be related back to push or force processing in the film world. We're taking the 1-stop amplified signal and *pushing* it further to 250 via internal signal processing. 320 ISO, however, is a result of taking the gain from 400 ISO and *pull* processing that down a third of a stop. That means we're taking the amplification and then processing it *backwards* slightly to get the lower ISO. This results in less noise, but also a slight sacrifice in highlight detail in the camera's dynamic range. The pull processing slides the window of dynamic range downward slightly so that you gain just a bit in the shadow detail and lose just a bit in the highlight.

Yes, it is electrical voodoo. No question.

From this test, you can clearly see that amplification of the signal—increasing ISOs—results in considerably more noise, but there are certainly stages within the scale that are worse than others. This may be entirely different for any given camera. Even cameras with the same sensors, but different processors, can deal with amplification and noise differently.

The Canon EOS C300, for instance, actually has a published base ISO of 640. You can set one stop slower than 640 to 320 (slowest the camera can go), or select ISOs above that. Although Canon reports 640 as the base, it also reports 850 (an atypical slight increase above 800) as the optimum setting for the camera with the lowest noise, best color fidelity and dynamic range. This has a lot to do with the signal processors inside the camera and how the math is calculated to create the final image.

Remember, also, that dynamic range is affected at "off" ISOs. With my Canon 7D, after careful testing, I determined that 160 ISO was the cleanest-looking grain, with the most extended dynamic range that the camera could represent. The difference in dynamic range between any of the ISOs on the 7D is incredibly small—but there is slightly more shadow detail in at 160 than there is at 100 ISO. This leads me to believe that the native ISO for the 7D is actually 160. However, like the C300, it could be that 100 is the true base, but 160 is the optimum setting for the 7D.

In addition, very close examination between 250 and 320 ISO resulted in cleaner noise at 320 than 250. Based on this testing—and shooting real-world (not manipulated) images of test charts and texture patterns—I determined that my best ISO settings for the 7D were 160, 200, 320, 400, and 800. I would avoid the use of 100, and, especially, 125 and 640.

Continuing, 1,600 ISO is actually cleaner than 1,250, but beyond that—the results are pretty linear (and pretty bad).

It's important to note that these tests were conducted to bring out the absolute worst in the camera performance. In real-world applications, the differences between the stages of ISO are miniscule, to say the least. Generally speaking, anything under about 800 ISO in modern cameras is an incredible image. In traditional video terms, that would be an increase of +18 dB of gain, which would almost never be acceptable!

Thanks to Chuck Westfall, technical advisor for Professional Engineering and Solutions Division, Canon USA for his help with this article.

How to Determine Your Camera's ISO

Continuing where we left off in the ISO discussion , if your camera does not represent gain in ISO, you can still determine the camera's base ISO by following a few easy steps. You're going to need:

- An evenly lit 18% gray card
- Light meter
- Your camera
- Waveform monitor

If your camera has an auto-iris mode that actually displays the *f*-stop, fantastic! This is going to be very easy and you won't need a waveform monitor. If the *f*-stop is not displayed in auto mode, you're going to need a waveform monitor to find your ISO.

If your camera shows the *f*-stop when you auto iris, follow these steps:

1. Make sure your camera is "zeroed" out: no gain, set at your preference for 24fps or 30fps, shutter at 180° or equivalent (if your camera shows shutter speeds instead of shutter degrees then set the speed as close to 2× the frame rate as you can, IE: 24fps $\frac{1}{48}$ or $\frac{1}{50}$ second, $\frac{1}{60}$ for 30fps), normal gamma settings, no ND filters inserted, and so on.
2. Evenly light the gray card.
3. Point the camera at the gray card and zoom in until the card fills the frame.
4. Auto-iris the camera and take note of the *f*-stop. Make sure that the auto setting is not changing the ISO, shutter speed, or gain controls, only the *f*-stop.

5. If you have an incident meter, take a reading at the card's position with the "ping-pong" ball facing the camera. If you have a spot meter, from the camera position, take a reading of the center of the card.

6. Adjust the light meter's ISO until the *f*-stop on the meter matches the auto-iris *f*-stop on the camera. This will be your camera's base ISO.

If your camera does not show the *f*-stop when you auto-iris, you'll need to hook the camera up to a waveform monitor. Use steps 1–3, and then adjust the camera's *f*-stop until the waveform reads 50–55 IRE and take note of that *f*-stop.

Finally, use Steps 5 and 6 to determine your base ISO/EI for your camera.

Remember that there is *always* a base sensitivity to any sensor. There are no magical sensors that can create any sensitivity. Any adjustment beyond the base ISO will always involve some form of signal manipulation, not always to the benefit of the final image. The only way to really be sure what will happen with any given camera is to test it yourself. The results of my Canon 7D test do not necessarily reflect those of other HDSLRs, each sensor and processor combination will have its own attributes and quirks.

Knowing the base ISO of your camera gives you a powerful edge into understanding how manipulation away from that base will affect the image you're shooting.

The Tools of Digital Exposure, Part I— The Waveform Monitor

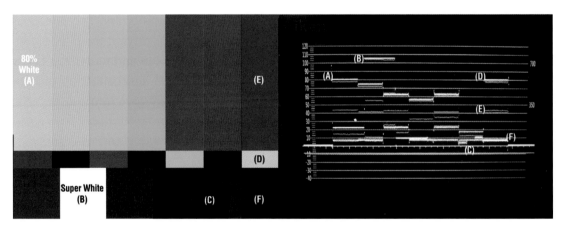

A look at SMPTE color bars as represented on a waveform monitor. Note the designated areas and how they fall on the waveform.

Back in my day (yes, you can visualize me sitting in a rocking chair with a smoldering pipe in one hand, an afghan on my lap, peering out at you over the tops of half-moon spectacles, if you so wish) the light meter was a cinematographer's best friend; a most primary tool and an invaluable asset. Although there were some exceptions—the late Douglas Slocombe, ASC, BSC, could famously call out the exposure just based on looking at the back of his hand—they were extremely rare. Even the top-notch, most experienced and revered cinematographers used a light meter to evaluate the exposure levels of their scenes.

Enter the digital realm. As the early days of digital motion picture cameras evolved out of their ENG (electronic news-gathering) predecessors, many of these emerging digital camera systems utilized an RGB-encoded recording format. One plus-side to working within this format was the extraordinary benefit of being able to actually *see* the final image on set. Digital became a WYSIWYG (What You See Is What You Get) medium, and cinematographers could make instantaneous decisions—not suppositions from reading a light meter—by actually seeing the image; live. In the days of motion picture film this was unheard of. Sure, we had video taps, but those were only a representation of the composition of the shot; not of the exposure, color, latitude, etc. All of those factors had to be inside the cinematographer's head through knowledge and experience.

In the world of WYSIWYG video, the light meter started to fade into obscurity—although it is still a very viable tool and many cinematographers still carry one—and judgments were made off of the monitor on set.

Today, we're moving more and more toward raw formats being preferred for scripted narrative, commercials, and music videos. This trend toward raw shooting has pulled us away, somewhat, from a WYSIWYG working environment and back toward the days of film where the cinematographer has to know how to interpret the image and understand how it will eventually look. Although the cinematographer can see an approximation of their final image on set—via the camera's RGB-encoded output or a LUT generator—it isn't the actual recorded image being viewed as it is with a true RGB-encoded format.

This doesn't mean that the cinematographer is blind and simply has to make decisions based on the approximate picture he/she is seeing. Instead, there are a plethora of tools available to make image evaluation—and, more specifically, exposure judgments—on set. These tools are often features built into the camera's functions, integrated into many monitors, or available as third-party additional tools. Now, as raw recording becomes more prevalent, exposure evaluation tools are even more important than ever.

One of the most ubiquitous tools available for exposure judgments is the waveform monitor. Waveforms have been around since the early days of analog video and have been used by video engineers to monitor the values of an image for over half a century. These devices used to be fairly bulky monitors that would be fed a signal from the camera on set. Today, many monitors, and some cameras, now have built-in waveforms to analyze their image on the screen.

The waveform is fairly simple to read and understand. There are three primary display modes on most waveforms monitors: luminance, luminance with chrominance and parade. We'll start with the first.

The waveform monitor starts with a grid marked out on the screen. The primary section of this grid is marked in horizontal delineations from 0 to 100. This represents the signal intensities from 0% (black) to 100% (white/peak). The markings actually represent IRE values (Institute of Radio Engineers), which translate to percentages of luminance in the image. Some waveforms have a scale that goes beyond the standard 0–100 and has below 0 values (generally to –40) and above 100 values (generally to 120). The lower values are for sync pulse signals and line-blanking intervals, and are of no importance to us in judging exposure. The area above 100 is the "superwhite" area, generally any signal in this area has complete loss of image detail. In addition, some waveforms have a marking at the 7.5 IRE level for "setup." This was required for getting solid blacks in standard definition, but can be completely ignored for HD and cinema camera signals.

Although waveforms do consider chrominance information, they are primarily for measuring luminance information.

The scale of IRE represents a percentage of luminance of the image. When you see areas of the waveform above 100 IRE, you know those areas are "clipping." They have become pure white and cannot be brought down later in post-production. If areas of the scene are shown on the waveform below 0, they likewise are pure black without detail.

In fact, where whites really lay on the scale is between 80 and 100. Generally a well-exposed image will have its white ranges between 80 and 100. If we have a scene of a wedding, the bride's dress should fall around 80–85 IRE to maintain detail in the material, but still keep the feel of the dress white.

Medium gray should be set between 45 and 55 IRE. Caucasian faces generally fall between 60 and 70 IRE.

The X-axis on the waveform (horizontal scale) represents the image from left to right. However, since the Y-axis (vertical) represents percentage of luminance, it cannot represent the vertical portion of the image. Therefore all pixels in the vertical column of the image are represented in the vertical of the waveform. If we're photographing a white piece of paper in the upper half of the frame and a black piece of paper in the lower half, each point along the waveform will register both white and black.

This aspect of how a waveform monitor displays information in the frame can make reading the waveform just a little bit tricky in real-world situations. Likewise, if we have a grayscale chart positioned vertically in the frame, you'll notice that each point on the waveform has a line that represents the steps of that scale.

You can use the waveform monitor like a light meter if you put an 18% gray card out into your scene, where the talent will be. Then zoom in on the gray card to fill the screen

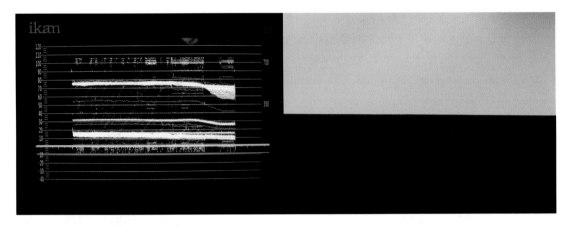

A look at half an image with a white piece of paper and half with a black. Because the waveform displays the image horizontally, but the luminance range vertically, notice that there are two main lines across the waveform screen, one representing the white paper luminance and one representing the black.

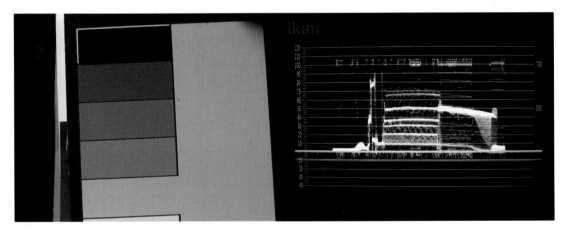

Again, an example of the horizontal being accurate to the image, but the vertical being accurate to the luminance. Where we see the grayscale in the image, we see several lines representing the different luminance range. Even though the grayscale is black at the top and white at the bottom, the lines on the waveform remain dark at the bottom and light at the top.

and then adjust your aperture until the waveform reads between 45 and 55 IRE. This will give you a proper exposure for that area, the same as if you took an incident light reading in that space.

The waveform is a solid tool for seeing your overall exposure range. In a very low light scene, you'll notice that the signal is crowded to the bottom of the waveform. In this area, you're likely to be picking up a lot of noise and it's generally better to open up, expose a little higher on the waveform scale, and then, if needed, reduce the brightness later in post

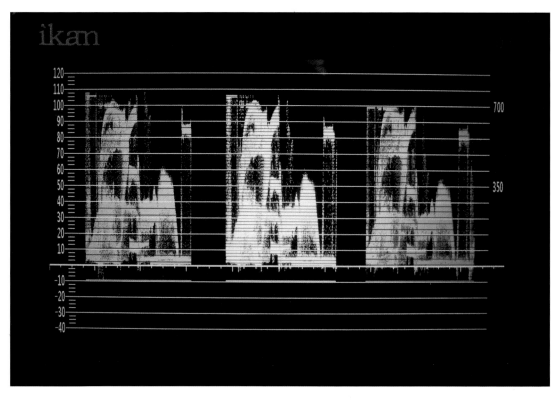

Showing a waveform in "parade" mode: red, green, and blue luminance are separated side-by-side.

during color correction. The waveform is a tool to help you keep a more solid signal-to-noise ratio in your image.

In addition to just looking at the luminance information, we can combine luminance and chrominance on the waveform screen. This can get kind of messy and hard to read, so if your waveform has adjustments, it's better to set it to IRE or Luma only and ignore the chrominance unless you're in "parade" mode.

Parade mode on a waveform separates red, green, and blue into their individual components allowing the luminosity of each color channel to be looked at side-by-side. It's a quick way to see if you're overexposing your skin tones too much: is the red channel running hotter than green and blue? Also, keep in mind that blue is generally the noisiest channel in an RGB signal so if you are low in blue information, you may want to adjust your lighting or even add a blue filter to the lens and re-white balance to make sure the sensor is getting a healthy blue signal.

The Tools of Digital Exposure, Part II: The Histogram

The histogram has a long history—dating back to the 1700s, although the term "histogram" wasn't coined until 1895. Webster's Dictionary defines histogram as "a bar graph of a frequency distribution in which the widths of the bars are proportional to the classes into which the variable has been divided and the heights of the bars are proportional to the class frequencies." Basically, early "histograms" were merely bar graphs—and, actually, that's all a histogram is: a bar graph representing a spectrum of data. In our case, the data represented is the luminance distribution in an image from black to white.

Unlike waveforms, the histogram doesn't represent the image in a pictorial fashion, it merely displays the number of pixels that are at a given luminance range. On the image histogram, the far left represents black and the far right represents white. If there were to be a scale on the histogram, the X-axis would be bit values (in an 8-bit system) from 0 (black) to 255 (white). The Y-axis would be a percentage or pixel count.

If the image was nothing but a white screen (top portion of the image below), the histogram would be one straight white line at the 255 point (far right) (see right-hand side of top portion of the image below) and the rest would be flat (no reading). If the image were a 50% gray box, then the 128 mark (the middle of the histogram) would be a straight line and all else would be flat (see the third section down in the image below).

Luckily, however, most images are not one pure tone. Rather they're a combination of many tones and variations between black and white—and that is what the histogram shows us. How many pixels in this image are at a given luminance between black and white? The histogram also works on a bell curve, so that whatever pixels in the image represent the

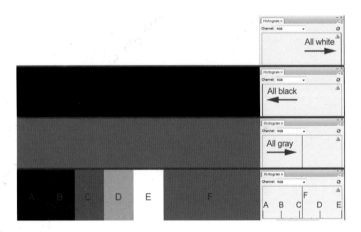

This image represents several different luminance ranges. At the top, a pure white box and the histogram shows a straight white line all the way to the right. Second is a pure black box and the histogram shows a straight line all the way to the left. The third is middle gray and the histogram shows a straight line right in the middle. Finally, a grayscale from black to white with a large chunk of middle gray and you see the representation of the pixel luminances denoted in the histogram. The line at F is significantly taller because there are many more gray pixels in the large gray box compared to the smaller boxes.

majority luminance value, that value will be at 100% on the scale and everything else will be a percentage of that. If we were looking at a ten-pixel image and two pixels were 70 bits and five pixels were 128 bits and three pixels were 255 bits—the line in the middle of the histogram, at 128 bits would be all the way to the top of the histogram and the line at 70 bits would be about 40%. How does that figure? Well, if 128 bits (gray) were the majority of the image (five out of ten pixels), then that line representing 128 bits goes to 100 on the histogram. What's left are five pixels and of those five pixels, two of them are at 70 bits (dark gray), so two is 40% of five and the remaining three pixels at 255 bits would be about 60% (three is 60% of five).

Histograms can also represent individual red, green, and blue channel luminance values, either separately or superimposed over each other. This is very handy as it is often possible to overexpose one color channel, but not the others—especially with flesh tones, which are high in red, but not so high in green and blue.

The following image of actress Lisa Jay from *Tranquility, Inc.* is indicative of many of my personal aesthetics in exposure—weighted more toward the shadow end, with flesh tones slightly under the normal exposure range and strong highlights. We can see this represented in both histogram options—the grayscale luminance values along with separated red, green, and blue, and the superimposed RGB values—also with separated channel information.

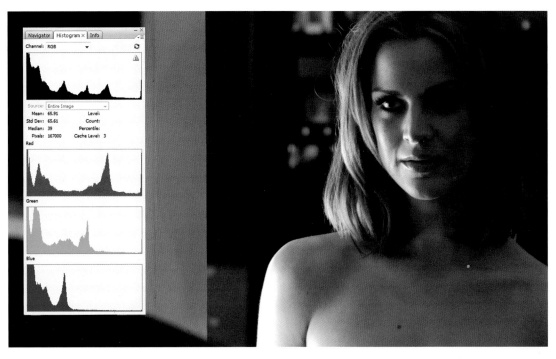

Actress Lisa Jay in Jamie Neese's *Tranquility, Inc.*, a short film I shot with the Canon EOS 7D. The histogram of the image of Lisa Jay. Luminance range is at the top, followed by red luminance, green, and blue. Tranquility, Inc. © Adakin Productions.

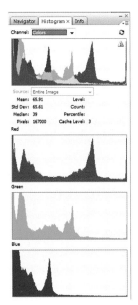

Sometimes the RGB superimposed histogram can be hard to read, which is why the traditional luminance histogram can be preferable with separated channel information.

In a "properly" exposed image, there should be a fairly even distribution (primarily weighted toward the center of the histogram) of the luminance range. "Properly" is subjective, however, and greatly depends on the effect you are trying to achieve—and the contents of the image itself.

Showing color histogram superimposed over itself—so RGB is represented in a single scale (at the top), which can make it hard to read.

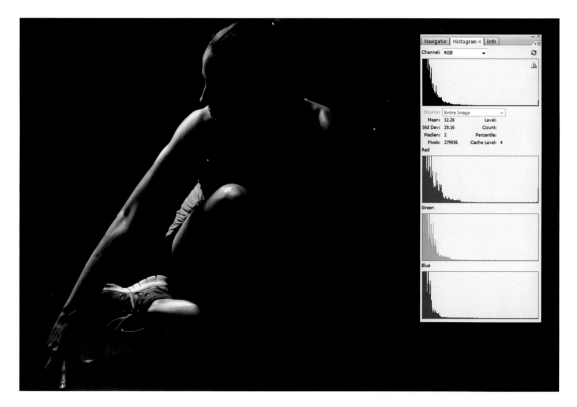

In this image of actress/model Becka Adams, a very moody, contrasty feeling is achieved by rich blacks and underexposed flesh tones.

In the dark image of Becka Adams stretching, I wanted to highlight the strength of her arms and define the silhouette of her body, but keep the overall feeling dark and moody.

The histogram for this image clearly shows that nearly all of the image falls into the blacks and shadow range with very little mid and highlight range. If you were just looking at the histogram and not considering the overall creative choices in the image, this would appear to be grossly underexposed.

In the photo of Alexandra Preda, the choice was made to slightly overexpose her skin tone to give it a more creamy quality. The histogram here shows a bias toward the highlight—especially in the red channel—in what might otherwise be considered bordering on overexposure.

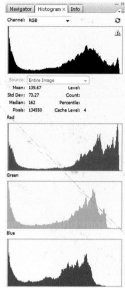

A high-key image of model Alexandra Preda, photographed by Claudiu Gilmeanu.

The choice is made, however, to push the overall luminance range toward the whites to achieve an effect. Contrast is naturally obtained through Alex's dark hair and eyes, which frame the brighter skin tone very well making this a balanced image—even though it is weighted toward overexposure.

Happy little dandelions on my front lawn, silhouetted against the afternoon sky.

In this image of a pair of dandelion flowers on my front lawn, I decided to silhouette the flowers and seeds against a cloudy sky and work to maintain as much detail in the sky as I could. Although it would appear to be a very shadow-heavy image, because the majority of the sky actually falls into the middle gray zone, the histogram represents a more "proper" exposure overall with the majority of the pixel information in the middle gray area.

Many camera manufacturers allow you to see a histogram of your image on the onboard monitor or LCD screen. Many HDSLR cameras can do this, but, with some, you need to shoot a still photo first, as they cannot display a histogram on a "live" or video image.

As another tool to aid in your exposure choices, the histogram can be very helpful to give you a quick assessment of the overall luminance values in your image.

When is White Not White? A Look at White Balance

Physiologically speaking, we see colors in the world based purely on the wavelengths of light reflecting off the object we're looking at. Each object is, literally, a different color based on the light falling upon it; although the human mind has the innate ability to reconcile these differences through adaptive color interpretation and color memory. To most people, a sheet of white paper is white no matter where they see it because their mind *knows* that it's supposed to be white. Their brain will therefore render it as white. In truth, that paper can be blue, orange, green, or yellow, depending on the light falling on it.

Digital sensors are nowhere near as adaptive or forgiving as the human brain. A digital sensor needs to be informed as to what wavelengths of light are present in order to "correctly" render the colors in a scene. The digital sensor will see the white paper for the color it truly is at any given moment, which can be undesirable, at times.

It is important to understand that not only is "white" subjective, but white is a combination of all colors of the rainbow equally reflecting off of a surface. What we perceive as white, is actually red, orange, yellow, green, blue, and violet all reflecting off that surface in equal amounts. Sunlight has all of these colors in it, to varying degrees, depending on the time of day, place on the globe, and atmosphere. In the early morning, when the sun is just rising, the angle of light to the atmosphere filters off most of the short wavelengths in greens, blues and violets to give a very warm light (2,000–3,000K). At noon, with heavy cloud cover, the atmosphere is filtering off much of the longer wavelengths creating a very cool light (9,000–15,000K).

Although digital sensors need to be "informed" as to what wavelengths of light are present at any given moment, they are extremely adaptive to rendering those specific wavelengths to a natural "white" wherein the colors will represent, digitally, roughly as they are seen to the human eye.

I'm talking, of course, about white balance. This term is originally derived from old-school video cameras wherein the imager was "informed" as to what colors were available by adjusting, individually, the red, green, and blue sensors and measuring the results on a waveform monitor in "parade" mode. White balance was achieved when all three signals— red, green, and blue—lined up in an equal balance.

This is exactly what modern cameras are doing, they just do it automatically. When you white balance, you are forcing the camera to adjust its sensors so that red, green, and blue are seen equally off that object (presumably white or neutral gray).

Most digital cameras have several white balance settings: factory preset "tungsten," "daylight," auto white balance (AWB), and custom. Some prosumer cameras have additional settings for fluorescent, daylight shade, and cloudy daylight.

Personally, I would never recommend AWB unless you're in a completely uncontrollable run-and-gun situation where you don't have the time to balance correctly. AWB, like auto-exposure, is a compromise based on average values seen by the camera. In an AWB situation, the camera has to guess what elements of a frame are actually white in order to render them correctly. In many cases, this can lead to an acceptable setting, but rarely will it ever result in a preferred setting.

The factory presets for daylight (5,500K) and tungsten (3,200K) are handy for a number of run-and-gun situations, but will often require color correction in post to really generate the look the videographer is after. Rarely is daylight ever specifically 5,500K and rarely are artificial incandescent sources specifically 3,200K.

The real power of the digital camera is in custom white balance. The ability of the videographer or cinematographer to define what should be seen as white in any given scene.

What you use to white balance can be just as important as what light you white balance under.

Generally, people seem to white balance off any "white" source they have handy. I've been known to use typing paper on a number of occasions (or the back of a script), but to be precise with your white balance, you should use a calibrated source; whether that be a calibrated white card, or an 18% gray card (my preference). Earlier this year I reviewed an extraordinary product called the ExpoDisc—a product that I now carry with me on every shoot. It is plastic disc that goes over the camera lens and, when pointed at your source light, creates a perfect 18% grayscale lit by your source to white balance off of. Quick, simple and incredibly precise. In my tests, the ExpoDisc produced the most accurate whites.

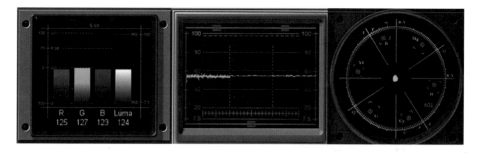

A screen capture from Adobe OnLocation showing (left) the red, green, and blue levels of the image, next to luminance (center) waveform and (right) vectorscope. The results of white balancing through the ExpoDisc.

This is a screenshot from Adobe's OnLocation, a program that analyzes DV signals and puts them through software simulated analysis devices. In this case, I'm showing a spectrum analysis (red, green, blue, and luminance), a waveform in "parade mode" (showing luminance, RY, and BY) and a vectorscope. In this first image, this is a custom color balance from a Canon XL2 set with the ExpoDisc under natural daylight through the window in the late afternoon. Note how extraordinarily close the image analysis is—red, green, and blue are nearly identical. In the waveform, we've achieved a perfect white balance with all three signals (luminance, red, and blue) lining up in the center. Finally, the vectorscope signal is dead center—perfect neutral.

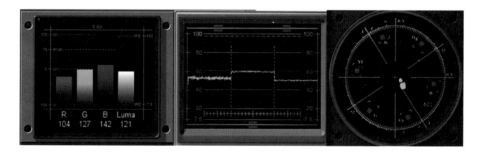

A screen capture showing the camera's auto white balance—through the ExpoDisc, notice the disparity of balance between red, green, and blue showing unbalanced white.

In the second capture, this is the camera's auto white balance setting—still through the ExpoDisc, meaning the entire image is a perfectly calibrated 18% gray, but the AWB cannot render it cleanly. There's considerably more blue in the image and much less red. The waveform doesn't line up and you can see the vectorscope signal biasing toward blue/cyan.

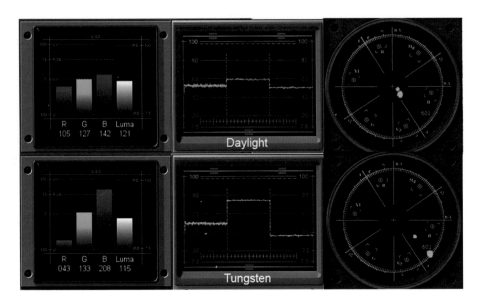

Screen captures showing camera's factory daylight (top) and tungsten (bottom) through the ExpoDisc.

In this final capture we see the preset "daylight" (5,500K) and, below that, the "tungsten" (3,200K) settings. Obviously the tungsten setting is way off and will be very blue. But even the daylight setting is off because the natural daylight at that time in the afternoon was warmer than 5,500K.

When balancing through gels, I've found the Lee Cinematographer swatchbook to be very handy as the gel pieces are 2" square, sizeable enough to fit over most lenses. These aren't easy to find these days, so you may have to cut your own.

As an alternative, a couple of manufacturers make specially calibrated white balance cards with warm or cool tints built in to achieve the same effects. DSC Labs (www.dsclabs.com) offers a calibrated white balance card and a warm balance, which gives the effect, roughly, of an 81A filter. Vortex Media (www.vortexmedia.com) offers WarmCards 2.0, cards that are calibrated in various strengths of warm or cool bias.

Always make sure, if you're using gels on your lights for effect, to white balance *without* the gels in place, otherwise the camera will counteract the effects.

It is also, sometimes, preferable to utilize the incorrect white balance setting. Is the natural sky a little too overcast and gray looking for your scene? Want a really deep blue sky? Set the camera to tungsten balance, light your shot with tungsten fixtures, and the natural daylight will naturally render a much deeper blue.

Another technique is to choose, specifically, what in the scene you want to be rendered white and white balance off of that. Shooting a commercial product that has a white package and the client insists it be as white as it can be? Use the product itself to white balance after you've lit it. Shooting a wedding or a wedding sequence? White balancing off the white wedding dress will make sure it stays pure white. Keep a keen eye on your flesh tones if you utilize a practical item to balance off—it can create some odd results that may not be desirable.

There are times when it will not be possible to achieve white. This is especially true under non-continuous spectrum illumination, such as sodium vapor streetlights. Shooting under low-pressure sodium vapor street lights will never render white. As they have no other wavelengths than orange (589nm), there is no red, green, or blue wavelengths in the light so the camera will never be able to render that single band as neutral white.

Hopefully this little white balance opus provides you with some new thoughts on a relatively boring step in your videography. Happy shooting!

FIELD NOTES

Different Colors in Time

Setting a custom white balance for any given location will help render the scene as the videographer wishes it to be experienced. That doesn't always mean making it "white." Sometimes having a scene that appears warmer or cooler than white is desirable. If you're shooting a scene at sunset, the last thing you want to do is white balance under the setting sun and "correct" out the warmth of the sunset! In that instance, it's best to utilize the standard "daylight" camera setting, which will render the sunset in a pleasing orange/red warmth.

On a number of occasions, I have white balanced through a piece of color correction gel—CTO (orange) or CTB (blue) of varying strengths to bias the camera in the opposite direction.

This scene below with actress Chanel Marriott was lit with tungsten light. Instead of white balancing "clean" or using the preset "tungsten" setting, I set a custom white balance kelvin to 5,400K to give the scene a very warm feel (it's also deliberately underexposed in the skin tones to give it a very dark, dim-lit room feel).

FIELD NOTES

An example of using misaligned white balance for creative results. Here, under tungsten lighting, a high daylight-range white balance is used to make the scene appear very warm. Image of actress Chanel Marriott.
These 4 Walls
© ActionGroup LA.

The opposite effect, in this shot of actress Megan Reinking, I'm using natural daylight through a window in the room and a daylight balanced 1 × 1 LED panel behind her, but setting the camera to 3,400K to give the scene a very cold look.

Another example of misaligned white balance, here under daylight lighting conditions with a low, tungsten-range white balance to make the scene appear very cold. Image of actress Megan Reinking.
These 4 Walls
© ActionGroup LA.

In these two examples, I'm using white balance to the opposite of what my actual lighting is to achieve a narrative effect.

Seeing the Invisible, Part I: Dealing with Infrared Contamination (Red Epic Test)

Let's take a brief trip back to high school science class and talk a little bit about the electromagnetic spectrum.

Sound waves, radio waves, or gamma waves are all part of a larger range of waves called the electromagnetic spectrum, which covers from one angstrom (one ten-billionth of a meter or one tenth of a nanometer) all the way up to AM radio at over 100m in wavelength and beyond. A tiny little portion of this spectrum, from about 400nm to 700nm is light. This is how we

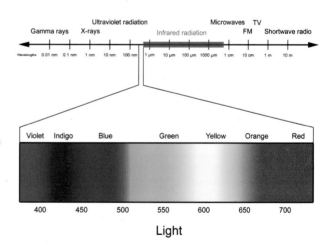

A look at the electromagnetic spectrum, the area of light, and the area beyond light—infrared radiation.

see the world—these wavelengths in this small area of the spectrum—interacting with physical objects around us. This is sometimes referred to as *visible light*, but that's a redundant term. All light is *visible*. If it's not visible, than it's not light; it's radiation. Just before the spectrum of light is ultraviolet radiation (UV), which we know as the harmful rays from the sun that fry our skin! Beyond light is infrared (IR) radiation, which takes up a large portion of the scale from 1,000nm to 1mm. Our eyes are not sensitive to radiation, at least not that we can visually interpret, but digital sensors are, which causes some problems. Remember that both light and radiation are forms of heat and it can be very difficult for an electronic circuit to differentiate between the various forms of heat as to what is good light and what is bad radiation. All digital cameras (except those specially designed for "night vision") feature infrared cut filters inside the camera to limit the amount of infrared radiation that strikes the sensor and that can be interpreted as light.

Ordinarily speaking, the IR cut filters inside the camera do a good job of keeping IR contamination out of our imagery. However, sensors are becoming more and more sensitive—our ISOs are increasing substantially—and counter to that, our apertures' openings are also expanding. Many artists behind the camera prefer to shoot with a wider aperture in order to minimize depth of field. If you're in a situation where you're faced with a lot of light—say a daytime exterior—and you want a large aperture for minimal depth of field, you need to incorporate neutral density filters to reduce the light striking the sensor.

ND filters are great for cutting down light without substantial color bias in the image, but the problem arises when you're cutting down high amounts of light passing through

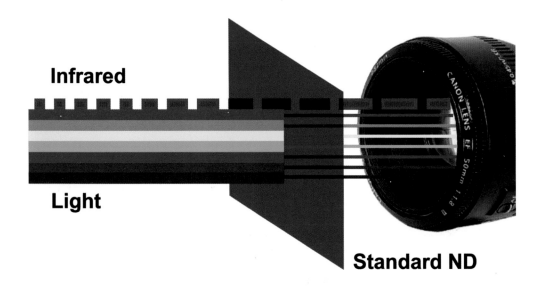

Infrared

Light

Standard ND

A visual depiction of the colors of light passing through a neutral density filter, which are reduced, equally, by the filter, but infrared radiation is unattenuated by the filter and passes through full strength.

the lens, you are *not* cutting down on infrared radiation. The higher the light levels, the more chance there is also high infrared radiation. This is true for high-key tungsten lighting, HMI lighting, and natural daylight, among others.

Since you're cutting down on the visible spectrum, but not the radiation spectrum, this infrared radiation is seen by the camera's sensor and captured by the photosites on the sensor closest to those wavelengths, namely the red photosites. The more actual photons of light you have in a photosite's well, the less IR contamination is noticeable. When you have less photons in a given photosite, then you'll see the contamination. This means you primarily notice the problem in shadows and dark colors. Blacks start to look more reddish with IR contamination and it can skew the image substantially.

Luckily there are tools available to cut down the IR radiation from entering the lens and combat this problem. Unfortunately every camera sensor reacts differently to IR radiation and no single tool is perfect for every system.

Recently I spent a day with cinematographers Christopher Probst, Phil Holland and Jesse Brunt at Camtec Motion Picture Cameras in Burbank to take a look at several IR cutting options on both the Red Epic and Arri Alexa cameras.

Our testing methodology was very simple: take several different black fabrics—including black cotton, cotton blend, nylon, and velvet—in addition to several calibrated color charts and light the objects to a very high stop: f/16 at 500 ISO. Then we would incorporate ND filters and various ND/IR filters from various manufacturers to reduce the light passing through camera to a T/2 or T/2.8 (depending on the strength of ND we had available) to see which combination worked better to cut the light *and* cut the IR contamination from each camera.

Filters tested:

- **Tiffen ND 1.8:** Traditional neutral density filter in 1.8 (–6 stop) density with no additional infrared filtration, used as a control basis.

- **Tiffen Full Spectrum IRND 1.8:** This filter series cuts down wavelengths equally until 680nm where it drops off sharply to eliminate IR contamination.

- **Tiffen Hot Mirror:** Introduced in 2008, the Hot Mirror is a filter that only cuts IR radiation and does not affect light. These filters start at 700nm and continue to block IR all the way through to the 1,000nm range.

- **Tiffen T1:** An IR cutting filter that also incorporates a slight green hue that helps to reduce oversaturated reds that can bleed and cause troubles in standard definition signals.

- **Formatt Hitech Prostop IRND 1.8:** Introducing a slight blue cast to a neutral density and infrared cutting filter, Formatt states their design is specifically intended for outdoor photographers to optimize the image while reducing IR contamination.

- **Formatt Hot Mirror ND 1.8:** A neutral density and Hot Mirror combined in a single filter.

- **Schneider ND 1.5:** Classic neutral density without any added IR filtration. Used as a control.

- **Schneider True-Cut IR-750:** Schneider's version of a Hot Mirror that allows light through but blocks wavelengths starting at 750nm, allowing more red wavelengths through before cutting infrared.

- **Schneider Platinum IRND 1.8:** With a cut starting at 700nm, Schneider's premium line of IRND filters incorporate IR filtration into standard ND.

In this first piece (of two) on infrared, we'll look at the results of testing various filter combinations on the Red Epic MX. To further simplify presentation, we'll only concentrate on the bottom left of the test image including the black nylon material and the x-rite Color Checker color chart.

This first image is the control image, with no filtration and T/stop of 16. Here we are not attenuating light at all, except by the iris, so there is no IR contamination in the image.

The control image, how proper correction *should* look if it's working properly and eliminating IR contamination. This is the reference to refer back to when interpreting the quality of the filtration being used.

The next two frames show the results of using only basic ND, which stops the light but allows the infrared radiation to pass through. You can see the ugly bias, not only in the blacks, but in all of the colors in the image. This is a significantly compromised image.

Utilizing traditional ND filters, without additional IR control, we easily see the effects of the IR contamination in the image.

We'll start with select combinations from the Formatt line of filters. Generally the Formatts do an excellent job at curbing the infrared contamination, and although the Formatt Prostop IRND alone isn't enough, the combination of the ND 1.8 and Hot Mirror obtains excellent results. Note that the Prostop filter deliberately introduces a blue cast into the image to help counteract the red corruption. This is mostly evident when used alone, but also visible when used in combination with a Hot Mirror.

Schneider's IRND, again, isn't enough to combat the contamination—it's actually worse than just the Schneider ND, but combining a Hot Mirror or True-Cut IR filter cleans up the image considerably. There is, however, a magenta cast to the image with the Schneider ND + True-Cut and the ND + Hot Mirror combinations. It is certainly correctable, but the Schneider Platinum IRND and the True-Cut were the cleanest option for the Epic in the Schneider family.

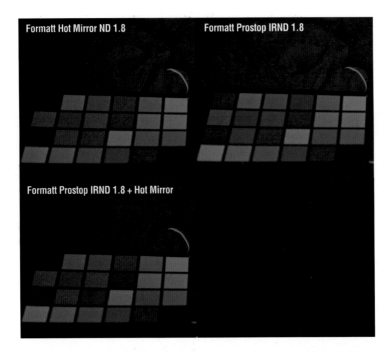

Three Formatt filter combinations.

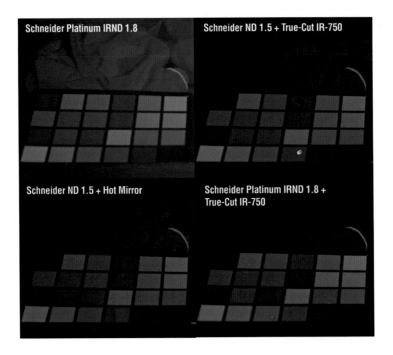

Four Schneider filter combinations.

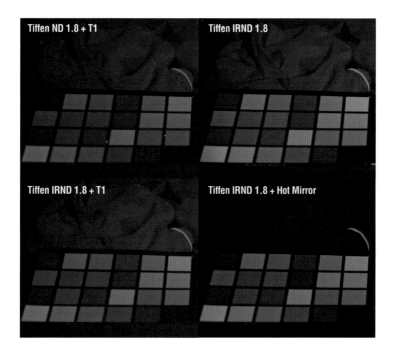

Four Tiffen filter combinations.

Finally, Tiffen was a bit surprising. Tiffen's IRND filter and T1 filter were not strong enough to combat the contamination, but the combination of the Tiffen IRND 1.8 + a Tiffen Hot Mirror gave us the cleanest, most neutral image of all the combinations for the Red Epic. The slight green cast that the T1 introduces, deliberately, is definitely visible in both iterations top and bottom left.

The key to the Epic seems to be a Hot Mirror with any other ND filter (Formatt's ND or Prostop IRND, Schneider's ND or Platinum IRND, or Tiffen's ND or IRND) to really combat the contamination for the Red Epic.

A very important factor here is that these particular filter combinations that worked well or didn't work well for the Red Epic will be entirely different for a different camera and a different sensor. Every camera requires its own filtration solutions to combat IR contamination and, really, only testing can tell you what the right combination is. Although some of these filters were less than effective for the Red Epic, that doesn't mean the filters don't work—they may work wonderfully for another camera system.

In Part II, we'll take a look at the results from the Arri Alexa.

Seeing the Invisible, Part II: Dealing with Infrared Contamination (Arri Alexa Test)

In last month's column, I discussed the problems of infrared contamination with digital cameras. We went into the problems of IR radiation, especially when you severely attenuate light with neutral density filters. A couple of months ago I spent a day at Camtec Motion Picture Cameras with cinematographers Christopher Probst, Phil Holland and Jesse Brunt to test a number of infrared cutting filters on both the Red Epic and the Arri Alexa. This month will look back at that test again and see the results of our filters on the Alexa. (For a detail of filters tested and methodology, see the previous article.)

I'll reiterate that although some of these filters are more effective than others with either the Epic or the Alexa, every sensor reacts to IR differently and you need a different filter or filter combination for each camera in order to best eliminate the contamination in your image. While one filter might not work for one camera, it's highly possible it will work perfectly for another.

We shot the Alexa to SxS cards in ProRes 422 to simplify our workflow.

For the Epic, the key was to incorporate a Hot Mirror filter. Any manufacturer's IRND filter in combination with a Hot Mirror or a True-Cut 750 produced amazing results, although we found that the Tiffen IRND + Hot Mirror combination yielded the best results.

For the Alexa, Arri has incorporated a very effective IR cut filter that acts the same as a Hot Mirror on the sensor's filter stack, so the Alexa already deals with IR contamination extremely well. If we look at the Epic with just straight ND compared to the Alexa (page 183) with straight ND you see that the Epic's image is severely compromised while just the reds in the Alexa image are biased, but the rest of the image still retains its color fidelity and contrast. Because the Alexa already incorporates an effective Hot Mirror, adding a second Hot Mirror in front of the lens has no effect. If anything, it slightly desaturates the reds, but that is an extremely subtle result.

The control image, how proper correction *should* look if it's working properly and eliminating IR contamination. This is the reference to refer back to when interpreting the quality of the filtration being used.

The next two frames show the results of using only basic ND, which stops the light but allows through the infrared radiation and you can see the ugly bias not only in the blacks, but all of the colors in the image. We can see with the IR cut filter inside the Alexa, it does a considerably better job at dealing with infrared contamination even without additional filtration. The blacks in the image are still compromised, but the overall contrast and color fidelity is much more sound.

After that, we move on with select combinations from the Formatt line of filters. All three of the Formatt Prostop filter iterations had excellent results with the Alexa. The T1 does, deliberately, add green to the image, and I don't see an immediate benefit to that. Perhaps in a different situation with a lot of red in the scene, that additional green factor can help tame it, but that's supposition, and not seen in our test here. The Prostop IRND, alone, does

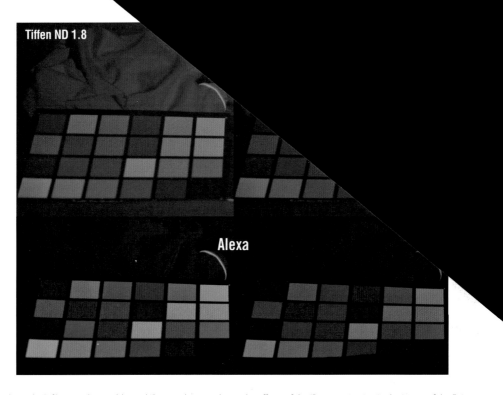

Utilizing traditional ND filters, without additional IR control, we easily see the effects of the IR contamination in the image of the Epic camera (top left and right) and the considerably less, yet still noticeable, contamination on the Alexa (bottom left and right).

very good work with the IR and the addition of the True-Cut has no real discernible effect on the IR or overall color. The clear winner here is the Formatt Prostop IRND filter, without any additional filters required.

Interestingly the T1 plays a strong role in the first iteration combined with just straight Schneider ND we see there's a bit of a deeper loss of light (we should have opened up another ⅓ stop), but the T1 cleans up the red in the blacks pretty well. The Schneider straight ND with the True-Cut 750 filter doesn't get the job done; we still see quite a bit of red contamination in the image. Basically the True-Cut is cutting the same range as the Alexa's internal IR filter, so it's ineffective as an additional tool here. We get a significantly better result with Schneider's Platinum IRND filter—this clears up the red, trues up the colors, and is an exceptional filter for use with the Alexa. Finally, combining the T1 with the Platinum IRND puts too much green in the image for my taste. Although this is correctable, it's not necessary. The Platinum IRND does the job fine by itself and doesn't need additional help!

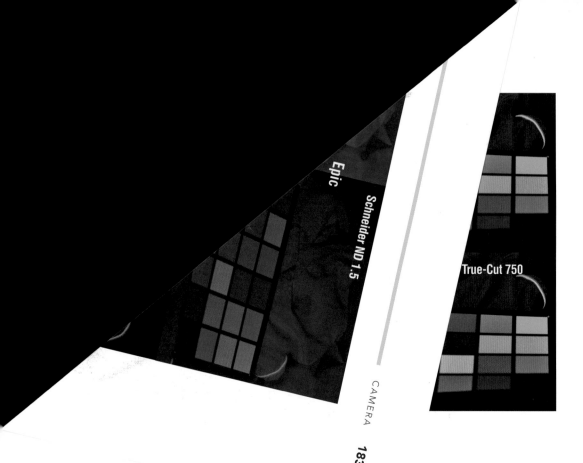

When it comes to Tiffen, ... Hot Mirror and True-Cut 750 have no effect. The T1 still puts green into ... I don't see as a benefit when it comes to the Alexa. The clear winner with Tiffen is the.. IND filter which cleans up the contamination beautifully.

The key to the Epic was clearly to use an IRND in combination with a Hot Mirror or a True-Cut 750. With the Arri Alexa an additional Hot Mirror is of no benefit, nor is a filter like the True-Cut 750, it needs a wider range of IR/red cutting to eliminate the contamination.

The internal IR filter in the Alexa does a great job all by itself and there's little to no need for any additional IR cutting if you're using ND of 0.9 or less. Above 0.9, you need an additional IRND filter with a wider cut range than the internal, which cuts off somewhere above 700nm. Arri specifically left that cut higher, just outside the visible range, because the higher wavelengths of red light are necessary to obtain pleasing skin tones.

So the filters that worked well for the Alexa were the Tiffen IRND, Formatt Prostop IRND and Schneider Platinum IRND. I saw no real benefit in incorporating the T1 with any of those filters.

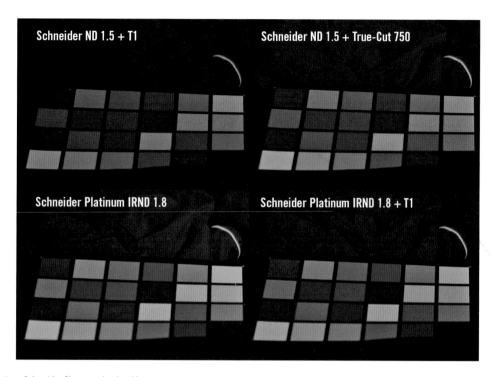

The various Schneider filters on the Arri Alexa.

The clear Tiffen winner, their IRND filter.

The Alexa, across the board, does better than the Epic because it already has a good IR filter built into the sensor's filter stack. Only wider-range IRND filters add to that cut to clean up further contamination with heavy ND use.

Again, it's important to reiterate that these particular filter combinations that worked well (or didn't work well) for the Arri Alexa or the Red Epic will be entirely different for different cameras and sensors. Every camera requires its own filtration solutions to combat IR contamination and, really, only testing can tell you what the right combination is. Although some of these filters were less than effective for the Alexa or the Epic, that doesn't mean the filters don't work—they may work wonderfully for another camera system.

of DV). He simply put the camera
the tripod in the air by the lo
surprisingly effective. Simpl
whole apparatus at its cer
out the bumps and sh
Fast forward to 19
a music video for
courses in New
During our p
(which, if I
The hea
Stead

I clearly remember the first time ⌐ ⌐
eight when it was released theatrically): I wa⌐
"movies" for years. Watching the horrifying film, I was comp⌐
operation. How on earth did that camera follow little Danny Torrance's ⌐⌐
throughout the Overlook? My own experience with makeshift camera dollies ⌐⌐ ⌐
had taught me how difficult it was to move a camera smoothly without track. Obviously
Kubrick and cinematographer John Alcott were not using dolly track as the camera was
following directly behind the big wheel and you could see the floor all the way down the
halls. With the wide lens choice, you could also see the ceilings and it was obvious that no
track was mounted on the ceiling. There was no way it was a free-wheeling dolly as the
Big Wheel travels from hardwood to carpet over and over again (creating an incredibly
iconic sound *hmmmm-thumpthump-wrrrrrrrrrr-thumpthump-hmmmmm*).

At that time, the Internet was only a sci-fi dream and finding answers to my cinematographic questions in Scottsdale, Arizona, was no small feat. If the answer wasn't in
my small stockpile of *American Cinematographer* magazines, chances are it would remain
a mystery.

Alas, it wasn't until several years later that I read about cinematographer, operator, and
inventor Garrett Brown who created an incredible tool called the Steadicam. Aha! *That's*
how *The Shining* was shot! They used this amazing science-fiction tool (indeed it was used
as a prop in James Cameron's *Aliens* as a heavy machine gun body-mount for the Colonial
Marine soldiers), that allowed a camera operator to perform dolly-like smooth shots with a
"handheld" camera.

During my short stint in "film school," a friend of mine shared with me his "Poor-Man's
Steadicam" solution for small cameras (in this case it was a Super8 camera, before the advent

on a tripod with a telescoping center post and then held
w end of the center pole. It was incredibly simple, but also
y adding the tripod as a counterweight and then holding the
ter of balance, far below the camera itself, was enough to smooth
kes of walking with the camera.

96 and I am now working as a cinematographer in Los Angeles prepping
irector Tobias Heilmann. Toby, who had gone through Steadicam training
ork, had rented a rig for the shoot and would be acting as his own operator.
ep period, I tried on the Steadicam harness fitted with a Sony Digital Betacam
recall correctly, was the DVW-970) for about 15 minutes and was incredibly tired!
vy rig is quite a strain on your back and I gained significant sympathy for the
cam operators I worked with from then on.

Director Tobias Heilmann working with a Steadicam rig.

The primary attribute of any stabilization system or tool is to isolate any external movement from affecting the camera movement. In terms of body-mounted or handheld stabilizers, the primary goal is to isolate the movement of the operator's body as they walk or run (most notably the vertical movement that is nearly impossible to eliminate when one shifts weight from one foot to the other while walking).

When considering a stabilization tool for your own camera the first choice should always be a body-harness system. A full body-harness system has four major components: shifted center of gravity for fluid operation, gimbal head at the center of gravity, iso-elastic arm to isolate the operator's body movements from the camera and counterbalance the weight, and weight-distribution body-harness. The body-harness is part of what separates the high-end systems from the inexpensive ones. As exemplified by Garrett Brown's original creation, the Steadicam harness distributes the combined weight of the camera, rig and monitor to the operator's shoulders and waist. There is nearly no strain on the operator's arms, leaving his hands as mere tools to refine the composition and operation. Distributing the weight of camera and rig to the body allows for greater control, smoother camera shots, and more operation stamina.

There are several manufacturers who make body-harness stabilization tools, which include Steadicam's Ultra, Archer, Clipper, Flyer, and Pilot; George Paddock's Pro Sleds; Glidecam's Gold, X, and V series; VariZoom's Black Hawk, FlowCam, Aviator, and ProLite; and Movcam's Pro, Avant, and knight series, among others. Each successive model/series from an individual manufacturer is designed for use with a different weight class of camera systems. The top-of-the-line systems, such as the Steadicam Ultra, Glidecam Gold, VariZoom Black Hawk, and Movcam Pro-Max, are for use with film cameras or large HD systems, generally above 25 pounds. The small end—Steadicam Pilot, Glidecam X-10, VariZoom ProLite, Movcam knight D201—are all designed for small camcorder systems, generally less than eight pounds.

All of these systems include the four principal components: modified center of gravity, gimbal head, iso-elastic spring counterweight system, and a body-harness. It is the combination of these elements that make for the best camera stabilizer. These are, of course, going to be the most expensive options, but—in qualified hands—will always yield superior results.

Next in line of both effectiveness and cost are non-body-harness gimbal stabilizers such as the Steadicam Merlin and Steadicam JR, Glidecam 4000 and 2000, VariZoom FlowPod and Ultralight, and Movcam Handfinder 190 and 350. These systems forgo the body-harness and iso-elastic arm and require the operator to handhold the entire rig, taking all of the weight of the camera and stabilizer on their arms. Not only does this become very fatiguing very quickly, but it also eliminates one of the principal benefits to a camera stabilizer tool—isolating the operator's movements from the camera. These simplified rigs are merely a step up from my old friend's hand-carried tripod technique as they alter the camera's center of gravity to a more neutral position and they incorporate a gimbal handle for more fluid movement of the camera.

The third category of camera stabilizers are the most simplified, eliminating the body-harness weight distribution, isolating arm and gimbal to merely alter the center of gravity to allow for more fluid operation. These are the least expensive, yet least functional of the stabilizers. The PanPilot or StabilizerFLEX are two non-gimbal versions and there are many, many online articles on DIY stabilizers, most of which are just variations of the old tripod technique. Some DIY models do incorporate a gimbal handle and, if you look hard enough, you can find a full DIY rig with isolating arm and body-harness.

One variation of the center-of-gravity change is the innovative Fig Rig, designed by director Mike Figgis, and offered by Manfrotto/Bogen, the Fig Rig disperses the camera's weight laterally by putting the camera in the center of a steering-wheel-like configuration where each hand is off to the side of the camera. This device, although incredibly fatiguing to hold for any length of time, is surprisingly effective to smooth out handheld camera operation. A similar device is the Quad-Pod, which has two handles set out at nearly shoulder-distance apart, with the camera mounted at various positions between them. This final rig borders on the edge between hand-held stabilizer and shoulder-mounted rigs, which are not stabilizers, but merely weight distribution systems.

It's important to note that with *any* stabilizer—high-end expensive model with all the bells and whistles or cheap DIY model—takes time and practice to understand and operate properly. No tool is going to solve your stabilization needs all by itself. All of them will require refined operator skill to make them function and it behooves any owner/operator of any stabilization tool to spend as much time—away from the actual shoot—practicing their operation as possible.

PART 4
LIGHTING

Adventures in Lighting: Light Sources 101, Part I—Tungsten

With a wide variety of illumination sources available to cinematographers these days, this sub-series of *Adventures in Lighting* will break down and explain the different kinds of illumination and their uses to help readers make more informed choices about their lighting needs.

We'll start with one of the most ubiquitous forms of illumination in our world: tungsten or incandescent bulbs.

Incandescent means light from heat and, although the sun and fire are both incandescent sources of light, the most commonly used form of incandescent light is the traditional filament light bulb.

The light bulb, originally refined (although *not* invented) by Thomas Edison, features a base (traditionally a medium screw base), two electrodes, a filament coil (most commonly of tungsten), and a glass envelope (bulb) to enclose the filament in an oxygen-free vacuum. When electric current is applied to

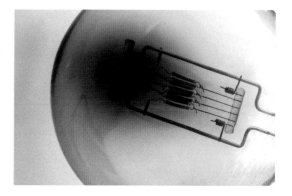

Top: An older 2K tungsten bulb. Bottom: A standard medium-base photographic bulb designated PH212.

the electrode, electrons pass from the electrode through the filament and on to the other electrode. This electrical movement through the filament, along with tungsten's resistance to the flow of electrons, causes the filament to heat up to the point where it begins to incandesce—or glow— and emit light from the heat. The hotter the filament grows, the higher the color temperature is emitted from the filament. This color can be altered by the shape and tightness of the coil of the filament in the lamp as well as the amount of current drawn.

Tungsten (also known as wolfram), a naturally occurring metal, is a very brittle substance, but it has the highest melting point of non-alloyed metals and the second highest melting point of all elements on the periodic table (3,421°C/ 6,191°F). This makes it perfect for the source of incandescence as the standard tungsten filament can heat up to temperatures of more than 5,000°F.

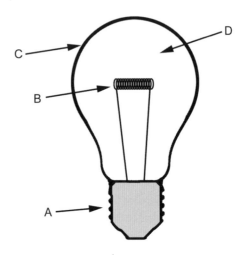

The components of a standard tungsten bulb: A) the base; B) the filament; C) the envelope; D) inert gas filling the vacuum inside the envelope.

A standard, clear, tungsten bulb next to a "soft-white" bulb.

With that extreme heat, if oxygen were present inside the bulb, the filament would simply burst into flames and burn out. Instead, we fill the bulb with inert gases, most often argon and/or nitrogen. Since tungsten is a delicate and brittle substance, it will start to deteriorate through usage, especially during the extreme moments of sudden current flow changes when the light is turned on or off. Small particles of tungsten will fall off of the filament and collect on the coolest part of the bulb (this is the blackening you see on older light bulbs). When the filament loses enough tungsten and becomes too brittle, it will break and the bulb will no longer light.

The glass of the bulb—called the envelope—must also be able to withstand the intense heat inside the bulb. Common bulbs have a borosilicate envelope—and the glass bulb is large enough to provide good space from the hot filament, or the glass would actually melt.

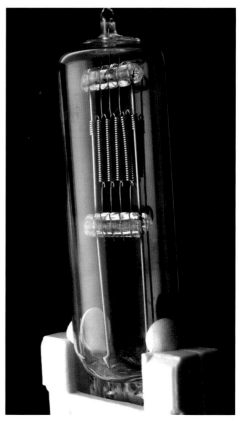

Many manufacturers also create "soft white" tungsten globes in which kaolin, or kaolinite, a white, chalky clay in a powder form, is blown into the envelope and electrostatically deposited on the interior of the bulb. This white coating diffuses the light emitted from the filament helping to make a softer and more pleasing light.

TUNGSTEN-HALOGEN

Many people misuse the term "halogen" with regard to incandescent lamps. This refers to a specific class of bulb, not the standard light bulb. Tungsten-halogen or merely halogen (also called quartz-iodine) bulbs are filled with a halogen gas (in addition to the argon and nitrogen), most commonly iodine (sometimes bromine, chlorine, fluorine, or astatine). This additional iodine gas, when heated by the filament, captures loose particles of tungsten that fall off the brittle filament and then re-deposits them back onto the filament, which prolongs the life of the bulb. This process requires the filament to burn at a

A tungsten-halogen bulb has thicker, higher melting point glass (quartz), more compact nature, and contains an iodine gas to prolong the life of the bulb.

higher temperature than a standard incandescent bulb and, as a result, requires a much thicker and robust envelope; generally quartz glass. Since these bulbs burn hotter, they actually have a higher color temperature than standard household bulbs. A standard tungsten bulb will burn around 2,600–2,800K, whereas halogen bulbs will burn between 2,900 and 3,200K. This makes them more beneficial for use in photography—creating illumination closer to what is regarded as "white" for incandescent sources. The thicker, higher melting point, quartz glass also allows for less required space between the envelope and the filament, making tungsten-halogen bulbs much more compact than their standard cousins. Halogen bulbs, because of their intense heat, require special fixtures to house them. Although some household fixtures utilize halogen bulbs, most do not. Nearly all professional lighting instruments for film and video utilize halogen bulbs.

PROS AND CONS OF INCANDESCENT LIGHT

Pros

- The sun is an incandescent light source. It is a great ball of fire that emits light from burning gasses. This light contains all of the colors of the rainbow—red, orange, yellow, green, blue, indigo, and violet. An incandescent light bulb functions on exactly the same concept. The light emitted from the heated filament is what is called a "full spectrum" light source; meaning it contains the full spectrum of colors of the rainbow. Although tungsten lights are a lower color temperature than natural daylight (which is combination of direct light from the sun and ambient skylight to raise the color temperature), they still contain all the colors and will render "true" colors to photographed objects (as long as the camera is set to the correct white balance).
- Incandescent bulbs can be easily dimmed using standard dimmers. The color temperature lowers as the bulb is dimmed, but they require no special hardware in order to dim.
- They are easy to manufacturer and inexpensive.
- They require no additional regulating equipment, such as a ballast.
- They work equally well on alternating and direct current.
- The standard medium-screw base is one of the most ubiquitous fixture connectors on the market.

- They are available in a wide variety of intensities (wattage) from as low as 5 watts to as high as 20,000 watts.

- For most common frame rates, even high-speed, there is no problem with "flicker" with incandescent lamps.

- The heat emitted from a tungsten bulb can be a benefit—especially in terms of livestock incubators (poultry or reptiles, for instance). In addition, some cooler climate locations are finding problems with modern LED streetlights during the winter months. The warmth emitted from traditional tungsten bulbs would melt the snow build-up in the stoplight whereas the LEDs do not, making the lights difficult to see as snow accumulates.

Cons

- The primary problem with incandescent illumination is that it must first have intense heat before it can emit light. Somewhere between 80% and 90% of the energy used is wasted on heat with only 10–20% of that energy actually emitting light. This is where the incandescent lamp has been vilified in recent years by the environmental and green movements. They are not efficient in their usage of electricity—as most of the electricity is lost to heat. Incandescent bulbs are *not*, however, the black mustache-twirling bad guy that the environmentalists would have you believe. Their natural light is often more pleasing and comfortable for human beings and photography. They contain no dangerous gases and, other than sharp glass, are not a danger to the environment or personal health if broken.

- The second biggest con to incandescent light is the immense heat they generate. With enough of them—at high intensities—you can significantly raise the temperature of the space you're shooting in. This can make it uncomfortable for talent and even dangerous for children or animals. It can also make food photography very challenging. The lamps themselves heat up considerably from the bulbs inside and make them difficult to handle when they're hot.

THE BAN ON INCANDESCENT LIGHT BULBS

As I mentioned above, environmental movements have created a legal "ban" on standard incandescent light bulbs—in the United States this is the Energy Independence and Security Act of 2007, but there is similar legislation in other countries all around the world. It's not a true ban, *per se*, the law requires a certain efficiency of electrical usage: 25 lumens per watt by 2013 and 60 lumens per watt by 2018; standard incandescent bulbs have an efficiency of about 10–20 lumens per watt, so they just can't meet the new standards. This phase-out has been happening since 2008. In 2012, 100W bulbs were phased out. In 2013, 75W and, as of January 2014, 60W and 40W bulbs are being phased out.

This ban only covers standard household bulbs. Specialty bulbs, like those used in professional lighting fixtures for our industry, are not affected. Also—"rough duty" bulbs are still legal to manufacturer and sell; as are bulbs with unusual bases. Some clever manufacturers have found a way around the ban by inserting small halogen "special duty" bulbs inside the envelope of a traditional medium base bulb. These have the benefit of being more energy efficient than standard tungsten light bulbs and, for us, they burn at a more "pure" color temperature than standard tungsten—win, win!

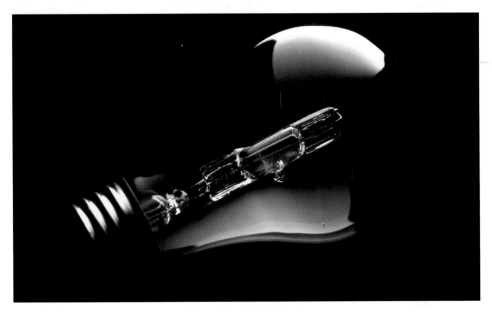

One of GE's "sneaky" new tungsten bulbs that gets around the new environmental laws. Inside the standard envelope is a smaller tungsten-halogen bulb. It's a bulb within a bulb.

Adventures in Lighting: Lighting Sources 101 Part II—Fluorescents

Last month, I broke down the elements of tungsten light sources. For this second installment in Adventures in Lighting: Light Sources 101, we'll take a look at fluorescent fixtures.

Once upon a time, fluorescent light was the bane of the cinematographer's existence. The light produced by these ubiquitous lamps was often greenish, ugly, and unflattering. However, modern advances in multi-phosphor mixes have made fluorescent fixtures feasible and efficient tools to light with.

The benefits of fluorescent lighting are that it is naturally soft, it consumes very little electricity, and it puts off nearly no heat. These are all strong pros in the digital video world.

The cons of fluorescent lighting are: the inconsistent mixture of different types of tubes you're likely to encounter in any given location, the high green content still common in many manufacturer's tubes, the non-continuous and false color spectrum, and the flicker associated with shooting at non-standard shutter-speeds or frame-rates.

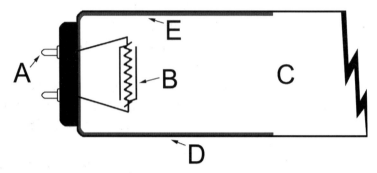

The components of a fluorescent tube: A) terminals; B) electrode; C) mercury gas; D) glass envelope and E) phosphor crystal coating inside the envelope.

A fluorescent tube is made up of five primary parts:

- Electrode
- Mercury gas
- Phosphor crystals
- Glass envelope (bulb itself)
- Metal terminals

Fluorescent light is derived from electrons that are emitted by an electrode at one end of the tube that collide with a free electron in the outer orbit of an atom of mercury (a metal/conductor in gas form) inside the tube. This collision, which happens at high speed, produces ultraviolet radiation. The radiation, in turn, excites the phosphors coating the glass tube, which then emit light.

Fluorescence is unlike incandescent light and doesn't produce a full spectrum of color. Although fluorescent lighting is energy efficient and doesn't create the heat that standard incandescent lighting does, the lack of color spectrum can cause cinematographers a number of headaches. Instead of providing a smooth, even distribution of color from the

A standard compact fluorescent lamp (CFL). The twists in the lamp allow for more surface area for a brighter lamp in a more compact space.

full spectrum, fluorescent light provides spikes of specific color wavelengths. Although fluorescent bulbs may simulate a specific color temperature (called CCT or correlated color temperature) equivalent to incandescence, it is never perfect. That being said, with careful selection of your lamps, you can still use them very efficiently to light your scenes.

There are many types of fluorescent lamps, from the popular compact fluorescent lamps (CFLs) to Slimline, to the ubiquitous T-12 tubes. The most important aspect of the different shapes and styles of bulbs available is that you find the right lamps for whatever fixture you're working with.

By nature of their operation, fluorescent lamps require very precise control over the electrical current delivered to the lamp. Without this control, the lamp would nearly immediately die, possibly in a very destructive manner. A fluorescent lamp is a negative differential resistance device, which means that, unlike metal conductors, as more current flows through the tube, the electrical resistance within the tube actually *drops*. If the lamp were connected to a constant supply of electricity, it would most likely explode, or at least quickly burn out the electrode. Regulation of electricity, then, is provided by a ballast, which provides an initial high burst of current to cause the electrode to spark, and then carefully regulates the flow. After the initial spike, the ballast needs to carefully regulate the electricity to keep the lamp lit, but not allow it to overheat the electrode or allow too much flow of electricity. Ballasts are specifically designed to work with a particular size and wattage of fluorescent lamp. If you ever need to replace a ballast, make sure it's designed for the specific types of lamps in your fixture.

Light Output Flux Lumineux Rendimiento Lumínico	3200 LUMENS LUMENS LUMENES
Life Duree de Vie Duracion	20,000* HOURS HEURES HORAS
Color Rendering Index Index de rendu de couleur Destaca los Colores de Forma, Indice	70 CRI
Color Temperature Couleur Froide Apariencia de Color	4100K

*See side panel for details. *Voir les détails sur le côté.

Technical information on a fluorescent lamp package. Important to note is the CRI of the lamp and the color temperature.

Most important to digital cinematographers are the CCT (correlated color temperature) and CRI (color rendering index) ratings of the lamps you work with. CRI, while somewhat of a controversial topic beyond the scope of this column, is a scale from 1 to 100 by which non-continuous spectrum light sources are measured. The number denotes how accurately they simulate a full spectrum of color and, in turn, allow objects to be seen in their "real" colors.

A CRI of 100 would be natural daylight, which renders an object's true colors. A CRI of 50 might mean that reds seen under that light will appear more maroon or greens will appear more gray. Now you *can* white balance under low-CRI lamps, but you're still not going to get true colors in your scene because not all wavelengths of light are there, regardless of how neutral your camera makes the whites.

Low-CRI lamps are often seen where inexpensive, long-lasting illumination is needed, but where true color is not a priority. The worst-case real-world example is the low pressure sodium vapor street lamps that permeate many cities. These fixtures emit a very specific wavelength of yellow/orange light and, effectively, have a CRI of 0 or 1.

In the late 1980s, gaffer Frieder Hochhiem created a custom-made high-output fluorescent fixture for cinematographer Robby Müller while shooting the film *Barfly*. This creation eventually evolved into a whole new career for Hochhiem as he founded Kino Flo, Inc., a company dedicated to the art and science of fluorescent (and now LED) lighting. These fixtures set the standard in the industry and brought fluorescent technology out of the taboo and into vogue. Research and development into specific recipes of phosphor blends, first with third-party vendors and then through Kino Flo's own creation, resulted in color correct tubes with very high CRIs of >95.

In addition to getting the phosphor mixes perfected to work seamlessly alongside tungsten and daylight color temperatures, Hochhiem also incorporated several aspects into the Kino Flo fixtures to solve the other problems of fluorescent lighting in motion pictures. One of the primary differences is Kino Flo's high-frequency ballast that cycles the lamp 25,000 times a second (as opposed to a standard ballast that cycles the lamps 60 times a second). This makes Kino Flo fixtures virtually "flicker free" at any shutter speed or frame rate.

Today, there are many other manufacturers who are making fluorescent fixtures, including Arri, Lowel, and Mole-Richardson, to name a few.

Commercial and residential fluorescent lighting normally has a moderate CRI in the 70–85 range. This makes the light more comfortable for people to work and live in, but it doesn't necessarily make it photographically precise. These commercial fixtures are moderate at representing natural colors, but can often have a high concentration of green/blue in them.

However, advancements in phosphor combinations have led to some really great options for fluorescent lighting in general. Look for lamps with high CRI ratings—in the 85–95 range and for a CCT that most closely matches the lighting you'll be mixing the fluorescent source with.

In the last few years, especially with the heavy environmental movement, CFLs have become very popular. Their efficiency is twice to four times that of incandescent bulbs, which lose 80–90% of their energy to heat. Since fluorescent fixtures get their brightness primarily from the surface area of the glass, manufacturers designed a way to twist the glass into a tight spiral to compact it down and get a lot more surface area in a smaller space. CFLs incorporate their ballast directly into the base of the bulb to create a single device that can be screwed into any standard light bulb socket. The smaller size and all-in-one construction meant that people could now replace their tungsten bulbs with fluorescent bulbs and not have to change out their fixtures.

These are very efficient sources and are fairly inexpensive; although they are typically much more expensive (about five to ten times) than the equivalent wattage in tungsten bulbs. They are not, however, manufactured for use in photography. Most CFL globes do not have published CRI ratings and there are considerable differences between manufacturers and even individual product lines and shapes within a single manufacturer. They also can take longer to switch on than a normal incandescent bulb. Regular CFLs won't work with dimmer switches and they can interfere with radios, cordless phones, and remote controls due to the infrared radiation they emit.

You can certainly use CFLs to light with, no doubt, but it's best if you're going to use them to use them exclusively—and stick to one manufacturer and specific model of CFL. In that case, you can white balance away any green cast and achieve some good results. If you're combining these with any other sources, however, I'd recommend staying away from CFLs altogether.

There is also a danger with fluorescent fixtures that environmentalists seem to like to ignore. Each bulb contains mercury—which is a poison to humans. Although this danger might be overexaggerated as the standard bulb only contains a small amount (which has been equated to the equivalent amount one is exposed to when eating a piece of tuna), one only needs to look at the Environmental Protection Agency guidelines for safe cleanup of a broken fluorescent bulb to understand that it's important to take the risk seriously:

Before Cleanup

- Have people and pets leave the room.
- Air out the room for 5–10 minutes by opening a window or door to the outdoor environment.
- Shut off the central forced air heating/air-conditioning system, if you have one.
- Collect materials needed to clean up broken bulb:
  - stiff paper or cardboard;
  - sticky tape;
  - damp paper towels or disposable wet wipes (for hard surfaces); and
  - a glass jar with a metal lid or a sealable plastic bag.

During Cleanup

- **DO NOT VACUUM.** Vacuuming is not recommended unless broken glass remains after all other cleanup steps have been taken. Vacuuming could spread mercury-containing powder or mercury vapor.
- Be thorough in collecting broken glass and visible powder. Scoop up glass fragments and powder using stiff paper or cardboard. Use sticky tape, such as duct tape, to pick up any remaining small glass fragments and powder. Place the used tape in the glass jar or plastic bag.
- Place cleanup materials in a sealable container.

After Cleanup

Promptly place all bulb debris and cleanup materials, including vacuum cleaner bags, outdoors in a trash container or protected area until materials can be disposed of. Avoid leaving any bulb fragments or cleanup materials indoors.

Fluorescents In-Shot

Fluorescents aren't just good sources for lighting your subject, they can also be very beautiful in-shot. Back in my gaffing days, I worked on a number of music videos with director/cinematographer Joseph Kahn. Two stand-out videos were Montell Jordan's "I Can Do That" and Monica's "First Night."

For Montell, Joseph had a fantastic set built that we integrated 15″ daylight (5,600K) Kino Flo tubes into the structure itself. There were 32 of those, eight on top, eight on bottom, on both sides of the curved

A shot from the set of Montell Jordan's "I Can Do That," directed and photographed by Joseph Kahn.

From the set of Monica's "First Night" music video, directed and photographed by Joseph Kahn, the art department built a false, raised floor that my team filled with 108 Kino Flo fluorescent tubes.

A shot from the set of Monica's "First Night" with the dancers on the lit floor.

A shot from the set of Monica "First Night" showing the number and variety of Kino Flo fluorescent tubes placed on the iron railings of the famous Bradbury building in downtown Los Angeles.

FIELD NOTES

structure. Above the car is an old fluorescent fixture that Joseph found somewhere that we put standard cool-white tubes into. On the floor behind the car are some bare daylight tubes and there's a 12″ tungsten-balanced tube wrapped in Lee Canary Yellow gel on the center counsel in the car below Montell. I really love the effect of all these lamps in-shot and in the reflections of the car.

The Monica video was a *huge* Kino Flo order. This video was shot in the famous Bradbury building in downtown Los Angeles (featured prominently in *Blade Runner* and other movies). We built a false, raised milked-Plexiglas floor and put Kino Flos under it to up-light the floor.

There were 18 4′ × 8′ floor panels each lit with six tungsten-balanced Kino Flo tubes. I wanted all 8″ tubes, but Kino didn't have that much in stock so we went with a combination of four 6′ tubes and two 8′ tubes in each floor panel. That was 108 individual tubes in total!

Then we strapped a 4′ or 8′ single Kino Flo tube on every banister in the center court of the building. That was another 110 individual tubes. For those, we alternated between clean tungsten and tungsten wrapped in Lee Canary Yellow gel (a favorite of mine). The result was a very unique party dance video.

Both of these works can be found on YouTube.

Adventures in Lighting: Light Sources 101, Part III—HMIs

In the world of luminaries, the carbon arc used to be the king, but his time has faded and left room for the HMI to be king of the power and utility.

HMI is an acronym for hydrargyrum (the Latin for mercury and the basis of the periodic chart symbol Hg) medium-arc iodide. HMI is actually a trademark of the Osram corporation, the original manufacturer of metal-halide gas discharge lamps, but it has been adopted as a common colloquialism for any mercury-based metal-halide fixture.

The conceptual design of a halide gas discharge lamp dates back to 1912, but it wasn't until the 1960s when the German television industry asked Osram to produce more efficient and less-expensive daylight

A specialty HMI fixture manufactured by Arri, the 1,800W HMI—the brightest fixture that can be plugged into standard 20A "household" power. Image courtesy of Arri.

color sources that the technology was really perfected. The HMI was introduced in 1972 for the European television industry and quickly adopted by television and film professionals worldwide. They were a little slow to be adopted into the United States as they were designed to operate at 50Hz, and adjustments to 60Hz, which include modifying the lamp arc to a shorter distance and changes in bulb configuration, took some time.

HMIs use mercury vapor to create light, not unlike a fluorescent lamp, but employ a continual electrical arc, as opposed to phosphor coating, at very high intensity to create a very powerful light. Addition of halide salts help to define the color and consistency of the light. A halide is a chemical compound of halogen with an electropositive element. Each halide salt (mercury, AgCl, AgF, AgBr, and AgI) glows a different color and the combination of the halides, together with the blue glow of the main mercury arc, help to create the precise color temperature. HMIs burn at a very high temperature and the gas inside the envelope is at a very high pressure (around 50psi), which makes them very dangerous when they fail. Safe handling of HMI bulbs is of a paramount concern—not to mention they're very expensive (as compared to standard tungsten bulbs). HMIs sometimes fail catastrophically and actually explode, but this is a rare occurrence.

As with all halogen lamps, care must be taken when handling the bulb. If you touch a bulb with your bare hands, the oils from your fingers leave a coating on the lamp that heats up and actually acts like an acid on the quartz glass. A single fingerprint can cause a lamp to fail. It's a good practice to clean off a lamp with an alcohol wipe and allow the alcohol to evaporate before starting the lamp.

Double-ended HMI lamps have a nipple—a small extrusion—on one side of the bulb. It is of paramount importance that this nipple face *away* from the fixture reflector and towards the front of the fixture (not up or down). Any other configuration can cause a reduction in lamp life and a possible catastrophic failure of the bulb.

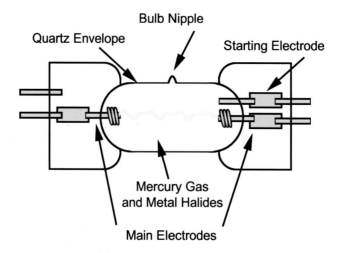

The components of an HMI bulb: quartz envelope, igniter, electrodes, mercury gas and halide salts, nipple.

The HMI lamp is a sealed vacuum with a quartz envelope. The lamp has three electrodes, one that is a starter, or igniter, and two main electrodes that form the lamp arc between them. When the lamp is first struck, which requires a high burst of electricity, the igniter sparks between itself and one of the main electrodes, then the arc spreads to the other electrode. It is, initially, very dim. The small arc spreads across the gas in the lamp to the other electrode and, at first, the arc fills the lamp until it warms up and starts to get smaller and brighter. As the lamp heats up, the mercury starts to vaporize, then enough heat is made to start vaporizing the halide salts. This is why it takes a few minutes for an HMI to come up to temperature and why you'll see various colors emitted from the lamp as it does before it finally settles on a clean 5,600–6,000K (depending on manufacturer) daylight color.

The HMI requires a ballast to maintain proper voltage to the lamp. Older magnetic ballasts were very heavy, noisy, and created a smooth sinusoidal transition in the arc that caused problems with flicker at various frame rates. As with fluorescent lamps, the arc itself is actually sparking 60 times a second. We can't see this with our eyes, but when shooting at shutter speeds of greater than ⅟₆₀ of a second (30fps at 180° shutter angle), the camera *will* catch moments of the arc sparking and the result will be a flicker in the image. Later electronic ballasts created "flicker free" HMIs with a square wave that had a very hard transition between on and off to eliminate most flicker problems. At high frame rates, HMIs still have flicker problems, but most electronic ballasts are acceptable for standard use.

HMIs come in a variety of sizes and intensities from 200W to 18,000W and have high efficiency, much more so than tungsten, of light output per watt, so they are much brighter than a tungsten at the same wattage—about four times as bright. Typical HMI wattages are 200W, 400W, 575W, 800W, 1,200W, 2,500W, 4,000W,

A battle-scarred 1,200W HMI PAR on the set.

6,000W, 12,000W, and 18,000W. Note that most of the HMI wattages are different from tungsten wattages (commonly 150W, 300W, 650W, 1,000W, 2,000W, 5,000W, 10,000W).

HMIs put out a high amount of UV radiation and, therefore, require a UV filtering glass to protect people from the harmful rays. Modern HMI fixtures have safety switches inside them so that the lamp will not operate if the UV glass lens is opened.

HMIs come in "open face" (with just UV protective lens), Fresnel, PAR, and soft light varieties.

Electricians prepare a 12K HMI Fresnel in the basket of a 60' condor crane for an upcoming night shot.

The beauty of the HMI is that it is very efficient in light output, very bright, and it burns at a natural daylight color balance, which means that the HMI fixtures can be used to augment—and even replace—natural daylight. HMIs are often used at night, as well, from high and faraway places—such as a condor or cherry-picker crane, to light a large area.

Although they are substantially more expensive than their tungsten cousins, HMIs are powerful and versatile tools in your lighting arsenal.

Adventures in Lighting: Light Sources 101, Part IV—LEDs

One of the woes of location shooting, especially on small productions when you can't afford a generator or a qualified electrician to tap into existing power, is being limited to wall-socket power in the 15 Amp or, at most, 20 Amp variety. This limits you to, at most, a 2,000W fixture (which is definitely stretching the boundaries of safety). In the HMI world, you're limited to 1,200W fixture (or perhaps the

Arri M18 1,800W fixture), if you can afford the HMIs. Fluorescent figures are a great alternative, but you're limited to soft lights and they're not necessarily compact or easy to transport.

LEDs came on to the scene several years ago, but for quite a while they were small units without much output. Although they consumed much less power than their tungsten or metal halide cousins, their output was a fraction of the traditional sources.

Finally, that is starting to change. LED is coming of age.

LED is an acronym for light-emitting diode. The modern LED was originally invented in the early 1960s, based on technological discoveries made at the turn of the twentieth century. Early LEDs were only capable of emitting a red light and at very low intensity, but further advancements paved the way to brighter red LEDs then orange, green, and, finally, in the mid-1990s, the blue LED. As technology improved, creating brighter LEDs, techniques were employed to coat the inside of the plastic lens with phosphors to turn the bright blue light into "white" light.

LEDs create light by electroluminescence in a semiconductor material. This process happens when an electric current is passed through the semiconductor and individual electrons fill "holes" in the material. These holes are created when an atom lacks electrons (negatively charged ions) and, therefore, has a positive charge. Semiconductor materials like silicon can be "doped" to create these electron holes. Doping (no, not what you're thinking) is the adding of additional elements into the silicon semiconductor to change its properties. Doping allows the manufacturer to create two separate types of semiconductors in the same crystal—positive and negative—with a boundary between the two types called the "p-n junction." This is why they're called diodes—meaning two terminal.

The p-n junction only allows current to pass through it in one direction. As electrons move from negative to positive through the junction, they fall into the "holes" and emit photons of light.

A somewhat psychedelic image of an RGB LED fixture and its reflector. The combination of red, green, and blue LEDs allow the user to create nearly any color from the fixture.

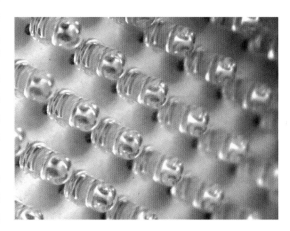

A close up of LED lamps in a fixture.

As blue/white LEDs emit the most practical light, most LED fixtures are naturally in the daylight color balance family, although with phosphor coatings, LEDs can also match the tungsten spectrum. High-end LED fixtures manufactured for the photographic industry are mostly very clean, with little to no green spike. Consumer grade, or inexpensive LED fixtures, often have a very high green content that needs to be filtered out.

LEDs require very low power, output no heat (from the lamp itself) and have extraordinarily long lamp lives; typically in the 50,000–100,000-hour range. As a result of this efficiency, many long-term installations have already switched over to nearly exclusive LED technology.

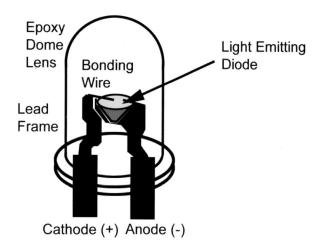

The components of an LED: epoxy dome lens, bonding wire, lead frame, light emitting diode, anode, cathode.

In the United States and Canada, all traffic signals have been switching over to LED lamps since the mid-1990s. Once the three primary color LEDs were perfected, large screens could be manufactured with red, green, and blue diodes clustered together in "pixel" formations to form pictures, like a television screen, and many outdoor giant screens are now made from LED lamps including Megascreen, D-Lite, Starvision, Monsterscreen, and Sony's massive Jumbotron. These screens go as large as the Adi iConic 100, a 41' × 23' LED screen with a 47' widescreen diagonal picture—it's an outdoor television larger than most cinema screens.

The advancements in LED technology have moved them into the viability range for film and video applications. Companies such as Litepanels, Nila, Element Labs, Zylight, Arri, and more, are manufacturing LED fixtures specifically for production use. The typical LED is a 5mm cylindrical shape, although they can come in larger sizes and rectangular shapes, larger doesn't necessarily equal more light.

The LEDs themselves are a fixed color, generally in a very narrow bandwidth, and they are not capable of changing color. Film and video fixtures therefore, just like their incandescent, gas-discharge or fluorescent cousins, are available in a specific color temperature. However, the small size of LEDs allows for many varying color diodes to be clustered together and activated at various intensities to create nearly any color in the visible spectrum with the possibility of dimming from one color to the next. This is the real benefit of LED fixtures—being able to have both daylight and tungsten in the same

The Litepanels Sola Fresnel fixtures. Image courtesy of Litepanels.

fixture and transition to any approximate Kelvin temperature between by dimming between the two colors. This nearly negates the necessity of color correction gel and makes a single lightweight and compact fixture, extremely versatile for many different types of shooting environments.

The real maturity of LED technology is just starting. Fixtures like the Litepanels Sola Fresnels, which—despite their enormous size—can output the intensity and quality of a tungsten Fresnel at a fraction of the power consumption and heat generation.

A final note about LEDs, just as with the danger associated with mercury in fluorescent lamps, LEDs may contain arsenic. Since this is the case, never handle a dead LED with your bare hands and dispose of them as you would other hazardous waste.

EMERGING TECHNOLOGIES

Electroluminescent technology, in a thin sheet, was popularized in the early 1990s by the Timex Corporation and their Indiglo watches. Afterward, it began popping up in household devices such as nightlights and digital clocks and in vehicle instrument gauge panels. Further developments in efficiency of the EL material led to architectural applications where the paper-thin material was carefully crafted in different colors to create lighted signs that were cooler, more efficient and had a significantly longer lifespan than their neon counterparts.

The Bridgewater, Massachusetts company Being Seen Technologies, Inc. manufactures electroluminescent products for a wide variety of uses. One of the most popular is their EL Cable, which comes in varying colors and widths from .1″ to .15″. These illuminated cables look much like lighted neon and can be bent into any shape easily. Bridgewater also offers EL sheets in 24″ × 17″, 17″ × 12″, 12″ × 8.5″, or 6″ × 17″, all of which can be cut to virtually any shape and size. These sheets and cables are available in up to 15 different colors and are fully dimmable, don't emit heat, and have extraordinarily long lifespans.

As of yet, there are no electroluminescent manufacturers creating colors with high CRI in the tungsten to daylight Kelvin range for use in film and video, but that hasn't stopped creative filmmakers from utilizing this new technology.

While puzzling over how to unobtrusively light the practical taxicab interiors for Michael Mann's *Collateral*, cinematographer Paul Cameron turned to electroluminescent sheets that he could cut into any shape and merely tape onto strategic locations around the cab's interior to light up the film's principal actors. Working with high definition cameras and high gain settings, these battery operated pieces of illuminated paper became the key source for both Tom Cruise and Jamie Foxx while driving in the cab. The green-cyan hue that the EL paper emitted fell perfectly in line with Cameron's (later Dion Beebe's) palette.

Screen captures from *Collateral*, directed by Michael Mann, photographed by Paul Cameron, ASC, and Dion Beebe, ASC. Cameron used EL paper in strategic positions within the cab to light the actors. Collateral © DreamWorks, LLC.

PLASMA LIGHTING

The latest in lighting technology is the plasma light source. A ridiculously tiny lamp—the size of a Tic-Tac—puts out incredibly powerful light in full-spectrum daylight. Although the evolution of the technology dates back to Nikola Tesla, the practical application of plasma for the production industry is brand new and, at the time of this writing, really only being developed by two companies: Hive Lighting, Inc. and Photon Beard Limited.

One of the Hive Lighting plasma fixtures.

Plasma combines the high intensity output of HMI sources with the energy efficiency of LEDs. Unlike most LEDs, plasma units are single-source fixtures, with just one tiny bulb. They work from a combination of noble gases and metal salts that, when excited, shift from gas to plasma to create light. There are no electrodes or filaments, so they call the plasma fixtures "solid state" and they have a very long lifespan of up to 10,000 hours. Hive's lamps boast a CRI of 94 with a full spectrum color temperature of 5,600K (although CRI and full-spectrum are contradictory terms, we'll let that slide for now).

Photon Beard's plasma fixture.

Plasma fixtures can be double the efficiency of light output to energy usage just like HMI fixtures and up to eight times the efficiency of tungsten fixtures. Plasma is still in its infancy, but it's certainly a technology to watch.

Adventures in Lighting: Fixture Types 101, Part I—Through the Eye of the Fresnel

The sea of lighting hardware can be confusing water to navigate. There are so many different options, so many different types of fixtures, qualities of light, and methods of creating light. How do you know which is the right one to use?

To help a bit in understanding the different types of fixtures and their applications, I'm going to discuss one specifically, identified by the type of lens it uses: the Fresnel.

In a fixture without any lens, commonly called "open face," the light emitted spreads out in all directions, more or less evenly, from the source. Most of the time, this creates a large, uncontrolled, and unrefined field of light. A lens is required to concentrate the light rays and make the fixture more efficient for controlling the light.

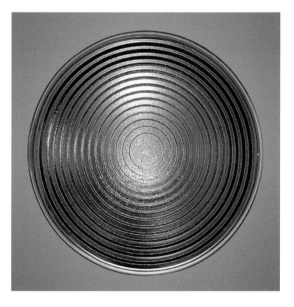

A Fresnel lens.

With a flat piece of glass, a light ray will strike one side of the glass, refract (bend or deflect) slightly passing through, and then refract again on its way out. The combination of these two refractions results in the light ray continuing on in exactly the same path it started. A lens, in any form, is designed to refract light in a specific manner so that its exit path is different from its entrance.

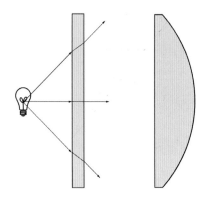

One of the most basic types of lenses is the plano-convex lens. As the name describes, the plano-convex has one flat side (plano) and one curved side (convex). Light passing through the lens refracts considerably, but the direction of the exiting light rays depends on the specific distance to the actual source.

When the source is set at the proper distance to the plano side of the lens, the light rays are refracted and exit from the convex side of the lens in a parallel fashion. If the source is moved farther away from the lens, the resulting light rays are refracted to converge upon themselves, forming a tight pool of light. If the light source is moved closer to the lens, then the rays diverge, forming a wider pool. In all three cases, the introduction of a lens forces the light rays into a more efficient and controlled path.

Above left: When light rays pass through a plane of flat glass, they are refracted by the first surface of the glass, and then refracted again by the second surface to continue in the same direction as they entered.

Above right: A standard plano-convex lens. One side is flat (plano) the other is curved (convex).

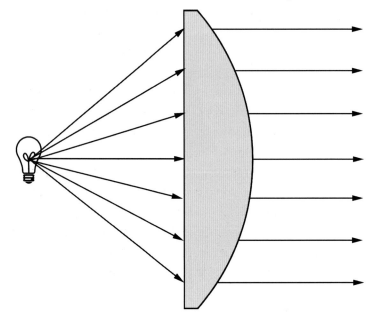

When the lamp is placed at a specific position away from a plano-convex lens, the light rays exit the lens in a parallel fashion.

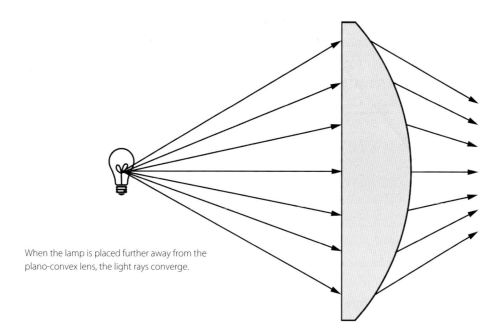

When the lamp is placed further away from the plano-convex lens, the light rays converge.

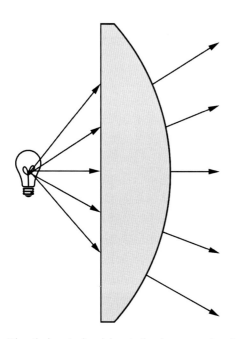

When the lamp is placed closer to the plano-convex lens, the light rays diverge.

In the early 1800s, French physicist Augustin-Jean Fresnel was working to create a large lens for lighthouses. The challenge with the plano-convex lens was that it was impossible to create a large diameter lens for large applications as the amount of glass involved became far too heavy and impossible to work with. By starting with the plano-convex shape and cutting away the mass of the lens in concentric circles, Fresnel determined he could retain the qualities of the lens while greatly reducing its mass.

The Fresnel lens was adopted into theatrical and film lighting almost as early as artificial light itself. Relatively lightweight, this workhorse lens allows light to be efficiently utilized in a soft, even field. Fixtures with Fresnel lenses most often have a "flood" and "spot" function on them, which literally moves the lamp and socket inside the fixture further away or closer to the fixed lens. This forces the light rays to converge or diverge, making them into a tight, smaller circle (spot) or a large, wide one (flood). Of course, spotting in a fixture intensifies the brightness of that smaller spot whereas flooding (diverging) spreads out the same light rays over a larger area and reduces the overall intensity of the light at a given distance.

Mole-Richardson, one of the oldest manufacturers of lighting fixtures for the motion picture industry that is still in operation today, has many Fresnel instruments to choose from; each with a different aperture and lamp wattage—in addition to fun and funky names that have become ubiquitous in the industry.

In the Mole-Richardson incandescent (tungsten) line, they offer the Midget (200W 4$^{15}⁄_{32}$" Fresnel lens), Tweenie (650W 4$^{15}⁄_{32}$" Fresnel), Baby (1,000W 6" Fresnel), Junior (2,000W 9$^{7}⁄_{8}$" Fresnel), Senior (5,000W

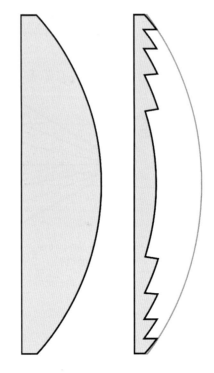

Fresnel took the plano-convex lens and cut it down in concentric circles to maintain the properties of the larger lens in a much smaller shape.

14" Fresnel), and Tenner (10,000W 24$^{3}⁄_{4}$" Fresnel). Even though the "Big-Eye" 10K fixture has a 2' diameter Fresnel lens, whereas the Midget has a 4$^{15}⁄_{32}$" Fresnel, they both refract light the same through their Fresnel lenses. In both cases the lens performs the exact same function, just with widely different intensities (determined by lamp wattage) and sizes of the light beams (determined by size of the lens). Other manufacturers, such as Arri, DeSisti, and Altman offer their own line of tungsten Fresnel fixtures. Fresnel lenses are also often seen on HMI fixtures, even as an accessory to a PAR (parabolic aluminized reflector) fixture.

The Fresnel offers an even field of light that is considered "pleasing" on the face. It can be used clean (without diffusion) on a person, without creating a harsh or unappealing look. A Fresnel doesn't have the same "throw" that a spotlight does, meaning the light doesn't necessarily travel well over great distances, but is more often used closer to talent or subjects. The Fresnel can, of course, be used through diffusion or in a softbox—such as a Chimera— but they aren't necessarily as efficient behind diffusion or in a softbox as an open-face fixture might be.

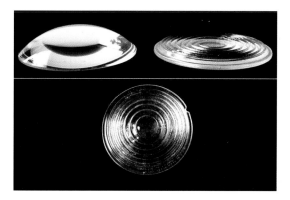 

Photographs of a plano-convex lens next to a Fresnel lens and looking directly at the tell-tale concentric circles of a Fresnel lens.

A Fresnel fixture.

Because Fresnel fixtures have their flood and spot function, they are very versatile fixtures, adapting to coverage and intensity needs without requiring additional hardware. Since the rays of lights are refracted in a focused pattern, they can be easily cut with flags. Fresnel lens fixtures require a single source, point source, such as an incandescent bulb or a gas discharge lamp (HMI). Since they're a single-lamp source, there's no danger of multiple shadows from a single light.

The Fresnel is a true workhorse in film and digital lighting. They are versatile enough to work in many applications and having a few of them in different sizes and wattages will cover many possible scenarios you'll encounter in your lighting.

Adventures in Lighting: Fixture Types 101, Part II—The Ellipsoidal Reflector Spotlight

I was originally introduced to the world of lighting in high school with legitimate (live) theater. There we had four primary types of lighting fixtures: the Fresnel—used onstage and over-stage for general wash, backlight, and some selected area lighting; the cyc light—used primarily for color wash on the rear cyclorama; large scoop lights—used primarily for work lights; and ellipsoidal reflector spotlights (ERS) fixtures—used for more focused and shaped light, generally from the front-of-house position. ERS lights are more commonly called Lekos or sometimes a Klieglight (by the real old-timers), but both nicknames are based on two manufacturers brand names: Strand (now Century) and Kliegl Brothers, respectively.

Many film and videographers today know the fixture by a new brand name,

An ETC Source Four ellipsoidal reflector spotlight hanging, ready for duty.

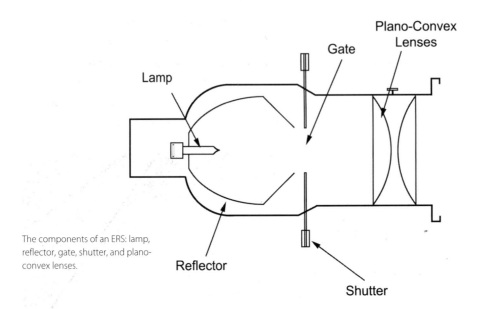

The components of an ERS: lamp, reflector, gate, shutter, and plano-convex lenses.

the Source Four, an invention of the ETC (Electronic Theater Controls) company, who manufacture a high-quality, advanced and versatile version of the ERS.

The ERS features a built-in reflector in the shape of half of an ellipse. By positioning the source light within the ellipse, rays of light emitting from the source are bounced off the surface and reflected to a single point called the conjugate focal point. At the CFP, the light rays converge and then diverge from there. By placing lenses just past this point, it allows us to refract and focus an intense concentration of light and create a very efficient spotlight that can project light over great distances.

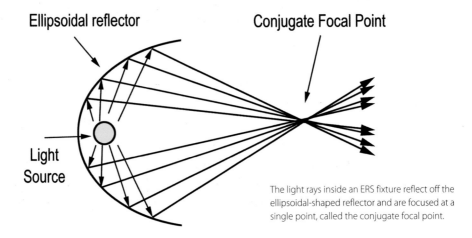

The light rays inside an ERS fixture reflect off the ellipsoidal-shaped reflector and are focused at a single point, called the conjugate focal point.

In addition, the ERS features an aperture, called the gate, just before the CFP that will cut off unfocused beams of light and form the shape of the light to be projected through the instruments' lenses. As an additional feature of ERS fixtures, the gate has four adjustable shutters; solid metal blades that can be inserted into the gate to further shape the beam of light. This is like building in four flags into the fixture to allow the user to cut the light off of unwanted areas and shape the beam into almost any simple linear shape.

An older Altman ERS fixture and (right) looking down the throat of the fixture at the gate, shutters, reflector, and lamp inside.

The various shapes that can be made by adjusting the four in-gate shutters in an ERS fixture.

Taking this gate further, as any interruption of the light at this point can be precisely focused in the fixture's projected beam, we can insert a template or "gobo" (officially a "gobo" is any object that cuts or shapes light) into the fixture. This will project whatever pattern is cut into the template onto the surface being lit. This can be the pattern of a window frame, light through leaves of trees, stars—pretty much anything you can imagine. There are thousands of templates available from several different manufacturers: Gam, Lee, and Rosco all make their own templates in pretty much any shape you can imagine.

All ERS fixtures feature a series of lenses to focus and project the beam. These lenses, generally just a pair of plano-convex lenses, can be adjusted closer or further from the CFP to sharply focus or defocus the beam at different distances.

ERSs come in various sizes, generally described by two numbers, the first is the diameter of the lens and the second is the length of the barrel. The longer the barrel, the farther the lenses are from the CFP and the narrower the projected beam will be. The final number is the field of projection for the beam angle (center, hottest portion) of the light. The smaller that number, the more pin-point the beam is.

3½″ × 6″ = 25°		6″ × 12″ = 16°
3½″ × 8″ = 18°		6″ × 16″ = 15°
3½″ × 10″ = 16°		6″ × 22″ = 8°
4½″ × 6½″ = 33°		8″ × 9″ = 7°
6″ × 9″ = 24°		10″ × 12″ = 7°

ERS fixtures are available in 250–1,000W varieties with the most common now being the 750W ETC Source Four fixture.

I have often used ERS fixtures to spotlight some object in the background, to give a specific shape of light on the set or to introduce a pattern and breakup of light.

It's important to note that the lenses in ERS fixtures are incredibly simple. They're the most basic form of optics—the plano-convex lens. No chromatic aberration correction has been worked into the lens system, which means that sharp patterns often have color fringing around the high contrast areas. To fix this, we do the same thing we do with camera lenses and stop down the aperture. In this case, we place a "donut" in the front color frame holder of the fixture. A donut is merely a solid piece of metal with a small circle diaphragm cut into the center. This reduces the exit pupil of the lamp in the same way that an aperture in a lens reduces the entrance pupil. This helps to reduce the effects of chromatic aberration significantly.

The ERS is a versatile fixture that works great for lighting specific portions of sets or locations with patterns, specific cuts of light—they're very controllable and efficient lights.

Night For Day

One of the most creative executions of an ERS on a film set that I ever witnessed was when I was a gaffer for cinematographer Robert Humphreys on a film called *The Invisibles* starring Portia De Rossi. We were on the second floor of an apartment building shooting at night, but the scene called for daylight. We didn't have the time or equipment to light through the windows from the outside, so Humphreys used an ERS to create a daylight look from the *inside*. The windows were covered with a sheer drape, so we focused an ERS on the drapes, cut the shape of the light to the shape of the window, inside the drapes, and the effect looked exactly like light was coming through the window instead of being simply projected on the curtain. By placing other instruments in the room to mimic what natural light would be like coming through the window, we sold the effect simply, quickly, and quite effectively. I used this effect several times later in my career, the first time I pulled it out of my bag of tricks when I was a cinematographer on a film called *Mothman* in Point Pleasant, West Virginia in a nearly identical situation: second floor, no access to lighting through the window, so we lit the window from the inside instead.

A shot from the set of *Mothman*, directed by Douglas TenNapel, photographed by myself. Here we see actor Ed Schofield and "Gordon" seemingly in a morning scene, but this was shot in the dead of night with an ERS fixture in the room lighting up the window curtains to make it feel like sunlight streaming in. Photo by Christopher Probst.

The scene, pictured above, was shot at night. Outside that window is a very cold, very dark West Virginia night. It was easy to light the room to feel like daytime, bouncing a 2K fixture into the ceiling to give me a nice soft, even, morning feel. The real key to selling the look was using an ERS on the curtain sheers. The ERS is inside the room, beside camera, shining directly at the window sheers and the shutters are adjusted to cut the light to the shape of the window behind the sheers. Even though the light is in the room, it doesn't look like that—it looks like bright daylight shining through the window. As long as no one moves between the light and the window, the effect is quite convincing. If you look carefully, however, you'll see just under the window sheers is a deep dark shadow that wouldn't exist if there were natural light coming through the window. That little area snuck by me!

Adventures in Lighting: Fixture Types 101, Part III—The PAR

The next in line in our examination of lighting fixtures is the PAR—which is an acronym for parabolic aluminum reflector.

The classic PAR is a reflector and lamp all-in-one, it is a sealed-beam lamp, like old-school car headlights. The rear of the envelope (the glass enclosure of the bulb) has a parabolic shape and is coated in an aluminum material for a built-in reflector. The filament of the lamp is placed in the precise focal point of the parabolic reflector so that the light rays exiting the lens are parallel. This creates a focused beam of illumination from a compact, lightweight lamp.

The PAR has four major components—the lens, the reflector, the base, and the filament.

As the PAR has a fixed relationship of reflector, lamp and lens, the only way to change the spread of the light is to change the bulb (or, in higher-end HMI PARs, change the lens). PARs typically come in: very narrow spot, narrow spot, medium flood, and wide

A standard household PAR lamp. The reflector is built into the fixture.

flood varieties. The quickest way to tell the difference is the more "crap" you see on the lens, the wider the spread of the light.

As a standard bulb, a PAR is typically used as a wide, intense flood light. You'll see them often used for exterior illumination, particularly security lights. Small PAR fixtures are great for "spotty" and intense practical lighting on a set. You often see PAR lamps in overhead recessed lighting in commercial and private venues.

PARs have a size designation: PAR36, PAR64—which is a reference to the diameter of the lens in ⅛" increments. Take the number, divide it by eight and that will give you the lens diameter in inches. So a PAR64 has an 8" diameter lens (64/8 = 8).

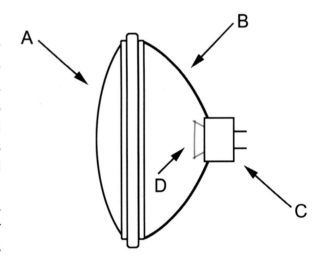

Components of a PAR lamp: A) lens; B) reflector; C) base/terminals; D) filament.

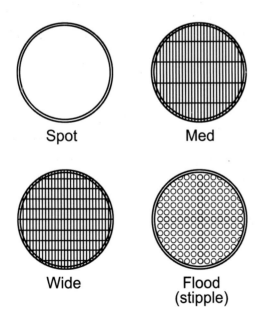

Spot

Med

Wide

Flood
(stipple)

Diagram of various lenses from a PAR lamp fixture.

A photograph of a lens set from a small HMI PAR. In the bottom row from left to right: wide, medium, very wide, spot. In the top row, left to right: very narrow spot and diffuse.

The simplest professional PAR fixture is the PARcan which takes the PAR globe and encloses it into a simple metal snoot to make it more of a spotlight fixture. The PARcan is used more often in theatrical and concert lighting than it is in film and television. The last time I used PARcans on a shoot was at the Encounter Restaurant at Los Angeles International Airport (the spaceship-looking building in the center of the airport that most people mistakenly believe is the control tower). I used 112 PARcans on the ground, pointing straight up, circling around the entire structure to light up the outside wall. They're a workhorse fixture, but the light is often too harsh for direct use on faces.

The next most common usage of PARs is in a multi-lamped fixture. We use PAR64s in four-lamp, six-lamp, nine-lamp, 12-lamp, and even 24-lamp configurations, all in one fixture. The six- or nine-light configurations are often called Maxi-Brutes. The 24-lamp variety is called a Dino or Wendy light. These

A six-light PAR fixture.

are often used for nighttime exteriors off a condor or cherry-picker for wide, broad backlight. PAR64s are 1,000W lamps, so 24 of them in a fixture provide a considerable punch. The individual lamps in the multi-array fixture can be swapped out for very narrow spot (nicknamed "firestarters" for the intense heat they project in a very tight beam), narrow spot, medium flood, or wide flood for different uses. It's possible to have some wide, some medium, and some spot in the same fixture to cover greater distances with the spread of light.

The light beam that comes from the PAR is elliptical in shape and, often, can be rotated vertically or horizontally by spinning the physical lamp itself.

The back of a "Maxi-Brute" nine-light PAR fixture at work. Photo by Otto Kitsinger.

HMI Pars have a sealed beam reflector and clear lens and require an additional lens to be placed in the fixture—they are, typically, spot (near clear), medium (some facets in the lens), wide (more facets), and stipple, or very wide (the most facets in the lens).

The only other real oddball in the PAR world is the ETC Source Four PAR, which features the same lamp as the ETC Source Four ellipsoidal reflector spotlight, precisely positioned in a parabolic reflector and separate, interchangeable, lenses for spot, medium, and flood.

Finally, FAY PAR lamps have a dichroic filter to raise the color temperature to 5,000K from a tungsten lamp.

Mixology: Additive and Subtractive Color Mixing

A few weeks ago I was asked to lecture at a college for a course in advanced cinematography. The professor requested that I include color theory in my lecture and at first I was a little overwhelmed at the concept. Color theory could fill an entire curriculum in and of itself—yet I only had a scant three hours to speak, and that was to be just one of the topics. I asked the professor for more detail on what he'd like to have covered and why and he told me that some of his students were having trouble grasping the idea of colored light and the way it interacts with colored sets and costumes. Aha! OK! So I can cover an introduction to additive and subtractive color mixing and help clear up that concept a bit.

Since that's still fresh in my mind—that shall be our adventure this month.

We cannot see light. This is a concept that generally provokes quizzical stares from my lecture attendees—but it's a hard fact of the physics of our world. We cannot see the wavelengths (or particles) of light traveling through space. What we *can* see is light reflecting or refracting off of objects in our world. You don't see the light falling on the page as you read this, you see the light reflecting off the surface of the page to reach your eye. Some people argue that they can see light beams in the air, but we only see light beams because that light is refracted through or reflected off of something in the air; be that dust, moisture, or smoke. What our eyes see is the reflection of light off of objects and that light reflecting off the object is altered by the object itself. Every object in our world reflects a certain amount of light, but it also absorbs a certain amount. The colors that you see are based on wavelengths of light that are reflecting off of the object, while others are absorbed. We see a basketball as orange because the pigments in the leather of that ball are rejecting (reflecting) off certain yellow, orange, and red wavelengths of light while absorbing green, blue, and violet.

The natural source of light in our world is the sun. The sun, as an incandescent source—that is light from heat—projects light waves in all sizes so that light from the sun contains all of the colors of the visible spectrum: red, orange, yellow, green, blue, indigo, and violet (like Pluto, Indigo was downgraded some time ago as not an "official" part of the spectrum—but I still include her for old time's sake). Under normal circumstances, all of these wavelengths of light strike all the objects in our world that are lit by the sun. Each object absorbs some wavelengths and reflects others. If we deprive that particular object of the wavelengths of light that it rejects, we will significantly alter the appearance of that object. This is, also, a hard concept to grasp because humans have wonderful color memory. If I take a strawberry, which we all know is red, and I put it in a dark room and light it with light that contains no red wavelengths, the strawberry will appear blackish. Most people look at that and say—it's just dark. But the truth is the colors aren't there to reflect back to our eyes. Cameras don't have this wonderful color memory, they only record the truth.

There are two different categories of color mixing: subtractive and additive. Subtractive color mixing is what happens when you mix paint pigments together. For anyone who ever took art classes as a kid, you were taught the primary colors were red, yellow, and blue. I'm here to tell you that's an outright lie. I think they teach kids this because magenta and cyan are difficult words to grasp at an early age. The pigment primaries are magenta (not red), cyan (not blue), and yellow (they got that one right). When you mix pigment colors together, every addition of a new color darkens your result. In subtractive mixing, every addition of

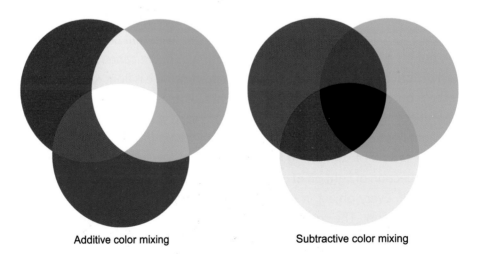

Additive color mixing   Subtractive color mixing

The left diagram shows additive color mixing (light), with red, green, and blue primaries that, combined, make white light. The right diagram shows subtractive color mixing (paint pigments, filters) with magenta, cyan, and yellow primaries that, combined, make black.

a new color brings the result closer to black. The combination of all colors is black and the absence of color is white.

Additive color mixing, such as with light, has different primaries. We deal with red, green, and blue and if you keep in mind that every addition of a light source makes the result brighter, it's easier to grasp that as you add colors in additive mixing, you get closer to white. White light is the combination of all colors and black is the absence of light.

These two behaviors of color mixing work together. When you mix pigment primaries (also called secondaries), you get the lighting primary colors. Mix cyan and magenta together to get blue. Mix yellow and cyan together to get green. Mix yellow and magenta together to get red. When you mix enough equal parts of yellow, cyan, and magenta, you get black. Likewise, if you're using the primary colors of light, you can mix red and green to get yellow (remember in additive, the result is brighter than the two colors you're mixing), you can mix green and blue together to get cyan and you can mix blue and red together to get magenta. When you combine red, green, and blue together, you get white.

Here's an actual photograph I took looking at real-world physics of color in action. Using red, green, and blue light mixed together, you can see the secondaries and a close approximation of white at the center. My sources weren't the most pure sources so the color mix isn't perfect, but it's definitely a real-world example.

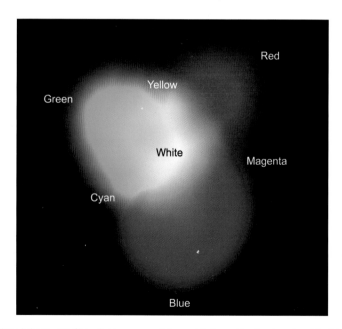

An actual photograph of three light sources, filtered red, green, and blue and their combination to make white light.

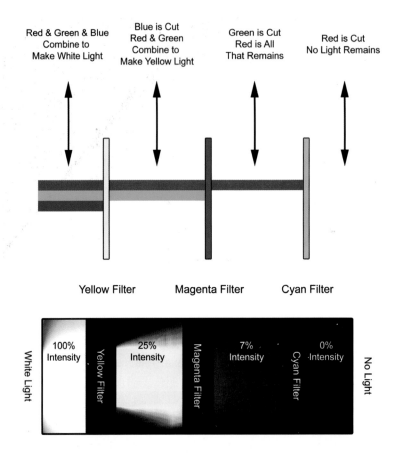

An illustration of subtractive color mixing. At top, full spectrum light passes through a yellow filter, which stops the blue spectrum, but passes through red and green. A magenta filter stops the green, passing only red, and the final cyan filter stops the red, so no light passes through. The bottom is an actual photograph of this happening. Notice with subtractive color mixing (filtration) we are losing light levels because we are stopping portions of the light from passing through. We start with 100% intensity, then down to 25%, then down to 7% and, finally, 0%.

The second photo shows subtractive color mixing using colored gels. Gels are subtractive because they stop certain wavelengths of light from passing through. In essence, they absorb those colors and allow others to pass through. So we start with white light (red, green, and blue) and pass that through a yellow filter. The yellow stops the blue and lets red and green pass through. The result is yellow light (red and green light combined make yellow). Note that the intensity of the light is reduced because we're filtering out some of the wavelengths, so we're down to 25% original intensity now. Then we put a magenta filter in front of that. That stops the green light, but allows the red to pass through. Now we only have red light— and it's 7% of the original intensity because we've filtered out all the other wavelengths.

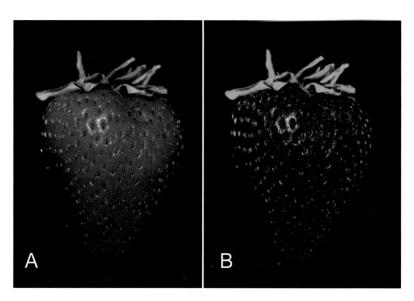

A real-world illustration of how light affects the colors we see. We see the strawberry as red (A) because red wavelengths of light reflect off the surface. When we filter out the red from the light with a cyan filter (B), the strawberry appears nearly black because it is no longer receiving red wavelengths to reflect.

Finally, we put a cyan filter in the path of the red light and the result is 0% intensity. The cyan filter doesn't allow the red to pass through, so we have no light on the other side.

Where this intertwines is when we realize that we only see objects in our world as their colors because they are reflecting those wavelengths back to our eyes. So if we go back to the example of the strawberry and we light it with white light, we'll see that beautiful red (yum!). But if we put a cyan filter in front of the light source that stops red light from reaching the strawberry—it will no longer be receiving red wavelengths to reflect back—and it will appear nearly black (there are other wavelengths of light mixed in with the red, so not pure black).

You have to keep the principles of both additive and subtractive color mixing in mind when you're lighting a set. The colors of the walls, set, props, products, etc., are all biased by the colors (and integrity of color) of your light sources. One student at the school had a set that was painted all brown and they wanted a moonlight feel with blue light and were confused when the walls became black in their image. The walls were black because the blue light didn't contain the red and yellow that the walls wanted to reflect, so they went black.

This whole topic is further complicated by white balance and picking your white point, which biases the way the camera sees colors even further—but that's a subject for another day.

Color Temperatur

Our world is filled with color—deep reds, cool blues, vibrant yellows—
because the light from the sun contains all of the colors of the rainbow a
objects in our world reflect certain colors back to our eyes.

Human vision is incredibly flexible with regard to color. Our eyes and our
together to interpret many different lighting situations and see them as natural and

The color of light is measured on the Kelvin scale, originated by British scientis
William Thomson Kelvin in 1848. Lord Kelvin theorized that if you take a perfect black b
radiator—which is a theoretical material that neither reflects nor refracts light—and you
slowly started to apply heat, the radiator would start to glow. It would first start to glow
red, then orange, then yellow, then blue, and so on. In his scale, which started at absolute
zero (−273°C), he was able to define the colors of the visible spectrum by specific temperatures.

When color film emulsion was invented—and then the CCD and CMOS chips much
later—it did not have the flexibility to see "white" light as versatile as the human brain. Film
and digital sensors have a very small window of temperatures they can see as "white" before
colors will read as "false."

To combat this, the creators of imaging mediums picked two "target" points of color
temperature that would be seen correctly. These were an average of measured daylight
color temperature at high noon, which is about 5,600 Kelvin, and tungsten incandescent
fixtures, which burn at about 3,200K.

Neither of those numbers are infallible, unfortunately. Daylight is rarely ever exactly 5,600K
and incandescent lamps are rarely, if ever, 3,200K. But the numbers represent a "close enough"
approximation that allows for slight manipulations in color correction later on to create the
right look.

The right look is, more or less, capturing the world how it is seen to the human eye.

Although we may be able to stand in a room lit with tungsten (3,200K) light at night and
see everything "normal" in white light, if the camera is set to see daylight (5,600K) as "white"

ep orange. This is because the
ee the higher Kelvin tempera-
a longer, warmer wavelength,

r "indoor" color balance and
daylight is going to appear

emperatures. If you have
to pick your approach:

of "neutral";

ᴊ with daylight color-balance lighting fixtures.

.. you let the camera make the choice—it will go with option C and white balance somewhere between the 3,200K and 5,600K marks. This will mean your indoor lights will be slightly warm and your daylight will be slightly cool, which will rarely be the best solution. In this scenario, nothing is rendered "correctly" as your eye sees it, but rather the entire image is compromised.

If you go with option B then you choose to set your white balance either to the daylight, which will render the indoor lights very orange, or to tungsten, which will render the daylight very blue. For some applications, this may not be a bad way to go.

Option D isn't always possible as daylight color-balanced lighting fixtures are, often, very expensive or unavailable. In most situations, the supplemental lighting that is most readily available is tungsten lighting. Tungsten, on the whole, is more prevalent and less expensive than artificial daylight sources. Daylight fixtures, most commonly in the HMI variety, require more complex electronics and more complex bulbs and are therefore considerably more expensive than tungsten fixtures. You can incorporate fluorescent fixtures with daylight color-balanced fixtures with high Color Rendering Index (CRI), or incorporate LED fixtures, HMI gas-discharge fixtures, or tungsten with dichroic (color corrected glass) lenses. These are all specialty fixtures, and not always available.

A shot of Model Alexandra Preda lit with tungsten (3,200K) light, but photographed with a daylight (5,600K) white balance. The wrong setting makes the tungsten light appear very orange. Photo by Claudiu Gîlmeanu.

The same shot of Alex, lit with daylight (5,600K) and photographed under tungsten (3,200K) white balance. The wrong setting makes the daylight appear very blue. Photo by Claudiu Gîlmeanu.

The same shot lit with daylight (5,600K) light and shot with a daylight (5,600K) white balance. The colors rendered appear normal and proper in the end result. Photo by Claudiu Gîlmeanu.

The least expensive solution is A. Although "least expensive" is relative because color-correction gel isn't cheap. However, if you take care of your gel, it can be reused and last for a while (keep it rolled up in a cool dry place, if it gets moisture and then dries it can smell *really* bad and some of the color can fade, rendering it less effective). In this case, you make a decision as to which color temperature will be your main source and you filter the other light to match that temperature. The best way to do this—in this scenario—is to filter the natural daylight to match the tungsten color temperature. You do this by adding CTO gels to the windows to filter out the blue wavelengths and correct the 5,600K color to 3,200K.

The reason it is better to filter the windows, rather than the lights themselves, is that any filters (gels) that you use will block certain wavelengths of light and reduce the overall intensity of light passing through the filter. CTO gel ("correct to orange" is a good way to remember) blocks out about two-thirds of a stop of light, or about 33% of the light passing through the filter. As daylight is, most often, the brightest thing around you, this isn't too much of a compromise and is often desirable to bring the intensity of the daylight down closer to the intensity of the artificial lights. You can even get CTO combined with neutral density gels (ND0.3, ND0.6, ND0.9, or ND1.2) which will correct the light *and* reduce the light even further, making the balance between exterior and interior even easier.

Inversely, if you filter the tungsten lights to match the daylight, you will use CTB ("correct to blue") filters, which block out the red, orange, and yellow spectrums. CTB gels are much more saturated than CTO and they reduce the light by as much as 75% (two stops). So if you have a 500W tungsten light, when you put full CTB on it, it effectively becomes a 125W light. If you then bounce that light or put it through diffusion, then you're reducing it even further and you can easily end up with the brightness of a 30W bulb from your 500W fixture. Typically your artificial lights are already much dimmer than the natural daylight, so cutting them down by 75% is going to make them even more powerless against the light of the sun.

A fifth option, which I did not include above, is to shut off all the indoor lights and use bounce cards and reflectors to light only with daylight.

Although a lot of people seem to overlook it, bouncing light is a great technique for not only creating soft light, but for optimizing what is already there. Bounce materials range considerably with each different texture creating a different quality of light. The smooth surface of a piece of foamcore (available at any arts and crafts store) will create a "harder" bounce light and return a high percentage of the light to the scene. This is great for taking light from the window and bouncing it into your subject to fill them. A piece of beadboard or Styrofoam will also bounce light back, but the broken-up (beaded) surface is much more

I'm a big fan of mirrors. Mirrors are a wonderful way to optimize natural light (as well as double-duty artificial light). I always carry a package of 1' × 1' mirrors with me. They're fairly inexpensive and can be found at any home supply store—normally in the tiling section. You can get some nail-on baby plates (flat plates with ⅜" spuds on them) or configure your own mounting system to be able to position the mirrors in stands. These are great for taking light through windows and bouncing it to highlight areas around the scene. I also carry some plastic mirrors (intended for use in showers) that are lightweight and can be taped up easily. These kind of compact mirrors allow me to multitask either existing lighting or what small fixtures I do have.

diffuse and will return a softer light with a lot less efficiency in intensity—meaning you'll lose more light off a beadboard than you will off a piece of foamcore. Many people use silver reflectors, which have an even higher efficiency of return than foamcore, but can produce some hard, spotty results and need to be used carefully. Inexpensive car sun blockers can be purchased at auto part stores and used as flexible bounces.

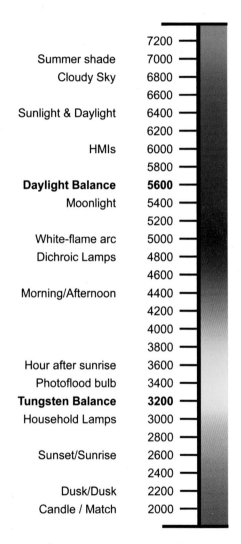

	7200
Summer shade	7000
Cloudy Sky	6800
	6600
Sunlight & Daylight	6400
	6200
HMIs	6000
	5800
Daylight Balance	**5600**
Moonlight	5400
	5200
White-flame arc	5000
Dichroic Lamps	4800
	4600
Morning/Afternoon	4400
	4200
	4000
	3800
Hour after sunrise	3600
Photoflood bulb	3400
Tungsten Balance	**3200**
Household Lamps	3000
	2800
Sunset/Sunrise	2600
	2400
Dusk/Dusk	2200
Candle / Match	2000

A spectrum of color temperatures and sources that create that color of light.

4.10 LIGHTING

The Magic of Mireds: To Gel or not to Gel, That is the Question!

In several of the previous articles I've talked about color correction filters for lighting. Especially when dealing with combinations of daylight and tungsten sources, I always advocate correcting the daylight to tungsten as opposed to vice versa. This month, we're going to delve a bit deeper into color correction filters.

Color correction filters for lighting are often called "gels" as they used to be made from natural animal-product gelatin (just like Jello!) but are now most often a poly-carbonate plastic, which lasts longer, is more robust, and has a higher melting point than traditional gelatin.

There are four major types of color-correction gel: CTB (blue), CTO (orange), plus green (green), and minus green (magenta). In addition you'll find CTS (straw) from most manufacturers. CTS has the same color-correction properties as CTO, but provides a slightly more yellow tone that some users find more pleasing. There are several primary manufacturers of color filters: Lee, Rosco, and Gam. All companies make a fantastic product and the decision to go with one over the other most often comes down to personal choice and regional availability. There are, however, differences between the companies and between the specific correction filters, as I'll discuss in a bit.

Color correction can be somewhat confusing for many people. Not only is there blue, orange, green, and magenta to deal with, but there are various strengths to each! All the primary correction filters come in ⅛, ¼, ½, ¾, and full versions—each variation providing greater color shift in their correction.

So, how and when do you break these out? Wouldn't you just always use full CTO or full CTB? Well, no. The first thing is that real world daylight is almost never 5,600K and tungsten is almost never 3,200K. In fact, you'll often see individuals refer to daylight as 5,500K, 5,600K, or even 6,500K—because there is no real set temperature and each manufacturer or individual will use their own base number. These numbers are theoretical standards that rarely happen in the real world. Natural daylight can range from 3,000K to 10,000K or more depending on where you are on the globe, the cloud cover, the time of day, the season, the pollution, and so forth. Tungsten lights can range from 2,000K to 3,600K depending on the manufacturer, age of bulb, reflector, lens, and so forth. Even putting two tungsten lights right next to each other from the same manufacturer and you're more likely to get two different color temperatures out of them than you are to get them to match!

So, because there are so many variables, color-correction filters come in variable strengths to help compensate for the discrepancies. Understanding how these various strengths integrate into real-world applications requires the introduction of a little math.

Most people understand that a full CTO filter will convert daylight (5,600K) to tungsten (3,200K), a color temperature shift of 2,400K. However, what if the daylight, at the time of your shoot, is actually 7,000K? Does that mean that full CTO will make it 4,600K (7,000 − 2,400)? Actually, no. To get a better understanding of how much a particular filter will affect the color, you need to get into *mireds*.

A mired is a microreciprocal degree. It's derived by dividing 1,000,000 by the Kelvin temperature. So 5,600K has a mired of 179 (1,000,000/5,600 = 179). If you look at the manufacturer swatchbooks for lighting filters, you'll see that each filter has a mired shift factor. Lee's full CTO has a mired shift of +159. 179 + 159 is 338; 1,000,000/338 = 2,958, which rounds to 3,000K. So Lee's full CTO actually corrects 5,600K to 3,000K, not 3,200K. If, in the example above, you actually had 7,000K instead of 5,600K, 7,000K has a mired value of 143; 143 + 159 is 302; 302 mired is 3,300K. So Lee's full CTO on a daylight source of 7,000K would give you a color temperature of 3,300K.

This system of mathematical calculation is important to understand so that you can compensate properly. It can also be used inversely. If you have a color temperature meter and you read the daylight coming through a window at 9,000K, you can determine that is a mired value of 111. You want to correct that to 3,200K, which has a mired value of 313. Subtract 111 from 313 and you need to have a mired shift of 202. Looking through the Lee swatchbooks, you can see that a full CTO plus ¼ CTO will get you to +223 mired 9,000K to 3,000K, which is close enough. Anything less than 100K isn't really discernible by the human eye and it really takes a shift of about 500K or more to make a noticeable difference. Anything within 500K should be totally acceptable for most applications.

Where things get a little surprising is in understanding that not all filters are created equal. A Lee full CTO has a mired shift of +159, but Rosco's full CTO has a mired shift of +167 (slightly warmer than Lee) and GAM is +146 (slightly cooler than Lee). Each manufacturer has a different compensation depending on what they determine is standard real-world "daylight" and real-world "tungsten."

Plus green and minus green are used for different applications. Non-incandescent lighting sources, such as fluorescent fixtures and HMIs, often have a tinge (or more) of green to them. Green is a challenging color because it typically is unflattering on skin tones. Generally you want to get the green out, but if you do so later in color-correction, this adds magenta to the image and that can make flesh tones appear overly pinkish. To compensate for this additional green, you use minus green filters—which are various strengths of magenta color. This blocks the green light while letting through the rest of the colors. Inversely, if you find yourself in a situation where you can't correct the green—perhaps you're shooting in a huge industrial warehouse with thousands of fluorescent ceiling fixtures—then you can *add* green to your own lighting to even the playing field which will make color correction go smoother later. That's where plus green comes in.

It's important to note that color correction filters are not just for technical applications. They're not just to correct one source to another—and you won't always *want* your lighting to be in the same color range. You may decide you want your daylight to be very cold and blue and you may even *add* CTB to that daylight to make it deeper blue. Or you might add CTO to your tungsten sources to make them warmer!

There are also hundreds of "party" colors as most film and video people call them. These are filters in every color of the rainbow that can be used for many different creative effects. The caution, however, is that because these are not calibrated colors, they often cut non-linear wavelengths and can often appear very different on camera than they appear to the human eye. If you're monitoring your image with a properly calibrated professional monitor, however, then you'll see the end results and can use these filters to your heart's content!

White Balance On-the-Fly

On a tangential topic for television lighting, this month's column will discuss color temperature—not just the basics of "tungsten" and "daylight," but how we dealt with rapidly varying color temperatures while shooting a reality show. For the past 25 days I've been traveling through Canada and the US doing home visits for a show I'm producing and directing called *My Hollywood*. The show is a documentary-style reality series where we're following kids (aged 8–17) who have dreams of making it in Hollywood. My two primary cameras are the Panasonic AG-HPX500 and the AG-HPX370, both shooting DVCProHD. We're constantly on the move: indoors, outdoors, day, night, fluorescents, tungsten,

Shooting on *My Hollywood* in Central Park, my director of photography Benjamin Molyneux utilizes a Litepanels Croma fixture on top of his Panasonic HPX500 camera to help fill the subjects with the right color balance.

neon—you name it, we've got it captured in the show. Following kids from interiors to exteriors, kitchens to hallways to bedrooms, riding in cars, in restaurants, out at night—it begs the question: "When you're really running and gunning, how do you keep up with the color temperature?"

For *My Hollywood*, I lent my director of photography, Benjamin Molyneux, my ExpoDisc—one of my favorite never-leave-home-without-it tools. It's a precisely calibrated piece of semi-opaque plastic that only allows 18% of light to transmit through it in a perfectly neutral gray. You pop the ExpoDisc in front of the lens, point the camera at your primary light source (or mixed source) and white balance through the card: *voilà*! You've got the most accurate white balance I've ever found.

A shot of an ExpoDisc, one of my favorite tools for maintaining great white balance.

In the home of the Kaufmans, *My Hollywood* cast members Jada and her mom, Jane, participate in a singing lesson while camera operator Rachel Lippert captures the action. Perched on top of Rachel's HPX370 camera is a Litepanels Croma fixture.

But . . . that takes time. And we only had one ExpoDisc on the show, so Ben would have to balance his camera and then hand it off to our "B" camera operator, Rachel Lippert, so she could balance hers.

When we could, the ExpoDisc was the way to go—great neutral color balance, even in mixed situations. When we *couldn't*, things got a lot trickier. Discussing the look and our efficiency with Ben, we decided on a camera preset of 3,200K (tungsten) with an "A" white balance at about 4,200K and the "B" balance at 55/5,600K. This gave us three quick looks for when we were really on-the-go: indoor, mixed, and outdoor, which was often enough to keep us rolling in mixed situations—or moving around a house with a shockingly varied mix between dark tungsten-lit areas and near-nuclear daylight areas.

Color balance is further complicated by the fact that the HPX500 has a black-and-white viewfinder. This required Molyneux to be hyper-diligent with his color choices as cameras moved from one area to another on a continual basis.

Augmenting further, we carried a set of Litepanels Croma fixtures, which are small LED panels with both 3,200K tungsten and 5,600K daylight LEDs. I went with the Cromas as they're the lightest dual-temperature LED fixtures I've found with very accurate color rendition and with very little to no green content. They're simple to use, with one knob to adjust brightness and one knob to adjust the blend between 3,200K and 5,600K. These came in handy on both "A" and "B" cameras to add a little fill when things got too dark. They run on six AA batteries, which is really convenient—although the fact that they *burn* through the batteries isn't so convenient. Worse, when the batteries get low—the lights *flash* on and off—not just dim—which is a sure-fire way to ruin any take. Running them sparingly—and not at 100% (which was rarely needed)—kept them running on a set of batteries pretty much all day. What we really needed was Litepanels' D-tap battery cable to plug directly into our Anton Bauer mounts on the cameras, but, alas, we didn't have those with us. Next trip, we certainly will and that will solve that problem and make the Cromas a perfect choice. We traveled with a Croma "flight kit"—three Croma panels with light stands, shoe mounts, and miscellaneous accoutrements to support the small fixtures, all packed in a small rolling Pelican case. We only pulled them out to do off-camera lighting with the Cromas just once during the shoot, in a small, confined kid's bedroom where our Arri kit would have been way too obtrusive and intense.

Inverse Square Dancing: A Practical Look at the Inverse Square Law

When the venerable Bill Klages last left the pages of *TV Technology*, he was discussing some mathematical esoterica regarding the inverse square law and I was a bit inspired to pick up, somewhat, from where he left off.

We all know inverse square law as the rule of physics regarding point sources where the intensity of the source will diminish by the square of the distance traveled. For most lighting professionals, this is a rule to determine falloff of a fixture at a specific distance. This works two ways, if you have a fixed relationship between your fixture and your subject, then using inverse square can aid in determining the size of fixture necessary to light your subject to a specific stop. The opposite of this is if you have a fixture that is providing too much intensity, knowing inverse square can help you quickly determine how much light you can reduce by simply increasing the distance to the subject to obtain the intensity you're looking for.

For the mathematically inclined:

$$I = \frac{1}{d^2}$$

(The intensity is equal to one divided by the square of the distance.)

Although the actual formula and hardcore physics only apply to point sources—that is sources without lenses to focus the light, without diffusion, that derive from a single point (like tungsten lamps or HMI lamps as opposed to fluorescent, a large light source that is not one point, or LED, which are multiple-point sources), it can be applied to broader, softer

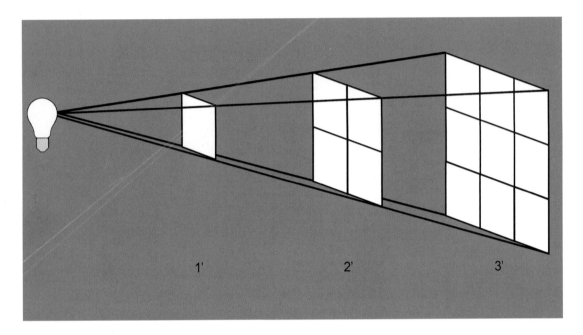

Light rays emanating from a point source diverge out in all directions equally. The further they travel from the source, the more physical area they cover and the more the overall intensity is diminished.

sources as well—although the math will never be as clean. Softer sources will have a greater falloff than just the inverse square.

Looking at some photometrics for lamps, a typical 1K open-face fixture has an intensity of 1,000 footcandles of light at 4′. If we increase that distance to 8′, our intensity drops to 250 footcandles. We have doubled our distance, but our intensity is now a quarter (or the inverse square the distance traveled) of the output.

If we look at the diagram above, which is typical to illustrate inverse square, we see that as light rays diverge from a point source, they travel outward in all directions and the further away from the source, the more they diverge and cover a larger physical area. So at 1′, what might cover a 1′ square area, at 2′ will now cover a 4′ square area. At 3′, that same light is now spread out over a 9′ square area. If we continued to 4′, we'd see the light spreading over 16′ square of area—so from 1′ to 4′, the light has diminished in intensity ¹⁄₁₆ of its initial power because it is spread over that much more area.

When you're dealing with a fixed subject, say a news anchor sitting at a desk or a seated interview subject, the relationship of that subject to the light source doesn't change. If, however, that interview subject is very animated and leans forward in their chair, their

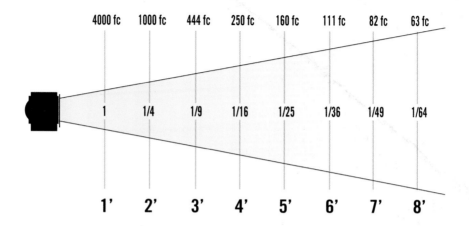

Illustrating the diminishing intensity of a point source fixture over a given distance. Top numbers represent the theoretical footcandle intensity at that given distance (bottom row of numbers) and the center row of numbers shows the fraction of light – relative to the 1' measurement – of light at that point.

relationship to the light source can change substantially. This is where understanding inverse square can help us alleviate problems before they arise. If we're lighting that interviewee with a 4' softbox from 4' away and the subject leans forward during the interview, moving 1' closer to the fixture, that subject has changed their relationship to that light by 25%— or the reverse of inverse square there is about a 75% increase in intensity on that subject; definitely a noticeable brightness increase. If, however, you increase the size of the light source to an 8' softbox *and* increase the distance to the subject to 8' away, the subjects movement of 1' is now only an increase in 30%—substantially less.

This is a situation where bigger is better. The 4' soft source at 4' has the same quality of light as the 8' source 8' away, but the spatial relationship to the subject is substantially different.

This also works for lighting groups of people—the further away and larger the source is, the more evenly the light will spread among the people. From 1' to 2' away from a fixture there's a drop off of 75% light intensity, but from that same source, the distances from 8' to 12' (room for three people to stand), there's a drop-off of less than 1% among them (see chart above).

If we have the ability to increase that source to a 20' source 20' away, then the intensity difference between our subjects is absolutely negligible and they can move within a substantial area without changing light intensity and exposure.

A shot from *The Event Premiere*. I used a 20′ by 15′ soft source (lit by two nine-light Maxi-Brute PAR fixtures) to light 16 kids seated on the bleachers. Photo by Otto Kitsinger.

In the image above, I'm lighting a group of 16 kids from a single key source that is 20′ wide by 15′ tall and about 20′ away from them. The large source, at that distance away, gives me an even field of light on all of the kids from the same source.

The practical lesson here is that the larger and further away the source is, the larger an area we can cover with relatively equal illumination from a single source—this is what I like to call the lighting inverse square dance!

4.13 LIGHTING

Adventures in
Part I—Beauty

In the location, there were
windows in the backgro
I decided to work w
sten white bala
natural dayligh
go very b
Litepa
pos

This month we're going to take a look at some ......ic and discuss how each was lit and why. In most of these, I concentrated on incorporating "alternative" lighting sources such as Litepanels LEDs, Kino Flo fluorescent fixtures, and Barger Baglites.

The first setup I'm going to discuss is a fashion shoot. This was actually a digital still shoot, but the concepts of lighting are equal for stills or motion. I have often preached to aspiring cinematographers to use stills to hone their skills and advance their cinematography; a practice I have utilized myself over the years.

For this shoot, I used four fixtures and a combination of color temperatures to achieve the end result. My key light was an Arri 650W Fresnel through a 4' by 5' stretch of light gridcloth diffusion. The 650 is positioned so that it fills the four foot diffusion area evenly at about half spot/flood. If the camera is in the 6:00 position on a clock dial and the model is in the 12:00 position, this key source is in the 4:30 position to get a little modeling to the shadow side of the face, but to be close enough to the camera to achieve the flattering "fashion" lighting. Often this fashion look is very flat, from as near the camera position as possible, to achieve the "Revlon" look.

The final shot of model Jennine Dwyer—a combination of tungsten, LEDs, and natural daylight.

...some ...und and ...ith a tung... ...ce to let the ...t in the background ...ue. Then, using two ...els 1 × 1 spot fixtures, I ...tioned them at 10:00 and 2:00, roughly, to give me a dual, crisp backlight on the model's hair and body. I let the Litepanels work in the shots on quite a few shots as I really liked the look of the fixture and the blow-out/flares it was giving me. I used a ¼ CTO on these two spot fixtures to start to correct them, partially, back to tungsten/ white for this setup so the background would slightly shift from deep blue to closer to white on the model.

Finally, for a fill, from the 7:30 position, I used a Litepanels 1 × 1 flood fixture, fully corrected with full CTO and a ½ white diffusion insert on the model's shadow side. This was dimmed down to somewhere around 50% to just slightly fill in the shadows and round out the modeling on her face.

The setup of the shot of Jennine, a 650W Fresnel into a sheet of diffusion with two 1x1 panel LEDs in the background.

The 650W Fresnel gave me the most punch to go through the diffusion. The key to creating soft light sources is increasing the physical size of the light—the 4′ × 5′ piece of diffusion is considerably larger than the 4.5″ lens on the Arri Fresnel, and creates a beautiful soft source. The light gridcloth is fairly dense, so I needed a light with some good punch to get through the diffusion and still give me enough light for my exposure.

Equipment:

Two 4' × four-bank Kino Flo
    fixtures with 5,600K
    daylight tubes
One C-stand

A second shot of model Jennine Dwyer, lit with two Kino Flo fixtures.

The Litepanels are versatile fixtures, but weren't enough punch to be corrected to tungsten (loss of two-thirds of a stop of light) and through the diffusion (about two stops loss) and still get me an exposure, so I elected to use them as backlights, and fill. They're portable, lightweight, and give off no heat. The dimming function, without changing the color temperature, is also a great feature of LED fixtures.

For the second shot, it required a different approach. I'm still working with "Revlon" fashion lighting, but now I'm approaching it in an alternate fashion toward the modeling and shape of the light. Using just two fixtures, I was able to achieve a very moody, gritty feel to match the makeup, hair (done wonderfully by Danielle Thompson), and wardrobe.

I positioned one 4' × four-bank Kino Flo on a C-stand above the model and tipped it down at about a 45° angle. Closing the top barn door about three-quarters, I lit only the top two tubes in this fixture, trying to keep the light off of the background, but provide me soft toplight on the model.

For the second fixture, I put it directly on the floor, using the mounting bracket to position it in place at a slightly up-angle toward the model. I lit only the bottom two tubes on this fixture.

Generally speaking, under-lighting is a no-no unless you're looking for a scary feeling but, sometimes, the right kind of under-lighting can be truly beautiful. Here, the Kino fixtures provide a very soft, wrapping glow under her that highlights her features beautifully. The fluorescents react well to the sheen of the makeup on her skin and make it almost look like she's glowing. These two fixtures were all that I used for this shot. Both Kino fixtures are about 3' away from the model. I underexposed these shots about a stop to a stop and a half to give them a very deep and grungy feel. Even in normal situations, I'm generally

The very simple setup for the shot of Jennine.

Equipment:

Two Barger Baglites
Two large quarts Chimera softboxes
Two combo stands
Three Japanese lanterns with 95W bulbs
One dimmer for Japanese lanterns
One 4′ × four-bank Kino Flo
One C-stand
One piece of 216 diffusion for Kino Flo

putting skin tones about half a stop to a stop and a half underexposed as I find that's the most pleasing place to put them.

The final shoot was a scene between a couple who were broken up and the man crashes a party to try and get her back. It was romantic, but also with an edge as it doesn't end happily and it doesn't get all mushy. I knew I wanted large sources to create soft wraps, especially for the actress, but I didn't have a large grip/electric package and had very limited power at the location. We used Barger Baglites on this one. Designed by Ed Barger, the

A shot from the set of *Tom and Sophie*, directed by Jamie Neese, photographed by myself. Here actors Lauren Waisbren and Brian Glanney are bathed in soft light from large sources. Photo by Carlis Johnson.

Baglite is specifically manufactured to work with Chimera softboxes and, in this case, I went with the large quartz boxes—the biggest I could get. We had two of those fixtures. Although the Baglite has six globes in it, we were usually only running two or three at the most. My gaffer, Andrew Korner, had his fixtures lamped with 750W and 300W globes, so we could burn any combination of those intensities to get what I was looking for. One wall of the location was covered with shrubs and I elected to drape this wall with Christmas lights. I'm a big fan of Christmas lights, especially for backgrounds. They do wonderful things when they're out of focus, but they also provide beautiful warm light if the actors get near them—which they did here. We used a 4′ × four-bank Kino Flo up high with some 216 diffusion on it as a very soft backlight for some positions and, finally, I used three Japanese lanterns (China balls) above the gate entrance to the pool area both for light and in-shot to add a more party-like atmosphere.

Behind the scenes on *Tom and Sophie* showing the large quartz Chimera softboxes lit from Barger Baglite fixtures. Photo by Carlis Johnson.

Actor Brian Glanney in soft key with a hot edge light. Photo by Carlis Johnson.

I generally tried to key the actress, Lauren Waisbren, from three-quarters front (the 7:30 or 4:30 positions on the clock dial) and then give her a soft edge light from the 9:30 or 2:30 positions. For the man, Brian Glanney, I tried to key him from the 10:00 and 2:00 positions to give him a more rugged, contrasting look.

The Barger lights with the large quartz Chimeras gave me nearly 6′ square soft lights that I moved around as we shot the scene. A blessing here was that the background, with the dark green foliage, was a very deep color, which is wonderful for soft lighting. If your background is a deep color, you don't have to worry about light spilling everywhere, you can hit your talent with soft sources and still have them separated from the background without washing it out with their key light.

Adventures in Lighting, Part II—The Gleaming Specular

By definition, a specular highlight is a mirror reflection of the light source in your subject. This can also be described as direct reflection. Properly utilized specular reflections help to define the shape of a glossy or highly reflective surface such as glass or chrome.

The classic example of this is a wine bottle. Here I have a beautiful bottle of 2003 Francis Ford Coppola's Rubicon Cabernet Franc (a favorite of mine), which is a lovely dark bottle with very little fringe decoration. I'm going to use two Arri 650W Fresnel lamps to light this bottle.

If I use the lamps clean, what we see is a specular highlight of the lamps reflected off the black glass of the bottle—and they're just a point of light. It's not pleasing and it's not helping to define the shape of the bottle. We have light on the bottle, it can be exposed, but we're not doing this beautiful, simple bottle any favors by just pumping hard light onto it.

What we need to do is to increase the apparent size of the light sources so that they become a very large source reflected down the length of the bottle.

The first shot of the bottle. Here I'm just lighting with two bare Fresnels and the result is two pinpoints of light in the bottle.

Converting the Fresnels to bounce light off two large sheets of white foamcore helps to shape the bottle beautifully.

Equipment:

Two Arri 650W Fresnels
One Arri 150W Fresnel
Two 40" × 60" white
 foamcore sheets
Two 24" × 36" black
 foamcore sheets
One 18" × 24" black
 foamcore sheet
One roll duvetyne
Six C-stands
Three light stands

In this case, I'm going to bounce the Fresnels into two large sheets of white foamcore. By evenly filling the foamcore with light from the 650W Fresnels, I turn a 6" pinpoint of light into a 40" × 60" source of light.

Now what we're seeing is the mirror reflection of the large sheets of foamcore in the glass of the bottle. The large reflection helps reveal the shape of the bottle and is a much more pleasing look than just the two spots of light. This is using specular reflections to our advantage.

This setup was a lot more complicated than just bringing in two large sheets of foamcore. The entire bottle is, for all intents and purposes, a mirror that reflects any source of light. I had to build up a lot of black around the bottle to not reflect myself (or the room I was shooting in) on the surface glass. Using duvetyne (black fabric), hanging on C-stands, I surrounded the bottle in black. The bottle then reflects the black, which has no specific detail, and makes the overall glass of the bottle appear smooth and clean.

I also had to put up "siders," which are solid, black flags on the sides of the 650W Fresnels to keep the lights themselves from being reflected in the glass. For these siders I simply used 24" × 36" cuts of black foamcore on C-stands.

The camera itself, and me behind it, was also reflected in the bottle, so I had to remedy that by hanging a large piece of duvetyne in front of the camera and cutting out a small hole to fit the lens through. This erased any reflection of me or the rest of the room from the face of the bottle.

Finally, finishing off this photograph, I shot this as if it were an advertisement. In which case, the name on the bottle is very important. Bringing out those gold letters against the glass was no easy task. I used a 150W Arri Fresnel positioned very high and pointing down at the

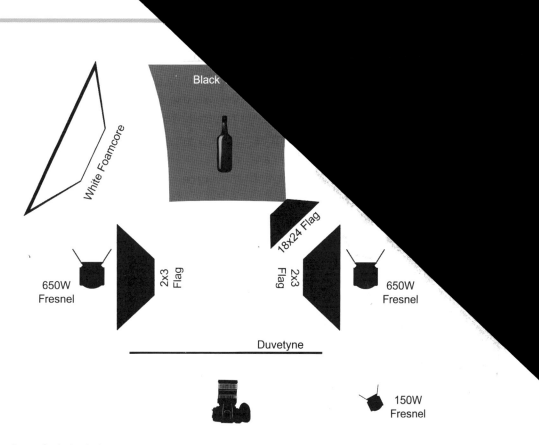

The lighting diagram for the bottle shot.

bottle, spotting in the light on the gold letters. I then brought in another black foamcore flag—as close to the bottle as I could get it without being in the frame—and used that to cut off the specular reflection of the 150W lamp from the upper curve of the bottle. You can see that specular reflection in the second photo, but it's cut out of the third and final image by using the flag.

When you're dealing with direct/specular reflection, it is handy to remember the laws of physics whereby the angle of direct incidence is equal to the angle of reflection (see the next section). This means that the precise angle that light strikes a glassy/glossy surface is the angle at which it will be reflected away. This is an important rule to remember when using specular reflections, or when trying to remove unwanted reflections. Look at the reflection from the camera's position and note the angle the camera is to the glossy surface, then trace that angle back to the offending (or creative) source. This can be a considerable challenge on a curved surface, such as the wine bottle, but with some practice you'll understand the principle.

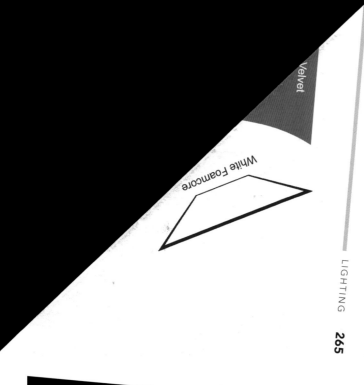

Velvet

White Foamcore

ɔcular reflections applies
reflective surface. In car
concept, but we utilize
larger) bounces or light
lection in the surface of

ə specular reflection in a
ɪrger the light source, the
he shape of the surface.
:e as it is very smooth, has
ɪ smooth highlight. You can
al to create your specular
reflective the surface is—if
or texture to it, that can be
ɪve used a softbox to create
ɪ any wrinkles in the front
show up in the highlight as

The final shot with the label lit.

Take a look through your favorite magazine. You'll see advertisements for cars, jewelry, drinks, silverware, even electronics— all employing specular highlights to show off the product's beauty. Looking at these ads and deconstructing how you think they were lit is a great way to expand your knowledge and experience when you don't have a chance to play with the lights and toys yourself.

The three lighting stages side-by-side.

Adventures in Lighting, Part III—Unwanted Reflections

I was giving a reprisal of my "Lighting from Home Depot" lecture, on which I based my book *A Shot in the Dark: A Creative DIY Guide to Digital Video Lighting on (Almost) No Budget*, last week for Hollywood Shorts, and one of the attendees asked me how to deal with reflections on set.

I floundered for a minute, trying to find the best way to answer her question, but the variables involved in "reflections on set" were just too vast for my mind to immediately grasp. It took a few questions back and forth to get what she was talking about and I thought up a few tips to help her understand how best to deal with those unwanted reflections—mostly from light sources—in your shot.

It's part of the camera operator's job to keep an eye out for "bogeys" in the shot—that is unwanted elements, be they a crew member's water bottle, an abandoned apple box or electrical cord, a roll of gaff tape, someone's script pages (production crews are notoriously messy), or the silent—and often missed—shot-killer, a reflection of a light in the shot!

The problem of an unwanted light reflection in shot.

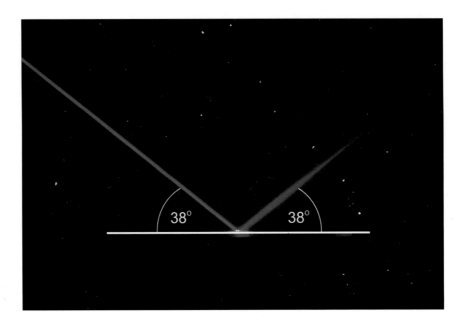

A real-world demonstration of the angle of incidence is equal to the angle of reflectance. A laser light is shone onto a mirror and reflects off at the exact same angle it hits the mirror surface.

I've seen many inexperienced crew members scramble to try and solve a reflection problem, but they aren't hard to track down. Luckily, light follows a few set rules of physics, one of them being: *the angle of incidence is equal to the angle of reflectance.*

So, let's use that law of physics to help track down the offending source of the reflection. In order to do this, we stand at the lens of the camera (if it's a particularly stealthy reflecting offender, put your head right in front of the lens so that your eyes are level with it) and note the angle of our vision to where the reflection is. If we walk in a straight line from the lens toward the reflective surface, the angle at which we arrive at the surface is the exact angle the offending source of the reflection will be at in the opposite direction.

This process is sometimes easier if you have a laser pointer. From the lens position, point the laser at the reflection and wiggle it around a little—you'll find the laser point dancing on the offending source of the reflection like a red-faced tattle-tale. This sometimes works, but if you're dealing with glass or reflective surfaces where most of the laser light will pass through the surface, it isn't as effective.

Now we've found the offender!

Time to solve the reflection!

Sometimes this reflection comes from light leak around the sides of a lighting fixture; either out of the ventilation holes, or between the lens and the barn doors. This can generally be solved by wrapping that side of the light with a piece of black wrap to stop the light spill from traveling toward the reflective surface. Be careful not to wrap the lamp too tightly and don't wrap the entire fixture (especially if it's an incandescent source) as you can trap heat and damage the fixture or, worse, start a fire. Just use enough black wrap to cover the one side and the offending light leaks. An alternative might be to place a flag alongside the lamp to cut the light from hitting the reflective surface.

Sometimes the reflection is from the face of the light itself, in which case you can't necessarily cover or flag the offending reflection as you'll cut the light off of whatever it is lighting. If you can move the lighting fixture, that's one of the best solutions; move it to a new location where the angle of incidence to the reflective surface does not end in an angle of reflectance to the lens. Sometimes this means moving the fixture only a couple inches or a couple feet to one side or another.

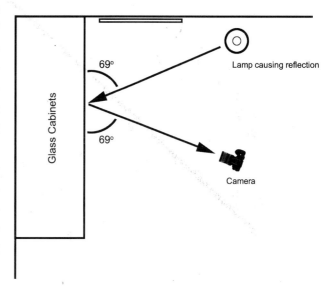

An illustration of the light causing the problem. Here we see the angle of incidence of the light falling on the glass of the cabinet is the same angle that the camera is shooting the glass, so we see the reflection in the shot.

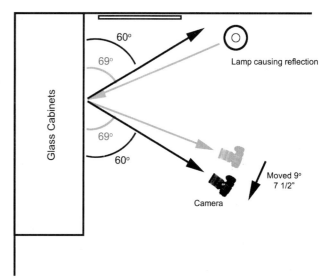

In this case, our solution is to move the camera a mere 7 1/2", which changes the camera's angle to the glass by a mere 9°, just enough to hide the reflection.

The result of our fix, the reflection is gone.

A tape ball made from rolling up a long piece of blue painter's tape.

The tape ball positioned behind a hanging poster to change the poster's angle.

Another alternative is to change the angle of reflectance by changing the angle of the reflective surface to the camera. If this is a glass door that is reflecting the light, opening or closing the door slightly can eliminate the reflection from view while leaving the lighting in the same position. If it's a glass frame on the wall, sometimes wadding up a little ball of paper or gaff tape and placing it between the wall and a lower corner of the frame will tip the angle of the glass in the picture enough to eliminate the reflection; but not enough to be noticeable to the camera.

Finally, and—in my opinion—the least desirable solution, is to alter the reflective property of the surface giving you the offending reflection. You're generally doing this by making the surface more diffuse. Most commonly this is done with dulling spray or hairspray, which will "gunk" up the reflective surface and eliminate the specular nature of the reflection. This can, however, make the reflective surface look odd, unnatural, and unrealistic and should be a last resort in most cases.

COMPOUNDING PROBLEMS

Definitely something to watch out for are compound reflections, where a light source is reflected off of multiple surfaces.

This can easily happen if you are shooting towards a corner and there are reflected surfaces on both sides of the corner, the light can actually be reflecting off of one surface into the other and then toward the camera. Keep in mind that the same laws of physics apply, trace the path of the reflection based on the angle of incidence being equal to the angle of reflectance.

The problem, a light reflection in the shot.

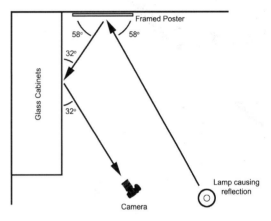

A diagram of the problem. Here the light is reflecting off two different surfaces, the framed poster on the wall and the glass doors of the cabinet. The compound reflection can make the problem light difficult to find.

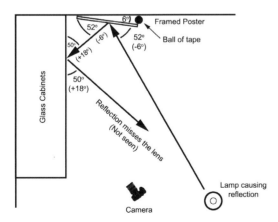

By putting the tape ball behind one side of the poster, it changes the angle of incidence, and, therefore, the angle of reflection of the light, which now misses the camera lens and is removed from the shot.

The result of the tape ball fix, the reflection is gone from the shot.

Smoke and Fog

When you mention smoke or fog, most people immediately conjure up images of a misty, creepy cemetery at night, fog crawling around the ground like the undead, or of dark, black smoke billowing out of windows of a burning house; generally practical special effects. Fog can be your friend photographically, however, as it adds atmosphere and defines light in a very special way.

The first thing I need to note is the difference between smoke and fog.

Smoke is a chemical process, a changing of one form of matter into another that is usually a byproduct of combustion. When you burn something, the chemical change happening to that object creates smoke. The particles released into the air from smoke are a mixture of gas, liquid, and solid particulates. With smoke you can have various colors— black, red, etc.—depending on the chemical composition of the material being burned. These particulates, however, are dangerous to humans. According to the United States Fire Administration and the Federal Emergency Management Agency, more than 79%

Light reflecting and refracting off of fog particles in the air.

When we backlight particulates in the air, we get to see the shape of the light beam.

of injuries sustained from indoor fires come from smoke inhalation. Smoke particulates are dangerous—and most special effects smoke (especially the really cool stuff like smoke cookies or burning tires) is generally illegal for use today or requires a special permit and a licensed effects artist.

Fog, on the other hand, is liquid particulates that adhere to imperfections in oxygen molecules in the air. Artificial fog works the same as naturally occurring fog—with water particulates that are small enough to adhere to oxygen molecules. Artificial fog is generally glycol based and is relatively harmless to humans. In standard foggers, water, glycerin, or propylene glycol (fog juice) is passed through a super-heated nozzle at high pressure and atomized into the air in a fine mist. Fog will generally cover a wide volume of space and will "hang" in the air. If you waft the fog (flap a large board or fan), you can create an even, featureless concentration of fog in an enclosed space.

Fog and mist can also be created with liquid nitrogen or solid carbon dioxide (CO_2 or "dry ice"—named so because when it "melts" it merely evaporates—turns into a gaseous form—not liquid like regular ice). The extremely cold nature of CO_2 or liquid nitrogen causes the fog to be considerably denser and heavier than air (or glycol fog, for that matter) and, as a result, it "hugs" the ground and is more susceptible to the forces of gravity (you can create a fog waterfall with liquid nitrogen, but not with glycol fog).

Since CO_2 and liquid nitrogen are used more for visual effects, or to create natural low-lying mist, for the purposes of this discussion, I'd like to stick with glycol fog and, most specifically, using fog less as a special effect and more for atmospheric effects.

We can't see light. Light, in and of itself, is invisible to the human eye. What we see is the reflection and/or refraction of light. We see light bouncing off our skin, the floor, the computer keyboard. We can't see light in the air, *unless* that light is reflecting or refracting off of something.

Enter fog! When you have liquid particulates in the air, light can refract and reflect off these particulates to define the shape of a light beam. When you see shafts of light in movies (and even in real life) it is because the light is interacting with some atmospheric "crap" to show up.

It's also important to understand that in order to see these shafts of light, we need to *backlight* the atmospheric material. The light needs to be directed toward the lens (not necessarily *into* the lens, but toward the camera). For the shape of the light to be seen in the fog, we need that light to refract from about 45° on either side of the lens.

If it comes from behind the lens, the refraction of light on the particulates in the air will simply wash out the scene and massively reduce contrast, not show the shape of the light.

Reduction of contrast, however, is one of the primary reasons to use fog for a scene. The level and density of the fog will determine how much the contrast is reduced. Too much fog and you'll reduce your contrast down to almost nothing but a gray blob! Just enough can help take some of the "video curse" off digital images and add more depth and atmosphere into the scene. This isn't like additional depth of field—more the opposite, it tends to create a "hazy" effect so that the background seems to be further away. This requires a light, but consistent level of fog. You spray the fog into the room in small doses and "waft" it around until it dissipates into a single, consistent layer of haze without any definition to the fog. The closer your subjects are to the camera, the less they will be affected by the fog. It creates a wonderful depth and feel.

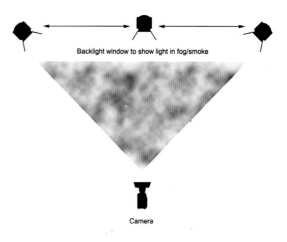

Backlight window to show light in fog/smoke

Camera

An illustration of the area of lighting to reveal particulates in the air. This area of backlighting applies to smoke, fog, water, dust; any particles in the air will be seen by backlighting them.

Recently I was brought in as a director to help finish a feature film called *Black Tar Road*. Although a large percentage of the film had already been completed, additional scenes were needed and the original director was no longer available. I brought in a young Russian cinematographer, Ashley Barron, who came to Los Angeles by way of Australia. We decided to incorporate fog for several of the scenes that we were shooting at a private residence in North Hollywood. We rented a Rosco fogger and used Rosco glycol-based fog juice to add atmosphere to several of the scenes that we shot over two days this last month.

There are some alternates to the glycol-based foggers, and some legal uses of smoke. Burning incense or sage can create smoke that isn't too offensive to most people—although people with sensitivity to fragrances can be bothered. For fog there are some companies that make aerosol sprays that are the same kind of

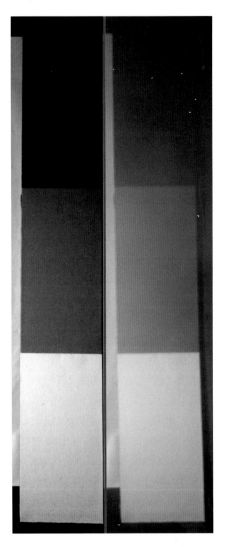

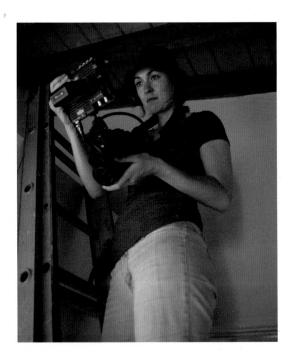

My director of photography for *Black Tar Road*, Ashley Barron, working with a Canon EOS 7D and an iKan D7 onboard monitor.

On the left, a grayscale with no atmosphere, on the right, the addition of smoke in the air reduces the contrast considerably.

Writer/actress Amber Dawn Lee and producer/actress Noelle Messier on set for *Black Tar Road* before we added fog into the air. Black Tar Road © Abovo Films.

The same shot after fog was added. The contrast is reduced and the room has more "atmosphere." Black Tar Road © Abovo Films.

fog-like haze from a can, both Diffusion Cloud in a Can and Fantasy FX Professional Haze use a medical-grade ("white") mineral oil in an aerosol can to create a good haze in an enclosed space. They're generally available from film or theatrical expendable suppliers.

Hazers are foggers that release a much more fine amount of diffusion into the air so less "wafting" is necessary.

I once had a fogger stop working on me and had a number of people light up cigars to replace the atmosphere—although I do *not* recommend this technique, it worked in a pinch.

It is important, also, to know that even though fog is not a product of combustion, the fine particulates in the air can confuse some smoke detectors and trip alarms.

Many years ago, before I made the move to Hollywood and started working in movies, I worked in theater in Arizona. I had the privilege of working as a master electrician with a brilliant lighting designer named Ed Brown. On a ballet version of *Dracula*, Ed had the brilliant idea of creating a light curtain. Utilizing 30 ellipsoidal reflector spotlights above the front of the stage and 30 more directly below them on the floor—both sets aiming directly at each other—when we added fog into the air and turned all 60 on, the light refraction/reflection was intense enough to create a completely opaque wall of light that acted like a physical curtain blocking the stage from the audience. By programming different fade patterns, we could "open" the curtain or have it "drop" or just magically fade in and out. The effect was beyond beautiful and something I'll always remember. An example of the power of fog to create incredible visuals.

Using a Light Meter to Maintain Atmosphere

This month I want to share a technique I have developed over the years to utilize a reflected light meter to maintain a consistency of fog or atmosphere in a location over time.

Many cinematographers like to use fog or haze to help add atmosphere and reduce contrast. Maintaining a consistent level of atmosphere, however, can be an enormous challenge. Back in the stone ages, when I was a gaffer, I developed a methodology for maintaining that consistency with excellent accuracy.

Since fog or haze adds particulates in the air that reflect and/or refract light, the way to maintain the proper level of atmosphere is to measure that scattering of light. I would do this by placing a black flag in an unused portion of the set or location, but within sight of the camera. It's best to put the flag in a dark corner, away from activity. Often the best place is behind camera, or perpendicular to the lens. You want the flag to be at a distance from you, but as close to the photography area as possible without being in the way.

I put the flag up perpendicular to the ground, but flat to my position at the camera. Then I take a Tweenie or similar small, focusable light, and put it on the floor in front of the flag with the light beam shooting straight into the air. Using barn doors on the light, I cut the light off of the flag so that the light path is passing in front of the flag, but not touching it.

It's also important that the light from the Tweenie isn't bouncing off the ceiling back into the metering area. If you've got a white ceiling, then it's best to use another flag above your existing flag to absorb the light and eliminate bounce.

Since the light beam is passing in front of the flag, when there is no atmosphere in the air, you cannot see the light, the reflected reading off the flag should be zero. The more fog or haze you put in the air, the more defined (brighter) that beam of light will be.

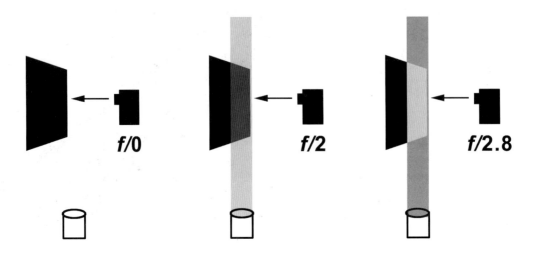

The left image represents the setup—a lamp on the floor shining up in front of a black flag. The light meter reads 0—no light from the flag. When a little fog is added (middle) then the light beam is revealed and we start to get a light reading off the reflection of light off the particulates. Adding more fog (right) reveals a higher reading as more light is scattered.

When I've set the level of atmosphere that looks good to me on the set, I then take a reading of the light at the flag and note the reading. Let's say that's an f/4.

Then we shoot the take.

By the time we get to the next take, the level of atmosphere has most likely changed. Air current from people moving around, air leaks in the location or set, air conditioning, doors opening and closing, open windows, vents—all of these things will alter the atmosphere. When we're ready for the next take, I take a quick reading of the flag. If my reading is, say, f/2.8, I know my atmosphere is too low and we have to add in more. If my reading is f/5.6—I know I've got too much and we've got to let it dissipate a bit before we shoot.

If you really have to be incredibly accurate with the atmosphere, it's best to have multiple flags set up at different points in the location. It's possible to hide these little metering zones within the set as well, you just have to be more creative about where you put them. Also, be sure that the flag is big enough to cover your degree of spot meter with plenty of safety room—you don't want to be accidentally getting light values from something behind the flag biasing your control.

Utilizing this relatively simple technique, I have been able to maintain very accurate control over atmosphere in scenes in many different applications.

More Adventures in Lighting: When Daylight Fades

While I was working with the Canon EOS 7D for my review, I was looking for a practical test to put the camera through and I tapped my friend, director Jamie Neese, to come up with a short project we could shoot in a day. He came back with a five-page script called *Breaking Up is Hard to Do* and enlisted the help of actors Mark Gerson (*2 Million Stupid Women*) and Lisa Jay (*Days of Our Lives*). After reading the script, I decided to go with a look that felt like late afternoon warm sunlight. I planned to augment natural day-

A screen capture from *Tranquility, Inc.*, written and directed by Jamie Neese, photographed by myself, of actress Lisa Jay. Using low bounce to create the feeling of late afternoon sunlight streaming in the room. Tranquility, Inc. © Adakin Productions.

light with low, soft, three-quarter back keys and nice warm sunlight feel. I had a very small lighting package available to me, an Arri Fresnel kit with a 650W, 300W, and two 150W fixtures.

The scene was all interior in an apartment living room. Anna (Lisa Jay) is visited by Derek (Mark Gerson) who has been employed by her boyfriend to break up with her. I had a roll of full CTO gel and planned on covering the windows to convert the natural daylight to

3,200K so I could use my tungsten fixtures at their natural color temperature. The idea was to make the most of natural daylight and augment where I had to with the small fixtures.

Unfortunately, the rains came to Los Angeles that Sunday afternoon. The day was very gloomy, cloudy and sunless. Ambient color temperature was in the high 9,000K range. We also got off to a late start, not rolling until after 3pm with the January light fading quickly. Therein was my challenge. Could I get the look I wanted with a small kit, all tungsten units, and fading daylight?

The answer was "yes."

I was working with some slow EF lenses, an 18–55 and a 28–135, both in the F4.5–5 range. Luckily, the sensitivity of the EOS 7D was certainly in my corner as I was able to shoot a clean image at an ISO of 2,500.

The key here was to get the wide shots as early in the day as we could—while we still had natural daylight to help—and carefully compose the tighter shots to make the best use of the kit I had.

We started at the apartment door where Anna opens it to greet Derek. The lobby of the location features a French-paned front door that I knew I couldn't fake daylight outside of, so that dictated where we started. I first covered the door with a sheet of full CTO to help reduce the color temperature of the natural daylight. I then created a "book light" in the corner outside the apartment door by bouncing a 300W into the corner and then taping 250 diffusion behind the fixture so that the light would bounce off the walls and then pass through the diffusion.

This technique allowed me to create a large soft source in a very tight space. The light from the "book light" created a key on Mark from his left side. On his right side, I used a 150W bounced into an 18″ × 24″ piece of white foamcore. Inside the apartment, I kept it low, with just a 150W bounced into the ceiling behind Lisa to help bring up her shoulders and the back of her head from the shadows.

As the scene progressed, Derek sat Anna down and explained to her that he had been hired by her

Actor Mark Gerson lit with a little natural daylight augmented by a book light off to his left side and a soft fill from the right. Tranquility, Inc. © Adakin Productions.

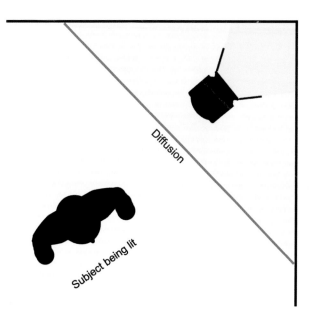

An illustration of a "book light", here utilizing the corner of the room—the light fixture is focused into the corner, bouncing the light into the room and that bounce is further softened by a sheet of diffusion spread between the walls behind the fixture.

boyfriend to "dissolve" the relationship. By the time we got to this coverage, night had fallen. The front wall of the location had three windows, but I explained to Jamie that I only had enough fixtures to light one window and the inside. We adjusted the composition so that the actor was squarely in front of one of the windows and the other two were out of the shot. I covered the outside of the window with an opaque white shower curtain and lit it with the 650W from about 4' away, covering primarily the lower third of the window that would be seen in the

Light was gone by the time we shot this shot. A single 650W Fresnel into a shower curtain outside the window gives us the hot window behind Mark and I'm using more low bounce for the late sunlight feel. Tranquility, Inc. © Adakin Productions.

shot. This created a hot, bright white world outside the window that passed for natural daylight. To continue this feel, I used a 150W high and behind Mark to get hot light on his shoulders, as if coming through the window. I used the second 150W off his right shoulder with some 250 diffusion to continue that "window" light around the right side of his face and create a hot three-quarters back-edge. Finally, I used the 300W into a 3′ × 3′ piece of white foamcore that was positioned low, about his knee height, to create the soft key bounce as if it were coming from hot natural daylight bouncing off the floor onto his face. I snuck in a Litepanels Micro on top of the 7D to get a little glimmer in Mark's eyes.

Close-up of Lisa, more of the low bounce. Tranquility, Inc. © Adakin Productions.

The same technique, roughly, applies to Lisa's coverage in this scene, except that she's sitting opposite the window so I eliminated the hot edges. She's lit from the 300W bouncing into the 3′ × 3′ foamcore as her key, again low, and the 150W with the 250 diffusion high and off her left shoulder for fill.

The confrontation comes to a head and she leads him to the door where he pleads with her to

At the door, there's no natural daylight left, this is all artificial. I'm using the 650W into the bookshelf to create the hot spot and to bounce light off the floor. Tranquility, Inc. © Adakin Productions.

Tranquility, Inc. © Adakin Productions.

succumb to reason. For the two-shot here, I stretched out the white shower curtain on the floor and bounced the 650W into it from behind Lisa. I made the 650 do double-duty by opening the barn doors and making sure the edge of the direct light also hit the bookshelves and door to mimic the feel of natural daylight through a window behind them. The hotspot of the light is focused onto the shower curtain and lower part of the door to reflect back on them as a low side key. The camera-side is filled with the 300W into the ceiling to provide a base level "room tone."

The package:

One 650W Arri Fresnel
One 300W Arri Fresnel
Two 250W Arri Fresnels
One Litepanels Micro LED fixture
One 18″ × 24″ foamcore card
One 3′ × 3′ foamcore card
One roll of Lee 250 diffusion
One roll of full CTO correction
Five C-stands
Four Arri light stands

This same technique tracks into the close here, with Lisa's main key coming from the floor and lower portion of the white door to her right. Her left side is filled from the 300W bounced off the white ceiling and, again, I pulled out the Litepanels Micro on top of the camera to get the sparkle in her eye.

Lighting with a small kit is definitely a challenge, but entirely doable if you're careful about how you use it. The additional trick here to this particular look is to try and keep the keys as more backlights and, when possible, on the off-camera side. I rarely use low positioned sources as key sources, but sometimes it can create really beautiful light.

The Composition of Sunlight

I was recently invited to give a guest lecture on narrative lighting for the Bay Area Professional Videographer's Association in San Jose, California. During the discussion a member brought up the question of how to create believable looking sunlight.

We all know that the color temperature of daylight is 5,600K (on average), but that 5,600K figure is actually derived from a combination of direct sunlight and ambient skylight. It's the two distinct sources that create the daylight we see every day—and that's the key to creating believable artificial sunlight: two sources.

When I was working on my book *A Shot in the Dark*, I sat down with my good friend, Dr. Jeffrey Crane, an astronomer, and talked to him about the real color of the sun. It was a much more complex discussion than one might imagine. The color that we see of the sun itself varies greatly depending on your location on Earth, the atmospheric conditions, weather, and the time of day.

Those of us who shoot out in the real world on a constant basis know that sunlight is, rarely, truly 5,600K. It varies during the course of the day, it varies based on cloud coverage and pollution. I've seen desert sandstorms in the distance that dropped the color temperature of the sun so drastically that we couldn't keep shooting.

The key, however, to understanding how to create believable daylight is in understanding the two different color sources: the direct light from the sun itself and the ambient skylight.

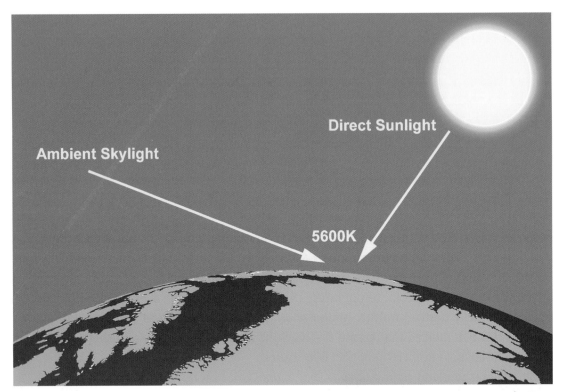

Daylight color temperature is the combination of direct sunlight and light reflecting off the atmosphere creating ambient daylight.

I was pondering a way to illustrate this, in nature, when I noticed the late afternoon sunlight coming through my closed curtains in my living room. One portion of the curtain was a bright warm glow, the other portion was a very cool, dimmer glow. Right there I had the exact illustration of the two colors of sunlight.

A real-world illustration of the two colors of sunlight. Part of the curtains is hit by direct late afternoon sunlight, the other part of the curtain is lit by cooler ambient skylight.

Generally I'll use two sources when trying to create daylight—whether exterior or interior. The first is ambient skylight. This is, generally, a cooler color temperature than my key "sun." During the demonstration in San Jose for the Bay Area Professional Videographers, I used a 650W Arri Fresnel with ¼ CTB bounced into a white textured ceiling as my ambient skylight and an Arri 300W Fresnel, clean, as my direct sunlight. I bounced the 300W into a counter in the kitchen to give a little uplight glow on Amber Myers, the talent modeling for the demonstration. Letting just the edge of the 300's field angle hit Amber below her shoulder, it put a hot source on her torso. The combination of the two sources—cool, soft overhead bounce, and more direct clean tungsten bounce—created an absolutely believable daylight look.

Model Amber Myers poses in the kitchen as I create the feeling of daylight through a combination of color temperatures.

To accentuate this look, I aimed the 650W bounce to be just above where the 300W Fresnel was. This way the bounce had some general directionality from the same direction as the hot spot. It made it feel like both sources were coming from the same large window off-camera. There's also a 150W Fresnel from off-camera right, pointing right at the microwave oven behind Amber. Without this, that was a dark area in the frame that belied the daylight look.

It's the combination of these two sources—a soft bounce, generally cooler in color temperature, to mimic ambient daylight, and a more direct, generally warmer, source to mimic direct sunlight—that serve to create a very believable natural daylight look.

After this column appeared in *TV Technology*, a reader wrote in with the question:

> "Just found your article on re-creating sunlight. Very informative. Thanks! How do you white balance in those situations? Do you put your white card at the subject's face with just the bare 'sunlight,' call that white, and then turn on the fill? Or do you balance with both sources? Thanks, Barry, New Orleans."

My response to Barry, printed in the following month's issue:

> It really depends on the narrative situation. Generally, I like my white balance to be between the two color sources so that the direct sunlight is a little warm and the fill is a little cool. In the scenario of the kitchen scene from San Jose, I was working with all tungsten units. Guessing the bare tungsten is about 2,900K and the ¼ CTB on the fill gives me about 3,200K, I'd probably set my white balance around 3,000–3,100. If you can't select an exact Kelvin, then I'd lean more toward the cooler side (white balance to the cool fill) so the sunlight has a warmer look and the fill feels white.

Art of Darkness: No Light Lighting

If we were to listen to the hype from some camera manufacturers, lighting isn't necessary anymore and cameras can shoot in total darkness! Although that certainly isn't the case, today's digital cameras are considerably more light-sensitive and *can* shoot in less light than their predecessors, but there is a trade-off.

Cinematography, by definition of the word, is "writing with light," but the art of photography is just as much about lack of light as it is about the light itself. The balance between light and shadow is where the science of photography meets the art.

Today's cinematographers seem to frequently find themselves in situations where light is a rare commodity. This is partially due to the marketing hype and partially due to an erroneous thought process that small cameras don't require the big "hoopla" that larger, professional cameras do. Most people readily associate motion picture cameras with big lights and big sets, but then they seem to feel that smaller cameras don't require the same accoutrements. That is, of course, a complete fallacy. Good photography requires careful control over light—no matter what format you're using. However, whether you're shooting with 35mm movie film or you're shooting with a consumer palmcorder, you *can* get away with creating a beautiful image in very little light if you're careful with how you do it.

THE SCIENCE STUFF

All cameras have a base sensitivity to light. This is defined in different ways, but as a former cinematographer I will always use the International Organization for Standardization (ISO) method of base sensitivity, which is the minimum amount of light at which a "proper" exposure can be achieved. "Proper" exposure for a digital video camera is defined as an 18% neutral gray card exposed at 50–55 IRE on a waveform.

Most digital camera manufacturers don't readily offer their camera's ISO, as this number can vary slightly from situation to situation. Instead they most commonly use LUX, which is a metric version of footcandles. One LUX is one lumen over a $1m^2$ area. (1 LUX = 10.76FC).

Whichever system of measurement you prefer, it all equates to nearly the same thing: how much light do you need?

FUMBLING IN THE DARK

When you're underexposing an image that means you are shooting in less available light than is required to achieve a "proper" exposure. Sometimes this is done deliberately for aesthetic reasons and sometimes it's done out of necessity because of lack of light.

At proper exposure, most light values and colors within a certain range will be represented pretty nearly as they are seen by the human eye. When you are underexposing an image, the camera is struggling to translate light photons into electronic signals and the direct result is a compromise in the image. In an underexposure situation, you begin to lose contrast and color saturation. The image will become more and more monochromatic as you get deeper and deeper into underexposure.

Digital cameras have a gain function that artificially amplifies the light passing through the camera's imager to achieve more exposure. This is akin to an audio amplifier, which takes an electronic signal and boosts it, but these tools can only boost so much.

Gain is measured in decibels (dB), a relative logarithmic scale of amplification based on the values of illumination before gain and after. Gain is typically represented in steps of +3dB or −3dB and with each successive application of gain, you are amplifying the signal more and more. Gain is a relative scale that equates to, roughly, one stop increase per +6dB of gain. A by-product of this amplification is noise, a distortion of the image with what looks like static. The more gain you apply, the noisier the image will become.

Although the noise that results from overamplification of the image may be part of your aesthetic choice for the image, generally, it is considered objectionable. How much noise is appropriate is, more or less, a matter of personal aesthetic and varies considerably from camera to camera. Some shooters feel that even the slight amount of noise generated at +3dB is objectionable; some find +12dB to be completely acceptable. It all depends on your project and the choices you are making for your image.

In low lighting situations, gain will help considerably, but it isn't the only tool that you have at your fingertips. Of course the first thing you'll do is to open up the camera's iris (f-stop) as much as possible before applying any gain.

The next tool you have available is your shutter angle or your shutter speed. Shutter angle is an attribute that is available on many high-end cameras and shutter speed is a combination of frame rate and shutter angle that is more typically available on consumer and prosumer cameras. If you can adjust your shutter angle, this is a more precise function that will alter the exposure time for each frame of video. A typical shutter angle is 180°. Increasing the number opens the shutter for a longer period of time per frame of video and allows in more light. A 270° shutter will add half a stop of light to the image. Some digital cameras can shut the shutter "off" (360°) to gain a full stop of light. It's important to note the larger the shutter angle, the more motion blur will result with any action in the frame as you're exposing each frame of video for a longer period of time.

Many consumer and prosumer cameras have shutter speed adjustments, represented in fractions of a second. This is a mathematical combination of your frame rate and your shutter angle. In many consumer and prosumer cameras, there is no option for slowing down the shutter speed, only increasing it. This won't help you in low-light situations—in fact it will do just the opposite and cut down on the light passing through the camera's imager. If you can slow down the shutter speed, this will help your exposure. Slowing down the shutter speed effectively increases the shutter angle and will allow more light per frame of video.

For typical motion blur and exposure, 180° shutters are the norm. This equates to a shutter speed of 2x the frame rate. If you're shooting at 24 frames per second (with a 180° shutter), your shutter speed will be $\frac{1}{48}$ of a second. If you're shooting at 30 frames per second, your shutter speed will be $\frac{1}{60}$ of a second. If you have the ability to "open" the shutter speed further, that will help your light levels considerably: $\frac{1}{24}$ (at 24fps) or $\frac{1}{30}$ (at 30fps) will give you an additional stop of light—a doubling of your available light. This is doing exactly the same thing as adjusting your shutter angle, it's just a different mathematical representation for it. As with larger shutter angles, it's important to understand that slower shutter speeds will create some motion artifacts as you're exposing each frame for a longer period of time; you may see more motion blur than is acceptable to you. Again, this is a personal choice.

A LITTLE GOES A LONG WAY

All of these techniques will help to gain a more acceptable exposure from the little light you have available, but you can help yourself by understanding how to utilize existing light better.

It should stand to reason, when possible, to look for areas of your location that are better lit than others. If you're in a dark parking lot, try to stage your action around where the lot's lights are. Any kind of light is often better than no light at all.

Going a step further, you can position your talent or subject in a way to maximize on the amount of available light in a way that will be pleasing. Typically front-light is the worst for low-lighting situations. Front-lighting your subject calls attention to the lack of light in the scene and will have your audience squinting to see details in the subject.

Actress Debbie Diesel poses in front of a tiny miniMag flashlight. Front-light is the least effective use of extreme minimal lighting.

In order to demonstrate the concepts here, I went into an extreme situation with only a miniMag flashlight, a model, and a camera.

Using just that little flashlight, this is what front light looks like (at left).

The flatness here belies the little light, it is the least effective use of the small source.

In the exact same lighting situation, if you can position your subject in such a way as to put the available light alongside them, or slightly behind them, this edge-lights your talent keeping their face in darkness, but the image becomes more readily recognized as "low light" and becomes more acceptable to an audience. It becomes an artistic choice rather than a limitation.

Here, I've moved the light to be a sidelight. We get an effective dramatic look that feels like night.

To this same end, a little light goes a long way. If you can have *any* aspect of your frame be relatively lit—even close to "proper" exposure or, better yet, *over*exposed—this small area of the frame will carry a lot of weight, tricking the eye into believing there is more light available than there really is. This is how you get contrasting backs in a very low-lit scene. Just putting one light somewhere in the background (preferably so that it backlights or edge-lights your subject), it will increase the overall impact of your low lighting situation immeasurably. I'm doing that with the flashlight here (top right), keeping the light itself in the shot. I've also added in a small 18″ by 24″ piece of white foamcore off to actress Debbie Diesel's left side to help bounce some of the flashlight back into her face so that we can *just* make out some detail in her face.

Here, lighting the wall behind Debbie, we get a silhouette feeling, very ominous and mysterious.

In addition, look for situations where you can establish separation between your subject and the background by positioning them in *front* of lit areas. This creates a silhouette effect and immediately gives the audience a shape to associate with the action. The audience understands that it's dark and we accept that, if we can still clearly understand what is happening.

In a low lighting situation, you'd be amazed what you can do with something as simple as a strategically placed flashlight.

GOING EXTREME

In extreme situations, you can turn to a different method of low light exposure, utilizing non-visible infrared illumination. Infrared is still part of the electromagnetic spectrum of light, but it is not visible to the human eye. Film and video imagers are naturally sensitive to infrared light and often require filters to *not* allow infrared waves to bias the common visible-light exposure. Cameras that can shoot in infrared have the ability to shut these filters off. It's important to understand that infrared doesn't react like visible light. Visible light reflects off surfaces and the wavelengths of light that reflect back establish the color and brightness that reaches our eyes (and cameras). Infrared radiation does not reflect back the object's color. Therefore infrared is a monochromatic (often black-and-white) image. Although digital cameras are naturally sensitive to infrared, they are optimized for visible light and will struggle to achieve a "proper" exposure in an infrared mode. Shooting in this mode will almost always result in a "noisy" image.

Infrared is not to be confused with night-vision, which is a combination of infrared with additional amplification of available light through specialized optics.

In the best-case scenario, you have full control over your lighting and can create the image you want. However, if you're careful and you take all these tools into consideration, you can make the most out of a situation where light is at a premium.

Night Lighting

One of the oft-touted benefits of digital cameras is their amazing light-sensitivity. As CCD and CMOS technologies continue to improve, the low-light abilities of newer cameras (especially the larger-chip cameras) are also improving.

This doesn't mean, however, that when shooting a night scene you don't have to light. When it comes to image acquisition, lighting is still the art that separates the pros from the amateurs. There is an art and science involved in lighting to make things look dark, but lighting for night isn't as complicated as many people make it out to be. With a few easy techniques in your bag, you can have the fundamentals to tackle almost any night lighting situation with ease.

Night lighting was a bit of a conundrum for me in the earlier parts of my cinematographic career until my buddy Christopher Probst, a fellow cinematographer and I, began to dissect cinematographer John Bartley's incredible work on the early *X-Files* TV series. Bartley (along with Thomas Del Ruth on *The West Wing*), is one of the most influential cinematographers in television who helped to really change the landscape and visual language of primetime television into a more "feature film" world. Breaking down Bartley's night lighting, Chris and I developed a simple three-step system that became the basis for much of the night lighting we did from then on. Although I'm not typically a proponent of teaching classic three-point lighting, as I find it far too limiting and not always practical, this particular technique falls exactly into that definition.

The first step is edge-light. One of the key factors that sells the "night" look is a sharp, well-defined edge on your talent's face. This is often best achieved with a three-quarter backlight above the head height of the talent and it is normally the brightest area on your talent's body, with the edge slightly overexposed by a stop or a stop and a half. This hard edge, along with surrounding darkness and underexposure, is immediately recognized as moonlight, high streetlights, or even no-light and evokes a feeling of darkness, as long as you keep the rest of the talent's face and body underexposed.

Actress Andrea Fellers hides in the dark. The key to creating this "no-light" look is using edge-lights and deep shadows.

Soft front light for a dark moonlight feel on actress Andrea Fellers.

That leads to the second step, which is soft, underexposed fill light. I'll generally put this a stop and a half to two stops underexposed. This can be on the camera side of your talent or on the off-camera side, depending on the scene and your taste, but it should be soft. I'll typically use a bounce card in this situation and beadboard seems to serve best. This fill should just start to bring out the detail in the talent's shadowed face, without giving us too much detail. The fantastic benefit to shooting digitally is that you can see exactly where your exposures are falling on a calibrated monitor and adjust accordingly.

The final step in this technique is backlight for the background. This isn't the same as the specific edge on your talent and can often come from the opposite side or even directly behind the talent. This is your environment lighting and you're better off making this a sidelight or edge-light for the environment just as you edge your talent. Front-lighting or washing the background can tend to look false and artificial.

This overall technique also applies for an interior scene. On my first 35mm feature as a director of photography, many years ago, I was confronted with a situation in which the main character was in his apartment and the bad guy kills the power. How the heck do I shoot a scene in an interior location when there's no light? The answer is, again, edge-light. Using the technique I've discussed here, create a hard edge on your talent to pull them out of the darkness.

A scene from *Mothman*, the evil Man In Black investigates evidence of the creature in the West Virginia forest. Strong backlight with soft front fill and some background light creates a wonderful night feel. Photo by Christopher Probst.

This doesn't necessarily have to even been explained or motivated. The audience generally accepts this without question. A soft front fill, underexposed, will help to bring out the details in the talent. This can even be a half light fill from the same side as the edge to keep half of your talent's face in complete shadow. The third step in an interior is actually what the late, great, Conrad Hall, ASC, used to call "room tone." This is often a light bounced into a white ceiling or a large white bounce card up against the ceiling and set to several stops below key to just *slightly* bring up the detail in the room. If the light is large enough (the light fills a large portion of the ceiling or a large bounce card) it will feel "sourceless" and just provide enough information in the shadow details to make out an environment. When shooting a dark interior scene, this is generally the very first light I'll set up. Creating this overall base-level "room tone" sets the rough base level exposure for the rest of the scene and gives me something to work off of. You keep this room tone very low, three stops underexposed is not uncommon.

Over the years, I've had a number of rather passionate discussions about the color of moonlight. I recall one cinematographer who fervently asserted that he had read moonlight with a color temperature meter and it was around 4,000K. Although I disputed whether or not his standard color temp meter could actually get a reading off of moonlight, I didn't necessarily dispute the results. As the moon is nothing more than a reflection of the sun and it is not necessarily biased by ambient skylight, it seems logical that the moon would be warmer than typical daylight. However, people don't *perceive* real moonlight as blue. When you're out at night and you're standing in moonlight, it doesn't look like blue light—it almost looks black and white (which is a factor of the rods in your eyes, which are more sensitive to low light, but less sensitive to color wavelengths) or "silvery." I've never really been a fan of deep blue moonlight and I think it has become something of a visual cliché, but that's not to say that your personal preference for or against blue is right or wrong. I will generally cool my "moon" lighting slightly, if it's a tungsten unit and I'm shooting a tungsten balanced scene, then I'll probably use a ¼ to ½ CTB on the moonlight to cool it off from the rest of the scene a bit. Oftentimes I'll then desaturate that blue a bit in postproduction and pulling the color tends to create that more "silvery" monochromatic look. In any case, I find the front fill is best if it is more neutral/white and as close to your proper color temperature as you can get.

One of the problems I've seen in lighting tutorials—including this one—is that they primarily address a stationary subject. One of my main objections to teaching classic three-point lighting is that it typically only works for a subject that stays in one place. In practice, that's rarely the case. If your subject is moving throughout a location the best technique is to create "pools" of light for the character to move through. Don't be afraid of having areas of darkness intermixed with areas of light. If your scene is a killer quietly breaking in through the front door, you might start with edge light out in the hallway and no fill on his face as he moves into the doorway. Then as he moves into the room he can move into darkness and then, perhaps into silhouette in front of a dim window as he reveals his murder weapon and then back into a pool of darkness before landing in the three-light night look near the victim's sleeping body. This variation in lighting creates mood and ambiance and feels realistic. Just be sure to highlight the moments the audience needs to see to understand the story points, and don't be afraid to vary your techniques!

4.22 LIGHTING

Natural Day for Night

In general, the most popular type of question that I get asked is "Can I light with inexpensive gear?" or, a variation thereof, "do I need all of that Hollywood equipment?"

The answer is yes.

And no.

Lighting is, without a question, the primary aspect in controlling a photographic image. Manipulation of light is one of the greatest tools that you have to convey mood and emotion through the image. Depending on what you're trying to accomplish, *sometimes* you need the Hollywood hoopla, but not always.

For this column, I decided to challenge myself to create a "night" look utilizing natural daylight (day for night) without any augmentation with artificial lighting.

Day for night is, generally, achieved through gross underexposure. You're rendering your highlights down to below middle gray and plunging your shadows into the abyssal blackness. Day for night works best when the natural light is backlighting the subjects and when you can keep the sky *and* the ground out of the shot—two things that will give away the cheat very quickly.

Many people use day for night filters from manufacturers like Tiffen, who make two options, the classic blue Cool Day for Night and a much more subtle Day for Night Monochrome that doesn't hit you over the head with James Cameron BLUE, but rather filters it out to give a more "realistic" desaturated night look.

In this case, I elected to not use any filtration. I was also experimenting with day for night on an *interior* shot. Using the Canon EOS 7D, I set my white balance all the way down to the basement at 2,500K. This puts the camera's white point at a very low color temperature and—since I was only working with natural afternoon daylight—it rendered that light a deep "moonlight" blue automatically without filters on windows or the camera.

Actress Debbie Diesel peeks around the corner in this natural day-for-night shot, rendered to feel like night by adjusting white balance and exposure only.

For the first shot, I used no bounces, no augmentation at all, but rather merely utilized the light coming from a window at the end of my hallway as a backlight, raking across the hall wall and the soft light coming from my partially opened kitchen drapes as a key source. The trick here was to not see the window at the end of the hall in the shot, because it would have been too bright and given away the "night" feel. After that, the image was totally controlled through exposure. In this case, I shot this at ISO 1,250 at an f/2.8 at ¼₀ of a second.

For my second shot, I got a little craftier. I wanted to utilize the natural daylight as blue "moon" light, but I also wanted a little hint of white light on her face. How could I accomplish this using no artificial lighting?

The answer is mirrors.

An odd challenge I set for myself—can I create a day for night image incorporating two different color temperatures from just natural daylight? Actress Debbie Diesel poses for my experiment.

Reaching into my bag of tricks, I pulled out two 1' × 1' square mirrored tiles and mounted one on a C-stand outside the window. I bounced direct sunlight into the window, behind the position where Debbie would be standing.

Inside, I used another 1' × 1' mirror, on another C-stand, on Debbie's right side. This bounced the direct sunlight from outside onto the right side of her face. Now, for this shot, I changed the white balance to "tungsten" 3,200K, which still made the natural daylight blue, but allowed me some room to get white light on the right side of her face.

To achieve "white," I placed a sheet of Rosco ½ CTO on the surface of the inside mirror to color correct the bouncing direct sunlight to tungsten, which the camera would see as white. In this case, I only used ½ CTO because the light would be filtered *twice* through the same gel. The light coming from the mirror outside would pass through the gel receiving one layer of correction, then it would reflect off of the mirror and pass *back through* the same gel again—receiving *double* filtration from one sheet of gel, hence turning ½ CTO into full CTO by the nature of it being placed on the surface of the mirror.

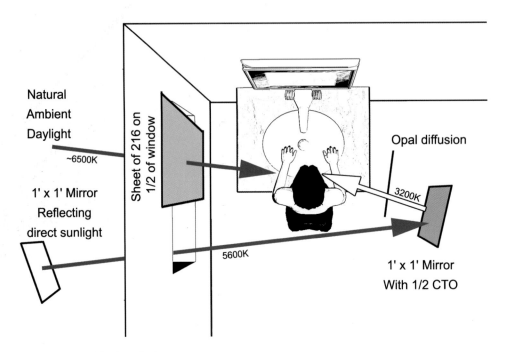

The lighting setup for the natural day-for-night shot.

The bounced sunlight from the mirror on Debbie's face was way too harsh for my taste, so I hung a piece of Rosco Opal diffusion in the space between the inside mirror and Debbie's face to soften the light quite a bit.

In addition, to reduce the intensity of the natural daylight through the window, I placed a sheet of Rosco Full Diffusion (216) on half of the window nearest Debbie to diffuse and reduce the intensity of the light there, but avoid diffusing the mirror light coming through the window behind her.

That did the trick and the result, again, considerably underexposed to achieve the "night" feel, was accomplished by using only natural daylight, but achieving two different color temperatures from the same light source.

Ghostly Lighting: Cinematographer Bill Roe, ASC, Discusses Lighting for *The X-Files*

This story originally appeared in the March 2000 issue of American Cinematographer *magazine as part of a series spotlighting television cinematographers and lighting breakdowns from specific scenes in their shows. I include it here as cinematographer Bill Roe, ASC, utilized several of the techniques I discuss in this book and incorporated them together.*

For this scene, aired in the second part of a two-part episode, FBI agents Mulder (David Duchovny) and Scully (Gillian Anderson) believe they've found out more information on Mulder's long-lost sister, Samantha. "This particular plotline is deeply rooted in *X-Files* lore," says Bill Roe, cinematographer on the supernatural series. "When Mulder was about 12, he witnessed what he believed to be the alien abduction of Samantha. This single moment was one of the strongest inspirations for him to begin investigating the FBI's paranormal cases.

"Mulder has gradually come to believe that Samantha was not abducted by little green men, but by government agents who used her as an experimental subject for their mysterious plots. In this episode, titled 'Sein Und Zeit II: Aliatope' [later renamed 'Closure'], Mulder and Scully have tracked Samantha's past to an abandoned Air Force base, where she is thought to have lived. Through the help of a psychic medium (Anthony Heald) who has the ability to sense past events, the two are led to a deserted house at the edge of the base.

"We shot the exteriors at an actual abandoned base in San Bernardino, California, and then built the interior on Stage 6 here at 20th Century Fox. Mulder, Scully, and the medium come into the house and find traces of Samantha as a child. The medium then brings the two agents together and asks them to hold hands with him in a circle while he begins an impromptu séance, attempting to summon some answers about Samantha's past. During the séance, Mulder opens his eyes and sees that the room is filled with ghosts. One of the spirits, a young buy, approaches Mulder, leads him down the hallway and shows him where Samantha once lived.

Screen capture from *The X-Files*, Bill Roe, ASC, director of photography. The X-Files © 20th Century Fox.

"The shot that reveals the ghost is a long, double-360° shot that begins in the middle of the séance circle. As the move begins, the camera spins all the way around to cover all three actors; it then spins outside the circle, and we see the ghost appear during the second 360° rotation. Eventually, the camera moves back into the circle. The only way we could pull this off was by using a Frazier lens on a motion-controlled crane above the set, so my first challenge was to light the set to a stop of T8 for the Frazier. For the most part we shoot the show with Kodak EXR 5298 [500T ISO] stock, which I rate at 500, so at least I had some help in the speed department.

"Because we were working with children in the scene, we were forced to break up the shooting order a bit more aggressively than we might otherwise have done. We shot the ghost sequences with the minors first, and then went back and covered the rest of the scene.

"To create the ghosts, we did a pass with the extras in shot, and then we did a clean pass with no one in frame to make them transparent. We then did another pass with the main talent in the shot.

"For the most part, I lit this sequence by pure process of elimination; the accompanying diagram shows the only places where gaffer Jono Kouzouyan and I could put lights! About 99.9% of the time, I never have a light over the camera. I'm always working with sidelight or even low light coming up on the actors, never toplight.

Screen capture from *The X-Files*, Bill Roe, ASC, director of photography. The X-Files © 20th Century Fox.

"In this situation, though, I was stuck. The deserted base ostensibly has no power, so there was no practical lighting at all—everything was motivated by moonlight. During their séance, the trio ended up in the middle of what would have been the living room. To get some light in there, we pulled out a ceiling panel from the set and keyed through the opening with a 20K on a scissor lift. We broke that light up with a bunch of Japonica 'branchaloris' rigs and cutters to help shape the light and make it a bit less sourcey.

A photo of the Japonica branches that were used to break up the light on the set.

"I also had to hit the walls with a bunch of little slashes of light, which is something I wouldn't normally do, because they're completely unmotivated. In this case, we had to have light on the walls to be able to see the walls through the extras. I usually like to use light on the set as separation, but for this shot I had to do even more of that than usual. If the walls were completely black, we wouldn't be able to tell that the ghosts were transparent, and the whole gag wouldn't work. I justified the use of slashes via the magical nature of the moment. I had a few 2K Baby Juniors raking up the walls in strategic positions from behind the desk and couch and whatnot.

"To me, the direction of the light is everything. Keeping light motivated is what keeps things real. The 'no light' situation is always the worst to do, because it's always a cheat. The audience has to be able to see something, so you have to create a source of light. It all comes down to what you can and cannot get away with. What is justified and what is not justified? Most of the time, we try to use windows or practicals as justification for everything. A lot of times, I'll shoot purely with practical lights. I'll just put them on a Variac and dial them in so that they work as keys and practicals at the same time.

"With this scene, though, we were just sort of making it happen as we went along. I hit the windows with quite a bit more moonlight than I normally would, but it was all in ratio. When there's no other source to compete with, the moon can be pretty bright. I had to be careful, though, because the art department frosted the windows with a kind of Fuller's Earth solution, and if I hit them too hard the scene would start to look as if it was playing in daylight. That required a fine balance that I pretty much achieved by eye.

"I dealt with all of the above to make the scene appear as if all of the illumination is coming from the windows. Even though most of my sources were coming from above, I don't think it reads that way on the screen. I tend to use a lot more silhouettes when we're in 'no light' scenes. That way, you can get a good feel for what the action is without really seeing details, and it also helps to sell the idea that the characters are in the dark.

"For the motion-control shots, I lit the set to about a T5.6/8, and exposed at a T8 to put the lit details down a bit. We had a 20K coming in through the open panel in the ceiling, and 5Ks and 10Ks coming in through the windows. When the characters enter the house, they leave the front door open, and we had a 20K outside cutting through the open doorway. All of the sources had ¼ CTB on them to cool the whole look down just a bit. The real finesse was coming from the Japonica branches, which helped to shape all of these lit areas and make them feel more real.

Actor Anthony Heald as Harold Pillar, a medium helping Mulder contact his lost sister. The X-Files © 20th Century Fox.

"When I look at a shot, I'm looking for two things: does it look real, and does it look good? If it looks good, then I can get away with fudging reality quite a bit. If it doesn't, something is wrong—either I've cheated reality too much or I've not cheated enough.

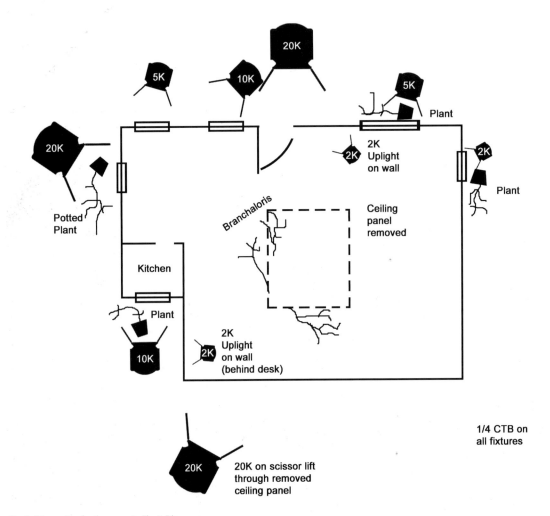

The lighting setup for the scene in *The X-Files*.

"For the most part, I find that I'm always bringing in the light from the complementary camera angle—meaning the opposite side of the line of action. If I'm doing an over-the-shoulder shot, which favors the right side of an actor's face, I'll bring the light in from the left side. I don't like to bring the light in from the same side as the camera—it doesn't have the right feel to me. I don't always get to follow that rule, but I do try to plan for it.

"The hard part of this sequence was reconstructing it and ☐ already shot to cover other parts of the same scene. After the dou☐ Steadicam shot that carries the actors from the kitchen area into the liv☐ hold their séance. It's practically another 360° shot, but it starts in the p☐ we were previously using for lighting! For the ghost shot, we could cheat ☐ even though it was a 360° shot in the living room, there were parts of the dining☐ kitchen that we weren't seeing in the shot. I took full advantage of those areas b☐ them for lighting.

"Now the frustration was that we were going back and seeing into those areas and ☐ the same time, we were moving in to the living room where the ghost shot happens. ☐

Screen captures from *The X-Files*. The X-Files © 20th Century Fox.

going back to what we'd
ble-360 move, we did a
ng room where they
rt of the set that
a bit, because
room and
y using
at

d set up before without being able to light from
ere we'd had lamps were now in shot. It became
the nooks and crannies that I could use to dial

as the kitchen. The medium finds Samantha's
and we had initially covered it in a raking over-
o the medium. In that shot, we only saw a small
indow on the back wall, which wasn't in shot,
he counter. In our subsequent Steadicam shot,
ter in the same shot. The window is frosted just
nd a way to hit the counter with the same hard
light when we couldn't light from the window. In the end, we decided to cheat the beginning of the shot slightly so that only half of the window will be shown. We also had the art department scrape the frosting off the other half so that we could light through the window and match what we'd done before."

Directed by Kim Manners, this episode of *The X-Files* (7th season, #11) was the second in a two-part series.

Adventures in Lighting, Part IV—Eternal Flame

A shot of model Becka Adams lit purely by the road flare she's holding.

Stanley Kubrick, the famous introverted filmmaker, wanted to shoot his baroque-style drama, *Barry Lyndon*, as realistically as possible—including the use of candles as the only means of illumination at night, as would be historically accurate. In 1975, the year he shot the film, this was an extraordinary technological achievement for cinematographer John Alcott, BSC. To accomplish this seemingly impossible feat, Kubrick scoured the globe looking for exotic super-fast lenses. He procured a trio of 50mm Zeiss *f*/0.7 lenses and had Ed DiGiulio of Cinema Products retrofit them to a BNC mount for his Mitchell cameras. Alcott used 100

ISO film pushed one stop to 200 ISO (for those of you keeping score at home, 24fps at 180° shutter, 200 ISO at an f/0.7 requires a mere 3⅛ footcandles of light for an exposure)—and the result is as beautiful as it is amazing.

Today, we have sensitivities 10,000 times greater than 100 ISO and although f/0.7 lenses are extremely rare, we do have fast lenses commonly available in the f/1.3 to f/2.8 range, combined with fast ISOs—you can easily shoot in the light provided by a single candle.

In the image below of model Becka Adams, she is lit purely by the three candles in front of her. Shot with a Canon EOS 7D at 1,600 ISO ⅟₃₀ of a second at an f/2.8. Although she has a good, natural, exposure on her face, the candle flames are completely overexposed and clipped with no texture or color to them—this is a common problem when your light source is in the shot: you can have good exposure on your subject, but the light source itself will be vastly overexposed. This is as true for practical lamps as it is candles and flame and it is not always desirable to have that in-shot source burn out so brightly.

Here Becka is lit only by the three candles in front of her. We get a good exposure on her face, but the candles themselves burn out bright white. Candle light alone, tungsten white balance, ISO 1600 1/30 Shutter f/2.8.

Fire can be very beautiful—with amazing colors and great animated texture, but when you're using that fire as your practical source of light (or creating the illusion of lighting from the flame), it takes a little more care—and more light—to bring your subject *and* the flames to life.

That brings us to a rather counterintuitive aspect to shooting around flames that will help to bring out the real color of the fire.

Many years ago when I was just a wee little burgeoning cinematographer, I saw *Backdraft*, directed by Ron Howard and photographed by Mikael Salomon, ASC. The fire in *Backdraft* is a living breathing character in the film—and it was immensely important that it have all of its true-life texture and colors and not just be white-hot, shapeless flames on the film. To do this, Salomon used a *ton* of light on all of the fire sequences to bring the base exposure way up so that the flames would fall closer to middle gray within the film's dynamic range

and you would be able to see all of the beautiful yellows and oranges and reds within the flames. For *Backdraft*, Salomon used a 250 ISO film stock, but went the opposite direction from Alcott and rated it at 100 ISO (for a stop and a third of over exposure). Further, Salomon shot the fire scenes at an *f/4*—requiring a base level of 200 footcandles, 64 times as much light as Alcott used on *Barry Lyndon*!

These same approaches, Alcott's and Salomon's, can apply to shooting by candle or firelight. Yes, you can use the actual flame as your source light for your talent, but if you want a little texture and life in the fire, you've got to increase your base lighting to compress the contrast range within the scene into your camera's dynamic range. This is where it's counterintuitive because you're shooting a dim candle-lit scene, but it requires *more* light to really render those flames a beautiful orange instead of hot white.

From the set of *Sharon's Secret*, a ridiculously brave (or crazy?) stuntman is lit on fire during the shooting of the dramatic climax.

Although the theoretical light from one candle on a 1' square surface, 1' away from the flame is one footcandle, when taking a spot meter reading of the flame itself you'll see that the flame is much hotter than the light emitted from it. Here, I was reading 2.8 footcandles of light from the three candles on the model's face (just about 1' away). It's always impressive when theory is actually proven in reality!

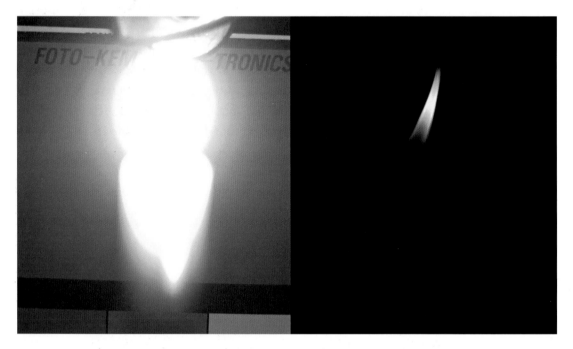

Setting a gray card 1' away from a lit candle. The left side of the image was exposed to put the gray card at middle gray. The right side of the image was exposed to put the candle flame near middle gray. When exposing for the subject, the light source is too bright. When exposing for the light source, the subject is unseen.

One trick you can employ when working with candles is not using standard store-bought candles, but by using specially made candles that have two or three wicks for a brighter flame—the flame, itself, will still be the same exposure at its center, but the light emitted from the candle will be more. Then, by stopping down and exposing more for the heat of the flame, you'll get deeper, richer color to your fire.

Additionally, to really get some color out of the flame, you're going to have to add light to the scene. This can easily be done with tungsten lighting, as it's closer to the color temperature of the fire and you can incorporate dimmers or color filters on your tungsten lighting to drop that color temperature further to better match the fire. Depending on the source of the flame, fire burns at about 1,500–2,000K. Some types of flames burn deeper orange/red than others. Gasoline, for instance, creates a very deep orange and red flame, much lower in color temperature than a natural gas fire, which burns a rich blue (unless there's extra oxygen in the mix, in which the flame turns yellow). Your typical paraffin wax candle wick burns in the neighborhood of 1,900K at the tip of the flame, with deeper blues toward the base of the flame where there's less oxygen and hotter temperatures. Most of the time, when you see big explosions in movies, they're using gasoline in the explosion to get the deep orange fireball.

In addition, you can cheat the color of the fire even more. With such low color temperatures from the flame, using standard tungsten (3,200K) white balance would seem to be the right thing to do—getting nice orange/yellow fire. However, if you adjust your white balance to daylight (5,600K), the color of the flame will be considerably richer in red/orange and have much more depth and texture.

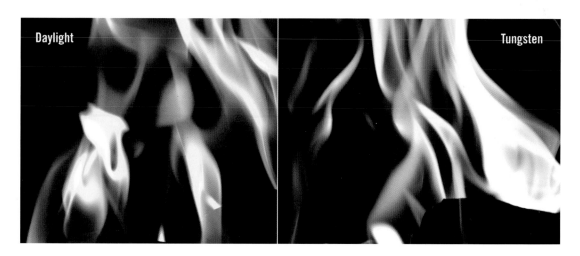

When fire is exposed under daylight color balance, it has more rich warmth to it than if exposed under tungsten balance.

Doing this white balance cheat, you do have to be careful about your talent's skin tones. The additional light that I bring into the scene is, generally, closer to daylight—more around the 4,000K range to keep it feeling warm (as if emanating from the flame source), yet not so warm as to turn the talent into a bright red tomato.

In this second shot of Becka, I've switched to a daylight balance and stayed at an f/2.8 at ⅟30 of a second, but dropped my ISO from 1,600 to 320 (two and a third stops down from the first exposure) and also brought in a tungsten Fresnel through a 4 × 4 diffusion frame

Now augmenting the shot of Becka with some artificial light to add to the candles so we can stop down the exposure to gain color in the flames. Candle light with tungsten key with 1/2 CTB. Daylight white balance, ISO 320 1/30 shutter f/2.8.

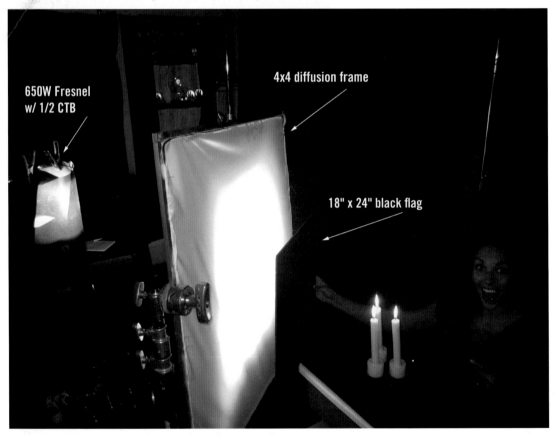

The lighting setup for Becka.

for fill. I added ½ CTB onto the frame so that the 3,200K isn't so orange on Becka's face under a daylight white balance.

When it comes to candlelight, I also like to use strands of Christmas lights stretched around an open frame. They create a very warm and soft light that very nicely matches the feel of the fire/candles without having a "sourcey" feel that you can get from a single light source. The falloff from the Christmas lights is also very pleasing—so there's less spill to contend with. For the Christmas lights, I switched back to a tungsten white balance as I didn't want to add CTB and lose the light output.

When you're adding in additional light, it's important to use flags to cut the light off of the candles themselves as that can be a dead giveaway that you're supplementing the candlelight—especially if the supplemental light causes a shadow of the candles to be cast on the talent as that can't happen naturally.

These "rules" don't always apply, of course. For the opening image in this section, I shot with Becka in a dark garage with only the light from the road flare. With a daylight color setting on the camera, the color from the flare is a rich red that really adds dramatic flair (forgive the pun) to the image. In the second shot of that image, below, I opened the garage door slightly to let in some daylight and stopped down a bit, I gained a touch of color in the flame, but lost a lot of the

Using Christmas lights to augment candlelight Tungsten white balance, ISO 320 1/30 shutter f/2.8.

I strung Christmas lights between two C-stand arms with a sheet of diffusion between to help reflect the light.

The Christmas lights in action.

dramatic feel by filling with daylight. In this case, my personal preference would have been to shoot with the flare alone, although the second image—with more daylight fill—would, traditionally, be considered a more correct exposure.

The shot of Becka with the flare, again, this time augmented with some natural daylight, but much of the dramatic feeling is eliminated by the daylight.

Additional sources used in this column:

Fisher, Bob (1991) The Heat is On in Backdraft. *American Cinematographer*, 72(5): 42–50.

DiGiulio, Ed (1976) Two Special Lenses for Barry Lyndon. *American Cinematographer*, 57(3): 276.

It Ain't Easy Being Green: Estimating Green Screen Lighting

I received an email question the other day about lighting a green screen and I thought it might be of use for me to share my response and thoughts here.

The question seemed simple: "Can I light an 18' wide by 12' high green screen with two Kino Flo Image85 units, or do I need more?"

I suppose I could have responded with a simple: "yes, you can, but I'd recommend three" and called it a day—but that answer was inadequate (and it's very unlike me to be simple in any response!). To be thorough, I had to ask a few questions: how far away from the screen can the Kinos be and what stop (brightness) do they need from the screen?

Keeping in mind that you want to keep your talent as far away from the green as possible to avoid spill and corruption, you want the biggest green you can afford (both cost and space). If your space is limited and your talent has to be very close to the green then you're going to have a lot of problems with spill.

The Kino Flo Image85 is a great workhorse fixture for lighting green screens. They're very soft, broad, DMX addressable, even have Pole-Op options with a yoke that is adjustable from below with a long pole. I started with a refresher on Kino's published photometrics for the Image85 (available on KinoFlo.com), which state that the fixture has an output of 160 footcandles at 6'.

As a general rule-of-thumb, your fixtures—especially with Kinos—want to be at least half the screen height away from the screen. This will give you a pretty even field from top to bottom. In this case, we were talking about a 12' high screen, so the fixtures, in an optimum

The Event Premiere, a recent job I produced and directed on the UVS1—Universal Studio's customized virtual stage. This screen is pre-lit with 29 Kino Flo Image80s and 21 6K spacelights. Photo by Otto Kitsinger.

setting, should be 6′ away. However, the further away you position your fixtures, the more you can optimize even coverage, at the compromise of your exposure level.

The real question here is how wide will the coverage from the Image85s be? Unfortunately, here, the published photometrics aren't going to help. Kino doesn't readily say how wide their field of illumination is—but my experience tells me I can hang Image85s on a 66″ center (gives me a foot between fixtures) to get great coverage. The reflectors in the 85s are optimized for vertical spread, not horizontal spread—so the closer you get the fixtures together, the better you are in terms of smooth coverage across the screen from the optimum distance, but that's not to say you can't move them further back and spread them out a bit.

As with many things in our industry, there are a nearly infinite variety of green screen material, colors and saturations. I, typically, estimate a 25% to 35% reflectivity off of green, which covers most typical greens from chroma to digi. Some darker, less saturated green material will have less reflectivity but 25–35% is a comfortable range for estimating.

Now 6' away is a bit of a ruse, because you're going to be focusing your fixture at the center (or lower third, depending on your preference) of the screen to get a good even field of illumination from top to bottom. To figure out our real throw distance, we've got to do a little geometry and pull out some Pythagorean Theorem here. If our wall is 12' high and we're focusing at the middle of that wall (6'), and we're positioning our fixture 6' away from the wall, that's two sides of a right angled triangle. To figure out our hypotenuse, we've got to remember that $A^2 + B^2 = C^2$. Our A, in this case is 6' (mid-height on the green screen) and our B is 6' (distance away from the screen). That's 36 + 36 = 72. The square root of 72 is 8.48. So at 6' away from the screen, the center focus of our Kino is 8.48' away. Utilizing one of my favorite iApps—Michael Zinman's PocketLD—I can calculate the output of an Image85 at 8.48' to be 84.83FC. If my worst-case scenario is a screen with a reflectivity of 25%—that gives me an illumination of 21.2 footlamberts off the screen. At 200 ISO, 24 frames per second with a 180° shutter, 21 footlamberts will give me an f/1.8 (1.4 + ¾).

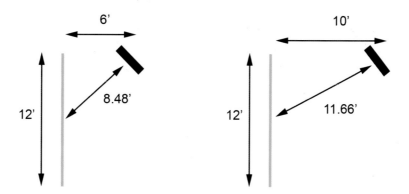

Figuring out the math of throw distance utilizing Pythagorean Theorem to estimate the fixture's output and reflected light for our exposure.

Not too bad, but a quarter of a stop shy of an f/2 at 200 ISO is only a fair exposure. In this scenario, it would behoove me to get a screen with a better reflectivity, for sure. A 35% screen reflectivity would give me 29.69fl of light, which would give me an f/2.2 (2⅓). The better, brighter screen will help a lot in this situation.

If we're figuring that at the optimum distance away, with 1' between fixtures, I've got even coverage—that means that my light extends out 6" on either side of my fixture evenly. So two fixtures, side-by-side at optimum distance away will give me about 10.5' of coverage—not enough to cover the 18' field. I either need to add an additional fixture, or pull the lamps back to get more of a spread. Of course, pulling them back will also reduce the intensity of light on the green.

How much light do you need on the green? That depends on the software you're using to pull the key. Some effects supervisors ask for the green to be one stop over your key, some ask for one stop under. In my experience, over is better than under to pull a better key.

If we went to 10' away from the screen, recalculated our Pythagorean, we'd have a throw of 11.66'. At that distance, our output drops to 44.87FC or 11.21fl (off the 25% reflective screen). That gives us an *f*/2 at 400 ISO. In some situations, this might be enough (the brighter screen is still better), but we *could* cover *most* of the 18' with two fixtures. I would, however, recommend adding in a third fixture, putting them back at the 6' range and going with a high reflectance screen to get the best results.

This is all a long-winded way of saying "yes, you can probably get away with two (with compromises), but I'd highly recommend three." Yet, knowing my thought process and the math involved might help you, dear reader, in the future!

Adventures in Lighting, Part V—12 Pages, Four Scenes, 12 Hours: An Exercise in Lighting Simplicity and Versatility

I was approached by a Los Angeles actor's networking collective to direct and shoot some scenes for the group and help their members build their reels. ActionGroupLA is a membership of actors of various disciplines who get together monthly to pool their resources and shoot shorts and specs. After directing a back-alley-gangster short for the group, they approached me to direct a series of intimate dramatic scenes that take place over different eras within one room. With no

Actress Megan Reinking as Grace in *These 4 Walls*. This scene is shot with an incorrect white balance to deliberately give the scene a very cold feeling. These 4 Walls © ActionGroup LA.

budget, only a single day and some tangled Janga-esque balancing of actor schedule availabilities, we embarked on a day of production that would encompass 12 pages of script and four scenes covering 40 years in time from the 1970s to today.

I liked the challenge of working in one room with limited gear and getting four distinct looks. We couldn't make any alterations to the walls, so the changeover would happen with subtle set decoration, costuming, and my lighting and camera treatment.

Canon EOS 7D

iKan D7w onboard monitor

One Arri 650W Fresnel

One Arri 300W Fresnel

Two Arri 150W Fresnels

Two 4′ × four-bank Kino Flos

One Lumos 300MK 1 × 1
  LED Panel

One Litepanels Croma LED

Mostly natural daylight in the room—with some backlight from a
4′ × four-bank Kino Flo, gives the room a very moody and sad feeling.
These 4 Walls © ActionGroup LA.

First up for the day was a very somber scene. Taking place in 1994, Grace, as an adult, played by Megan Reinking, has just split from her longtime boyfriend and is crushed. She's staying with her sister, Sheila (played by Tamara Rhoads) in the house where they both grew up. The scene is dim, depressing. Grace hasn't left the room in several days—just sitting and contemplating her life. I decided I wanted venetian blinds in the room and purchased a set of black blinds from a local home improvement store and we temporarily hung them up off of an existing curtain rod with a pair of spring clips. I utilized the natural daylight coming through the window—adjusting the blinds on a shot-by-shot basis, but decided to color balance to make it feel cool, by setting the camera to 3,800K. Windows are only on one side of the room and the natural light, from the mostly-closed blinds, was great on Megan's face, but I needed a little shaping behind her, so I had my gaffer, Daniel Harvey, bring in the 4′ × four-bank Kino with daylight tubes and placed that behind Megan, with just two tubes on and the doors pinched down to give her a little edge as she sits on the side of the bed.

Tamara enters from the doorway, and just outside the door is a small window—I left that natural, but we bounced a 300W Arri into the ceiling in the hall with a cut of ½ CTB on it to brighten the world outside the dim bedroom a bit.

For details, I brought in the Lumos 300MK panel for a little needed fill on a shot-by-shot basis mostly just to lighten the contrast, and I worked in a small Litepanels Croma fixture as a little eye-light for both Megan and Tamara. I composed this scene for a 2.39:1 aspect ratio and letterboxed the footage in editing.

The second scene takes place in 1986 and we see Grace, a little younger, played by Areti Athanasopoulos (also the writer of the project) with her boyfriend Derrick, played by Nathaniel Edwards. They're visiting Grace's parents for the weekend and have just had dinner and are retiring to the bedroom. Nate is amorous, but Areti won't let him; she's uncomfortable here in mom and dad's house with thin walls. The scene is dramatic and reveals that she hasn't yet told her parents that she's living with a man, but I decided to go warm and brighter than one might expect. I wanted this to feel realistic—like a young adult returning to her teenage bedroom; nothing romantic or overly dramatic. I brought in a pair of practical lamps from elsewhere in the house and put one at a vanity we brought in for the scene

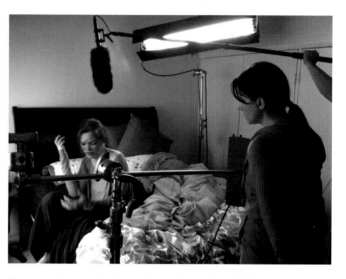

The setup with Megan Reinking and Tamara Rhoads. *These 4 Walls.* © ActionGroup LA.

and another by the bed. It's a nighttime scene, but we were shooting during the day, so we had to black out the windows. We used a technique I've turned to many times by using black seamless backdrop paper to tape up to the windows. It's cheap, opaque, and very quick to apply. For me, it beats trying to tape up duvetyne or—especially—trying to tent in the windows. Most of the

Actress and writer Areti Athanasopoulos (as a younger Grace) with Nathaniel Edwards in her childhood bedroom. These 4 Walls © ActionGroup LA.

time I'm not a fan of light coming through a window at night—it doesn't feel real to me unless it's in a city and you're looking at street lights or something coming through the window. Here, I didn't mind if the windows went black behind the curtains—so the covering was simple and Daniel got help from our first AD, Devi Brulé to make the job go faster.

The setup with Nathaniel and Areti. The 650W Fresnel (far right) is bouncing off the open white door, into the 3' diffusion frame to create an impromptu booklight for a soft key on the actors. These 4 Walls © ActionGroup LA.

Actress Chanel Marriott plays Grace as a young teenager in the late 1970s. Shooting with a very high white balance to get a very warm feel. These 4 Walls © ActionGroup LA.

The actors enter the room and go to the vanity where they're edged by the off-camera practical. It was a tight space, but I wanted a large soft light, so Daniel and I utilized the white door behind camera to bounce the 650W Fresnel into and placed a 3' square of silk diffusion in front of that, creating a "book light" that was very soft as the key for Areti and Nathaniel at the vanity. The quality of light was nice, but I was looking at an image that was a little flat to me. There wasn't any room for a negative fill on the actors, so I went the other way and had Daniel use one of the 150W Fresnels to put a hot spot on the wall behind the actors to give a little more contrast to the image. I played this scene in 1.78:1 aspect ratio—opening it up a bit more from the first scene.

The third scene takes place in 1977, where we see Grace (now played by Chanel Marriott) and Sheila (DaNae West) as young teenagers. I wanted to keep the same warm tone, but make it aged. I went with an ISO of 3,200 on the 7D to pick up some noise and degrade the image a bit. I also went with the Technicolor CineStyle picture profile—not to give me more latitude in color correction later (what it's designed to do), but to give me a more low contrast, washed palette.

I set the camera's Kelvin temperature to about 5,000 to make the tungsten-lit scene very warm. It's a dark scene, again, and I kept faces a stop underexposed. I utilized the same practicals as edges and brought in a 150W Fresnel to put a hot cut of light on Chanel, who is sitting on the floor, as if it's coming from the practical. We put the 150W Fresnel through the 3' × 3' silk diffusion, but only diffused the top half of the light beam so that the bottom half would be hot on Chanel, but the top half, on her face, would be soft (as if coming through the lampshade). I used the Lumos panel, dialing it a bit cooler than the practicals, for a little soft, low, fill that would complement the warm tones with a cooler contrast.

When the scene opens, Chanel is sitting on the floor by the side of the bed and DaNae is sitting on the bed. I edged DaNae with the 300W Fresnel from the side, as if it were coming from the practical on the vanity across the room. I also put a "puck light"—a little round low-profile tungsten light intended to be put up under a shelf in a kitchen or living room (purchased from an Ikea years ago in a kit of five) on the floor in front of the dresser in the background to give that a little texture.

The director/cinematographer ends up in the closet! The setup with a 150W Fresnel on Chanel's left partially hard light on the lower half of her body and partially diffused by the large frame of diffusion for the upper half of her body. A Lumos LED fixture provides some fill on Chanel's face. These 4 Walls © ActionGroup LA.

Actress DaNae West plays the young version of Sheila, Grace's older sister, with Chanel Marriott. These 4 Walls © ActionGroup LA.

This scene was, again, composed for 2.39:1. Space was tight in the room and I wound up having to sit in the closet with the camera to get the right shot of Chanel and DaNae on the floor.

The final scene takes place in modern day. A new family has moved into the home and we see a new story beginning. Mom (Glenda Suggs) and daughter (Karin Pyrak) bicker about the move. Karin isn't happy having to leave her school and friends and mom tries to console her. I wanted this scene to play very open, bright, new. We took all of the coverings off all the windows and utilized natural daylight. The windows have an Eastern exposure with a lot of tree cover, but by the time we opened the windows for this scene, the sun was on the other side of the house and

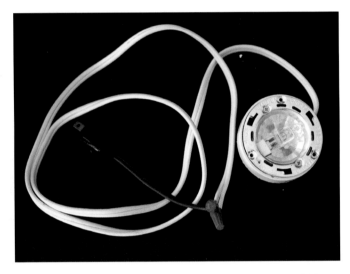

A "puck light." These are actually intended to be under-cabinet or in bookshelf lights, but I often use them as little detail background lights. lights. Note the alteration of the fixture with the addition of a quick-on Edison plug, I wired this on to replace the proprietary connection that came with the light - a simple alteration that makes this puck light useable anywhere.

I just got a very nice, soft light through the windows. I lit this scene 100% natural light—just let the sunlight be my key and let the room bounce it around to fill. I set the 7D at ISO 320, white balanced to the sunlight to keep it bright, white and framed, again, for 1.78:1.

The challenge, photographically, with this project was to create four distinct looks emulating different eras and overall emotional tones with a small kit and a camera crew of two. We covered all 12 pages in just under 12 hours.

Actress Karin Pyrak, lit by only natural daylight, is a new occupant of the room. These 4 Walls © ActionGroup LA.

Glenda Suggs plays mom, lit by natural daylight. These 4 Walls © ActionGroup LA.

A Motel-Room Meltdown: Shooting the Dollar Baby *Paranoid*

Paranoid is an eight-minute excursion into the mind of a paranoid-schizophrenic woman on the verge of a total breakdown. The short film was adapted from Stephen King's 100-line poem "Paranoid: A Chant," which appears in *Skeleton Crew*, a collection of his short stories.

I served as both director and cinematographer on the film, and my primary goal was to create a visceral visual experience that would plunge the viewer into the chaotic and disturbed first-person voice of King's poem. *Paranoid* was primarily photographed in the span of a single day.

One of my first choices was to shoot in the 2.39:1 widescreen format. Because this project was always intended to have a digital finish, and because I didn't have access to anamorphic lenses or a Super35 camera, I shot the film in Academy 1.33:1 (with a Panavision Platinum camera on 35mm film) and composed within the Academy frame for a 2.39:1 image. I knew the Cinemascope frame was particularly well-suited to a narrative such as this; a large portion of the storytelling comes from isolating the woman deep in a corner of a hotel room, and the expanse of the room fills the rest of the frame. I felt that Cinemascope was the best choice for the story, even though it forced me to a tape finish and pretty much eliminated the possibility of ever striking a print.

My second decision was to combine color and black-and-white imagery to differentiate between reality and the woman's delusions. King's writing is ripe with incredible imagery of "faceless men" with "eyes like silver dollars," and I wanted a canvas that would suit those images and bring them to life. All of the reality in the film is depicted in color, and all of

Screen captures from *Paranoid* starring Tonya Ivey. Paranoid © Adakin Productions.

the fantasies and delusions are depicted in black-and-white. To further control the palette, I kept the color sequences fairly monochromatic, working with a "dirty" palette to intensify the woman's destitute situation.

Although the film intercuts black-and-white and color, it was shot entirely on Eastman Kodak EXR 500T 5298 emulsion. Using one stock gave me greater flexibility later on with some inserts that were on the borderline of being real or delusion, and it also helped to cut down on the budget. The black-and-white sequences were desaturated in telecine at Riot Santa Monica by colorist Beau Leon.

My main objective with the lighting was to keep it simple yet graphic, tailoring the imagery to serve the story. For all of the black-and-white sequences, I pushed the contrast ratio to play best in gray tones. For all of the lighting situations, gaffer Michael Collins and I used as few instruments as possible to avoid complicated setups.

The main location, the woman's hotel room was lit with three fixtures. I used a 1K Baby fitted with Lee Super White Flame (#232) gel and bounced into the ceiling to give me an overall, sourceless room tone (the ambient level of light at the base of exposure, which sat at 2–2½ stop under key just to lend texture and color to the shadow areas). The Super White Flame gel is actually intended to take white flame arc sources to 3,200K, and it has a wonderful, deep amber color. Pushing a tungsten source through the filter creates an effect that is very similar to sodium-vapor lamps; this idea was inspired by a June 1995 *AC* article on *The X-Files*. Working from the overall ambient level, I was able to create a warm but dirty light that isn't very pleasing for flesh tones, which is what I wanted. The wallpaper on the set was carefully chosen to work well with that source color to suggest a very dilapidated look.

To light the woman in the corner, I had a straight sidelight raking down the wall, usually from a 150W Pepper gelled with the same Super White Flame. For one or two of the wider shots, I had a Mini Kino Flo on the side of the lamp next to her to get the same side-light feel. Outside of the window, I had a 2K Baby Junior coming through Rosco Medium Red (#27) on a Variac, and our best boy sat out there all day long, rolling the dimmer up and down to simulate a flashing neon sign. I also put two Tweenies on a single stand outside of the window; they were panned to emulate car headlights passing by, adding another layer of texture to the lighting.

The insert work was all done over the course of three nights prior to principle photography, and I kept those setups very simple as well. In fact, I had no crew at all for those shoots. I was able to make *Paranoid* because I was producing and shooting a number of other small projects that I had grouped together in order to pool resources. At the end of each shooting day, I'd take the camera package and a small lighting package home and shoot my *Paranoid* insert list before I went to bed. In the morning, I'd pack the gear up and take off for that day's job, and then repeat the whole process that night. Although it was a bit lonely working alone, I also found a kind of purity in each of the setups. Although I certainly don't want to work like that again, I enjoyed the experience.

The most important thing for me was to stay true to King's words. I spent a great deal of time studying the cadence of his text and carefully structured the whole film around his patterns of words. Where he broke paragraphs, I took visual breaks. Where be broke lines or deliberately formatted his text in a certain way, I strove to interpret that choice visually. It was imperative that his words be the driving force behind the film.

On the occasions when I've been both director and cinematographer, I've preferred to work with a camera operator in order to free my concentration from the viewfinder. However, I served as my own operator on *Paranoid*. Because the set was so small and compact, I didn't feel any lack of connection with my lead actress (Tonya Ivey), and I was very comfortable directing from the eyepiece. For me, however, working that way is a rare exception—I'm not a believer in the auteur theory. Filmmaking is a collaborative art that requires every position to really make the magic happen; we just happened to have gotten lucky and made magic with a very small crew.

Dancing in the Dark: Shooting Under UV Light

Bending over backwards to get the shot, model/actress Grace DeSilva in UV makeup. Photo by Maria Angelopoulou.

The past couple of months I wrote about the problems of infrared radiation when it comes to digital sensors and how to combat that infrared contamination with specialty filters.

This month we'll jump to the other side of light on the electromagnetic spectrum and talk about ultraviolet radiation—UV.

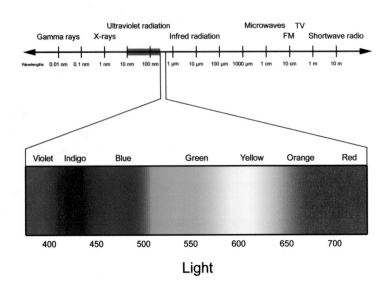

The electromagnetic spectrum highlighting light and ultraviolet radiation.

Ultraviolet radiation is what comes from the sun and burns our skin, giving us that awful sunburn in the summer when we forget to apply sunblock. UV covers a range from 10nm (ten one billionths of a meter) to 400nm, just to the edge of light. The very short end, from 10nm to 100nm, covers vacuum UV, extreme UV, hydrogen Lyman-alpha UV, far UV, middle UV, and near UV—all of which are of no real interest to us. From 100nm to 280nm is the range of ultraviolet C—this shortwave range of radiation is extremely dangerous, the most concentrated form of UV radiation. In fact, artificial lamps that emit UVC are used as germicidal instruments to sterilize medical equipment because germs and bacterial cannot survive the burst of UVC. A specific frequency of shortwave UVC at 254nm is often used to purify air, water, and food because it kills 99.9% of all pathogens. It is UVB, the range between 280nm and 315nm, that causes the pigments in our skin to darken—to get a suntan—and also the radiation that can harm the pigments in our skin and bring about burns. UVB is a known cause of skin cancer and can also cause blindness or lead to cataracts. If you're going to lie down (or stand, I suppose, depending on the model) in a tanning bed, the lamps surrounding you are emitting UVB, which will darken the pigments in your skin. The goggles you have to wear are to protect your eyes from the potential UVB damage.

UVA is the range of UV from 315nm to 400nm, the longwave range that is affectionately known as "black light." It is this range that we can utilize in photography for nifty effects.

"Black light" is, of course, a misnomer. We know that "light" defines only the range of the electromagnetic spectrum that is visible to human beings, anything beyond that—infrared or ultraviolet is *radiation*, not light. Ultraviolet radiation can, however, reflect off certain objects and create visible light, this is called fluorescence and it is this fascinating attribute of UVA that makes it a cool effect.

There are some elements, both natural and manmade, that are sensitive to UV radiation. When a "photon" of UV radiation comes in contact with these elements, they absorb some of the UV wavelength and reflect off a slower (longer) wavelength that is in the light range of the electromagnetic spectrum. This means certain objects, when struck by UV radiation will actually fluoresce or emit *light* back from them. The object is actually glowing because it is being struck with radiation and it is reflecting light. Materials that are not sensitive to UV radiation will appear black under UV.

Recently I directed a small spot, working with cinematographer Ashley Barron, that utilized black light effects. During prep, we spent an afternoon at Wildfire FX in Torrance, CA, testing out various materials and makeup with makeup artist Desiree Falcon and stand-in actress Laura Manchester, who volunteered to be our guinea pig for the day. It had been a number of years since I had worked with black lights and the testing was certainly eye-opening, especially working with a digital sensor as opposed to film. It's fascinating how differently materials fluoresce under black light. Materials that look like they're identical under normal

light can react very differently under black light. The only way to really know what will work and what won't is to test. Test, test, test. When Laura showed up for the test she was wearing a white sweater over a white tank top. In normal light, the white values of both were nearly identical. Under the black light, the sweater had no UV sensitivity at all, but the tank top glowed so brilliantly it was nearly blinding. There's no way to know until you experiment.

On the day of the shoot we had the actress, Grace DeSilva, bring in several clothing options and we had to test them all under black light to see which responded best. The results were surprising. Certain materials

Guinea-pig Laura Manchester was a trooper for our testing at Wildfire FX.

I thought, for sure, would fluoresce went black while others that I would have otherwise dismissed shone brightly!

In addition, there's no way to know how vibrantly certain materials and colors will fluoresce until you test them. Making things even more complicated, digital sensors see vibrant, saturated colors differently—especially with a Bayer pattern sensor like the Red Epic, which we used on this project. Certain colors that were crazy vibrant to the eye—would be flat and underexposed on the monitor. Again—the only way to know for sure is to test, test, test, and test again!

Most black light fixtures, even the most efficient, still emit visible light and this short wavelength violet light can look fairly ugly on skin. Incorporating white light can help clean up skin tones. In our case, we avoided white light, but incorporated some heavily saturated gels in the background and as edge lights to add more color depth and help eliminate the sickly blue skin tones from the black light.

When Grace turns away from the UV fixture, the fluorescent effect dims away quickly. Photo by Maria Angelopoulou.

Another confusing factor of black light is that you can't think of your intensities like you can with traditional lighting. Although black light fixtures are rated in wattage, just as typical fixtures are, the wattage is purely power consumption and *not* "light" output. In fact the output of the fixture itself has significantly less to do with the overall effect than does the material that is fluorescing under the UVA radiation.

We used Kryolan makeup from Wildfire for Grace during the spot, which is specifically designed to fluoresce brilliantly under UV.

Motion picture film stocks are sensitive to UV radiation, so when shooting film it was necessary to incorporate a UV haze filter—although that might be counterintuitive, it was necessary to keep the image from "fogging" from too much UV contamination. With digital sensors, this is not an issue and the UV filter doesn't have an effect. I would, however, have liked to have tested out a

Hot Mirror infrared filter as most UV fixtures also emit a large percentage of infrared light—but that will be an experiment for another time.

A spot meter is really the only way to measure exposure off of a fluorescing object when dealing with film—but in the digital world we can see the image right on the screen and utilize waveform and histograms to help moderate exposure. Generally we set the exposure to the effect and lit the backgrounds to match with that exposure. For the most part, it didn't really matter how far the UV fixture was from the subject, only that it was as near to the lens axis as possible for the best effect. As Grace turned away from the UV beam, the effect would disappear very quickly.

There are lots of fun things you can do with black light materials. There are several companies out there who manufacturer "invisible" black light paints that cannot be seen under normal light, but fluoresce brilliantly under UV.

Makeup artist Desiree Falcon applies the final touches to Grace DeSilva. Photo by Maria Angelopoulou.

An angstrom UV fixture.

For this project—it was fun to dabble back a bit with black light—and if you decide to play in the UV world, be sure to test as much as you can before, it's the only way to really know what the effect will be on the day.

The full makeup effect on Grace DeSilva. Photo by Maria Angelopoulou.

Illuminating Workout: Lighting an Exercise Video Series

This past weekend I was called into action by my producing partner, Ryan Harper, who, along with his wife, Barbara, are venturing into a new endeavor to create a website filled with exercise tips and techniques that professional women can do while at work.

This is a fairly good example of a simple, quick, and easy industrial lighting setup using only five lights.

The set was constructed on a small stage near Long Beach, CA. A simple three-wall set was constructed out of typical 4′ × 8′ TV Flats (See Misc section for instructions on how to build your own). We had no lighting grid, and a very small clearance over the walls (about 8″) from which to light. I had my trusty Arri kit that contains a 650W, 300W, and two 150W Fresnels, a Kino Flo Gaffer's kit with two 4′ × four-bank fixtures and a Bron Kobold DW200 HMI. That was the sum total of our lighting package.

Our grip package was equally modest, six C-stands, two Cardellini clamps, six 8″ C-clamps with baby spuds, and four 4′ × 4′ floppies.

On the back wall of the set was a sign for *Working Girl Fitness* with a bit of a 3D relief to it, so I hit that from above and to the side with one of the Arri 150W Fresnels to give the relief letters a bit of a shadow.

Lighting the main area, I knew I wanted a fairly simple soft wash of light for her to work in. In a perfect world, I would have put both Kinos slightly overhead, just off to one side a bit and have a soft, flat wash. Unfortunately we had no way to mount the Kino's overhead. My only hardware was the C-stands and putting both Kinos side-by-side would put the stands in the way of the camera and dolly. I decided to take one of the Kinos off to camera left, arming it out horizontally on the C-stand as far as I could safely. The second Kino I put

Giving exercise tips—Barbara Harper on the set of *Working Girl Fitness*.

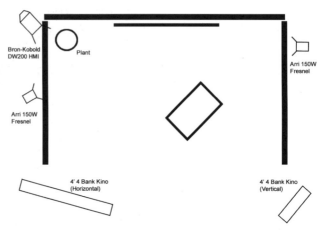

The lighting setup for *Working Girl Fitness*.

way off to camera right, vertical, more as a fill than anything else. I removed the egg-crates from both Kinos to give me the most punch from the lights. I elected not to use any diffusion as they were soft enough for my needs and I wanted to keep the light off the side walls as much as possible.

I used the Bron DW200 high in the far camera-left corner as a wide backlight. I used the Par attachment along with the CTO filter (to correct the daylight balance to tungsten) and the stipple lens. On the first day, we didn't have any blackwrap, so I had to improvise and use regular aluminum foil. I used the foil to create a "bottomer" to keep the spill off the walls and to create a "topper" to cut the light from hitting and flaring the camera. The foil wasn't enough of a topper, so we used a piece of black foamcore as a flag and grabbed that with a C-stand behind the wall to cut the backlight out of the lens. On the second day, I brought in a box of blackwrap to replace the aluminum foil. Finally, I used the second 150W Arri Fresnel over the camera-right set wall to give a little kiss of light to a plant in the corner. Without the additional light, that plant fell into dark shadow and just looked like a black blob in the deep corner.

On day two I also added a piece of Lee 250 ½ white diffusion to the Bron backlight to help soften the shadow it cast on the camera-right set wall and a sheet of Hampshire Frost diffusion to the 150W Fresnel on the sign, to soften that shadow a bit.

So that was my weekend. Simple, clean, cheap lighting.

Keeping the Lights On: Basic Electrical Management

Whenever you're using equipment in a practical location, there is always a concern about power consumption. Especially with today's technology and sensitive computer equipment, one blown breaker can mean a major hassle for the location owner and a black mark for you.

Understanding how to keep the lights on is not hard. It requires a basic understanding of electricity and just a *little* math (but I'll make it as simple as possible).

There are four main components of electricity: watts, volts, amps, and ohms.

To better understand their relationship and what they represent, I use the analogy of a bucket of water. If we have a large bucket filled with water and we have a spigot at the bottom of the bucket to drain the water, we have the beginnings of an electrical flow. If that bucket has barely any water in it, we're going to get a trickle of water out the spigot. If we fill the bucket, that water is going to shoot out of the spigot. This difference in flow is analogous to voltage or electromotive force. Voltage fluctuates, but within a given range. In the US, this range is between 110 and 130 volts for standard circuits.

Officially, volts are the measurement of the potential of electrical current between two points.

Now the diameter of the spigot is going to determine the rate of flow of that water. A very small spigot is only going to let out so much water whereas a big, thick spigot is going to let it rip. This is analogous to amperage. Amps are the ones you really have to pay attention to. Amps are the number of electrons actually flowing past a given point in a given period of time.

If we took the spigot and attached it to a long pipe and then bent and twisted that pipe all over the place—that would reduce the flow of water out of the spigot. In an electrical circuit, this resistance to the flow of electricity is measured in ohms. Ohms are the measurement of resistance in any element to the flow of electrons.

Finally, if we measure out how many gallons of water we actually get flowing out of this big bucket, that would be wattage. Watts are the measurement of the "work done" or the overall energy created. For all intents and purposes for any given component, wattage is a constant.

Flowing electrons have the side-effect of creating heat. Too much heat, of course, creates fire. Aside from electrocution, fire is the biggest danger of electricity. To help prevent that, every electrical component has an ampacity rating—that is the highest number of amps that component can handle safely. In most situations that is going to be between 15 and 20 amps.

When you arrive at the location, it's a good idea to first check out the breaker box. Right on each breaker will be a printed ampacity. Generally you'll find 15 or 20 amp breakers in most residential and commercial locations. That, however, rarely means that you actually have the full 15 or 20 amps to work with. In a perfect world, you have an amperage meter that you can clamp on to your hot lines for each breaker and see what is currently being drawn off of that circuit. Barring that, you've just got to use caution and try to take visual inventory of what else is running in the location. Anything plugged in draws power: computers, TVs, clocks, radios, appliances, etc.

Another important factor—and one that seems to surprise a lot of people—is that one circuit, protected by one breaker, covers a number of components within the location. Generally there are multiple outlets and lighting on each circuit (the exception is a red-colored outlet—usually found in hospitals or around sensitive computer equipment—which is a dedicated circuit).

Unfortunately, there is no rhyme or reason to the way that buildings are wired. You could have half of a room on one circuit and half on another, or the entire room could be on one circuit. Often half of one room and half of another room will share the same circuit. There are really only two methods of knowing, for sure, what outlets are on any particular circuit. The simplest, yet most intrusive method, is to turn all the breakers off and start turning them on one-by-one and checking the outlets. This is best done in a two-person team with one in the location at the outlets with a circuit tester or a simple lamp and one at the breakers. As the breakers are turned on you label the individual outlets (or breakers) as to what they control.

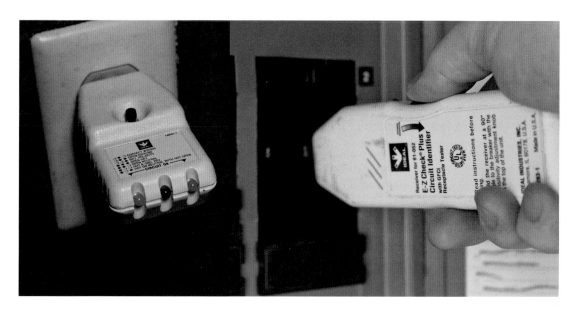

A two-device circuit tester helps to find the breaker associated with an electrical outlet.

The second, less intrusive, method is to use a circuit finder system. This is a two-component system with a plug and a receiver. You plug the tester into the wall, and then hold the receiver over the breakers and it will beep when it finds the breaker that the tester is plugged into. This way you don't have to disconnect power to map out the circuits. These kits can be found at any hardware or electrical supply store.

Now we get to the math part. Don't be scared—it's not that bad. There is a simple formula, easily remembered by calling it the West Virginia Law. Watts = volts × amps (W = VA). Wattage will always be a given for any specific component. A 100W bulb will always require 100W of energy. Voltage, for the most part, can be considered a constant, as well. Although, in actuality, voltage varies (in the US between 110 and 130), we can simplify the math and build in a bit of a safety net by assuming a constant. If we *presume* that the voltage is always 100 (in the US)—it makes things easier and builds in a little cushion.

So, let's say you have an interview you're setting up and you have a 1,000W soft light, a 300W Fresnel for a backlight and a 300W Fresnel for a background light. That's a total of 1,600W of electricity. If we plug that into the formula, W = VA (assuming 100 for voltage) then we find that we're using 16 amps of electricity. If your breakers are only 15 amps, this isn't going to work. You're going to have to run at least one of the lights (probably both Fresnels) on a separate circuit. If you're working quickly and don't have the chance to map out the circuits at your location, you can be confident that in any architecture erected after 1970, in the United States, the kitchen and bathrooms will always be on separate circuits from other rooms. Also, you can fairly safely assume that an outlet at least two rooms away will be on a separate circuit—but testing is always your best bet.

You see why we assume 100 volts in the US? First off because it makes the math easy, second—if you're working ahead of me—if we use 120 volts, then a 1K fixture (1,000 = 120 × A) is actually 8.33 amps. When we use 100 volts not only does it make the math easier, but it means we're *overestimating* the amperage draw and building in a little extra safety factor (by assuming 10 amps per 1,000W instead of 8.33 amps) . . . Watts = volts × amps West VirginiA (W = VA).

This applies to anything electrical you need to run. If you look on the bottom of anything electrical there will be a sticker telling you the voltage necessary to run the device and the wattage of the device. For example, a Sony PD-150 camera (sitting next to me) has the following information on the power pack: AC IN: ~ 100–240V 50/60Hz 23W.

This means this camera can run on voltages from 100V to 240V (but remember the voltage for the particular area of the world is relatively constant (in areas of Europe the standard is 220–240V as opposed to the US at 110–130V) at 50/60 Hz (this is the cycles of electricity per second—US = 60Hz, Europe = 50Hz) and—most important, 23W.

The PD-150, when plugged in, is 23W: 23 = 100 × A.

The PD-150 draws .23 amps (not even a quarter of an amp).

You *do* need to consider everything electrical you're plugging in: lights, cameras, sound, props, food service, make-up/hair, etc., in your calculations. Things that generate heat (coffee pots, hair dryers, lights) tend to have higher wattages than things that don't (cameras, sound gear, monitors, etc.).

Remember the byproduct of electricity is heat. Without fuses and breakers in place, if you were able to run 60 amps on a 20 amp circuit, you would—literally—overheat the circuit, melt insulation on wires, and, very possibly, cause a fire.

To be safest, remember the West VirginiA law (W = VA)—or even easier, every 100 watts is 1 amp—and you'll keep the location owners much happier and have a safer and more efficient shoot.

Not only do circuits have breakers and fuses with amperage limits, ***EVERY ELECTRICAL COMPONENT IN A CIRCUIT HAS AN AMPACITY LIMIT***. I'll be rather obnoxious with the caps, bold, and italics there because it's an important concept to understand. An electrical circuit is only as strong as its weakest link. Your breaker may have a 15 amp limit, your plug may have a 15 amp limit, the lamp that you're running may only be 13 amps, but if your extension cord is only capable of handling 8 amps, you're in a very dangerous situation. More than likely that cord is going to heat up and start a fire. The breaker isn't going to protect this circuit because you're not using more than 15 amps, but that extension cord is being heavily overtaxed and it's going to fail. Without a fuse or a breaker in the extension cord itself, it will continue to complete the circuit, continue to heat up and will, eventually, light on fire.

To avoid this, you need to be aware of all the components in your circuit. When you're working in a residence or commercial space, you can reasonably assume that all components of a circuit from the plug to the breaker are properly integrated. If it is a 15 amp breaker, the wires in the walls and the plug itself are going to be able to handle that 15 amp load. Commercial and residential wiring is designed so that the breaker or fuse is the weakest link in the chain and will trip long before any single component in that circuit hits a danger point. Where you need to be careful is how you connect to that circuit beyond the plug. Primarily that refers to your extension cords or, as we call them in the film business, stingers.

Keeping the lights on and not blowing breakers is a good way to maintain a good relationship with the location owners and to not be embarrassed by a dark delay.

The Perfect Travel Companion: Lighting Kits

Just about every other month, and especially when I do lectures and workshops, I get asked about the "perfect" lighting kit. Invariably someone will send me a link to something they found online or bring me a brochure or ask me about this kit or that "Is it a good kit?"

My answer, unfortunately, is nearly always the same, "Looks like it *could* be good . . . It really depends . . . "

Unfortunately, it does depend.

It depends on a lot of factors—such as:

- Your budget
- Your intended use(s)
- Your shooting style
- Your physical space/weight and size requirements

Budget is a biggie. Lighting is rarely, if ever, cheap. Although good, high-quality lighting fixtures will last you a long, long time and are, therefore, cheap in the long-run—that initial expenditure can be painful. In this regard, I highly recommend spending as much as you possibly can. There's a lot of truth to the old adage "you get what you pay for." Higher quality, and thusly more expensive, equipment will last you longer and provide better results. Does that mean the cheap(er) stuff isn't good? Does that mean it doesn't work? No. It just means it *might* not last you as long as the more expensive stuff. For high-quality Fresnel tungsten fixtures, expect to pay anywhere from $0.50 to $2.00 per watt, on average. A good quality 650W Fresnel should run you between $325 and $700. For high-end fluorescent fixtures, expect to pay about $100 per lamp-foot. Meaning if you have a 4' long, two-lamp fixture, expect to pay about $800. LED fixtures are harder to get a price fix on because they vary so much with their functions, electronics, and bells-and-whistles. Be wary of super-great deals on LED fixtures—or, if you do snag that bargain, be aware that you're probably going to have to invest in some minus green gel to cut down on the gross green spike from the cheap LEDs. These prices are, by no means, the be-all-and-end-all—but can be taken as a rough guide to what you should be paying for high-quality gear.

Your intended use is the second biggest factor in determining what kit works for you. Are you shooting all talking-head interviews? Are you shooting food? Are you shooting narrative material? Are you a run-and-gun documentarian? If you're all-of-the-above, or any combination thereof, there's no one kit for you. There's no magical light kit that works in every situation. Are you typically working in a controlled studio environment, or are you often working in practical locations with mixed lighting sources? Do your fixtures need to have battery power or will you always have electricity handy? All of these factors have huge impact on the lighting requirements.

Your shooting style has to weigh in here. Some people are die-hard LED aficionados: light-weight, low-power, low-heat. These are all great factors, but LEDs don't really have the power of their tungsten counterparts, especially when diffused—which they almost always need to be when used on people. Maybe your lighting style is incredibly soft sources, but you need a lot of "punch"—then open-face tungsten units are probably the best bet for you with large softboxes. If your shooting style is on-the-fly, you might be looking at on-camera lighting or very lightweight, portable and battery-operated LED fixtures you can pick up and run with.

Finally, your physical space and weight requirements. I've talked to a *lot* of professionals who are often one-(wo)man bands and are responsible for their own gear. One of their biggest concerns is that the gear needs to pack down tight and light. On the other hand, a professional with an equipment truck, or a large vehicle, might not worry about the size and weight of their gear—they just want the most bang for their buck. If you're traveling a lot, you'll want to look into hard cases to protect your equipment. Soft cases can be lightweight, but aren't as rugged dealing with the rigors of real-world production. In the post 9/11 world, excess baggage on flights can be a nightmare, and if you do a lot of flying, you'll want to try and keep your kit below 50lbs to save yourself some hassle.

So—what is the answer her[e]? What is the perfect lighting kit? T[he] truth is—there isn't one. If you['re] doing a lot of types of shooti[ng] you want a kit with the m[ost] versatility you can find. Gener[ally] you'll want at *least* three fixture[s in] a kit—to give you the ability t[o do] the classic key, fill, kicker lighti[ng. I] prefer four fixtures as it gives [me] just a bit more flexibility to a[dd a] background light to that cl[assic] scenario.

In 2004, when I was produci[ng] and directing a documentary, my producing partner and I purchased an Arri Fresnel kit that consists of one 650W Fresnel, one 300W Fresnel, and two 150W Fresnels, along with four stands and a small Chimera softbox. The kit came in an Arri hard-case and was about $2,500 at the time. In the seven years since, I have used that kit on hundreds of jobs and shoots. It has traveled all over the world and I've lit everything from studio portraits and interviews to feature films and television shows. Is this kit the be-all-and-end-all? No. But,

like them to be—but these lights have al[ways] I love the quality of the Kinos, but woul[d] tion for all situations. However, the c[ost] micro-budget productions for se[veral] The bottom line is to really [have a] equipment with the most v[ersatility] a few compact accessori[es]

The contents of the Arri kit, one 650W, one 300W, and two 150W fixtures in addition to four stands and a small Chimera softbox in a single 50lb case.

quite honestly, when it's what you have on-hand, you make it work. I would actually prefer two more heads: a 1K and an additional 650W for a little more punch and versatility, but the four-light kit works great.

In addition, a few years back, we purchased a Kino Flo "Gaffer's Kit" which consists of two 4′ × four-bank Kino Flo fluorescent fixtures. Just two large fixtures aren't as versatile as I'd

so worked non-stop since we purchased them.
never say that this two-light kit is a recommenda-
combination of the two kits has served me very well in
eral years.

look at what your needs are and go for the highest quality
ersatile assortment of fixtures that you can afford. Augment with
es, and you're off and shooting.

PART 5
MISC

A Twisty Tale: A Few Key Knots

And now for something completely different . . .

Here's a topic I've never touched on before—ropes and knots. Yup, ropes and knots!

This one reaches back to my days as a theater rigger and extends into my second passion (other than filmmaking): sailing. Over the years, the knowledge and ability to tie good knots has gotten me out of many jams and saved the day more times than I can count. It's a lot more than just wrapping two ends of a rope together—it's an understanding  of how putting bends and twists in ropes reduces the working load; it's knowing elastic limits and stress loads and it's knowing what knot is best for a given application.

So, for this section, set aside the cameras and lights and grab a piece of rope and work along with me.

There are two primary types of ropes: natural and synthetic.

Natural ropes are generally manila (also hemp), sisal, or cotton. Synthetic rope is commonly nylon, polyester, polypropylene, or polyethylene (usually the bright yellow, slick rope used in watery and dirty locations).

Understanding working load can be the difference between a safe application of rope and a potentially lethal situation. There's a general rule of thumb for estimating safe working loads of different types of rope used, but it requires a little math and a little memorization.

First, you need to know the size of the rope. Is it ¼"? ½"? ¾"? Easy to do with a tape measure—and I'm talking about diameter of the rope, not circumference or length. From there you need to convert the fraction to eighths (*shudder* fractions!). It's not too hard, divide eight by the denominator (bottom number) to get your conversion factor and then multiply both numerator (top number) and denominator by that factor. So if you have ½" rope: 8/2 = 4 (this is now our conversion factor). 4 × 1 = 4; 4 × 2 = 8 so ½ converts to ⁴⁄₈. With me? Instead of reducing fractions you're increasing them to something over 8.

Now, here's where the memorization comes in.

Safe working load (SWL) factors:

- Cotton = 10
- Manila fiber = 20
- Polyprop/polyethyl = 40
- Nylon/polyester = 60

Knowing those SWL factors, you then multiply that factor by the numerator of your converted fraction to get your estimated safe working load.

So, for example, let's say we have a length of ¼" nylon rope; ¼ becomes ²⁄₈; 2 × 60 = 120lbs. I can safely estimate the rope's working strength at 120lbs.

Now it's very important to understand that anytime you put a bend or a twist or a hitch into a rope, that weakens its strength. A rope, in otherwise excellent shape, will fail at the bend/hitch. A typical knot will decrease the rope's safe working load by 50%. An important thing to keep in mind.

There are two factors that make a good knot over a bad one:

- It must hold, under all conditions. A knot that comes loose on its own is "knot" of any use.
- It must come apart easily when you want it to. Here's a biggie. Nothing worse than struggling with a locked bad knot. Then you need your "rope-wrench" (a knife!).

There are three knots that I use on a nearly daily basis (other than the classic "shoe-lace bow" which is common for tying soft goods to frames) and they are: the square knot, the clove hitch, and the bowline.

THE SQUARE KNOT

The square knot is so very simple and yet so rarely properly executed. A square-knot is two half-hitches together, yet in opposing directions. When you get it wrong, you get a "granny" knot. When you get it right, you have a very strong knot that is *easy to remove*. That, boys and girls, is the key to a good knot—it's strong and yet easy to untie.

For the square knot, the rule to remember is right-over-left and then left-over-right.

You're creating two loops that intertwine together.

When you do this knot right, it forms a symmetrical shape that could be considered square. The beauty is—when this has been under load and tightened down, to untie it— you grasp the two ends and push towards the center knot and it will release. Different ropes release easier than others, but it's a heck of a lot easier than untying a granny knot (which would be right-over-left and then right-over-left again).

The square knot is used to bind two ends of a rope together or two different ropes of the same size together.

The square knot.

THE CLOVE HITCH

The clove hitch is great for wrapping rope around an object, like a pipe or pole or roof rack on a car. It's also great for using in cables to tie them off to the handle of the dolly to keep them out of the way of the operator. The clove hitch can be created in the middle of a line that is connected on either end, as long as you can slip it over the object you are connecting to.

- Loop the rope over the top of the object.
- As you close the loop, cross the tail over the top of the loop.
- Bring the tail around the object again
- Bring the tail UNDER the cross-over you just made and tighten. That's the clove hitch.

The clove hitch.

THE BOWLINE

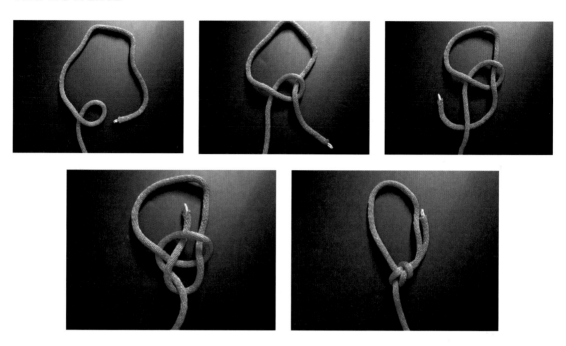

The bowline.

Next is the **bowline**. This is a lifesaver, literally. When search and rescue technicians have to get someone out of a hole or lift them up via rope or lower a body down, it's the bowline that is used to secure the rope around the person (or a figure eight with a follow-through, but that's for another lesson). The bowline is a little tricky, so it helps to keep the "rabbit" story in mind. You form a loop near the end of a line, leaving enough length that is twice the size of the loop you want to form, and then bring the tail of the rope (the "rabbit") up through the loop (rabbit comes out of the hole), then around the working end of the rope (rabbit goes around the tree) and then back through the loop (and rabbit goes back into the hole). This forms a loop at the end of the rope that can be wrapped around many things. Because the bowline has less harsh bends and hitches than a square knot, it only reduces the working load of the rope by 35%, not 50%.

These three knots are a great indoctrination into the world of working with rope. Master these three to the point that you can do them in your sleep—and it will help you immensely on any location and on any set and in everyday life!

Bring the Noise: Tips for Better Audio Production Recording

For those that know me, seeing that I'm writing an article on production sound would be quite amusing. In my early filmmaking days, I was notorious for making silent films so that I didn't have to deal with sound. Later, I made an infinite number of sound mistakes before I started getting it right. Coming up through the camera side of filmmaking, sound was never my forte. Cameramen and sound mixers have a kind of natural animosity between them; a bit like cats and dogs. We get along, we can even be best friends, but a lot of times we end up circling each other with our haunches up and trying to stay out of each other's way.

With that in mind, I spent some time researching and learning the best tips I could find about capturing solid production sound—and I learned quite a few things that I'll share with you here.

There are two classic methods of recording sound; single-system and double-system recording.

In the low budget world, single-system seems to often take the lead in most forms of production. This means that you're running your sound directly into the camera, whether or not it passes through another device, such as a mixer, beforehand.

There are several different ways to connect to the camera, but XLR connectors are the preferred method.

An XLR connector, male and female ends.

1/8" and RCA stereo connectors.

The balanced aspect of the XLR connector allows for longer cable runs without hum or frequency response in the line. Most higher-end prosumer cameras have XLR inputs. A step down from the XLR would be RCA stereo inputs and, finally, ⅛" phono jack plugs. Regardless, if you're going to get solid sound, you need to have a camera with an external audio input.

Most location audio is recorded with a shotgun microphone. This is an area where you really do get what you pay for and you should get the most expensive microphone you can afford.

Most shotgun microphones on the market are condenser microphones.

THE SHOTGUN MIC AND THE BOOMPOLE

A shotgun mic has terrific off-axis rejection; in other words it only picks up the sounds from the source at which it is pointed. This is what makes shotgun mics the best choice for production sound applications. Think of it like a telephoto lens; it has to be very carefully aimed or else you will wind up recording the passing traffic (or whatever) and not the dialog. As you get into the more expensive shotgun mics you will find that they have better off-axis rejection and greater sensitivity thus requiring a greater degree of skill to use.

You are going to need a boompole but they can be expensive, starting at around $250 and going up to over $1,000. You can make your own boompole with a painter's pole or a light bulb changer.

Firmly secure the cable to the boompole with Velcro straps or gaffer's tape so it doesn't rattle against the boompole, but leave a loop where the cable attaches to the mic. If you made your own boompole, you can use water pipe insulation foam to widen the grip, make it less slippery and provide some more sound insulation from your hands.

Most of the time you will want to boom from overhead. Come up from underneath if you have low ceilings or other height problems. Straight on is your worst option. You want to get the mic as close to the talent as possible (remember the inverse square law? Yup, it works here, too). Start with the mic in frame and slowly pull it up (or down) until the cameraman tells you it is out of the shot.

If you're going straight into the camera, it's a good idea to record the shotgun mic to both audio tracks in your camera (left/right). Set one channel to normal levels and reduce the volume of the other by a few decibels. In the event that there is a transient (a sudden volume spike) that could distort the audio of the "normal" volume channel it will (hopefully) not be distorted on the "reduced" volume channel.

Lavalier mics, also called lavs or lapel mics, are the small microphones that you see clipped to the tie or lapel of newscasters, etc. Smaller versions are used on film sets. They are used when a shotgun mic cannot be used effectively, or they're used in addition to the shotgun. They can be hidden in the clothing or even in the hair of the talent as well as being hidden on the set. When the talent is stationary, such as sitting at a table, the better option is to run the lav "hardwired," a physical cable run directly to the camera, mixer, or recording device. When the talent is moving around, it is common practice to connect the lav to a wireless transmitter/receiver system. This means having to conceal the transmitter on the talent as well as concealing the lav. This can be difficult if the talent is seen from all angles during the shot, so if you have decided to use a wireless lav you will have to experiment with the placement of the transmitter during the blocking of the scene.

Wireless systems can be expensive. They're dedicated to either VHF (very high frequency) or UHF (ultra-high frequency). VHF systems are less expensive, give you longer battery life and greater range, but they are very prone to interference, which can be a major problem when working in urban and suburban areas. UHF systems are more expensive, have shorter battery life and less range but are markedly less prone to interference. At the upper price range of wireless UHF receivers/transmitters you can find systems that are frequency selectable, enabling you to find frequencies with little or no interference at your location.

When using a wireless system, keep in mind that anything between the transmitter(s) and the receiver(s), including the talent, can cause a reduced or even a lost signal. It is not unusual to hide the receiver(s) on the set or even suspend it above the set and run a long cable to the camera, mixer or recording device.

Record each lav to a separate channel on your camera. Set the volume levels slightly lower than normal to protect yourself from transients (volume spikes) that may cause distortion.

HEADPHONES

Use a good pair of closed-back and over-the-ear headphones. Closed-back headphones permit less outside sound to reach your ears. Do not use open-back headphones. Have enough extensions for the headphones so the boom-op can hear what he/she is recording. You may want an additional pair for the director, so a "Y" cable may be needed.

ROOM TONES AND WILDS

Collect room tones. This is recording the sound of the empty set. You should try to record room tones for every angle from which you shot. So when you have finished shooting from one angle collect 90 seconds of room tone.

Dialog wilds are recording the dialog close up off camera. The talent is still in character and still in "rhythm." Do at least four takes of each line. This could save you from having to do ADR sessions.

Set wilds are recordings of sounds that emanate from the set. This includes doors, furniture, squeaky floorboards, tableware, sinks, toilets, cars (engines, doors, pull-outs, pull-ups, starts, stops, start-ups, etc.), elevators, ambiences, and crowd "Walla." For crowd "Walla" you can just roll for several minutes before you ask for quiet and begin shooting, it sounds much more natural.

These things will take some extra time on the set but will be worth your while when you get to audio postproduction.

SHOTGUN 101

A majority of the production dialogue recorded in major "Hollywood" theatrical productions and television series is miked from overhead, utilizing either a fishpole or studio boom.

Overhead miking provides a natural sound. Normal sound effects and some background ambiance are also picked up, and at a lower relative level than the dialogue, thus rounding out the total track. One of the big advantages of shotgun mics is the ability to capture sound with perspective. The sound perspective matches camera perspective when the boom mic is able to get in close on tight shots, and is further away on longer shots.

Microphone selection plays an important role in overhead miking technique, along with choosing a skilled and experienced boom operator. Just like camera lens focal length, there is no one choice of specific microphone that will be right for all situations. A professional package should include an assortment.

It cannot be stressed enough that, for best results, only the highest quality condenser microphones should be used in capturing dialogue. Although most electret condensers are very good microphones for their price and features, they simply do not perform as well as condensers for professional or theatrical dialogue applications. Top of the line condensers offer superior reach and sensitivity over the electrets, and that can spell out the difference on those more demanding shots between getting "rich" dialogue versus "weak" or "thin" audio.

Allow the extra room in the budget to purchase or rent a package of true condenser microphones along with the proper accessories (power supplies, shock-mounts, blimp windscreens) to make them work.

Similar to telephoto lenses, shotgun microphones tend to compress the distance between foreground and background. Avoid pointing the mic as if it were a rifle, unless you are totally unconcerned about bringing up the background. Be careful of what is in the "line of sight" behind the talent.

The best way to eliminate this "telephoto" effect is to aim the mic down from above, so that the only "background" in the microphone line of sight is the silent ground.

Miking from in front of the talent can pick up background noise, miking from above the talent picks up the floor and cuts down on background noise.

The most popular microphones for exterior use are long shotgun microphones. Long shotguns offer narrow pickup patterns and excellent sensitivity and reach. Deployed overhead of talent, tilted just slightly towards the mouth—these mics will eliminate considerable background ambiance while still picking up natural sound effects such as footsteps and hand business. Because of their directionality, these long shotguns can be placed at greater headroom above the actor when necessary (up to several feet depending on ambient noise), thus facilitating the wider frames more common on exterior setups.

The disadvantages of the long shotgun are its directionality and physical dimensions. The narrow pickup pattern requires that much more care be taken in cueing (aiming). Moving talent must be meticulously followed; multiple talent requires rapid and precise repositioning of the mic for each person's lines. The physical length sometimes becomes a problem, for example, in interiors with low ceilings.

The extended length of the shotgun is usually not a problem when working outdoors, although situations may arise where a shorter mic is necessary. Weight, on the other hand, can be a definite problem. Do not underestimate the strength and stamina required to manually support a fully extended fishpole complete with shotgun mic, shock-mount, and windscreen over the course of a long day!

The short shotgun is characterized by its more manageable length and wider pickup pattern.

The somewhat wider (although still very directional) pattern makes it easier to follow, or cue the talent. On the other hand, the effective working range (maximum distance) of the mic is diminished. Also, the wider pickup pattern tends not to isolate talent from ambient noise as well as the long shotgun.

Sound Advice: Interview with Emmy Award-Winning Post Rerecording Mixer Eric Lalicata

I grew up on the visual side of things. In the theater, although I held many jobs, lighting was a primary vocation for me—electrician, master electrician, and lighting designer. Then when I made the move to film, I started in Los Angeles as an electrician, made my way up as a best boy, gaffer, and then cinematographer—where I worked for nearly a decade.

Although I actually got my start in live entertainment, back in high school, working sound, I have spent very little time during my career in the sound department. I have a basic understanding of sound recording techniques and I've learned more over the years, but I am—by no means—an expert when it comes to sound.

To that end, in order to provide some, ahem, "sound" advice to filmmakers, I turned to a true professional, Eric Lalicata, an Emmy Award-winning supervising sound editor and rerecording mixer specializing in sound supervision and sound mixing for television and feature films. Eric is the co-founder of Anarchy Post in Glendale, California. Anarchy Post won the MPSE Golden Reel Award and Cinema Audio Society Award for their work on Sony's *30 Days of Night: Dark Days*.

I sat down with Eric on Stage A at Anarchy and picked his brain in order to provide some advice for fellow filmmakers.

Studio A at Anarchy Post in Glendale, CA.

Jay Holben: So, let's talk about some of the most common mistakes that independent filmmakers make when dealing with sound.

Eric Lalicata: One of the biggest problems that we see here is not having a common sync reference between digital picture and sound.

JH: I would imagine that's even more of an issue now with the popularity of HDSLRs, Reds, and the Arri Alexa, cameras that are pushing the digital realm back into the film world of two-system sound.

EL: Exactly. Filmmakers have to be sure that their cameras and the production sound recorder are jammed to the same timecode periodically in order to establish a link so that postproduction can easily resync the dailies.

JH: That generally just takes a few seconds and requires actually plugging the recorder or slate into the camera to make sure the sync is precise, right?

EL: Yeah. It's easy to do—and it should happen more than once during the day because it can get out of sync for various reasons. Also, in post, the picture editorial department may sync up only the mix track.

JH: That's the reference track from the on-set mixer that contains a rough mix of all the individual recorded tracks, but not any individual tracks, right?

EL: That's right. It's just meant for reviewing dailies and for the director and editor to use while cutting. It is meant to be used for reference only. It's originally mixed and recorded for the director to hear on set. Then, later, the sound house will reassemble all the individual mic channels for use in the final sound mix. This means we have to redo the syncing process, yet again, and if the timecode isn't correct—if it wasn't jammed properly on set, then these individual files have to be synced by hand, which can be very time-consuming and a waste of money.

JH: Especially since you're not just syncing one track, but four or six or eight tracks recorded for one scene.

EL: Exactly. The next problem that we see a lot is just not enough microphone coverage on set. Each actor should have a wireless body mic in addition to the boom. These mics are recorded on their own "iso" [isolated] tracks in addition to being mixed into the mix track. This gives the post sound mixer and dialog editor the most flexibility when trying to create a smooth sounding dialogue mix.

JH: That's obviously in a perfect world. I know there are a lot of times when lav mics don't work—either because of wardrobe or blocking. Do you have any quick tips for those kinds of situations?

EL: Having the wardrobe department assist with mic placement is always a good idea. An experienced sound utility tech will have a few tricks up their sleeve in order to minimize wardrobe rubbing against the mic. It involves gaff tape or these little premade mic head sleeves that really help when miking under clothing. You're right, of course. There are always special circumstances that prevent getting the proper sound coverage. That shouldn't prevent one from trying, however. Using "plant mics" hidden in the surrounding set is sometimes an option. Multiple boom mics can also help with coverage when lav mics are not practical.

JH: I know that I've been scolded by my post sound team before for shooting too many MOS shots—mostly tight inserts or shots we want to get quickly and can't get a mic in there right away.

EL: Shooting MOS is rarely a good idea. Mostly, don't do it. Establishing shots, maybe. Any shot with action, movement, or actors in it should also have sound rolling; even if it is only to give post a reliable "guide track" to what the shot sounds like. Sometimes, the actual sound makes it in the film, adding a sense of reality that library sound effects can't cover. Often, we see slow motion shots being done MOS. Sometimes, with the actors saying things, or making efforts or breathing. All of that will make the film seem more real. Record it.

JH: I would never have thought to roll sound on an off-speed shot. Very interesting.

EL: Be careful with the "We can fix it with sound" mentality. You can't. You can *change* it with sound, you can sweeten it with sound, but if your shot has problems to begin with, no sound work is going to fix that.

JH: That goes along with "fix it in post," which I generally avoid . . . about 98% of the time.

EL: On the same note, "We can fix it with ADR" is a dangerous thought process. *Sometimes* you can fix it with ADR. A lot depends on the actor's ability to get back to the same emotional place they were at on the day of shooting. Recording wild lines on set should be done for scenes that you think may need ADR. Often, those recordings match production much better than ADR can. No one likes doing ADR. No one likes editing ADR, and most people don't like hearing ADR in their film. The performances are often weaker and the sync is often loose. That being said, properly recorded and mixed ADR *can* really save a scene. There is a reason every film has ADR in it, but it should be a last-case scenario and a filmmaker should never depend on it in place of making good choices on set for sound.

JH: Good point.

EL: Multiple camera setups shooting a "master" and one "close up" angle at the same time seem like a good idea to a producer trying to save money and maybe to the picture department, but for the sound department it is a micing nightmare. The composition of the master shot dictates how close or how far the boom operator can get to the microphone actors. Often making the close-up angle sound very "off mic." Then when the second close up angle "reverse shot" is done, boom op can get up close. When this sequence is cut together, you end up with a master shot and one angle "off mic," and another close up angle "on mic." The makes it very difficult for post to make these shots cut together smoothly.

JH: This is a situation where lavs would certainly help balance that out, right?

EL: Absolutely.

JH: What else comes to mind as common mistakes?

EL: Do not rename the files created by your digital camera, or move them from their enclosing folder structure created by the camera. This isn't really a sound specific note, but this causes major re-connecting issues when you want to online your edit. After the footage is transcoded for editorial by the DIT an assistant editor needs to enter the scene and take metadata associated with each clip. This information is crucial to your post sound department. Without it, hunting for the correct dialogue take is virtually impossible.

Finally, turn off anything that makes noise on your set. This may seem obvious, but it's amazing how many filmmakers don't take this step. If you hear it, the microphone hears it. Relight refrigerators so the compressor can be turned off.

JH: Yeah, I know one sound mixer who will always put his car keys in the location's refrigerator to remind him to turn it back on when they leave.

EL: I guess that works. Really, think about anything in your shot that may make noise that will harm your dialogue and do whatever you can to minimize or remove it. Often, kitchen scenes will be shot with an actor actually cooking. Don't do that. If the shot requires the audience to see the food, pre-cook it and have the actor fake it. Pan sizzles will ruin your dialogue every time. If you are shooting a practical location, find out how to turn off the HVAC unit during takes. Put a PA in charge of that. Also make sure you cannot hear your generator on set. If you can, it is too close. Move it. Those are the biggest things that I can think of that are common mistakes that can be fairly easily avoided and make the post sound process a lot smoother.

JH: Some fantastic tips! Thank you, Eric, for your time—much appreciated!

EL: Absolutely, my pleasure.

Shoot the Moon: Tips for Celestial Cinematography

"Aim for the moon. If you miss, you may hit a star"
—W. Clement Stone

There have been a few times in my career when I've had the assignment to shoot the moon; the last time was for the opening title sequence for an HBO series. It can be a bit of a challenge to photograph the earth's only natural satellite.

The first thing to understand is that the way we see the moon with our eyes, especially when it is close to the horizon, is an optical illusion. The moon is not actually larger in the sky when it's near the horizon, it's not a trick of the atmosphere, either, it's just the way our brain interprets what we are seeing. It is akin to the Ponzo illusion, whereby two identically-sized parallel lines will appear to be two different sizes when they're placed over converging lines.

This is because our brain interprets converging lines as parallel lines going off into the distance. So when we see the lines across the converging lines—our brain sees the one closest to the convergence point as larger—because it is farther in the distance.

Your camera does not suffer this same optical illusion, however. Most people who try to photograph the moon are horribly disappointed when it appears to be just a

My shot of the moon for *Femme Fatales*.

small spec in their photo as opposed to the gargantuan glowing orb in the sky.

Photographing the moon, in all its glory, requires a long lens—the longer the better. In my last case, I used a Canon L 600mm *f/4* lens on my EOS 7D, which got me plenty close to the mystical ball in the sky.

Exposure of the moon is often a surprise for many people. You're more or less photographing a light source. The moon is just one big reflector in the sky bouncing back sunlight—so it takes a shorter exposure than one might imagine. For me, I set my ISO at 320, and my aperture between an *f/8* and an *f/11*. This exposure keeps good detail and texture in the surface of the moon. You also want to make sure you're manually focusing, autofocus can be confused and often not really sharpen in on the moon itself.

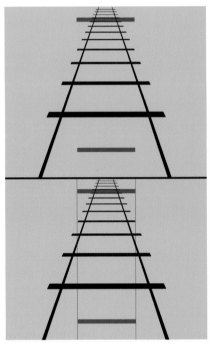

Illustrating the Ponzo illusion, whereby two identically sized parallel lines will appear to be two different sizes when they're placed over converging lines.

Shooting the moonrise with a Canon 600mm lens on a Canon EOS 7D. Photo by David Williams.

In addition to a good long lens and a deep exposure, you're going to need some careful planning. Moonrise and set times can vary by as much as an hour each day, so it can take some solid planning to make sure you're going to get the shot. Just because it's time for a full moon, doesn't mean that the full moon will actually be up in the sky at night! It could be up during the day—planning ahead will save you a lot of frustration.

Happy shooting!

Carnet Chronicles: International Travel with Equipment

I'm currently producing and directing a reality show called *My Hollywood* about kids pursuing their dreams to break into show business. The major leg of home-visits for this show has me on the road for 25 days from Alberta, Canada, to Manhattan to Pennsylvania to Ohio to Tennessee and Florida. Although I've shot in Canada once before, I did it a little surreptitiously by flying into New York and driving across the border with an SUV full of equipment, a field producer,

My boarding pass for my flight to Alberta, Canada.

and a cameraman. This show is a bit bigger, I've got a crew of six: a DP, a camera operator, a sound mixer, a story producer, my assistant/DIT, and our supervising producer. We've got a substantial amount of equipment (16 checked bags for each flight, woo!) and I've learned a ton while trying to negotiate the logistics of moving the crew and equipment across the border.

My first concern was work permits in Canada. Did I need to get permits for my crew to be able to enter and work in Canada? It was a little convoluted, but the answer became a "no." As a television production from America, with an American crew, who are being paid by an America production company—we were free to enter Canada without a permit. I learned this was part of Section 187 of the Immigration and Refugee Protection Regulation, which provides the general criteria for entry as a business visitor. As was explained to me by a representative of the Canadian General Consulate in New York, "The general criteria is as follows: There must be no intent to enter the Canadian labour [sic] market, that is, no gainful employment in Canada; The activity of the foreign worker must be international in scope, that is, there is the presumption of an underlying cross-border business activity; There is the presumption of a foreign employer—the primary source of the worker's remuneration remains outside Canada and the principal place of the worker's employer is located outside Canada as well as the accrual of profits of the worker's employer is located outside Canada."

Basically, since my crew is American, is paid by an American company, and isn't attempting to take any Canadian jobs—they don't need a permit. For some businesses in Canada, you have

Just some of our luggage we traveled with on *My Hollywood*.

to apply for a Labor Market Opinion, which evaluates your impact on the Canadian business market—if you're a benefit or have no impact, you're allowed to operate with the LMO.

I was elated to learn I didn't need an LMO or a work permit for my crew for Canada. What I *didn't* know, what that I needed a Carnet (pronounced car-nay).

It was actually my sound mixer, Kevin Bellante, who asked me "Are we doing a Carnet?" just two days before we were getting on a plane.

He said that to me and sirens went off in my head. I *know* I had heard that word before. I know it has significance. *What does it mean?*

Google is your friend! A quick Google revealed that we were, potentially, in trouble.

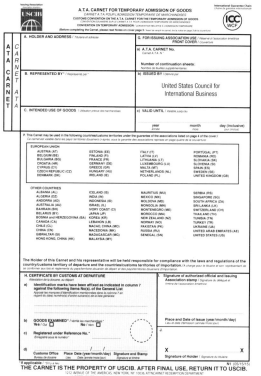
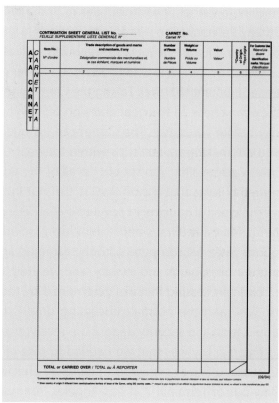

A Carnet provided by the United States Council for International Business

A Carnet is commonly known as a "Merchandise Passport." It is, more or less, a passport for your equipment. Countries frown upon individuals traveling abroad, purchasing expensive items like jewelry and electronics, not paying sales tax, and then bringing those items back into the home country (perhaps reselling them?). A Carnet is an official customs form that declares the ownership of equipment that is crossing borders—a proof that you had all the equipment before you left the country, when you entered the new country, when you left the new country and re-entered the old country. The Carnet is for the temporary importation of professional equipment. They facilitate international business by avoiding extensive customs procedures, eliminating payment of duties and value-added taxes (minimum 20% in Europe, 27% in China), and replacing the purchase of temporary import bonds.

Filing a Carnet, I was fortunate to find a wonderful service—CarnetsXpress.com, run by Tiffany Peterson. She was able to facilitate a Carnet for me same-day. I had to provide a list of all the equipment we were traveling with along with serial numbers and values.

Once the Carnet is issued, you get a folder of paperwork that lists the inventory of all of the equipment to travel. Taking the Carnet and the equipment to your local Customs office, they can check all the gear and sign off on your Carnet. I recommend doing this at least a day before you travel. The Carnet can include more items than you're traveling with, so if you are making several trips within the year that the Carnet is valid, and one is a big trip, others are smaller, you should list all of the equipment necessary for the big trip and then note the items that are on the list, but not included on a specific trip.

The types of equipment covered by Carnets: commercial samples, professional equipment, items for trade-shows and exhibitions, including display booths, in addition to ordinary goods such as computers, tools, cameras and video equipment, industrial machinery, automobiles, gems and jewelry, and wearing apparel.

Basic processing fees are determined by the value of a shipment. Fees range from $225 to $380 and the normal processing time is between one and two working days, if the application and security deposit are received according to the service provider's guidelines.

The real key was that we needed to take *all* of the equipment and the Carnet to the US Customs office at the airport *before* we checked in at the gate. This was a struggle as we flew out of Terminal 2 at Los Angeles International Airport—and the Customs office is at Terminal 4. The Customs agents need to see all of the equipment so that they know it's all in your possession when you leave the country.

When you arrive at your destination in the new country, their Customs agent needs to sign the "counterfoil" a document in the Carnet, to acknowledge that the equipment entered the country.

When you leave that country, you need to take the equipment to the local Customs office to have them inspect it and sign off on their counterfoil in the Carnet. One final signature is required by US Customs when you re-enter the country—although this step was done for me in Canada by a US Customs officer and I didn't have to do it after landing in the US.

It's a somewhat confusing process the first time—but if you understand *why* it's necessary, that makes following the steps a lot easier. The alternative is that the foreign country may make you post a bond (up to 50% the value of your goods) upon entering their country that, theoretically, is returned to you on your departure.

If you're planning on traveling abroad with equipment—be sure to look into a Carnet for your gear—it'll save you a *lot* of potential headaches.

Understanding Post Color Correction

I was at an industry networking function this past week and had a conversation with a young woman who was interested in producing films. She had been working as a PA for about two years and when she learned that I had previously been a cinematographer she asked me, "Can you explain color correction to me? Does that mean that something is wrong and it has to be fixed?" Before I could even start to reply, a young man standing next to us chimed in, "That's what happens when they shoot it wrong on set and they have to fix it in post."

I waited for the smile to crack on his face, but when it didn't, and I realized that he was serious, I had to wonder how many people in this business don't understand color correction.

I'll start with the basics: color correction—or as it used to be called color timing or grading—is *not* a step to correct errors. It is a requisite step in the production process—in *every* production process—to create a final, polished, and professional presentation. To skip color correction would be similar to building a car; making the chassis and piecing together the engine, putting in the interior and all the dash components, bolting on the wheels and then skipping the paint job. You've got a car—but it's unfinished. The paint isn't correcting any mistakes—it's simply the final stage in the creation of the car.

Color correction starts with *balancing* the image. This is where some people have the mistaken belief that color correction fixes errors. The majority of balancing isn't about fixing errors, it's about accounting for innumerable variables within shooting limitations: light changes due to time of day, light changes due to different fixtures, changes in image due to different shooting environments or matching shots that were shot days, weeks or even months apart, matching color differences between lenses, between cameras, and so much more. Especially in narrative shooting, where you're taking multiple camera setups (whether that be from one camera, or many) and editing them together to create a linear whole that appears to take place in real time—although the shooting might have taken days or weeks to capture—balancing between shots is very important to smooth out the scene and it is the most basic task a colorist does, but it is also the most complicated.

With today's digital tools, nearly anyone can take an image, fiddle with some filters and functions and create something "cool," but having the knowledge, experience and talent to apply that "cool" look to every shot in a sequence, and make them seamless, is of paramount importance. Many people who are new to color correction think they can just experiment to set a "look" and then copy and paste that look to the rest of the scene—but without balancing first—that will have disastrous results.

The general controls over the image are: blacks, mids, and whites, and then red, green, and blue color elements of the picture. Within each color, red, green, or blue, you can add that color, or subtract it by adding in its complimentary color. For instance, if you want to make a scene cooler, you might add blue to the scene, but if the scene is already too cool, you'll reduce the blue look by adding yellow. If you just adjust a color in the blacks, it will only change that color value in the shadow areas of the image. If you change the mid range, it will change those areas that are closest to proper density—or the middle gray area. If you change the whites, you will only affect the areas in the highlights of the image.

Once you've achieved a color balance, you can start to apply your "look," this is the creative part of color correction. Today's digital tools are versatile enough to take a daylight image and make it night; which happens from time to time. That's not to say that it was a mistake on the behalf of the cinematographer—but sometimes, in editing, the sequence of scenes might be changed and what was once a day scene might now need to be a night scene in the new order. With a good colorist (and the right image) this is possible.

Setting the "look" is normally done with the colorist and cinematographer (and sometimes the director) in the room. Most often, most of the look is set on location and in-camera, but it is further refined in the color-correction sessions. Should the "look" be a 1970s-era feel, with high contrast and washed, faded colors? Should the "look" be dark with reddish hues to match the alien planet where the story takes place?

A lot of high-end digital cameras now shoot in raw mode. The "look" that the cinematographer and director set during shooting is *not* recorded, but is saved as metadata in a look up table (LUT). The colorist can start by applying this LUT to the footage to get the best idea of what the director and cinematographer wanted the image to look like. Without the LUT, the image will be washed, low contrast and—often—with a sickly greenish hue.

I would always recommend that any serious project be taken to a professional, experienced colorist. Although some editors *can* do color correction, it's a lot like asking a veterinarian to operate on your mom. Sure, they're medically trained, but they are not skilled specialists in a very delicate and complicated trade.

Software like Apple's Final Cut Pro comes bundled with some basic, but pretty powerful, color correction tools. I recommend using the 3-Way Color Corrector filter in FCP and experimenting a bit.

Below are some screen shots from Final Cut Pro featuring a shot from a project I directed called *Amanda's Game* with actor Brian Glanney, shot by cinematographer Teri Segal. Although the warm, high-contrast image was our intention, for purposes of illustration I'm going to change that to a more sickly green—à la *Collateral*.

A screen capture from Apple's Final Cut Pro showing a scene from *Amanda's Game*, which I directed, with actor Brian Glanney. This is the way the scene was shot by cinematographer Teri Segal. Amanda's Game © Adakin Productions, Teri Segal, Director of photography.

Take a look at the left side of the screen capture at the three color spheres. The far left sphere represents the shadow range of the image, the middle shows the mids, and the right represents the highlights. Notice that each sphere has a small circle in the center of the sphere. This is the color position for that range of the image—center is a neutral position making no change to the image. The farther away from center you drag that circle, the more drastic the color effect you're adding.

Adjusting color-correction controls, I changed the feel of the scene from a warm look to a sickly green look. *Amanda's Game* © Adakin Productions, Teri Segal, director of photography.

In the final image, by adding blue/cyan into the highlights, I start to cool off those red/yellow tones. I added a moderate amount of cyan into the mids and then just a little into the blacks. The overall effect is a much cooler, more pale and sickly fluorescent look.

This example represents a creative choice in postproduction, which happens from time to time, not any fault or error in photography.

Even though the tools are available inexpensively, I would still always recommend working with a professional colorist to finalize your project.

Colorful Communication: Working with a Colorist

In today's digital age, the concept of "do it yourself" has been taken to a new level; especially if you listen to the product manufacturers. Ten years ago, what would take a small army of specialized individuals, can now be accomplished by a single person on their own home computer! However, just because one *can* do everything doesn't mean one *should* do everything. There are still aspects of creative production best left to specialized individuals and one of those remains firmly in the hands of the colorist.

As a former film cinematographer, the concept of a colorist or color timer is something that I've grown up with. When shooting film, it is an impossible step to skip; someone has to set the exposure values for red, green, and blue light passing through the negative to make a positive print. As it happens, a considerable amount of creative control comes with that seemingly arbitrary task. Adjusting red a few points one way or another can drastically alter the final look of that film print—and from that creative control was born a very symbiotic relationship between cinematographer and colorist.

When telecine (the process of transferring film to video) came onto the scene and telecine machines were able to transfer film negative onto videotape as a positive image, the same principles applied, but suddenly there was even more flexibility over the image. It wasn't just red, green, and blue densities, but yellow, cyan, and magenta in addition to gamma, toe, and shoulder control. It wasn't long before a telecine colorist had the ability, quite literally, to turn a day scene into a night scene. With this amount of control, very clear and concise communication was required between the cinematographer and colorist to make sure there was no misinterpretation of intentions. The cinematographer may have intended a scene to be underexposed and mysterious and the colorist interprets that as a mistake and makes it bright and clear. For years cinematographers and colorists worked to refine their own methods of precise communication, but nothing goes beyond the cinematographer actually sitting in the same room while the colorist is working and offering specific guidance on his or her intentions when the image was originated.

At its most basic, color timing, also known as color correction, is a technical process to iron out the kinks and inconsistencies in original photography. Inconsistencies arise from differences in exposures, lighting, color, film stocks, white balance, etc. In a particular scene, the sun might have passed behind a cloud for one take, rendering the shot slightly cooler in color than the other shots around it or a particular shot in a scene may have been shot months away from the next shot in the scene and the lighting wasn't exactly the same. These inconsistencies can arise from something as simple as the exact same model lighting fixture that has a slightly different color temperature than a previous model had months before. While shooting, no one would be able to see the difference, but when the shots are edited together side-by-side, the difference becomes much clearer. The color correction process smooths out these inconsistencies and makes the picture a cohesive whole.

Over the years, however, this basic technical process has evolved into an extraordinary creative tool. Digital color correction has gone way beyond a simple smoothing of inconsistencies to a further extension of creative image enhancement. A true, experienced and talented colorist can elevate your image to a whole new world.

Although many editing platforms now include powerful color correction applications, the software itself is not a replacement for the artist controlling it. During the course of my career I've had the luxury of sitting with some of the top colorists in the business and I can say, in no uncertain terms, the talent of the colorist is a considerable attribute to the success of the color session. Merely having the tools, and even a qualified understanding of how to use them, does not replace the talents of a good colorist by any stretch of the imagination.

With that said, the first session with a real colorist can be a bit intimidating for the new filmmaker. Understanding the basics of what is possible and what the colorist is doing to manipulate the image will help alleviate some of the trepidations you might have going in.

THE BASICS

At its most basic level there are three major image controls that need to be understood: the blacks, the gamma (or mid-range), and the whites. Blacks and whites, or shadows and highlights, are relatively self-explanatory. Brightening the blacks is often called "raising" or "lifting" and it will make the shadow areas less dense, less dark, and render the blacks more gray-like, lightening the picture. The reverse of this—"crushing" or "lowering" the blacks— takes the low-end shadow detail and eliminates it, strengthening the blacks and darkening the picture.

Adjusting the blacks of an image. From crushed to normal to lifted blacks. Notice the grayscale below the image of model Mason Rae. When the blacks are crushed, the darker chips blend together. When the blacks are normal, we can see each step of the grayscale. When they're lifted, we lose the black completely and they all become levels of gray.

Adjusting the whites/highlights.

The "whites" control the highlights of the image. It is important to note that, in the digital world, once you have overexposed an element—in the photography—beyond 100% white, there is no longer any detail information remaining and it can no longer be brought down.

Whereas underexposed elements of the image can be raised toward "proper" exposure and still have detail.

The trickier, but possibly the most important area is your gamma or mid-tone range. This is where most of your skin tones fall, with the exception of dark black skin. Just like the blacks and whites, you can lift and/or lower the mid-tone range to control the overall look of the image. If your faces are a little too overexposed, you may want to bring down the gamma a bit to correct that; or if they're a little dark, bringing up the gamma can help considerably.

Adjusting the gamma/mids/grays.

All of these areas have independent control, but they also all work together. A combination of crushing the blacks, popping (raising) the whites, and raising the gamma can result in a "poppy," contrasty commercial look.

Communicating your needs to the colorist is as simple as asking: "Can we raise the gamma here a bit?" or "Can we crush the blacks a bit?" and you'll see the results immediately.

Once you get beyond these basics, you have primary color correction, which is manipulation over red, green, and blue elements of the picture. In additive color mixing (light), these are your primary colors and any combination thereof can

create any color from pure black to pure white. Y...
green will do to the picture, you can simply talk in co...
example, you might say "I'd like this scene to be really w...
orange" or "I want this scene to be very cold, but more steely...
colorist work their magic.

It's a good idea to start with a defining shot for a particular sequ...
started shooting a scene with inserts or cutaways or coverage on a second...
most important shot for the scene is the close-up of the actress that happen...
tenth shot for the day. It's a good idea to start with that tenth shot, establish the...
you want for the sequence on that hero shot and then have the colorist go back and m...
the rest of the sequence to that key shot. This not only saves time—as the colorist can match...
the look quicker if they know where they're going with it—but it also sets the right tone
for the most important moments of a scene. Sometimes if you start setting the look on less
important shots, when you get to the important ones—the look you liked earlier just doesn't
work and you have to go back to the beginning, costing time and money.

The "frame store" is one of your best friends. Most color suites have a frame store option
where you can capture a single frame from a colored sequence and recall that frame later
for reference. This is used to match shots and sequences that don't sit right next to each
other on your camera rolls.

It's always best to establish your own working cadence with your colorist, but generally
it's a good idea to let them work on a shot first, let them get to a point where they've done
their technical adjustments and then start giving input. There's nothing more frustrating to
a colorist than having a filmmaker over your shoulder saying "No, no, that's too bright, that's
not what I want" when the colorist is actually setting a range for the whites and has no
intention of keeping it there, you're just speaking too soon. If you're not comfortable with
your cadence yet, simply tell the colorist your general idea for the scene then tell them "you
go ahead and work and let me know when you're ready for comments." They will appreciate
that more than I can explain.

Many digital shooters don't feel color correction is a necessary step, but that's a mistake.
Color correction, at its most basic technical application, can elevate the consistency and
professionalism of your image to a whole new level. Working with a talented colorist and
allowing them the creative input to help improve your image can elevate the final result
well beyond your imagination.

ou don't always have to know what a little
onceptual terms with your colorist. For
arm, but more yellow warm than
than deep blue" and let your

ence. You may have
ary actor, but the
ed to be the
look that
atch

Raising the Roof: How to Build a Flat

Carpentry isn't typically something I discuss here, but this is a skill that has come in handy on a number of occasions. Back in my theater days, I learned a number of great skills that I still carry with me today—and some of that is basic carpentry, specifically how to build a "TV" flat. These are the basic walls used in sets on nearly every TV and movie set ever built. They're lightweight, simple to construct, easily locked together with other flats and fairly easily transported or stored (I've currently got three in my garage).

To build a flat you'll need:

One 4' × 8' sheet of ¼" luan
Three 8' long 1" × 3" lumber
One 4' long 1" × 3" lumber
One box of 1¼" drywall screws
One drill with Phillips screwdriver bit
One tape measure (at least 8' long)
One bottle of wood glue
One pencil
One saw (skill, crosscut, band, back, etc.
   Something to cut/chop the 1' × 3's)

Alternately, if you have a pneumatic stapler you can build the flats with 1¼" staples, but if you have fancy tools like that at your disposal, you probably already know how to build a flat!

The flat has four major components: stiles, rails, spreader, and face.

Construction of the flat isn't difficult, but a few tips can help construction and handling easier. You'll basically be building a frame and then covering that frame with a face.

Step 1

We start with the first piece of 8' long 1 × 3 and cut that exactly in half so you have two 4' long pieces. These will become our rails, or the top and bottom of the flat. Rail is a clue—you want to be able to slide the flat across the floor, so the top and bottom should overlap the sides to make rails (like a train track).

If the sides overlapped the top and bottom, then when you slid the flat on the floor, it would be easy to split the seam connection and break the flat apart.

Step 2

1 × 3 isn't exactly 1″ by 3″, but it's close. Since we want to create a frame that is as close to 4' wide by 8' tall, and the rails will overlap the stiles (sides), we need to subtract the thickness of the rails from the length of the stiles. You'll be taking two of your other 8' long 1 × 3s and cutting 2″ off one end of each board to make two boards at 7' 10″ long.

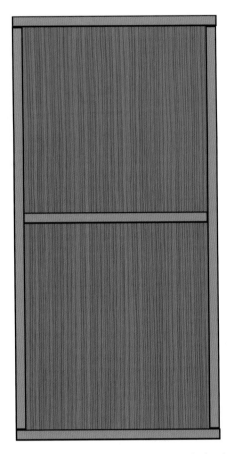

The back of a TV flat, showing the frame consisting of rails, stiles and a spreader.

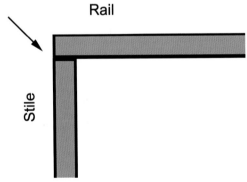

The corner of the frame of a TV flat. Notice that the rails (top and bottom portions) overlap the stiles (sides).

Step 3

On the final piece of 4′ 1 × 3 you're going to cut 2″ off one end to make a piece that is 3′ 10″ long. Set this aside for later.

Step 4

Now we'll start to build the frame. Take one of the 4′ long sections (careful to make sure it's actually 4′ long and not the 3′ 10″ section!) and one of your 7′ 10″ stiles. We're going to turn them on their long side, so the 1″ side is flat on the ground and they are standing 3″ tall. Put a line of wood glue on the tip of the stile and drive two screws into the stile from the outside of the rail. It's important to use two screws (or the stile may turn on you when you're handling it). You have to be careful not to split the wood—so you want the screw to be ¾″ from the top and bottom of the rail and ½″ from the outer edge. Screw down slowly and just enough to slightly bury the screw head into the face of the rail.

Step 5

Doing the same thing as step 4, secure the second stile to the other side of the rail.

Step 6

Now secure the other rail to the other end of both stiles. Don't forget the line of wood glue and wipe off the excess with a paper towel.

Carefully drive drywall screws into the wood, being careful not to split the wood.

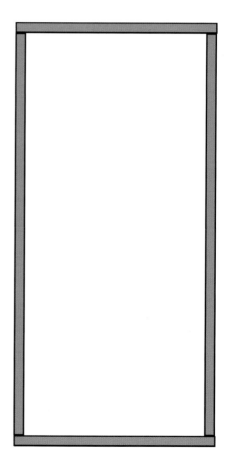

The finished outer frame.

Step 7

Drop the 3' 10" piece of 1 × 3 into the middle of the stiles, equally spaced away from each rail (dead center of the flat frame). Screw in two screws from the outside stile into the spreader from each side. This is your "spreader" it's meant to give structure to the frame.

Step 8

Run a line of wood glue all along the top of the stiles, rails and spreader. It doesn't need to be a lot—just a long bead of glue.

Step 9

Carefully—with the help of another person —align one edge of the 4' by 8' sheet of ¼" luan to one end of the frame and slowly lower it down onto the frame. Square up the edges to make it neat.

Step 10

Starting at one corner, begin to drive the screws from the face of the luan into the 1 × 3 below. You want the screws to be ½" from

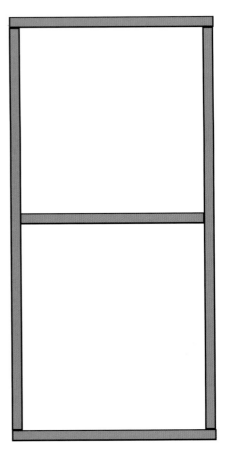

Adding the spreader to the middle of the frame to give it more structure.

the edge of the luan and place them about 4" apart from each other. As you secure the luan to the frame, continually check that the face is squarely aligned with the frame, adjusting the frame below, as necessary.

That's it! Stand her up and you've got your first TV flat! This can be easily joined to other flats to create walls.

The back of several TV flats attached together.

The set for my film, *Wall*, several very tall TV flats pieced together.

Carpentry Skills Save the Day

The carpentry skills I learned in the theater and, later, on my first short film, came in handy years later when cinematographer Christopher Probst and I were collaborating on a spec commercial. The gig was very impromptu, Chris called me in the early afternoon telling me that he had a film camera that night and he wanted to shoot something. Within less than six hours, we had a concept, a cast, a location, a crew, lighting and grip gear, film, and we were ready to roll! We shot a spec commercial (a fake commercial done on "speculation" to demonstrate your skills in the hopes of landing a real job) for Sharpie permanent markers in a pool hall/bar in four short hours and had a blast. Later, in editing, I realized that I was missing two really important shots to really tell the story correctly and Chris and I decided to do a pickup shoot to get those two shots. We went back to the location, but they were now asking $3,000 as a location fee—a price we certainly couldn't dream of affording. It almost seemed like a lost cause until I looked at the footage and said, "We can do this." We went to the home improvement store, bought some lumber, built a flat and painted it to match the wall behind the bar. We propped up some more lumber to fake a bar top, decorated it with empty glasses and bottles and shot the two missing shots in a garage. The two shots intercut seamlessly with the commercial and we did it for $50 in supplies. These odd skills do come in handy in the independent do-it-yourself world!

If you'd like to see this spec commercial, visit http://youtu.be/UsMni6NrY9Y.

To Film School or Not to Film School?

Over the years I've had several hundred aspiring filmmakers approach me, mostly online, seeking advice on how to break into the industry. The overwhelming majority of them want to know: should I go to film school?

The answer to this question is one of the most controversial topics in the film business with fervent supporters on both sides of the debate. In truth, the answer is that attending or not attending film school is a personal decision that no one can make for you. *You* need to determine what the best course of action is for you. A harsh reality of the film business is that there is no specific path to success. There's no ten-step (or 20-step or even 100-step) approach to guarantee your career. Each and every person in the business has to follow their own career trail. Some are lucky enough to stumble into the business, or start in Hollywood right after high school in entry-level positions; some attend less prominent film schools; some are graduates of the prestigious schools; some tried film school, but never graduated.

PROBLEMS WITH FILM SCHOOL

Personally, I am firmly in the anti-film school camp—for several reasons. Two biggest are:

a) Film school is extraordinarily expensive.
b) Most film schools don't teach you what you really need to know.

All higher education is expensive, without a doubt, but most trades, industries, and professions reward the expense and effort of higher education with the possibility of better salaries and better career potentials than they would have been able to achieve without the higher degrees. The motion picture industry, unfortunately, is incapable of caring less whether you have a degree or not. No one looks at a résumé and examines your education. In fact, in most below-the-line positions, a film school degree can be a liability to getting work. It's a bit of a cliché (although, as all clichés, it's based on a long history of truth) that film school graduates are generally know-it-alls who really *don't*. For the working professional, that can be very frustrating. The last thing you want is a production assistant on set who feels they can direct (or write, produce, shoot) better than you. This attitude is hard to defeat as many film schools, by design, instill their graduates with a kind of swaggering self-confidence— a degree that shows they know what they're talking about, but the reality is that the education most often received from a school rarely prepares you for real-world work.

Although an institution may vaguely reassure their student body that they can assist with job placement in the industry—believe them not, fellow filmies. No college can guarantee any form of placement in a creative field; it simply doesn't work that way. At best, your alma mater can set you up as a production assistant or with an internship in a selected discipline paying barely minimum wage for the length of a single project (from a single day to six months on average). People don't generally go to college to become PAs and interns, they go to college to become writers, directors, producers, and stars. Some might go for a more specialized trade such as cinematography, music composition, wardrobe design, production design, sound design . . . but the reality is, no matter where you graduate from, you'd better be prepared for five to ten years of scrambling, scratching, and scrounging for work—at the very least. In those five to ten years of scrounging, what do you have to show for your grand education? A humongous debt! A King Kong of fiscal responsibility saddled firmly on your shoulders, the likes of which forces most film school graduates to take full-time jobs *outside* the film business just to pay their bills. If you're paying more for your education than you can comfortably pay for a car then you're paying too much, in my opinion.

On the second note, most "film schools" don't teach you what you need to know. The harsh reality is that so many people *want* to be in the film business that film education is big business. Any major college that doesn't have a film department is simply losing money. So what do they do? They quickly create a "film degree" and—being an institution of higher learning—they shoehorn a film "education" into a pre-made academic mold just as they would a law, mathematics, chemistry, or business degree. They balance out categories of classes and credits exactly the same as they would for any other major, but the film industry isn't law or chemistry, it's a creative business and it works *very* differently from most industries. The education necessary cannot simply be shoehorned into an 18-credit semester.

ARE YOU SELF-DISCIPLINED?

So what do you do? Just jump in, drive to Hollywood and suddenly you're a big director?
  No.

  The bottom line is you need an education in the art and science of filmmaking, no matter
what your chosen discipline. However, my stance is that you *don't* necessarily have to learn
those ins and outs from a formal institution. If you're a self-starter, you can learn on your
own. If you're dedicated, motivated, and focused, then there are resources galore to give
you the solid education in film that you desire.

  People to whom I have recommended skipping film school are self-starters that already
know exactly what they want to do in the business: director, producer, writer, etc. Many
young filmmakers are so used to doing everything themselves—or foolishly think they can
even without trying—that they feel they can continue doing so professionally. The reality
is that the business revolves around talented experts who specialize in a specific trade.
Although there are hyphenates in the film industry (people who do more than one job), it
is extremely rare to be successful as an early hyphenate. You're much better off picking one
trade, pursuing that and diversifying later, if you so desire.

READ, READ, READ

With your mind firmly set on your future profession—start with books. There are myriad
books on every aspect of the film industry and I suggest starting with three basic books.
Get three that cover the same territory (read through the tables of contents and compare
before you buy). Choose one book as your first and read through it from cover-to-cover.
Take notes. *Seriously*. Keep a journal every day as you read through the book and jot down
the ideas expressed in each chapter. Try to expand on the concepts discussed and test the
ideas with your own practical examples. For instance, if you're reading a book about
screenwriting and the chapter discusses character histories—then write a history for a
character in a script you're planning to write. Work along with the book.

  If you come to a passage or concept in the book that just doesn't make sense, open the
second book, find the section of that book that discusses the same topic and read that. If
it still doesn't make sense, go to the third book and do the same. Nine times out of ten,
between the three separate authors discussing the same topic, the subject will become clear
to you. If it still isn't clear, you can turn to the Internet. Nearly every discipline now has a
forum and online society dedicated to it—and answers can be found to nearly all of your
questions. The more educated and literate you are on the question you're trying to ask, the
better responses you'll get from forums. Asking "What is an *f*-stop" in a cinematography

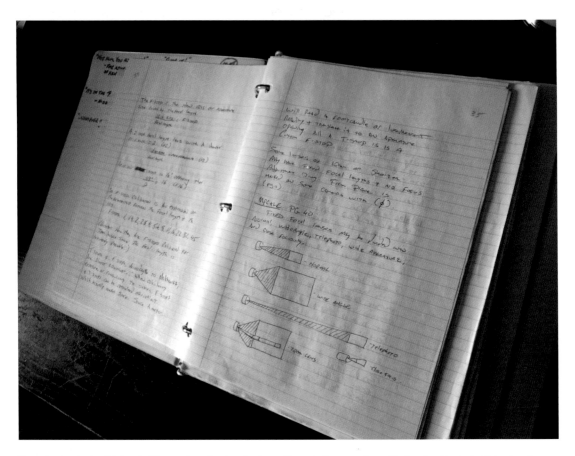

Please forgive the horrible handwriting—a shot of my learning journal from the first year of my self-education. I took plentiful notes of everything I learned.

forum is likely to invoke snarky responses like "Google it!" but asking "Why would I want to shoot a scene at f/5.6 to get better blacks?" should elicit much more detailed and thoughtful responses. When you have a clear understanding of the previously confusing or vague topic, return to the first book and continue reading. Be sure to journal your findings.

When you finish the first book, read the second book cover-to-cover and repeat the same procedure by referencing the third (and re-referencing the first book) if you get confused. By the time you get to the third book, it's your choice to read cover-to-cover (never a bad idea) or skim through the chapters to glean new information or new insight. It's also never a bad idea to re-read the first book when you're done with the third, you'll be surprised how much more you'll often pick up on a second read with a new perspective.

In addition, Internet sites such as Lydia.com offer extraordinary training videos for specific software key to many film disciplines. Look for forums, with other people discussing your specific trade and interest—although be wary of forums, there is a *lot* of misinformation and unqualified "experts" who *think* they know what they're talking about—but don't (see this book's introduction for a story of a precocious young tyke offering advice and filmmaking answers on the Prodigy network). There is a wealth of information out there to be had. Google is your friend, my fellow filmie.

MAKE YOUR OWN MOVIES?

A common suggestion that I've heard time and time again is to take the money you'd otherwise invest in a film school education and invest it into your own filmmaking. While I support this concept of get-out-and-do-it wholeheartedly, it is often unrealistic. Most people can't afford college to begin with and will need to take out heavy loans to pay for the education. Taking out heavy loans to make your own films is *not* recommended. Getting into debt is not a good way to get your education, in my opinion.

However, I do *highly* recommend making your own films—as many as you can: shorts, music videos, commercials, and features (if you can) to gain experience before you try to make it in Hollywood.

The best investment you can make in your career, and the best place to invest your money (besides building your library) is to get the tools of your given trade and to study/experience that trade before you try to make a professional go of it. If you're planning on becoming a screenwriter, you need your script formatting software and you need to *read* scripts. If you haven't read *at least* 200 screenplays, you haven't even started your homework yet. Many of the scripts to your favorite movies are available, for free, online. In addition, you should write at least ten feature scripts before you attempt to get one made or sold. The experience you gain from this process will be invaluable. If you want to be a cinematographer, you need a camera. You need to shoot. Want to design wardrobe? Get a sewing machine. Tools of the trade are important.

STILL GOING?

If you *do* decide to go to a film school, if you decide that you're not enough of a self-starter to make a go on your own or that you personally need the degree or formal structure, then it's best to pick a school in a major metropolitan city with a very strong film production community: Los Angeles, New York, Chicago, Austin, etc. I recommend finding a smaller college within those areas with *active* film programs. Study the faculty résumés—have they been or are they still active professionals? What kind of equipment resources does the school have? Can they provide you with access to tools that you cannot otherwise provide for yourself?

Once you're in school, it's your job to educate yourself. I'm going to repeat that, because it's of paramount importance: *it's your job to educate yourself*. Do not expect the school to give you an education—you have to work for it. Utilize the school's resources as often as you possibly can. Read on your own. Read ahead in the class textbooks. Ask the teachers/professors educated questions. You need to take an active role in your education whether you're in a formal setting or not. Participate in as many productions as humanly possible—in and out of school. Nothing can beat actual practical filmmaking experience. The three best things that you can get out of any film school are: connections with fellow students who may become your best allies in the "real world"; access to professional equipment and resources you cannot otherwise afford; access and networking with working professionals (affiliated with, or alumni of, the college).

BOTTOM LINE

You simply cannot make it in Hollywood without a solid clue of what you're doing, but just like the multitude of paths to filmmaking success, there is no one way to achieve that education.

See the appendix of this book for some additional book recommendations.

Learning From Mistakes: Block, Light, Rehearse, Shoot

Excuse me for a moment while I adjust my soapbox here . . . there, that's better—the view from up here is pretty nice. I feel justified in standing here. Even though I'm about to proselytize to y'all, I'm *really* about to lecture my own self. I should be so wise as to follow my own advice. So, bear with me, and we can both learn from my mistakes.

As a cameraman I used to preach to directors the mantra of "block, light, rehearse, shoot." If you've worked narrative productions, chances are you've lived this mantra (or you *should have*). It's a simple philosophy: block your scene with your actors, send them away to makeup and wardrobe or their trailers or the craft service table—anywhere but the set to give your cinematographer time to light the scene. Then bring the actors back, rehearse the scene and tweak the lighting, rehearse the camera, refine the whole shebang and then shoot.

It's really a tried-and-true methodology of production and it used to kill me when directors would try to shortcut this process.

"Can we block this scene?" I would ask with hope in my heart.

"Oh they're just going to be standing here and then they'll move here and that's it," the cavalier director would respond. "Pretty simple."

No.

Let's bring in the actors, let them do it, do the *whole* scene—not just what we're shooting today—and we're going to learn a phenomenal amount from this experience. We're going to be able to see problems before they happen; we're going to be able to make sure that we refine our plan of action for covering this scene. We don't just want to see the small portion of the scene we're shooting today—because seeing the whole scene might allow us to refine the schedule. I've saved productions a lot of money with this methodology by being able to refine the coverage and approach to a scene by knowing what we're going to be shooting in intimate detail.

Having the actors there, blocking out the scene with the director, new things are discovered. Suggestions are made. New directions chosen. In their head, the director might have visualized the scene one way, but when the actors start to perform it—it just feels *right* if they do it *this way*, which completely changes the initial plan. If we make this change *before* the lighting crew and art department has come in and made the world perfect for the *first* plan—we can save ourselves a lot of time and hassle and, sometimes more importantly, money.

It all makes sense, right?

Except when you forget to follow your own advice.

Recently I was hired by a lovely Dutch actress, Shanice Kamminga, to direct a short film she had written to showcase her

On the set of my film *The Night Before*. Photo by James Cole.

On the set of the short film *If* with cinematographer Jon Mahoney and writer/star Shanice Kamminga. If © Black Drone Media. Photo by Constance Abram.

performance abilities. It's a sweet little intimate love story that mostly takes place in a single location of a living room. It's a simple story and my coverage plan was simple. I had to laugh when the producer, good-hearted Devin Goodsell, asked me if I was going to storyboard the film.

"No, no. That's not necessary here. This will be pretty straightforward."

And it was.

As is my usual methodology, I line my script and create a shot list which is just a general plan for how I'll approach the film. I usually do my homework in detail and then allow myself the freedom to throw that all out when something organic and better happens on set. In this case, I shot-listed ⅚ of the script—all but the final scene, which felt a little convoluted to me. It takes place at the door to the character's home, but the character motivations for the blocking, as it was written, were a little fuzzy and I felt I would block this scene on-set and feel it out with the actors.

We shot the film, more or less, in order—both for simplicity and for integrity of the actor's performances. After spending a day working our way through coverage around the living room with my cinematographer, Jon Mahoney, doing a fantastic job, we finally came to the last scene, which was supposed to move the actors to the door. As we started to put the scene "on its feet" and block it out, my initial feelings were proved right: the motivations for the actors moving weren't working. We spent a good 15 minutes discussing and working out the scene and in the end we decided to shoot this final scene in the same living room. Even better—it allowed me to have a visual bookend to the short where the opening and closing images were very similar, strengthening the visual narrative.

This meant, however, that we were returning to the exact same setups that we started the day with. The *exact* same setups.

My stomach tightened. I'm not afraid to

Directing writer/actress Shanice Kamminga on the set of *If.* © Black Drone Media. Photo by Constance Abram.

Directing on the set of *If* with actress Shanice Kamminga. If © Black Drone Media. Photo by Constance Abram.

admit I had a little self-loathing going on. As a cinematographer, I would have grumbled a bit and chastised a director for making such a foolish and inefficient mistake.

"If you had listened to me and we blocked this whole scene earlier, we could have avoided this!"

It wasn't done for performance, it wasn't done for logistics—it was simply an oversight. If I had followed the mantra (block, light, rehearse, shoot; block, light, rehearse, shoot)—we would have blocked out this scene in the morning and realized that we could combine coverage to get it shot while we were shooting the top of the film.

It was a mistake that cost us time—the most precious commodity. It caused Jon and his crew to redo the work they had done in the morning. It caused Nate Brunel, our production designer, to have to rebuild the set and set dressing the way we started. There's no way to get around the feeling of walking in circles and making no progress when you have to do this. Sometimes there's no way to avoid the situation—you simply have to return to a previous setup for other reasons, but I was upset with myself that it was *my* fault we were returning.

So—there's the diatribe, dear readers: follow my advice (even if I don't)—learn the mantra. Live the mantra. Block, light, rehearse, shoot.

I'm Captain Kirk! Musings on the Role of the Director

Concentrating on the set of *The Event Premiere* on Universal's UVS-1 stage. Photo by Otto Kitsinger.

Contrary to what the headline might have you believe, I am neither delusional nor a Trekkie (or Trekkor). I've never really been much of a *Star Trek* fan. In fact, I'm in the opposite camp: I've always been a *Star Wars* fan. For those of you not familiar with the ageless feud between geeks—we reside on separate sides of the playground and jeer at each other over our lightsabers and phasers from different universes.

However, I have often used the example of Captain Kirk in discussions with film students and film outsiders as the perfect example of what a director is.

In the motion picture industry, since the dissolution of the "studio system" (and a bit before), the director is king. A producer may be the one to call the ultimate shots, as they're usually the one holding the purse-strings, but a good producer

Giving direction, shaping the project. Photo by Otto Kitsinger.

knows to let a good director do their job and when it comes to creative decisions in preproduction, production, or postproduction—the director's word is god.

This is the way it should be. This month, I'm going to discuss the roles of the director and the way the director integrates into various stages of production and relates with various members of his or her crew.

I use Captain Kirk as an example because he represents the epitome of what a director should be in a number of aspects—and nearly everyone has seen at least one *Star Trek* episode or movie and can relate. One can argue that many of the gazillion other ship leaders in the *Star Trek* spin-offs could also fall under this category, but most are less known and ubiquitous in the public consciousness than Kirk.

First: Captain Kirk is a charismatic man. He is likable, amiable, and personable. He gets along with a great variety of people from the lowest ranked member of his crew to weirdo alien people from some bizarre planet (that looks remarkably like a vacant lot behind a Walgreens in Burbank). He is, most of all, respected. His crew has the utmost respect for Kirk and they would willingly lay down their lives for him (especially those poor dweebs in the red shirts) in a heartbeat. The respect for Kirk leads to loyalty from his crew. They would, quite literally, follow him to the far reaches of the galaxy.

Second: Kirk is not a dictator, by any means, but he is decisive and he is bold. When decisions are to be made, Kirk is the man to make them—no matter how difficult that decision may be. He thinks outside the box, but he's always got the *Enterprise*'s best interest at heart and can see the grander mission quite clearly.

Third: Kirk is knowledgeable in all areas of the ship. He is not an engineer, doctor, scientist, pilot, or communications expert, but he understands their jobs quite well. He works with the best in their fields (Spock, Scotty, Bones, et al.) and allows them to do their jobs, but he knows enough about all of their jobs to be able to troubleshoot with them in a time of crisis. Kirk may not know the specific wiring schematic for the Dilithium Crystal generator on the *Enterprise*, but he knows Crystal theory, wiring theory and when the "fit hits the shan," he can suggest an uncoupling of the third cluster and combining that with the first (real *Trek* fans are, of course, cringing in their skins right now as I completely slaughter the language and terminology). Scotty, a bodiless voice from deep in the bowls of the ship's engine room, responds with "That's dangerous, Captain, *but it just might work!*" Kirk knows enough about everyone's job to be creative and offer solutions in troubled times—but he allows the experts to do their jobs and merely, ahem, *directs* from the helm.

Fourth: Kirk is on top of every department. All decisions funnel through Kirk. The *Enterprise*, like a film set, has a very military-like chain of command with a very clear hierarchy—but Kirk has the ultimate say on all matters.

These four Kirk-ian traits are exactly what it takes to be a good director:

- Mutual respect; respect the people working for you, and, in turn, they respect you.
- Bold, authoritative decisions in a non-dictator fashion.
- A clear understanding of the jobs/tasks of all those working for you to be able to troubleshoot with them.
- Being on top of the big picture, but still clear enough to oversee the tiniest detail.

DIRECTOR RELATIONSHIPS

Director and Producer

Perhaps the hardest to pin down is the first relationship on most projects, the producer/director relationship. Many directors are also their own producers, which is a smart idea, as it maintains creative and administrative control over the project. In a traditional workflow, an executive producer will acquire a project and hire a director. The executive producer oversees the entire production, but leaves the creative decisions to the director—hence why the director was hired in the first place. A director doesn't just call "action" and "cut"—they bring their own style, vision and perspective into every project. Each director will create a different project, execute a different vision. That vision, although it involves many players, is ultimately the *director*'s sole vision. There are some producers, such as Jerry Bruckheimer, who are very involved with day-to-day decisions and oversee the production very closely—

but these producers are a dying breed. This is a holdover from the old studio system when many directors were merely guns-for-hire. Today, the director is the driving creative force on the set and most producers handle the business side in support of a director and keep the director moving on time and on budget.

Director and Production Designer

Generally speaking, the second to be hired, on most large budget productions, is the production designer. This is purely a time-management decision as the designer needs time to create set designs, find the locations (with the location manager), and build any sets. This means the production designer, generally, has the most prep of any of the creative heads (with the exception, of course, of the writer, to be discussed later).

The creation of the sets, choosing of locations, and intended dressing/finishing of all shooting locations (whether practical or set) all fall under the direction of the director.

When interpreting the script, the director begins to visualize the movements (blocking) of the actors and camera throughout a location—be that the middle of the woods or a mansion in Beverly Hills or a prison in Dubai. The production designer's job is to provide a location that serves the director's needs and vision.

Director and Cinematographer

This is arguably one of the most important relationships on a film production. Without the camera, hence without the cinematographer, there is no movie. Without the camera, it is radio or live theater—the camera is what differentiates movies from any other art form. Everything that ends up on the screen—with the exception of completely computer-generated sequences—passed through the lens of a camera (and even most computer-generated sequences follow the physics of the camera). The cinematographer or director of photography is, traditionally, next to be hired.

The cinematographer's job is to visually represent the director's

Director Jamie Neese (right), myself, and co-cinematographer Jayson Crothers watch a rehearsal of a scene while shooting *2 Million Stupid Women*. Photo by Shannon Lee.

vision. This involves careful control over lens selection, lighting, exposure, composition, camera movement, and image manipulation. Some directors are very visual and will dictate precise camera placement, movement, composition, lens choices, and (rarely) specific lighting. Some directors are very actor-focused and leave the visual aspect up to the cinematographer. Either way, it's the cinematographer's job to bring the director's vision to life on the screen.

Director and Costume Designer

The clothes make the (wo)man. Wardrobe is key to identifying character and getting the right wardrobe for each character, whether that is custom-created or bought off the rack, is always a challenge and extremely important. The director works with the costume designer to define the looks for each character; their style and what their clothes say about them. You don't just throw an actor in jeans and a T-shirt—the colors, cuts, and fits of the jeans and T-shirt are crucial to that character and how they are perceived by the audience. It's up to the director to make sure each character is perfectly represented by the costume designer's choices.

Director and Actor

The classic relationship. In the theater, an actor rehearses a play with a director for weeks, or even months, before performing it for a live audience. The nuances of the character and the story can be meticulously crafted and explored and are presented within a linear time line during the course of the play from beginning to end.

Working with young actor Lucas Riney on the set of *The Night Before*. Photo by James Cole. The Night Before © Adakin Productions.

In a film, there is rarely time for extended rehearsals and as films are mostly shot out of continuity, the task of the director is to keep the actor focused on where they are at any given moment in the film. In the morning they may be shooting a scene from the end of the film and in the afternoon they're shooting a scene from the middle, then after lunch they're shooting part of a scene that happened just before the last and part of a scene that happens at the very end of the film. It's a confusing puzzle and the director needs to know not only how that actor's performance in one scene will cut with the performance in the scene immediately before and after it but how their performance is working for the entire arc of the film. Is this actor hitting the right "notes" in their performance at this given moment?

Further, the director needs to make sure that all actors are working towards a common goal and refine their performances so that—in the end—they're all in the same film.

Many years ago, in my theater experience, I was working as a master flyman in a professional roadhouse in Phoenix, Arizona. I had the chance to do two shows back-to-back. Both were five-character shows with limited sets and both shows had five fantastic actors in them—not a weak member of the cast. One show had an incredible director and one show had a very green, very distracted and very bad director. I'll never forget the lesson I learned in those few weeks watching those two shows. The show with the good director was a solid, cohesive, and incredibly effective show. The show with the bad director was a mess. The five great actors might as well have been doing five completely different shows. None of that show "gelled" and everyone had a sense of aimlessness, from the actors to the crew. It's the director that holds it all together and keeps everyone focused on the right goal—that particular director's vision.

This past summer when I was invited to visit the Sundance Director's Program and take a look inside an industry staple, they showed me a series of short films that each director makes during their first week in the program. Each director—every year—is given exactly the same script. They're assigned actors and they go shoot their scene. Every scene comes out completely different—and I got to see half a dozen examples while I was there. Each director brings their own interpretation to that script and they lead the cast and crew along the path to get their vision on the screen. That's what a director does. Many film schools do this same exercise and the results are always enlightening.

Director and Editor

This is where the rubber meets the road. Up until now, the movie is nothing more than fragments—pieces of a puzzle. It is up to the editor and director to piece this puzzle together to form a whole picture. Often the picture is much different from what was originally planned. Often the editor's work refines the story, characters and events to tell the best version of the story possible. The director works side-by-side with the editor, overseeing every detail, every moment, and refining the representation of their vision. Many times, new scenes are created or scenes that were shot are re-ordered to form new story elements. Dialogue is deleted or added and the film begins to take on its final form.

Director and Sound

I incorporate sound as one category here as it's difficult to easily differentiate all of the elements of sound artists who work on a film from location mixers to editors to Foley artists to loop/ADR artists or post mixers . . . there is a long team of experts who craft the sound of a film—and sound (as much as it is difficult for a former cinematographer to admit) is a major portion of the experience of the movies. Most audience members are more sensitive to sound anomalies than picture anomalies. The director works closely with all these sound artists to craft the sound

A shot of the sound mix session for my film *Alone* on stage A at Anarchy Post.

experience of the film. Every nuance, every breath, every footstep falls under the final discretion of the director.

Director and Composer

Like so many other elements I've spoken of, music is imperative to the film experience. A score is like a musical actor combined with a lyrical script—to craft and refine the story presentation and audience experience. The director works intimately with the composer to craft a perfect score that supports the final version of the film.

Director and Writer

Notice that I've held off on this category until the end. It's one of the most crucial relationships in crafting a film. Although films are a director's medium, the film lives and breathes—without a doubt—based on the script. The script—the story, characters, plot, dialogue—defines the film. The script sets the grounds for everything that comes next. However, in Hollywood, the script is rarely the result of a single writer's words. More than likely it is an amalgamation of many different writers, each who add their own two-cents on the original script (or the previous draft thereof). In a perfect system, however, the film has one writer, one voice who can work with the director. When a director comes on to a project, either finding a script themselves or being hired by a producer who has a script, the director's first job is to work with the writer to *develop* that story specifically to suit the director's vision and interpretation of that script. Already, at this stage, any director is refining the screenplay and honing it toward the big picture that director has in their mind.

That's an important note. This relationship is one of the most controversial in Hollywood as many writers feel that they, as the originators of the material, have an "authorship" over the final film. For many years in Hollywood, the "possessory" credit: *Alfred Hitchcock's Psycho* or *Martin Scorsese's Mean Streets* has been the source of heated, passionate debate between the writers and directors. This debate has received a lot of press in the last few years, but it is far from new.

Posing for a moment with James Cole, writer of *The Night Before*. We collaborated on developing two feature projects as well.

Many writers find this practice to be appalling. They feel it is belittling to their contributions as "authors" of a screenplay—the main source of the entire film.

The reality, however, is that the screenplay is just one part of a larger whole. The script, like so many other elements, is molded, crafted, formed, edited, and rewritten under the director's discretion to suit their vision of the film. Some people refer to a script as a blueprint, but it is more often than not a mere outline. A pencil sketch of what the final "building" will look like. In rare cases the original script survives the final stage unscathed—in fact, in my 21 years as a professional in this business, I have never known a single example of a perfect script that was made into a completed film and was completed exactly the way it was written.

It is the director's job to interpret that writer's work and bring it to life on the screen. Even if the writer's work is wholly original and the work of a single author (not based on any pre-existing material and not co-written by any other hand), it is still just *one* element in the otherwise finished film and the writer is *only* involved with that one element. The writer does not oversee the actors, cinematographer, production designer, wardrobe, sound, editor, composer . . . only the director follows the film through every step to oversee every detail and keep everyone on the same page.

Although a movie is the result of many, many expert craftspeople and artists who contribute their blood, sweat and tears to making a film—it is, primarily, the work of *one* person that brings all these people together for the common goal and directs them all toward the right path. In very rare instances, a film is directed by a team of two people (the

Coen brothers, Wachowski siblings, and Polish brothers are rare exceptions). This is rarely successful, however, by the very nature of the job. Just like my experience in the theater, without a single, strong voice—things get muddled. The teams who can pull off this one job are very close people who, in essence, can become one voice. Just as the example of the Sundance Director's Lab, each director will make a completely different film out of the exact same script. It is ultimately the director's decisions that shape the movie the audience will see.

At the end of the day, just as Captain Kirk is responsible for the lives and well being of every crewmember aboard his ship, as well as being responsible for achieving the overall mission goals, it is the director who is responsible for every detail of a film—every choice. After all, the *Enterprise* belongs to only one Captain (ahem, at a time, thank you Trekkers who started squirming again . . .), even though it is really the Federation's ship (producer) and it can't run without Scotty (writer) or Spock (cinematographer), Uhura (sound), Chekov (actor), or Bones (and the rest . . .) and the film belongs to only one artist—the director.

In 1966, the Writer's Guild of America, West, made a secret agreement with the Association of Motion Picture and Television Producers on a contract that states no artist, other than the writer, may take a "possessory" credit. Just a few short weeks later, the directors find out about this secret contract and a battle begins. A year later, with no adequate resolution having been met, the directors advise all their members to not work until the DGA contract expires in April. Just before a strike in April, the AMPTP announces a new contract that offers all directors the right to negotiate a possessory credit. This credit, however, didn't start in the 1960s, in fact it harkens back to 1915 when D.W. Griffith first put a possessory credit on *Birth of a Nation*. Between Griffith and the 1966 DGA contract, filmmakers like Alfred Hitchcock, David Lean, and Frank Capra, among many others, have used the possessory or "above the title" credit.

In 1981, in an effort to thwart excessive possessory credits on advertisements, the AMPTP and DGA agree that no "above the title" credit shall be afforded on any advertisement with more than six personal credits. Instead, the director would be afforded an "A Film By" credit. Since then, this new form of the possessory credit has been afforded to many directors—and the controversy reigns.

Great Relationships: Jack Green, ASC, Clint Eastwood, Bruce Surtees, and Joe Dieves

This was part of a series of small articles that ran in the September 1998 issue of American Cinematographer *spotlighting several great teams in film history. I include it here because I find great inspiration from this story and wish that more people would follow Dieves, Surtees, and Green's lead in helping others to progress in this business.*

A screen capture from one of Jack Green, ASC, and Clint Eastwood's collaborations, *Unforgiven.* © Warner Bros.

Jack N. Green is the cinematographer behind *Midnight in the Garden of Good and Evil*, *Serenity*, *The 40 Year-Old Virgin* and he was nominated for the Academy Award for *Unforgiven*.

Few professionals have had the extraordinary opportunity to work under two mentors who guided and shaped their future. Director of photography Jack Green has had the good fortune in that regard.

The son of a barber, Green was schooled and employed in the family business long before dreams of a profession behind the lens entered his mind. His father dabbled in photography, however, and maintained his own darkroom. He introduced young Jack to the enticement of images at a fairly early age. "Once I was old enough," recalls Green, "my father would allow me into his darkroom to watch. He built a little contact printer for me out of wood, a light bulb and opalized glass, and I'd make my own contact prints and do my own developing. I did this many times over the years, and as a result I have this wonderful affinity for the smell of chemicals and darkroom equipment."

Green's fascination with photography wasn't strong enough to keep him from taking a job cutting hair, until a repeat customer spurred his interest in moving images. "This was in the days when people came in for a haircut every two weeks or so," explains Green. "Through repeat business, I got to know a cameraman named Joe Dieves. He stopped in regularly and we would just talk images the whole time—he was just wonderful to me. At first I was just interested in what he did for a living because it involved photography, but the more we talked, the more intrigued I became. After six or eight months of cutting his hair I worked up the nerve to ask him if I could go watch him work.

"He went one better—he got me a job and asked me to come along as his assistant. The job has all of the elements that were inspiring to me—taking pictures, and the excitement of working in the movie business. After spending time standing around cutting hair, getting out to do something like that was pretty darn thrilling. I got some more jobs with Joe after that, and it was only a matter of time before I stopped being a barber.

"Joe was such a generous person. He would bring home equipment the night before a shoot, and I would go over to his family's house with my wife. They would feed us and we'd have a laughing time. After dinner he'd have all the equipment spread all over his living room floor and we would put it together. I had such a good time, I really got hooked on film. And he continued to cover my act—watching over me and seeing to it that I was always finding work, and that I was put with people who weren't afraid to instruct."

Green pursued work as an assistant on industrials, documentaries and commercials before landing a job with Wescam in Los Angeles working on the aerial unit for *Tora! Tora!*

Tora! Spending more time in the air, Gree[n] accepting more assistant jobs with such ASC ca[meramen] and Rexford Metz. The latter invited Green to wo[rk on] a film directed by Clint Eastwood. Further work with M[etz] on *Every Which Way But Loose*, also starring Eastwood. [...] *Bronco Billy*, would serve to form the foundation of an alm[ost...] the two filmmakers. Green continued working as an opera[tor] and eventually teamed up with director of photography Br[uce...] Angeles native and son of the late cinematographer Robert Su[rtees (Mutiny] *on the Bounty*—1965), the younger Surtees earned his own place in [...] Award nomination for Bob Fosse's *Lenny* in 1974. Surtees also worke[d with Gordon] Parks (*Leadbelly*) and Arthur Penn (*Night Moves*) before teaming up agai[n with Green on] *Firefox*. Previously, the duo had collaborated on eight films, including *Dirty [Harry, Play Misty* *for Me* (Eastwood's directorial debut), and *The Outlaw Josey Wales*. Surtees's e[xpert low-] key style earned him the nickname "Prince of Darkness."

"To be perfectly honest," Green confides, "at the time we did *Firefox*, Bruce just [knew] me. Clint and I had established a relationship that sort of infringed upon the trad[itional] hierarchy of the set. But Bruce and I did four pictures with Clint, and by the end of the[...] one we were really good friends. Clint, Bruce and I would discuss each setup and then dis[til] all of our ideas into the scene. When Bruce was hired to shoot *Beverly Hills Cop*, he invited me to be his operator and we commuted to work together every day.

"Bruce and I spent quite a bit of time together after that, and I went with him to his mother's house in Carmel. In one room of their home there was a display case with his father's three Oscars, and plaques for more than a dozen nominations. I stared at them in awe. I was face to face with Bob Surtees's Oscar for *Ben Hur*. Mrs. Surtees said, 'Go ahead, pick it up! It's wonderful, isn't it? Maybe you'll win one for yourself someday.' My feet didn't touch the ground for days."

Two years before Green worked with Surtees on *Beverly Hills Cop*, Eastwood had approached him with the prospect of stepping into the role of cinematographer on his film *Honkytonk Man*. Green politely declined, worrying that the promotion might damage his relationship with Surtees. But after their collaboration on *Beverly Hills Cop*, Green approached Surtees with the notion. "I told Bruce, 'You know, one of these days Clint is going to ask me to move up again, and I don't want it to affect our friendship.' He replied, 'Jack, don't let it bother you. I moved up over somebody, you're going to move up over me someday, and

his business. It would be a
riendship is all about, and

es. "I loved the minimal
leave a small footprint
ll making it dramatic.
on other projects he's
cting light. He often
urce and very little
st brilliant.
loe Dieves. I said
vered, 'The best
back.'
ge] whenever
nething back
reaching has its own
am also able to get so much out

toiled for a while with Tyler Systems before
eramen as Donald Morgan, Michael Watkins,
k as a B-camera operator on The Gauntlet,
etz led Green to the A-camera operating
Green's next foray with Eastwood, on
st symbiotic relationship between
or on most of Eastwood's films,
ce Surtees on Firefox. A Los
tees, ASC (Ben Hur, Mutiny
history with an Academy
with directors Gordon
with Eastwood on
Harry, Play Misty
extremely low-

didn't like
ditional
last
ll

Glossary

2:3 pulldown—name for the process of transferring 24 frames per second film to 30 frames per second video. A cadence of one film frame for two fields followed by one film frame for three fields expands the speed from 24 to 30.

216—Lee's number designation for "Full Tough White" diffusion, an opaque white gel. The number has been adopted by several other manufacturers.

250—Lee's number designation for "Half Tough White" diffusion, having half the opacity of 216, therefore half the diffusion properties. The number has been adopted by several other manufacturers.

3-chip—(3-Sensor, 3-CCD, 3-MOS, tristimulus) designation for a camera that features three sensors, one that collects red light information, one that collects blue and one that collects green.

Achromat—a second optical element in a lens designed to counteract chromatic aberration; a lens with multiple elements that eliminate chromatic aberration.

ADR—automatic dialogue replacement, the process of replacing an actor's dialogue after the fact in the studio.

Algorithm—a set of steps or computations that are required to calculate a mathematical formula.

Ampere (amps, amperage)—a measurement of the number of electrons passing a given point in a given period of time, represented mathematically by the abbreviation "I" (*intensity*).

Analog to digital converter—the component of a digital camera that translates electrical impulses sent from sensor photosites into digital bits.

Anamorphic—a photographic process whereby a cylindrical element within a specialty lens distorts the image to capture twice the horizontal width of a normal lens. An equal cylindrical element is in the projection lens to unsqueeze the image and project a very wide picture.

Antialiasing—a digital filtration process to combat the aliasing (artifacting by the nature of isotropic or linear sampling; creating curves and diagonal lines from squares) associated with digital sampling.

Aperture—the iris of a camera, most often within the lens, that restricts the amount of light passing through the lens to the sensor. See **f-stop**, **T-stop**.

Artifacting—image degradation, anomalies, generally as a result of digital sampling or image compression errors.

ASC—the American Society of Cinematographers, one of the oldest trade organizations in the motion picture industry. Formed in 1919, the ASC is an invitation-only membership of cinematographers who represent the best of the best in television and movies.

Aspect ratio—mathematical representation of the width to the height of a picture. Common ratios are 1.33:1 (4:3), 1.44:1, 1.66:1, 1.78:1 (16:9), 1.85:1, and 2.39:1

Bayer—a type of color filter array designed by Dr. Bryce Bayer that is a mosaic of half green and quarter blue and red colored photosites to gather RGB information from a single sensor. See also **color filter array**.

Bits—the basic unit of digital information. One bit can define two states, generally opposites. The addition of each bit doubles the number of states that can be defined.

Blue check—A function of a professional video monitor that can "turn off" the red and green portions of the image to only show blue. Used to balance out phase and chroma adjustments with calibrated color bars.

Borosilicate—a robust, high heat-resistant type of glass made from silica and boron oxide. First introduced in the early 1890s as Corning Glass Works and later sold in the early 1900s as Pyrex. An alternative to quartz glass.

Branchaloris—nickname for a branch that is placed in the path of a light to break up the light in a tree-like natural pattern of shadows. A combination of "branch" and "Cucaloris;" a piece of wood or wire mesh cut out or coated with an amorphous pattern intended to be placed into the path of a light beam in order to break up the single source into a random pattern of light, as if light was passing through leaves of a tree.

Byte—eight bits of information.

CCD—charge coupled device, an electronic light sensor used in digital cameras. Invented in the late 1960s, CCDs were the primary image capture medium in digital video cameras until the 2000s when advances in less-expensive, easier to manufacturer CMOS chips started to tip the balance. Generally more robust with less image artifacting, but extremely difficult to manufacture. In the mid-2000s there were only three manufacturers of CCDs and all cameras used chips from one of the three manufacturers.

Chimera—trade name for a brand of expandable soft boxes for lights.

Chroma—color; One of the two adjustments of a television monitor that define color presentation.

Chrominance—intensity of color within an image.

CinemaScope—trade name for a popular widescreen anamorphic process from the 1950s, often used interchangeably with any anamorphic process.

CMOS—complementary metal–oxide semiconductor. An electronic light sensor used in digital cameras. Patented in the late 1960s, CMOS sensor chips are an alternative to CCD image sensors and, generally, are less expensive to manufacture. Advances in CMOS technology in the 2000s made it a popular choice for a new breed of HD cameras. Simplified manufacturing meant that companies weren't locked into using one of the three CCD manufacturers, but could create their own CMOS chips to suit their own designs.

Color filter array—a pattern of color filters placed over photosites of a sensor to allow one sensor to capture multiple colors. See also **Bayer**.

Color temperature—a scale, defined by Kelvin temperatures, that describes a relationship between Celsius temperature of a theoretical black body radiator incandescent source and the general color spectrum combination that is emitted from that temperature.

Color Rendering Index (CRI)—a scale from 0 to 100 representing the accuracy by which a luminary will represent colors. A rating of 100 is natural daylight, representing colors with 100% accuracy. A rating of 1 would not represent colors at all.

Correlated Color Temperature (CCT)—a modified Kelvin scale for non-full-spectrum light sources to identify the simulated color temperature.

Crop factor—Mathematical calculation for altered field of view when utilizing a lens designed for a larger sensor camera on a smaller sensor camera. Determined by finding the diagonal (hypotenuse) of the sensor size of the larger camera divided by the diagonal of the sensor of the smaller size. Multiply the result by the lens' focal length to get the new field of view as compared to the larger camera.

CRT—cathode ray tube. Traditional television before flat screens.

Cyclorama—a large, generally curved, backdrop designed to create a seamless look. Most often painted white, but also green or blue.

Decamired—reducing mireds by dividing by 10. 313 is a mired, 31.3 is a decamired. See **mireds**.

Demosaicing—the process of interpreting and "filling in" the missing colors from a color filter array to interpolate the full color image.

Depth of field—the area of an image, at a given focal distance and a given aperture, that is within acceptable focus. Depth of field is greater at smaller apertures and longer focal distances.

Dichroic—a specially coated glass filter that cuts certain wavelengths of light.

Dichroic beam splitter—optical component of a three-chip camera that splits the light entering the lens into the primary colors red, green, and blue, sending each color off to a separate sensor. Physically it is a combination of two prisms and two dichroic mirrors that reflect some colors and allow others to pass through.

Diffusion—a medium, generally white and semi-translucent, that is intended to scatter the light passing through it.

Diopter—a positive supplemental image magnification tool that will reduce the minimum focus of a lens, thereby allowing for more extreme close-ups of a subject.

DIT—digital imaging technician, a part of the camera crew. Traditionally the individual who manipulates the controls of the digital camera and image; more commonly the individual who handles the image data between the camera and the editorial department.

DMX—digital multiplex. Officially DMX512, the digital communication language for controlling lighting dimmers and stage effects.

Donut—a metallic insert with a circular cutout in the center, essentially an aperture, that helps to eliminate chromatic aberration from an ellipsoidal reflector spotlight.

DSLR—digital single lens reflex, a term referring to a type of digital sensor camera wherein the viewfinder is of a reflex type utilizing a mirror and prism system of optics to view directly out of the taking lens of the camera. See also **HDSLR**.

Duvetyne—a soft woven dense black fabric used for cutting light.

Electrons—negatively charged atomic particles that orbit around atoms. To be a conductor, an atom needs to have a "free" electron that has its own orbit around the nucleus. The traveling of electrons creates electricity.

Electromotive force—the difference in potential between two points of a circuit akin to how many free electrons are available to move from one point to another. Also called voltage.

ENG—electronic news-gathering. Generally referring to a type of shoulder-mounted camera with a zoom lens used by news videographers.

Envelope—the glass enclosure of a light bulb.

f-**stop**—scale system for describing the size of a camera's aperture. A geometrical relationship between the focal length of the lens and diameter of the iris opening. See also **T-stop** and **aperture**.

FCP—short for the Apple non-linear editing software Final Cut Pro.

Flange focal depth—the measurement from the photographic sensor of a camera to the point at which the camera body physically contacts the lens body. See also **register**.

Foamcore—an artboard created from sandwiching a section of foam between two pieces of coated paperboard. This creates a rigid, lightweight board, sold in various thicknesses and colors. Generally used to bounce light (white) or to block light (black). Can be easily cut, taped, and shaped.

Footcandle—basic English unit of measurement of incident lighting intensity. Based on the theoretical light from one candle on a one foot square area one foot away from the flame. See also **lux**.

Frame rate—the speed at which a camera is photographing motion; typically 24 frames per second or 30 frames per second.

Frazier—a specialty borescope lens designed by Jim Frazier for Panavision, the Frazier has an articulating tip that allows the lens to pan and tilt without moving the camera in addition to having deep depth of focus generally associated with borescope lenses.

FTZSAC—focus, T-stop, zoom, speed-aperture, controller. A remote control device that controls camera focus, aperture, zoom, and start/stop functions. In addition, the T-stop control can be linked to the camera speed to ensure constant exposure with variable camera speeds.

Full raster—a term for three-chip cameras that record images equal to the number of photosites on the sensors. A full raster HD camera has three sensors at 1,920 × 1,080 photosites each to create a 1,920 × 1,080 image.

Gain—electronic camera function to amplify the voltage signal from the sensor and in order to increase the sensor's sensitivity to light at the expense of noise.

Gamma—representation of photographic contrast in the middle of the exposure scale between blacks and whites.

Gels—flexible and cuttable lighting filters impregnated or coated with specific color dyes. Most often with a polyester base.

Gobo—any object placed in the path of a light to shape the light by way of creating shadow. Can be a flag, net, cookie, or even a cut metal template in a spotlight used to project a pattern.

Gridcloth—a specific type of white nylon cloth diffusion with a square grid-like pattern. Can be sewn to create larger diffusion pieces.

HD/HDTV—officially, the definition given to exhibition image sizes of 1,280 × 720 or 1,920 × 1,080 pixels. Unofficially, HD is often used in marketing any resolution higher than SD (720 × 480).

HDSLR—high definition single lens reflex. A term coined for a new brand of digital SLR cameras that also shoot high-definition video.

HMI—Mercury (periodic element Hg) medium-arc iodide. A short-arc gas-discharge light source that generates a light source in the "daylight" Kelvin temperature range.

Hypercardioid—a pattern of microphone pickup that is shaped much like a heart in front of the microphone, but canceling out what is behind it.

Hyperfocal distance—optical phenomenon wherein at a specific aperture and focal distance combination the depth of field is half the focal distance to infinity. Every lens has a hyperfocal for every aperture, most are beyond the focal scale of the lens.

Hypotenuse—the diagonal edge of a right triangle.

Imager—see **sensor**.

IMAX—trade name for a large format motion picture camera and process utilizing 65mm film with fifteen perforations per frame and a 70mm print stock. The resulting single frame is, roughly, the size of a business card. Also, a trade name for specialty digital theaters that show a larger-than-usual image.

Interpolation—a mathematical process of creating new data based on known data.

IR—infrared radiation, the large area of the electromagnetic spectrum just after visible red wavelengths.

IRE—Institute of Radio Engineers, scale on a waveform monitor to define values of electrical current representing areas between black and white in the visual image.

Kelvin—see **color temperature**.

LCD—liquid crystal display.

Letterbox—the black bars above and below a widescreen image when presented on a smaller aspect ratio screen.

Lumen—metric system of measuring lighting intensity. One lux is equal to one lumen over a square meter area. One footcandle is 10.76 lux. See also **footcandle**.

Luminance—a measure of brightness.

Luan—a type of plywood less than ¼" thick (typically ⅛"). Sold in large sheets, typically 4' × 8'.

LUT—look up table, a digital color reference data table for converting from one color space to another. LUTs are often employed to emulate a final color corrected image on-set or during post-production.

Lux—metric system of measuring lighting intensity. A secondary measurement based on lumens, one lux is equal to one lumen over a square meter area. One footcandle is 10.76 lux. See also **footcandle**.

Metadata—data about data. Descriptive data connected to other data that helps to define how the main data should be interpreted. In images, metadata can include: white balance, color temperature, exposure, ISO, and much more.

Mireds—micro reciprocal degrees. A mathematical scale by which Kelvin color temperatures can be added, subtracted, and compared. Mireds are equal to 1,000,000 divided by the specific Kelvin temperature.

Modulation transfer function—the measurement of loss of contrast of light passing through a lens. Also, the measurement of the resolving power of a specific portion of a lens.

Moiré—an undesirable image artifact produced when repetitive scene detail exceeds the sensor resolution. The result is a wavy, often animated "dancing" pattern of anomalous lines in the image.

MOS—a term given to shooting a scene without recording sound. Legend tells of a German director with a thick accent who asked to shoot the scene '*Mit Out Sound*', but, more than likely it is an acronym for minus optical stripe, minus optical sound, muted on screen, mute on sound, motor only shot, motor only sync, among others. The true origins of MOS are unknown.

NLE—non-linear editor.

Noise—unwanted and random signal information in a digital image that often appears as static. Generally a result of over-amplification of an image or signal interference.

Nyquist theorem—officially the Nyquist-Shannon Sampling Theorem. Derived by Harry Nyquist and Claude Shannon, the theorem stipulates that in order to faithfully sample a signal, we must have twice the number of samples that we wish to reproduce.

Ohms—element of electricity that represents a conductor's resistance to the flow of electrons.

Opal—a type of diffusion gel with very little opacity that is very thin.

Optical backfocus distance—the distance between the imaging sensor and the rearmost optical element of the lens.

Pan-and-scan—the process of dynamically moving a 1.33:1 "window" within a widescreen frame (typically 2.35:1 or 2.39:1) to display the "important" parts of the cropped frame. Sometimes this dynamic movement creates a "pan" of the image that was not in the original photography.

Parabolic aluminized reflector (PAR)—a type of lighting fixture featuring a parabolic reflector. Most often a closed unit wherein the reflector is built into the bulb itself.

Persistence of vision—physical phenomenon; the ability of the human eye and brain to retain an image after it has gone. Erroneously associated with why human beings see rapid succession of still images as motion.

Phase—an adjustment of a portion of the color signal on a monitor; tint.

Phi phenomenon—the optical illusion of perceiving continuous motion between separate objects viewed rapidly in succession. One standing theory why human beings view rapidly presented still images as motion.

Photometrics—measurements of the intensity performance qualities of a lighting fixture over given distances.

Photons—tiny particles of light.

Photosite—the individual photosensitive element of a digital imaging sensor. Most sensors have multiple million photosites.

Pixel—an element of an image that is made up of values of red, green, and blue. Short for "picture element," a term coined in the 1960s.

PLUGE—picture line up generating equipment , namely the three black rectangles in SMPTE color bars that represent blacker than black, black, and just above black.

Puck light—a light fixture generally used under cabinets and within bookshelves, sold at home improvement and furniture stores. Often used by cinematographers and gaffers as a small, inconspicuous detail light in the background.

Raw—recording information straight from a single sensor without applying any image-creation mathematics or filters.

Rectilinear—a lens that yields images where straight lines are rendered straight, not curved. A lens with no curvature (barrel or pincushion) distortion.

Refraction—the altering (slowing) of the direction of a wavelength of light as it passes through a translucent material such as glass or water.

Register—the measurement from the photographic sensor of a camera to the point at which the camera body physically contacts the lens body. See also **Flange focal depth**.

Resolution—the measured ability of a system to render fine detail. Defined by the system's ability to reproduce high contrast lines of increasing spatial frequency. Closely tied to contrast reproduction. *Not* merely a measurement of the number of pixels in an image or photosites on a sensor.

RGB—red, green, blue, the lighting primaries—combinations of which are capable of creating any color in the visible spectrum.

Sensel—scientific name for the photosensitive element of a digital imaging sensor. See also **photosite**.

Sensor—a photosensitive photographic device in a digital camera that coverts photons of light into electrical voltages to create a photographic image.

SLR—single lens reflex, a category of camera whereby a mirror and prism allows the viewfinder to look through the taking lens of the camera.

SMPTE—Society of Motion Picture and Television Engineers. An international professional association created for the purpose of generating internationally recognized standards for the motion picture and television industries.

Spatial frequency—a measurement of the frequency of an occurrence within a given space. In terms of MTF/resolution, the increasing number of black and white lines within a millimeter of space.

Super35—a 35mm photographic process that used the full negative area between the perforations to record the image, ignoring the area set aside for the sound track as specified in the Academy standard. Super35 was the largest recording format of 35mm motion picture film and the category has been readily adopted by digital camera creators, although very few digital sensors are exactly the dimensions of a Super35 film negative.

Supersampling—gathering more samples (information) to create a smaller yet more faithful reproduction. See **Nyquist theorem**.

T-stop—calibrated scale of defining aperture sizes based on *f*-stop with consideration to the actual measured transmission of light through the specific lens. A more highly calibrated alternate to the geometric *f*-stop.

Telecine—the process of transferring film to video.

Transcode—the technical process of converting an image from one compression codec to another. Also used for taking raw data information and demosaicing to create an image.

Ultraviolet radiation (UV)—electromagnetic waves just below the light range. Invisible to the human eye. Reaction to UV can cause substances to glow or fluoresce. UV radiation is a component of sunlight (and gas-discharge arc lamps) that can cause damage to human skin, commonly referred to as sunburn.

Variac—short for variable AC. A device that changes voltage output, used most often to dim tungsten lights.

Vectorscope—a tool for measuring the color content of an image.

Volts—measurement of electrical potential between two points in a conductor. See also **electromotive force**.

Watts—element of electricity that defines the energy created by a specific device.

Widescreen—any image with an aspect ratio of greater than 1.33:1. Generally used to refer to theatrical aspect ratios of 1.66:1, 1.85:1 or 2.39:1.

WYSIWYG—what you see is what you get.

Suggested Reading

MORE BY THE AUTHOR:

A Shot in the Dark: A Creative DIY Guide to Digital Video Lighting on (Almost) No Budget. Boston: Course Technology PTR Cengage Learning, 2012.

Filmmaker in a Box: *An Intensive Case Study on the Production of a Micro-Budget Feature Film*. Los Angeles: Filmmaker in a Box, LLC. www.filmmakerinabox.com

BIBLIOGRAPHY AND SUGGESTED FURTHER READING

Ascher, Steven and Pincus, Edward. *The Filmmaker's Handbook: A Comprehensive Guide for the Digital Age*. New York: Plume, 1994.

Box, Harry C. *Set Lighting Technician's Handbook: Film Lighting Equipment, Practice and Electrical Distribution*. Boston: Focal Press, 1993.

Boyle, Geoff. *Cinematography Mailing List: CML—the First Five Years*. Devon: Boyle, 2005.

Boyle, Geoff. *Cinematography Mailing List: Lighting—January 2001 to January 2005*. Devon: Boyle, 2005.

Brown, Blain. *The Filmmaker's Pocket Reference*. Boston: Focal Press, 1994.

Burum, Stephen H., ed. *The American Cinematographer Manual*, 9th edn. Hollywood: ASC Press, 2004.

Carlson, Verne and Carlson, Sylvia E. *Professional Lighting Handbook*, 2nd edn. Boston: Focal Press, 1991.

Carter, Paul. *Backstage Handbook: An Illustrated Almanac of Technical Information*, 3rd edn. Louisville: Broadway Press, 1994.

Kingslake, Rudolf. *Lenses in Photography: The Practical Guide to Optics for Photographers*, revised edn. New York: A.S. Barnes and Company, Inc., 1963.

Long, Ben and Schenk, Sonja. *The Digital Filmmaking Handbook*, 3rd edn. Boston: Cengage Learning, 2006.

Malkiewicz, Kris and Mullen, M. David. *Cinematography: The Classic Guide to Filmmaking, Revised and Updated for the 21st Century*. New York: Simon & Schuster, 2005.

Millerson, Gerald. *The Technique of Lighting for Television and Film*, 3rd edn. Boston: Focal Press, 1991.

Rahmel, Dan. *Nuts and Bolts Filmmaking: Practical Techniques for the Guerilla Filmmaker*. Boston: Focal Press, 2004.

Stump, David, ASC. *Digital Cinematography: Fundamentals, Tools, Techniques and Workflows*. Boston: Focal Press, 2014.

Taub, Eric. *Gaffers, Grips and Best Boys: From Producer-Director to Gaffer and Computer Special Effects Creator, a Behind-The-Scenes Look at Who Does What in the Making of a Motion Picture*, 2nd edn. New York: St. Martin's Press, 1995.

Upton, Barbara London and Upton, John. *Photography*, 4th edn. Glenview: Scott, Foresman and Company, 1989.

Viera, Dave. *Lighting for Film & Electronic Cinematography*. Belmont: Wadsworth Publishing Company, 1993.

Wildi, Ernst. *Photographic Lenses: Photographer's Guide to Characteristics, Quality, Use and Design*. Buffalo: Amherst Media, Inc. 2002.

Index

Note: Page numbers in **bold** are for illustrations.